The Social Foundations of
Language and Thought

The Social Foundations of Language and Thought

Essays in Honor of Jerome S. Bruner

EDITED BY DAVID R. OLSON

JEREMY M. ANGLIN	ALASTAIR MUNDY-CASTLE
T. BERRY BRAZELTON	DAVID R. OLSON
ROGER BROWN	ROY D. PEA
ROSALIND CHARNEY	JEAN PIAGET
MICHAEL COLE	JAN SMEDSLUND
JACQUELINE J. GOODNOW	HENRI TAJFEL
PATRICIA M. GREENFIELD	COLWYN TREVARTHEN
PEG GRIFFIN	EDWARD TRONICK
BÄRBEL INHELDER	PETER C. WASON
KENNETH KAYE	DAVID J. WOOD

With a foreword by George A. Miller
and an afterword by Jerome S. Bruner

W · W · NORTON & COMPANY

NEW YORK   LONDON

Copyright © 1980 by David R. Olson
Published simultaneously in Canada by George J. McLeod Limited,
Toronto. Printed in the United States of America.

All Rights Reserved

First Edition

Library of Congress Cataloging in Publication Data
Main entry under title:
The Social foundations of language and thought.
   1. Psycholinguistics—Addresses, essays,
lectures. 2. Sociolinguistics—Addresses, essays,
lectures. 3. Bruner, Jerome Seymour—Addresses,
essays, lectures. I. Bruner, Jerome Seymour.
II. Olson, David R.
P37.S56   1980   401'.9   80–19844
ISBN 0–393–01303–0

W. W. Norton & Company, Inc., 500 Fifth Avenue, New York, N.Y. 10110
W. W. Norton & Company Ltd., 25 New Street Square, London EC4A 3NT

1 2 3 4 5 6 7 8 9 0

Contents

Foreword

Few psychologists have left and continue to leave a distinctive mark on so many different branches of their field. Over his career, Jerome S. Bruner—Jerry, to all who know him—has explored every important approach to a psychological understanding of humankind: social, experimental, physiological, comparative, clinical, developmental. Diversification in itself is no great thing, of course; the trick is to find a unity in the diversity. The unity of Jerry's work derives from his deep conviction that different approaches are but different ways to ask the same questions.

I once complained to Jerry that our intellectual life at the Center for Cognitive Studies was too rich; I felt drawn in too many directions; there was too little time to assimilate the ideas exploding around us. His reply was immediate and characteristic: "You must trust the integrity of your own personality." At the time I thought he meant that coherence would emerge, if only I would let it, from some kind of unconscious work. Now I think it was a reminder that psychology is as much art as science: reach down to the source of all arts and sciences. Perhaps he meant both.

In either case it was advice I needed to hear, advice I have since passed on to others. But Jerry lives by it more faithfully than I. Behind the apparent variety of his work are several themes whose persistence must reflect the integrity of his own personality. One of those integrating threads, his continuing concern with the social foundations of psychology, has been singled out for celebration in this volume.

Jerry Bruner returned from World War II to a Harvard that was cutting up Psychology, severing its social head from its biological body. He was never comfortable with that division. It was his effort to rise above it and to be a complete psychologist that attracted me. Early in his career Jerry fought for recognition of the social foundations of all mental processes. Later he took this synthesis for granted and exploited it in formulations of other problems. He knew that human cognition is a subject one divides at one's peril.

Divide and conquer is a motto of analytic science, but the dividing is usually easier than the conquering. For a scientific conquest you must get your divisions right. Be careful where you draw them.

Consider, for example, this traditional division: Cognition can be studied in terms of content or process—in terms of what people know or how people know. Traditionally, sociologists and anthropologists emphasize content and psychologists emphasize process. This division of labor parallels a division of psychology into sociotropic and biotropic components.

But does it make sense? The division between sociology or anthropology on the one hand and psychology on the other serves well the purpose of academic administrators, which is no small matter, but what is the evidence that cognitive content and cognitive process ought to be pursued separately? What evidence we have seems to argue for their closer marriage.

Imagine a psychophysical experiment on some perceptual process—size estimation, say—where you vary the content of the stimulus material. If you found that the process of judging size varied as a function of the content to be judged, would that count as evidence for not separating content and process? Suppose you could show that different content affects differently the judgmental processes of people from different socioeconomic levels. Would that persuade you?

Or suppose you gave people some kind of problem to think about and then found that the cognitive strategies they use to solve it depend as much on the content in terms of which the problem is phrased as on the problem's logical structure. Suppose you could show that the reasonable hypotheses people fall back on depend heavily on prior familiarity with the content of the problem. Would that persuade you that content and process should not be analyzed separately?

Since the dependence of process on content is only half the argument, you might also try to show how content depends on process. For example, you might study opinion formation as a function, not only of informational content, but also as a function of motivational processes.

Did Jerry Bruner consciously plan his experiments to demonstrate the folly of carving up psychology? No doubt his choice of research projects, like all complex human decisions, was subject to many influences. But his style of thinking has been consistent and has consistently led him into research enterprises that illuminate the social foundations of psychology in general, and cognitive psychology in particular. He has always respected the wisdom of culture as much as the wisdom of nature.

It is most appropriate that children play an important role in the following pages. The mutually cooperating, mutually limiting relations of body, mind, and society are nowhere so clearly revealed as in the developing mind of a young child. Infancy and childhood provide an optimal demonstration of the unity Bruner believes in.

I am confident he will take delight in this book, which so eloquently invites its readers to join in a unified approach to the foundations of human language and cognition.

GEORGE A. MILLER

Princeton University

Preface

The cognitive processes, particularly those higher mental processes concerned with knowledge, its acquisition and use, have always been construed as socially based. Partly this is because what any person takes to be normal or to be true has been seen as being socially determined. Yet experimental psychology, beginning with Wilhelm Wundt, has been biologically based and concerned, largely, with sensory and physiological processes which were believed to be fixed and common to all human beings. The basic dichotomy, rooted in Aristotle, has, of course, generated vigorous and productive but separate descriptions—the biotropic and the sociotropic as they were called at Harvard. For the past decade there has been a growing discontent with these fundamental categories and with the theoretical disciplines resting on them. This book, written as a tribute to the work and influence of Jerome S. Bruner, is an attempt to rediscover the common ground underlying these two traditions.

Jerome Bruner is one of those individuals who while examining any one issue—whether perception, intelligence, cognitive growth, or language development—does so in such a way as to elucidate the common grounds, the foundations, of many issues. That quality gives Bruner's writings not only a degree of interest that sustains reading and re-reading but also a stance toward a problem or problems that may influence readers profoundly. One of these foundations is the relationship between higher and lower levels of cognition. When it was conventional to treat perception as sensation determined, Bruner with Postman showed that it was expectancy or knowledge driven. When intelligence was treated as a quality of an organ, Bruner treated it as a set of strategies and procedures for solving problems, and when language was seen as the gradual unfolding of semantic and syntactic structures from an innate base, Bruner treated it in terms of its uses as an expression of intention and as a means of constructing and maintaining a social relationship between infant and adult. All of these concerns may be seen as reflecting the role of higher mental processes in relation to lower order ones, and as the higher ones were generally social, Bruner's work can be said to uncover the social foundations of language and cognition.

As French philosophers have recently pointed out, theoretical concerns must be seen not only in terms of their expressed content but also in terms of the relation of that theory to the individual or group that advances them. Bruner's theoretical concerns with social foundations of language and cognition find expression not only in his theoretical writings but also in his professional commitments and in his personal and social life. His professional commitments to social analysis and to social praxis take many forms, most important of which are those directed to educational theory and practice. *The Process of Education* alone has been translated into twenty-odd languages and compares in scope, significance, and impact with John Dewey's *The Child and the Curriculum.* His experimental school curriculum *Man a Course of Study* has been studied by hundreds of thousands of students in the United States. In addition he contributed to the development of preschool education in America including Project Head-Start and to the study and reform of childminding practices in Great Britain reported in the forthcoming *Infant Care in Great Britain.*

Bruner's professional and social life similarly reflect these deep social concerns. Jerry Bruner is a remarkably social being. He is a personal friend, not merely an acquaintance, of virtually every psychologist in the world. Not only that, he corresponds with most of them. Megan Kenyan, Bruner's secretary at Oxford, estimated that Bruner writes some fifty to sixty letters per week, some three thousand per year. Furthermore, he has friendly, personal relationships with hundreds of scholars whose work in other disciplines is often relevant to his own work. Not quite as many have enjoyed the warm hospitality and friendly conversation of a dinner party at the Bruner home, yet it is safe to say that, outside of a few institutional factors, Blanche and Jerry Bruner's dinner parties have done more to create a community out of individual scholars than any other activity. Finally, as almost everyone knows, conversation with Bruner is not only informative and challenging but also socially confirming and deeply satisfying.

The leadership and influence of Jerry Bruner is no more clearly indicated than by the authors and topics contributing to this volume. Virtually all of the authors involved were colleagues of Jerry Bruner and George Miller at the Center for Cognitive Studies in the early sixties. It is impossible to overestimate the significance of the Center on contemporary cognitive psychology. The leadership of Bruner and Miller—the association, argumentation, and collaboration they encouraged—helped to define both the primary conceptual issues of the discipline and some of the methods most appropriate to their examination and to establish personal ties between the scientists most concerned with those issues. The list of scholars who shared in the activities of the Center is impressive indeed and includes: Ernst Gombrich, Israel Scheffler, Marx Wartofsky, Nelson Goodman, Herb Rubenstein, Jerry Katz, Noam Chomsky, Jerry Fodor, Tom Bever, Jacques Mehler, Eno Flores d'Arcais, Pim Levelt, Philip Smith, Frank Smith, Molly Potter, Rose Olver,

Patricia Greenfield, Janellen Huttenlocher, Dan Slobin, Bärbel Inhelder, Jan Smedslund, Henri Tajfel, Al Bregman, Don Norman, Jackie Goodnow, Dick Hayes, Amos Tversky, Danny Kahneman, David McNeill, Douglas Carmichael, Norman Mackworth, Peter Wason, Ken Kaye, David Wood, Berry Brazelton, Ragnar Rommetveit, Zoltan Dienes, Donald Taylor, Helen Kenney, Paul Kohlers, Harry Savin, Nancy Waugh, Mary Henle, Sheldon White, Roger Brown, Daniel O'Connell, Art Blumenthal, Sam Fillenbaum, Tom Bower, Masanao Toda, Elaine Vurpillot, Doris Aaronson, Martin Richards, Alastair Mundy-Castle, Colwyn Trevarthen, Hanus Papousek, Phillip Liss, Larry Marks, Daniel Forsythe, Roman Jakobson, A. R. Jonckheere, Jerry Anglin, Susan Carey-Block, Judy Gardner, Ed Tronick, Eric Aronson, and others, as well as many visitors and students.

This volume represents only part of the profusion of ideas that grew, indeed thrived, at the Harvard Center for Cognitive Studies. The authors invited to contribute to this volume are perhaps representative of that larger group in that they see a decided influence of Jerry Bruner and the Center for Cognitive Studies on their work. But in addition, they are a few of the scholars who, from the limited perspective of the editor, were involved in work that contributed rather directly to the side of Jerry Bruner's work that this volume is intended to examine. Hence, this book reports some of that influence and acknowledges some of that debt.

This book is not a eulogy to Jerry Bruner. It is an attempt to pick up the problem central to his concerns and to carry it forward. It is a gift to Jerry Bruner on his birthday; it is a tribute to the energy and enthusiasm he brings, to the aristocracy of mind that he represents, to the social concerns he demonstrates, and to the personal friendship that we have all enjoyed. We join with him in recovering the social foundations of cognition and language.

Finally, I wish to express my gratitude to the authors of the chapters of this book both for their encouragement and cooperation and for letting me be the first to see their interesting and significant ideas. Special thanks are due to Jerry Anglin, Roy Pea, Patricia Greenfield, and George Miller, who helped in the planning; to Mary Macri, Nancy Torrance, and Angela Hildyard, of the Ontario Institute for Studies in Education; and to Don Lamm, Donald Fusting, Donna Seldin, and Sue Lowe of Norton, who helped in its execution.

DAVID R. OLSON

St. Croix Cove, Nova Scotia
August, 1979

A word about the Afterword. After the volume was complete, I began to wonder what Jerry Bruner would think of the way we, in this volume, addressed the problem of the social foundations of cognition and language. Because it is a birthday present to Jerry Bruner, he could hardly be asked to bring a present. But Don Lamm, the publisher, George Miller, and I decided that there was no reason why Jerry should not be invited to attend the proceedings, and indeed, be allowed to blow out the candles. Hence the Afterword.

D.R.O.

Toronto, Ontario
October, 1979

The Social Foundations of
Language and Thought

Introduction

David R. Olson

The study of human cognition is bounded on one side by considerations drawn from biology and on the other by considerations drawn from sociology. Because those considerations place constraints upon the central problem of cognitive psychology, the structure, acquisition, and use of knowledge by individual subjects, they may be taken as the foundations of cognitive psychology. Some students of cognition, notably Piaget, Lorenz, and Lenneberg, along with such neurophysiologists as Broca, Jackson, and Sherrington have made their contributions to cognitive theory from perspectives which are essentially biological. Piaget begins his book *Biology and Knowledge* by saying "Among leading ethologists today there is a realization that the problems of knowledge, including the higher forms of human knowledge such as mathematics, can no longer remain outside the scope of biology" (1971, p. 1). His own goal is to pursue "the rather striking parallel between the problems raised by organic embryogenesis and the kind of mental embryology which constitutes the development of individual intelligence, or perceptions and so forth. It is from these that we draw most of our facts about the nature of knowledge" (p. 14). In as much as knowledge is encoded in the physical and biological structures of the human brain, an analysis of those biological systems provides insight into the structure and acquisition of knowledge, as indeed, those studies have clearly shown.

But for other students of human cognition, Jerome Bruner in particular, attempts to account for human perception, thought, speech, and action by means of models based primarily on biological functions are somewhat unsatisfactory. They fail to honor, at least in a compelling way, what may be called "the world of ideas"—the "Geist" of Hegel and Dilthey, the "collective representations" of Durkheim. That is, what is missing is an account of, indeed a sensitivity to, the ways in which the conventions, artifacts, symbols, and ideologies of a culture influence the cognitive structures of the individuals who make them up and of the social relations—parent-child, teacher-child, and so on—that mediate that influence. It is these social relations and these cultural products which, inasmuch as they influ-

I

ence or perhaps even determine the structure of human cognition, may be considered the social foundations of language and cognition.

Traditionally, beginning with Aristotle, it has been assumed that the biological and the social foundations of language and cognition are oppositional. Indeed, as we shall see, there is a long tradition of treating the former as "of the flesh" and the latter "of the spirit," the former as lower level processes, the latter as higher level processes. That opposition is misleading for Piaget because "all knowledge presupposes a physical structure" (1971, p. 2) and for Bruner because "much of the structure of our cognitive models . . . of reality is already given in the innate nature of our . . . techniques for representing reality . . ." (1966, p. 319–20). Indeed, several papers in this volume, especially those of Brazelton and Tronick and of Trevarthen, show that one of the biological predispositions of the human infant is to respond to and to socially interact with a caretaking adult. They have as Trevarthen says "instincts for cooperative understanding." This reconciliation has not yet gone very far; the purpose of this introduction is to set the stage for such proceedings by reference to the work and influence of Jerome Bruner.

The social foundations of language and thought may be pursued in three somewhat independent ways, all of which are exemplified in Bruner's work. The first is in the social relations between the child and the adult caretakers, especially parents and teachers, and the ways these social relations contribute to and influence the form of language and thought of the child. In the cross-cultural studies that Greenfield conducted with the Wolof of Senegal, Greenfield and Bruner noted that, at least in traditional societies, even simple practical actions have a social component: "motor manipulations of the child are . . . interpreted as signifying a desire on the part of the child oriented in relation to some person" (1966, p. 371). This view, however, was soon generalized to all children growing up in any social order—physical actions were to be seen not only as attempts to achieve goals but also, simultaneously, as attempts to construct a social relation with another person such that in some cases "the social and physical constitute but a single level of reality" (pp. 371–72). The relationships between the mental representations of the physical world and those of the social world, especially the ways in which the latter are instrumental in the construction of the former, is a topic that is central to much of Bruner's recent writings (Bruner, 1975, 1978; Ninio and Bruner, 1978) and to the theme of the book.

Secondly, cognitive representations reflect the social relations between individuals, whether mother-child, teacher-child, individual-peergroup, or whatever, not only because those representations are constructed in a social context, but also because those representations adopt for their content the concepts, categories, and relations conventionalized in that culture. Bruner argues that "Man is seen to grow by the process of internalizing the ways of acting, imaging, and symbolizing that 'exist' in his culture, ways that amplify his powers. He then develops these powers in a fashion that reflects the uses to which he puts his own life" (1966, pp. 320–21). And again, "intelligence is to a great extent the internalization of 'tools' provided by a given culture. Thus, 'culture-free' means 'intelligence-free'" (p. 21). In a similar vein, Sir Peter Medawar (1973) has added that "what is human about man is his technology," including his symbol systems, artifacts, tools, and machines. This is an important claim and one that is central to this volume, and hence it is worth examining it in somewhat more detail. As mentioned earlier, the idea of a "world of ideas" or culture which exists independently of the knowledge of particular individuals is an old and somewhat mystical concept. But the idea that culture evolved is a more recent one. Samuel Butler in *Erewhon* (1872) developed the conception that there is a parallel between the evolution of organs and the evolution of tools and machines. Animal evolution is primarily *endosomatic*, the biological modification of organs. Human evolution is primarily *exosomatic*, the development of new organs outside of our own bodies. Popper adds: "But man, instead of growing better eyes and ears, grows spectacles, microscopes, telescopes, telephones, and hearing aids. And instead of growing swifter and swifter legs, he grows swifter and swifter motor cars. . . . Instead of growing better memories and brains, he grows, paper, pens, pencils, typewriters, dictaphones, the printing press, and libraries" (1972, pp. 238–39). Although Popper is quite indifferent to the cerebral requirements for "growing" such artifacts, he does make the important point that exosomatic organs are transmitted from generation to generation just as surely as endosomatic ones. Any account of the cognitive processes of humans will therefore have to take into account the properties of these cultural artifacts as well as of the biological organs. Cognition rests as much on a cultural foundation as it does on a biological one.

Regardless of whether we consider biological or cultural considerations to be more fundamental, the psychological problem is that of showing how those foundations come to be represented in the structure of the cognitive process of particular individuals. Biological foundations are usually described as having their effect through innate ideas and through predispositions for learning. Just how the social-cultural world comes to be a part of an individual's own cognitive processes has been much less clearly spelled out. As mentioned above, one critical route seems to be through social interactions. Martin Richards, who because of an unfortunate accident was unable to contribute a paper to this volume, says that the child "is a biological organism with biological propensities and organization who becomes social through his encounters with social adults" (1974, p. 1). The careful studies presented in this volume on mother-child communication, on the management of dialogue, and on tutoring clearly indicate both the motivations that lead to social interaction and the ways that this interaction contributes to the construction of a shared "intersubjectivity."

What about cultural symbols, tools, and artifacts? Bruner's preferred description, cited above, is that of "internalization" of the culture. This conjecture, though plausible, has received two types of criticism and extension. First, the concept of internalization implies that concepts, ideas, symbols, and conventions are imposed from the outside. This leads some writers in this volume, to consider Bruner an empiricist.

The second difficulty with a theory of the internalization of symbols and artifacts and their uses as "amplifiers" of the innate or internal mental operations is that while it may help to explain how culture affects cognition, it overestimates the differences between "naïve" and "educated" thought. Michael Cole and Peg Griffin in this volume argue that the cognitive resources of an individual remain relatively invariant across differences in culture, while the goals to which those resources are applied and the levels of performance which may be achieved may differ considerably. For this reason, they suggest that metaphors like the "amplifiers" are somewhat misleading.

The relation between the artifacts of a culture and the structure of the cognitive processes of individuals may be looked at in a quite different way. A culture cannot create and preserve conventions and artifacts, including languages, which are not congruent with the biological "biases" of the individuals who learn and use them. This fact provides a third perspective on the social foundations of cognition. Not only may social interactions be relevant to the construction of knowledge, and not only may the conventions and artifacts of the culture be internalized as modes of thought, but also social conventions and cultural artifacts may be seen as a window to the underlying cognitive processes. That is, the structure of the artifact may reflect the structure of the cognitive processes that created it. This widely held structuralist assumption has its roots in the "New Science" developed by Giambattista Vico in 1725. He argued that since language, literature, culture, history, and politics—the subjects of his new science—are man-made, we are able to understand them; but since man did not make the physical or the biological environments, we are not able to understand them: "Whoever reflects on this cannot but marvel that philosophers should have spent all their energies to the study of the world of nature, which since God made it, He alone knows; and that they should have neglected the study of the world of nations, of the civil world, which, since men had made it, men could come to know" (1961, p. 96). That is, there is a direct link between what people can make and what they can know and understand. Hence if we analyze what they *make*, their artifacts and conventions, we have a good indication of what they *know*, that is, of how their minds work. In his discussion of mathematical structures, Robin Gandy makes precisely this point: "It is of course one of the prime tenets of structuralism that the structures (of, for example, language, social codes, artifacts, systems of thought) which human beings create are far from random and have a high degree of order; and that by studying this order we can discover universal truths about the human mind" (1973, pp. 143–44). Or as Chomsky has argued, "The principles of formal grammar . . . express the properties of a basic component of the human mind" (1972, p. 43). Hence, the studies of the structure of language, the rules of conversation, as well as artifacts and conventions generally are of interest not only in their own right but also in that they provide further insight into the structure and functions of the mind. Although the structure of these artifacts, conventions, and symbols provide some clue to the structure of the minds that created them, again they fall somewhat short of the analysis desired by a cognitive psychologist. These cultural inventions are socially distributed; that is, one part of the system may be known by one person, and another by a second person, and still another by a machine without the whole structure being known by any one individual. Hence the relationship between the structure of the cultural artifact, say a language, and the mental resources of any one individual, remains an important problem in both psychology and sociology, which, interestingly have tended toward similar solutions.

In psychology, Wilhelm Wundt (1832–1920), who is generally regarded as the father of experimental psychology but who also had his roots in Hegelian philosophy, found it necessary to divide the study of the psychological processes into two quite distinct enterprises—the experimental psychology of the lower physiological and sensory processes and the cultural-historical study of the higher mental processes in man. The first, Boring says, was expressed in his lectures on physiological psychology, begun in 1867, which "were to become a book the most important book in the history of modern psychology, his *Grundzüge der physiologischen psychologie*" (1950, p. 322). The second, concerned with the higher psychological processes including voluntary remembering and reasoning, had to be studied as products of the historical evolution of human culture and society and became the topic of his ten-volume *Volkspsychologie*. As Cole and Scribner (1978) point out in their introduction to Vygotsky's *Mind and Society*, Soviet psychological writings grow largely out of Wundt's second concern with the ways in which the world of ideas and artifacts—the "Geist" of Hegel and Dilthey—came to be reflected in the mental life of the individual. This was an approach which Bruner found congruent with his own interests and which he greeted enthusiastically in his introduction to Vygotsky's *Thought and Language* by saying that the symbols of the culture, what Vygotsky called the "Second Signal System," "provide the means whereby man creates a mediator between himself and the world of physical stimulation so that he can react in terms of his own symbolic conception of reality" (1962, p. x). Much of Bruner's effort, like that of Vygotsky and Luria, is directed to examining the ways in which the structures of the culture become the thought-ways of individuals. In retrospect this effort can be seen as developing in two stages. The first was that of describing these influences in terms of expectancies, hypothesis-testing procedures, coding systems, and eventually as "symbolic representation"—a distinctive, culturally imposed, tertiary form of mental representation (Bruner, 1966). At the second, more recent stage, Bruner turned from the task of demonstrating the existence and significance of these cultural-social forms to showing how these forms are rooted in the biological nature of humans and therefore appear in proto-typical form in the earliest perceptions and actions of infants. That is, the contemporary enterprise for Bruner and for this volume is one of reuniting the higher and the lower psychological processes. It is a point that is articulated and empirically defined in the paper by Trevarthen. I shall return to this point.

These social foundations have undergone a somewhat similar development in sociological theory. The possibility that cognitive structures directly reflect the social and political structures of a society has an important place in the writings of Durkheim (1858–1917). In his authoritative analysis of the thought of Durkheim, Lukes (1973) points out that Durkheim, who was to some extent influenced by Wundt, differentiated the order of knowledge into two parts: "the senses and sensory thought"—organically based, personal, and private—and "the understanding and conceptual thought." "Conceptual thought was," he claimed, "social and nothing but an extension of society." Lukes goes on, "Thus concepts, including the fundamental categories, were originally collective representations being socially caused, modelled on society, impersonal, and common to a plurality of men." This duality of human nature, adopted from Descartes and Hegel, left an unbridgeable gap between the physiological and sensory structures of the body and the collective, transcendental, spiritual structures of the mind. Further, Durkheim argued that there was a causal relation between the social order and the conceptual order: "If the totality of things is conceived as a single system, this is because society itself is seen in the same way. It is a whole, or rather it is the unique whole to which everything is related." And again, "logical life has its first source in society" (Lukes, 1973, p. 441). Scheler (see Berger and Luckmann, 1967) too had emphasized that human knowledge was given in society as a priori to individual experience. If society determines both the appearance and the content of human ideation, the latter could hardly be examined as an explanation of the former. Hence the study of social relations moved away from a concern with the cognitive processes of individuals and toward a concern with society as an organism which can be studied without reference to individuals (see Talcott Parsons, 1949). Leach points out that what has survived is the "sociological part of the Durkheimian tradition—namely the thesis that society is an articulated system which exists in its own right independently of the individuals who make it up" (1973, p. 38). Consequently, it adopts an extreme and somewhat obsolete view of the relation between social and biological structures. It assumes a complete separation between the lower and higher mental processes and therefore between biological and social foundations of cognition. In a word it overlooks the fact that, as Vico had pointed out, social structures are man-made and they therefore have properties that reflect the cognitive properties of their makers. To the extent that these properties are common to all members of the human species, they can be readily learned by the young and readily represented in the minds of each individual member of the social group.

Some more recent sociological theories (see Berger and Luckmann, 1967) have moved in this direction, the work of Pierre Bourdieu being an important case in point (DiMaggio, 1979). Bourdieu makes two major contributions to the Durkheimian scheme. First, he relativizes the account so as to make modern society one form of social structure among many rather than the end point of evolution, as Durkheim had done. Secondly, he shows that the social structures are essentially psychological structures in that they are represented and managed symbolically by the individual members of those social groups.

Let us consider these points in turn. Durkheim had claimed that social organization determined the structure of religious belief; scientific knowledge he believed had become "disinterested" and free from social interests. Bourdieu, on the other hand, claims that all knowledge and beliefs are similarly socially conditioned: "Different classes and class factions including all institutions such as schools and all fields of endeavor such as art or science are engaged in a specifically symbolic struggle to impose the definition of the social and physical world most in conformity with their interests . . . the object at stake is . . . the power to impose (and even indeed to inculcate) instruments of knowledge and expression of social reality . . ." (1977, p. 115). That is, the attempt to symbolize or describe the world in a particular way, and to have that description taken as the "standard" view, Bourdieu argues, is the goal of competing social groups. However, these social groups compete for the right to assign a description to the world compatible with their collective interests only through the activities of individuals who are purposeful, reasoning, self-interested actors pursuing their own goals: "It is by serving their own interests in the struggle internal to the field of production (and to this extent alone) that these producers serve the interests of groups external to their field of production" (p. 115). Such views are important in that social structures are no longer seen as the cause of the cognitive structures of individuals as Durkheim and Scheler had argued. The relationship is not one of causality but of structural congruity—the individuals in serving their own personal ends serve the ends of the social group. Yet the theory fails to account for how one comes to perceive his own personal ends in any particular way—in a word it fails to trace these individual cognitions to the other structural congruity, that between the biological foundations and these social foundations. This, of course, is a problem for the cognitive psychologist—especially for Jerome Bruner and the authors of this volume. Cognition is rooted in the social life, not simply because of the imposition of culture—what is sometimes called socialization —but because the cognitive processes of individuals from the outset generate social relations as well as objective relations. How deeply these social processes are represented in an infant's biological makeup is a recent discovery, one partly due to Bruner's concern with the social foundations of the cognitive processes and to the leadership and inspiration he gives to the writers who contributed to this volume.

Bruner's own work has long reflected this joint concern with the biological and social foundations of language and, hence, with the relations between the higher and the lower mental processes. It is informative to note Bruner's own reflections on his attempts with this problem. In his "Intellectual Autobiography," Bruner describes his perception of the first decade of "social relations," Harvard having split the "biotropic" and "sociotropic" aspects of psychology into the Department of Psychology and the Department of Social Relations. He says of Social Relations, "What it did for me personally, this immersion, was to make me appreciate to what extent cultural and social forms and the rules that govern them become somehow internalized in the mental apparatus of the individual human being" (1980).

But, as we have noted, the alignment of psychology with sociology was not in itself a solution to the understanding of the higher cognitive processes. Bruner notes his increasing unrest with the domination of psychological thought by sociological theory; there was "a focus exclusively on psychological conceptions that would fit the requirements of a sociological theory" (1978, p. 44).

If the sociologically inspired theories of the cognitive processes seemed to be too insensitive to the biological foundations of cognition and the lower mental processes, early studies of the psychology of language seemed, to Bruner, to be too insensitive to social relations. Early psycholinguistic studies at the Centre for Cognitive Studies were devoted primarily to the syntactic/semantic meaning of words and sentences and the veridical relationship between sentences and the situations they represent. This is the aspect of language which most weakly reflects the social relations which were Bruner's greatest concern. Bruner expressed this concern, "My previous reluctance to get involved in language work stemmed, I think, from the feeling that formal syntactic analysis was only indirectly related to the psychological processes that interested me" (1978, p. 62).

More recent developments in speech act theory and in the pragmatics of language have done much to put Bruner's concerns with the social foundations of cognition and language back onto center stage. Utterances not only represent a particular physical reality but also express a social intention—to assert something as true, to request an action from a listener, to commit a speaker to a certain course of action, and so on. Bruner, Roy, and Ratner (1979) have argued that one speech act, requesting, is present in infants prior to the acquisition of its conventional grammatical form and may be decisive in its acquisition. Similarly, certain social relationships such as authority and dependency are preparatory conditions for using such gram-matical forms as commands and requests. Hence, in learning a language a child is learning both a picture of reality *and* finding his place in a social order. It is precisely this social sensitivity and social competence which has come to light in the recent studies of infants and young children. Further-more, the child's progressive mastery of the structure of language offers an important means of examining the interface between cultural artifact and human competence. This topic is one that has greatly concerned Bruner, who writes: ". . . language is a developed set of communicative procedures for fulfilling certain functions indicating, requesting, affiliating, and generat-ing possibility. Skill in realizing these functions is achieved by entry into dialogue with adult members of the linguistic community" (1978, p. 216). Both the structure of that human artifact and the means by which children and adults cooperate in the mastery of this structure are carefully examined by several papers in this volume.

The examination of biological roots for social skills may help to dissolve the Great Divide which, since the time of Aristotle and continuing through the writings of Descartes, Wundt, Durkheim, has been erected between the biological and the social, and between the lower psychological processes and the higer psychological processes. That goal is advanced not by deny-ing the social foundations of language and cognition, nor by reducing them to the biological foundations, but rather, by finding in the biological bias of the mind the seed out of which all of the formal systems of knowledge are constructed and by symmetrically seeing in these formal systems, the fundamental cognitive operations of the human mind. C. S. Pierce com-mented that ". . . man's mind has a natural adaptation to imagining cor-rect theories of some kinds" (1957, p. 238); it is a theme developed by the authors of this volume, and it is part of the legacy of the work and influence of Jerry Bruner.

This topic is reflected in three ways in the three sections of this volume. First, there is a concern with the cognitive structures which appear both in the minds of individuals, and are therefore psychological, and in the society, and therefore cultural. These structures whether of a linguistic, scientific, or political form are cultural artifacts which provide a clue, but only a clue, to the nature of mind. More critical is the task of describing which structures and which procedures for operating upon these structures are actually pres-ent in the mind of an individual at various points in his development. Four papers examine these structures. In the first of these Bärbel Inhelder, Fellow at the Center for Cognitive Studies in 1961–62, and Jean Piaget, "le Patron" of developmental psychology to whom Bruner dedicated *Studies in Cognitive Growth,* discuss the roles of structure and process in cognition generally. They point out that while there is some interchangeability between mental operations and mental structures, the basic distinction is that *procedures* are fundamentally temporal processes which use transformations to attain particular goals, while *structures* link transformations to form atemporal systems which are general and not directly goal related. By means of this opposition, they explain a number of fundamental binary pairs of descriptions including Ryle's famous distinction between knowing how and knowing that.

Peter Wason, who was a Fellow at the Center for Cognitive Studies from 1960 to 1963, reviews his long line of research on adults' comprehension of negation in terms of the evolution of the ideas and their development in the context of interactions with Bruner, Miller, and other Fellows at the Center for Cognitive Studies. The fundamental concept is that of differentiating the affirmation of a negative proposition (a "true negative") from the denial of an affirmative proposition and that the proper function of negatives is to make denials. But the construction of that solution depended upon a great deal of thought, research, and collaboration.

Jan Smedslund, who was a Fellow at the Center for Cognitive Studies in 1963–64, criticizes contemporary theories of cognitive structures including Bruner's theory of "coding systems" for their empiricist bias. Hence the truth of propositions about coding systems is assumed to be empirically determined. However, he argues, these propositions are essentially and irretrievably deductive; given the structure of our ordinary language in which these theories are couched they could not be false. He illustrates this point by proposing a formal, analytic theory of human action in terms of motives, beliefs, abilities, and effort which "represents an a priori rather than an empirical approach to psychology."

Henri Tajfel, who spent a year with Bruner at Harvard in 1958–59 relates some of Bruner's research on categorical perception to the perception of social groups and hence to one's own social identity. Following earlier perceptual studies which had shown that judgments of properties such as size depend upon the context of relevant alternatives, Tajfel has repeatedly shown that individuals' perception of themselves and others depends upon fundamental social categories such as *we* versus *they*: "We are what we are because they are not what we are." That is, properties which, from "a Martian point of view," are completely arbitrary are taken as significant features *if* they serve to distinguish oneself from others or one's own primary social group from other social groups. Or again, "one of the more powerful forms of social influence is to direct the individual's search towards the detection of those similarities and differences in the social environment which happen to fit in with the contemporary requirements of social adaptation." As such Tajfel's findings provide a key link in understanding how perception and knowledge are socially constructed. Knowledge serves the purposes not only of truth but also of defining and maintaining social groups.

My paper attempts to do for spoken and written utterances what Tajfel's does for social perception. These ideas benefited from my association with

Jerry Bruner at three different times and places. I was a Fellow at the Center for Cognitive Studies in 1964 and again in 1965–66, at which time I contributed to Bruner, Greenfield, and Olver's *Studies in Cognitive Growth*, and I did the research on diagonality that I published later in my book *Cognitive Development*. In 1974–75 I spent a year at Bruner's invitation at Wolfson College and the Department of Experimental Psychology, Oxford, where I first started to worry about the ways in which the social-pragmatic aspects of meaning could be related to my work on the relations between oral and written language. In 1978–79 both Jerry Bruner and I were Fellows at the Netherlands Institute for Advanced Study at Wassenaar, The Netherlands, where, with Melissa Bowerman, Robin Campbell, Manny Schegloff, Herman Parrett, Bea de Gelder, Paul van Geert, Moire Logan, Margrett von Ierland, and Claudia de Lamos, we spent many delightful hours discussing the vicissitudes of child language. In order to examine the social functions of language, I adopt the distinction advanced in speech act theory between propositional content and illocutionary force, the former specifying a relation between a symbol and its referent, the latter specifying a social relation between the speakers. My paper is concerned with the alignment of these two aspects of meaning in the oral conversational language of young children and in the reading and study of written school textbooks. I conclude that even the putatively true statements of school textbooks depend for their belief and acceptance not only on logical structure and empirical evidence but also upon the differentiation of speaker from speech and the attribution of that speech not to an equal but to the "authorities."

The second section of the volume examines young children's linguistic structures in the context of communicative discourse. Jeremy Anglin, onetime student of Bruner's and Miller's at Harvard and later the editor of Bruner's collected writings *Beyond the Information Given*, considers the acquisition of the ability to construct sentences as an example of early skill development. He presents evidence that language production is governed by an intention to communicate and can be viewed as requiring the orchestration of constituents in a serial order. The skill consists, basically, of the commitment to memory of a lexicon and the mastery of rules for combining these lexical units. This skill underlies the primary pragmatic function of language, that of "getting things done with words."

Getting things done with words—the social, or pragmatic, function of language—may mediate the acquisition of the lexical and syntactic structures suggests Roy Pea on the basis of his longitudinal examination of the negative expressions first produced by six children. Pea, a former graduate student of Bruner's at Oxford and a former associate of Miller's at Rockefeller, finds that his young subjects first used "no" for the social "don't" function of rejecting and only later did they come to use "no" for the "not" of truth-functional expressions. He suggests that the social function, rejection, therefore provides the foundation of the logical or truth-functional negation. Wason's chapter on negation can be read, or re-read, in this context.

Roger Brown, long-time colleague of Bruner at Harvard, examines the ways in which conversations with two-and-one-half-year-olds are maintained with a view of determining the relation between the mastery of structure of conversation and more traditional measures of the mastery of lexical and semantic structures. To this end, Brown compares the traditional measure of language development, the mean length of utterance (MLU), and a new measure, the mean length of episode (MLE). The MLE is the number of turns across which "a child may be said to hold up his end" of a conversation. Brown finds marked differences in children's ability to maintain a conversation. The discourse-related MLE was found to relate to non-discourse measures of linguistic ability, MLU. Furthermore, discourse competence appears to be a good indication of the degree of congruity between knowledge and expectancies of the child and the adult and hence a clue to the child's stage of linguistic development.

Kenneth Kaye was Bruner's student at Harvard. His colleague Rosalind Charney studied at the University of Chicago with a former Fellow of the Center, Janellen Huttenlocher. Their paper makes a further analysis of conversations between mothers and two-year-olds. They discovered that while these children participate primarily either by making requests (mands) or by responding to adult utterances (responses), mothers frequently combine these two types into a single turn, which they call a turnabout—an acknowledgment of the child's utterances and a call for a further utterance. Hence while these two-year-olds could fully participate in dialogue, the major responsibility for creating and maintaining that dialogue still rested primarily on the mothers.

Alastair Mundy-Castle, a Fellow at the Center from 1967 to 1970, compares the patterns of mother-infant interaction which occur in middle-class American families with those which occur among the Yorba and Igbo of Nigeria. While there are some important differences in the goals and games involved in such different cultures, the rules underlying joint action and joint attention in mother-infant interactions are "universal to human society, and are culturally encoded into all languages."

Patricia Greenfield, a former student of Bruner's at Harvard, then Fellow at the Center from 1968 to 1972 and co-editor with Rose Olver and Bruner of *Studies in Cognitive Growth*, examines infant discourse for a somewhat different purpose. Greenfield uses conversational exchanges with very young children to demonstrate that language is in the service of intentions, goal-directed activity with a specified end state. In so doing she both brings "intention" into cognitive psychology and shows that conversational and interactional exchanges even prior to language involve the setting up of an intention, an acknowledgment of the intention by the interlocutor, followed by the completion or fulfillment of the now jointly held intention. These intentions become visible not in single utterances but in an ongoing interpersonal exchange.

David Wood, a Fellow at the Center for Cognitive Studies 1970–72, shows that the structure of dialogue is important not only to conversation but also to tutorial instruction. In a series of studies of mothers teaching their children to perform complex tasks, Wood found that interaction and dialogue are critical to the establishment and maintenance of intersubjectivity, the sharing of intentions and understanding. Successful tutors play into this shared understanding by exploiting the fact that children can recognize correct solutions (comprehension) before they can assemble the means of achieving them (production). Comprehension then provides the goal or intention while the child's attempted performances gradually assemble the means. Furthermore, this shared understanding enables the tutor to play into the comprehension-production gap at just the right level of complexity to ensure their joint achievement of the goal.

The third section of the book is concerned with the general relations between cognitive processes and cultural products. It presents not only the view that the higher mental processes in some way reflect the structures and artifacts of the culture, but also the dissatisfaction with the simplistic notions of internalization of culture, socialization, and acculturation. Rather, some accommodation is sought for the vast cultural differences within a more limited set of cognitive universals. Hence, some meeting ground is sought between the operations of the mind and the structures of the culture. The former could be called the predispositions to culture.

Berry Brazelton and Ed Tronick, who with Bruner and Trevarthen began the Infancy Project at the Center for Cognitive Studies from 1966 to 1970, report on their pioneering research into infant interactions with the mother. These interactions are built on the infant's ability to defend himself from unwanted stimuli, control his internally generated activity in order to attend to important external stimuli, and respond to and elicit social responses. They show that the infant is attuned to dealing with the social world just as Bower, Trevarthen, and others have shown him to be attuned to dealing with the physical world. This theme is picked up and greatly expanded by Trevarthen.

Colwyn Trevarthen builds upon his own careful observations and the rising flood of information now available on infants' interactions with their mothers to show that there are powerful predispositions, or motives operative in the very young infant; one toward "subjectivity," the construction of a personal representation of the physical world, and one toward "intersubjectivity," cooperative, interpersonal structures which underlie the acquisition of language and other social forms. He concludes that "infants are clearly preadapted to take an active part in the development of the psychological functions of culture. They are intrinsically motivated to seek instruction and to share discovery of the conditions and techniques that make collective life effective."

Michael Cole collaborated on an important article with Jerry Bruner on cultural differences and inferences regarding cognitive processes and co-edited with Bruner and Barbara Lloyd a series of volumes entitled *Psychology of the Child*. Cole and his colleague Peg Griffin make a critical analysis of the relation between the artifacts of the culture and the structure of the mental process. They are wary of the naïve view of the "internalization" of the culture because of the misleading inferences it leads to in regard to the cognitive differences between individual members of vastly different cultures. For this reason they seek a more precise differentiation of the cognitive processes of any individual and the artifacts and technologies of the culture; rather than viewing the technology as having a comprehensive effect, they seek more local effects tied directly to the activities involved in using that technology. The cognitive resources including the structure and use of knowledge, they suggest, remain relatively invariant.

Jacqueline Goodnow—student, then colleague, or Bruner at Harvard and co-editor with George Austin and Bruner of *A Study of Thinking*—examines in a personal way how the social context, especially the pattern of thought encouraged by Bruner, influenced her own scientific development. She points out how Bruner encouraged a focus upon theories whether explicit or implicit that permit one to "go beyond the information given." Not only did he encourage others to formulate such theories, even as trial balloons, but he also encouraged the attempt to recover implicit theories, for example from childrearing practices or educational practices, in order to better understand and reform those practices. She shows how this social environment came to influence her own research and thinking about the structural and cultural aspects of thought.

In these ways, Jerry Bruner has threaded social considerations more and more deeply into the cognitive processes. The hypotheses that social processes are involved in the formation of intentions, in the planning actions, in learning a language, and in developing modes of thought are conjectures which invited the further thinking and research reported in this volume.

References

Berger, P. and Luckmann, T. *The social construction of reality*. New York: Anchor Books, 1967.

Boring, E. G. *A history of experimental psychology*. New York: Appleton-Century-Crofts, 1950.

Bruner, J. S. On cognitive growth. In J. S. Bruner, R. Olver, and P. M. Greenfield (Eds.), *Studies in cognitive growth*. New York: Wiley, 1966.

————. *Beyond the information given: Studies in the psychology of knowing.* Edited by Jeremy M. Anglin. New York: Norton, 1973.

————. From communication to language: A psychological perspective. *Cognition,* 1975, 3, 255–287.

————. Berlyne memorial lecture: Acquiring the uses of language. *Canadian Journal of Psychology,* 1978, 32, 204–218.

————. Intellectual autobiography. In G. Lindzey (Ed.), *A history of psychology in autobiography* vol. 7. San Francisco: W. H. Freeman, 1980.

Bruner, J. S., Goodnow, J. J., and Austin, G. A. *A study of thinking.* New York: Wiley, 1956.

Bruner, J. S., Greenfield, P., and Olver, R. *Studies in cognitive growth.* New York: Wiley, 1966.

Bruner, J. S., Roy, C., and Ratner, N. The beginnings of request. Mimeographed, 1979.

Butler, S. *Erewhon.* New York: New American Library, 1872.

Chomsky, N. *Problems of knowledge and freedom.* London: Fontana, 1972.

Cole, M and Scribner, S. Introduction to L. Vygotsky, *Mind and Society.* Cambridge, Mass.: Harvard University Press, 1978.

Di Maggio, P. Review essay. On Pierre Bourdieu. *American Journal of Sociology,* 1979, 84, 1460–1474.

Gandy, R. 'Structure' in mathematics. In D. Robey (Ed.), *Structuralism.* Oxford: Clarendon Press, 1973.

Jakobson, R. *Linguistics and poetics.* In T. A. Sebeok (Ed.), *Style in language.* New York: Wiley, 1960.

Leach, E. *Structuralism in social anthoropology.* In D. Robey (Ed), *Structuralism: An introduction.* London: Oxford University Press, 1973.

Lukes, S. *Emile Durkheim: His Life and Work.* Markham, Ontario: Penguin Books, 1973.

Medawar, P. Man: The technological animal. *Smithsonian Magazine,* May, 1973.

Ninio, A. and Bruner, J. S. The achievement and antecedents of labelling. *Journal of Child Language,* 1978, 1–15.

Olson, D. R. *Cognitive development.* New York: Academic Press, 1970.

Parsons, T. *The structure of social action.* Chicago: Free Press, 1949.

Piaget, J. *Biology and knowledge.* Chicago: University Press, 1971.

Pierce, C. S. *Pierce's essays in the philosophy of science.* Edited by Vincent Tomas. New York: Liberal Arts Press, 1957.

Popper, K. *Objective knowledge: An evolutionary approach.* Oxford: Clarendon Press, 1972.

Vico, G. *The new science of Giambattisto Vico.* Translated from the 3rd ed. by T. G. Bergin and M. H. Fisch. Garden City: Doubleday, 1961.

Vygotsky, L. *Thought and language.* Cambridge, Mass.: MIT Press, 1962.

————. *Mind and society.* Cambridge, Mass.: Harvard University Press, 1978.

PART I

Cognition and Language in Their Social Contexts

1

Procedures and Structures
Bärbel Inhelder and Jean Piaget

Any behavior that has a cognitive component also possesses a set of characteristics or properties that may be termed bi-polar, because while seeming somewhat antithetical they are interdependent. Procedures and structures are a typical example. On the one hand, every mathematical construction is based on structures, structures which are currently used or yet to be invented. Using structures or inventing them implies the use of procedures which Polya (1945) termed "heuristics." On the other hand, any strategy used by a child to solve a practical intelligence problem implies the use of procedures that necessarily call on structural knowledge, either already acquired or discovered during the task.

In this paper we intend to examine the relationship between these two fundamental components. To begin with, it is appropriate to show that this indissociable pair, subject to contradictions which are always overcome (as in a happy marriage), is far from being the only pair of this nature and is but one of a long list of similar pairs. The most general characteristic of these pairs is that they all, in different ways, relate to the central pair of "knowing how" and "knowing why."

Our aim is to present new problems suggested by current research pursued by one of the authors and her team,* and not, at this point, to provide solutions.

The most important of these pairs is undoubtedly the complementary pair *action* and *meaning of the action*. An action is an intentional act (as

---

* See Inhelder, Ackermann-Valladao, Blanchet, Karmiloff-Smith, Kilcher-Hagedorn, Montangero and Robert, 1976. For a discussion of experimental results, see Ackermann-Valladao, 1977, Blanchet, 1977, Boder, 1978, Karmiloff-Smith, 1979, Karmiloff-Smith and Inhelder, 1975, Kilcher and Robert, 1977, and Montangero, 1977. The problem of the relationship between action and meaning will be illustrated in a paper by Ackermann-Valladao: "Procédures de résolution de problème chez l'enfant dans une tâche de construction de chemins au moyen d'éléments articulés: étude des relations entre procédures et attribution de significations aux instruments."

opposed to laughing or sneezing for example), carried out on the external world or mentally, involving entities conceptually constructed by the subject, such as classes or numbers, themselves products of previous actions. In this sense, all actions have meaning. Reciprocally, all meanings are directly related to actions. Even the properties or predicates of an immobile object depend on certain mental actions, such as classifications, comparisons, and so on. In fact, all meanings stem from the attribution of schemes to objects or events, and reciprocally, all schemes are the result of construction-by-action. Our first pair exemplifies this very general principle.

Transformations and *comparisons* are a second pair that seems very similar to the first. Every action is either a transformation of an object or a comparison of an object to other objects. Carrying out a transformation also implies making comparisons between the initial state and the final state. Comparisons do not transform objects; if they did, the comparison would be invalid since the objects would be deformed in some way. Nevertheless, making comparisons transforms subject-object relationships by enriching them so that a large variety of new correspondences (bijection, injection, surjection) become possible.

A third pair may be termed *function* and *comprehension*. Function can be defined by the role played by a part of the goal-directed procedure or transformation in the construction of the whole procedure, while comprehension gives the reasons for the mechanisms involved (Piaget, 1974). However, a function cannot be cognitively complete as long as it is not "comprehended"; it must, sooner or later, also be "explained." Reciprocally, the comprehension of the process relies in part on structural aspects but does not become complete until the functions have been analyzed. On the biological level, this pair plays an evident role. Organs and their functions are both interdependent and distinct. The pair obviously also plays a role on a psychological level, from the most primitive behaviors to the most complex. Moreover, the well-known polemics between structuralists and functionalists, or, in other words, between those interested in studying the "why" and those interested in studying the "how" of human behavior, arise because of this fundamental distinction.

The fourth pair, an extension of the third, is of an even more general nature: namely *finality* and *causality*. Even though it appears that here we are dealing with a fundamental duality, an irreducible opposition, the link between the two poles, is just as strong as for the other pairs. The fundamental distinction between finality or "teleology" (which is based on the deceptive idea of "final causes," as if the pursuit of a goal in itself provides sufficient explanation) and "teleonomy" (sometimes defined by its partisans as a "mechanistic explanation of finality") serves to justify the link between the two poles.

More precisely, the tenet of finality is that the future determines the present, as Max Planck believed. Planck, though a physicist of genius, ascribed the inversion of the future and the past to the explanation of the principle of the shortest path traveled by light through the atmosphere. Teleonomy, however, does not reject the idea that the present determines the future and explains that the shortest path, in fact a curve, is the result of successive regulations.

From this point of view, the two terms are not antithetical but interdependent. In fact, in this cybernetic sense, every action has a finality. Even a mathematician demonstrating a theorem, though he is elaborating a structure, is involved in goal-oriented activity: his goal is to achieve a satisfactory demonstration. Because the goal precedes the action itself, the initial anticipatory representation of the goal is the cause (or part of a succession of causes and effects, if we are dealing with a series of sub-goals that follow one from the other). Goals thus partly, at least, determine the way the process is produced. Therefore, teleonomy and causal explanations, in their widest sense, are not opposed or contradictory, but interdependent.

Internal and *external* finality form a fifth pair. This pair deserves careful examination, as it is of some importance for understanding the relationship between structures and procedures. A subject attempting to obtain a result in the external world (as for example the balancing of weighing scales) has a clear external goal, which is immediately obvious to an observer. When the subject's activity is mental, reflective, and abstract (as in mathematics, even if the problem is "simple") it seems that despite appearances, he has a purpose, which is just as systematic as for the goals described previously. He is trying to satisfy an internal need. Internal needs do not necessarily lead the subject to perform actions in the external world but are related to the subject's internal mental activity. No matter how antithetical these two types of goals may appear, they are as interdependent as the other pairs described above. On the one hand, logico-mathematical instruments, previously constructed according to internal goals, are needed for fulfilling external goals. On the other hand, internal goals lead to the construction of new mental constructs (classes, numbers, morphisms, etc.) that will sooner or later serve for generating problems in physics that imply external goals.

It is appropriate to distinguish a sixth pair. The following two types of processes may seem antithetical but are readily seen to be interdependent. The first type of process shows the subject which are the schemes, previously constructed, that can be used for solving the problem. That is not a simple recognition process, to be interpreted in a behavioristic or associationistic fashion. Rather, calling on or using schemes that have already been constructed implies making assimilations to previous acquisitions.

The second type of process leads the subject to understand which gaps must be bridged by the construction of new schemes or by new accommodations. Clearly these two types of processes, one of "re-use" and one of construction, though they may lead to behavior which is oriented in distinct directions, always have to be combined and depend on each other. Once again, possible oppositions are overruled, and we clearly see that the two elements are interdependent. This interdependency is an interesting particular case of a more general link between what we may call "retroactive" and "proactive" processes, re-utilization and creation of novelties, or, in a wider sense, recursive or precursive processes.

A seventh pair can be formulated as the synthesis of the six pairs described above: *knowing how* and *knowing why*. These two processes, though they can easily be distinguished, always tend to support one another despite the fact that failures do occur and that their union is only progressively established.

As the seven pairs analyzed all play some role in the relationship between procedures and structures, we are clearly dealing with a complex problem. Nevertheless, we will attempt to solve it in a satisfactory manner, whatever the various personal sympathies for one or the other of these cognitive components may be.

The essential difference that distinguishes procedures and structures is the following. Although both procedures and structures are based on transformations, procedures carry out or make use of transformations in order to attain a great variety of specific goals. Procedures are thus fundamentally temporal processes. Structures, however, link transformations one to the other and extract connections to form atemporal systems. The only goal involved is the very general goal of understanding the nature of the system, common to all structures. Without a doubt, constructing structures is a certain type of goal-oriented activity, and it therefore entails the use of various procedures. However, once a structure has been discovered or elaborated, it loses its teleonomic dimension. Reciprocally, using a procedure to obtain a particular physical result (like finding the center of gravity of an object, Karmiloff-Smith and Inhelder, 1975) may lead to the discovery of a structure (of compensation for example). Once established, the structure becomes atemporally stable. It is also worth noting that when the subject uses some of the operations of a structure when carrying out a procedure, he uses the operation locally or momentarily, and this *is* a temporal procedure, or part of one. However, if the operation is re-inserted into the corresponding structure, its structural character is once more established. Let us point out that even the non-transformational structures such as elementary morphisms or correspondences can be used as procedures. This happens when a child establishes a one-to-one correspondence between elements of two sets to see if the sets are made up of an equal number of elements.

Before taking our comparison further, it is obviously appropriate to first counter an objection that is frequently made. If structures are systems that are or seem atemporal, it may be that they do not exist in the child's mind but are merely the product of interpretations made by psychologists or logicians who observe the child's behavior and that the child actually only makes use of procedures. This is somewhat like stating that even though children are aware of eating and breathing, their stomachs and lungs only exist in the minds of physiologists. Structures are related to the child's "know-how," independently of his awareness of them. If the child is aware of procedures rather than of structures, it is because it is easier to mentally track a temporal succession of processes or actions than it is to mentally combine the diverse connections of a structural totality in one cognitive set.

What the child considers possible, impossible, or necessary furnishes the best proof of the existence of structures in the child's mind (Piaget, 1976). In this respect, there are considerable differences between the types of reasoning of preoperational subjects and the reasoning of subjects in the concrete operational stage. Let us give an example. The child is given ten sticks of different lengths correctly seriated and is asked "How many sticks are there that are bigger than this tiny one?" The child easily shows the smallest stick and correctly counts the others. Then the experimenter shows the biggest stick and asks "And how many are smaller than this one?" The five-to-six year-old will then count the sticks again, whereas one or two years later he will laugh and immediately answer "Nine also, of course." The "of course" said by the child is the important indication (Berthoud, 1979). In another example, the experimenter is seated in front of two glasses containing an unequal number of beads, and one of the glasses is opaque ($x \neq x$). The inequality is brought to the child's notice. The experimenter then puts beads into the two glasses, one bead in each glass at the same time, using both his hands. In this situation young subjects believe that if one carries out the operation often enough, the quantity of beads in the two glasses may become the same ($x' = n$, $x = n$). Subjects of a more advanced level consider this impossible. Reciprocally, if $x = x'$ at the start, and if the experimenter keeps on adding $+n$ as described, young subjects no longer know if $x = n$ will always equal $x' = n$, whereas more advanced subjects consider this conservation necessary: "Oh yes, once you know, you know for ever!" as one of our subjects said (see Piaget and Inhelder, 1963, p. 66).

Conversely, examples of pseudo-necessities can often be observed in young children. A square must be "resting on" (viewed from) one of its sides to remain a square. If it is resting on one of its corners, it is no longer a square, but "two triangles," and its sides are perceived as unequal in length (Sinclair and Piaget, 1968). Judgments of this type show that even if the child is not conscious of the structures involved, structures do play an objective, systematic role that cannot be denied. The role they play and their effects are constantly visible in implications and incompatibilities. Of course, judgments concerning what is possible or necessary are not based on processes that are directly observable; they are the results of inferential processes. In short, structures play a role in the inferences a subject makes, while procedures are far more empirical. The elimination of contradictions or incompatibilities in the inferential process best reveals the structural nature of inferences.

A second fundamental difference is the result of the difference between structures as atemporal operations and procedures as goal-oriented temporal sequences of aims and means. Structures tend to become logically integrated one into the other, whereas procedures are chained sequentially. Procedures are chained and not integrated: they are only integrated when a sub-procedure (dependent on a sub-goal) becomes part of the complete procedure. The integration of structures, however, is a general mechanism that already occurs in sensorimotor behavior and gradually increases to the highest level of scientific thought. The scheme of searching for an object is a good example at the sensorimotor level. When a toy is hidden several times in front of his eyes, the infant will first look in the spot where the object was first hidden and found. Later, this scheme becomes integrated into the more general scheme of object permanency. That is, the child always looks for the object in the spot where it actually was seen to disappear. Later, the structural scheme of object permanency is integrated into the mathematical group of displacements. In short, even at the most elementary stages of development, simple structures are integrated into wider, richer structures. This process develops considerably in the preoperational and concrete operational stages. For example, the early conservations, such as that of matter, are integrated into observation structures of a more general nature, such as weight. Later, the first groupings—classifications and seriations—are integrated into groups that coordinate the two types of reversibility (inversion and reciprocity), as for instance in the explanation of the relationship between action and reaction in physics. These different integration mechanisms prefigure what eventually becomes the general rule of logico-mathematical thinking ("monoids" are integrated into groups, these are then integrated into fields, and so on).

As far as procedures are concerned, they do not integrate into each other in the same way but are rather chained one to the other in the following way. First of all, there is an unlimited number of procedures as new ones have to be constructed for every new goal, and every new problem implies a new goal. The chaining of procedures is made up of successive replacements and diversifications. Of course, procedures that are already known can be used if they are appropriate or if they can be modified to suit the new goal. Secondly, a series of successive procedures must be carried out if the goal cannot be reached immediately. For example, goal B must be solved by means x, and means x is at present not directly accessible to the subject. Means y must then be used to gain access of means x; means x is therefore a subgoal B_1. If means y is not directly accessible either, and one has to resort to means z, means y is then a sub-goal B_2, and so on. Such processes are the general rule for complicated problems, and the chaining that takes place is a succession of steps; this is a different kind of link from integration.

Now that we have described these two fundamental differences between procedures and structures we can return to the seven pairs we discussed in the beginning of this paper. The seven pairs can be found both in procedures and structures; however, they are closely linked in different ways and always remain distinct. The seventh pair (knowing how and knowing why), which summarizes the six other pairs, allows us to analyze the nature of the distinctions between procedures and structures. It is clear that knowing how plays a role both in the discovery and the carrying out of procedures and in the use of structures. However, understanding the reasons why plays a different role in procedures and structures. Carrying out one of the operations of a structure cannot be done without an understanding of the structural constraints involved, because structures are closed systems of operations (though they may nevertheless be integrated into larger systems). Classifying objects means consciously seeking out similarities and differences. Seriating them according to size or systematically carrying out an operation such as in + 1 means consciously searching for differences. This kind of knowing how cannot be disassociated from the corresponding knowing why: the subject feels that both his actions and their results are "necessary." By contrast, though understanding the reasons for using a particular procedure obviously promotes its use, such understanding is not strictly speaking essential, as noting the result of a procedure takes precedence over everything else. In most cases, procedures are thus constantly modified in the light of previous results. Sometimes subjects will even make a drawing (or use other figurative means) of a procedure that has been carried out, so that it may be corrected or used again later. Subjects will often make anticipatory gestures that favor the choice of the most appropriate means. On the whole, comprehension plays a secondary role, as the primary aim is to succeed. Subjects are able to achieve pragmatic success without being able to reconstruct the entire procedure or understanding the reason why certain links are necessary. However, it is impossible to structure contents without at the same time realizing "why" and "how." This holds for structures that are attributed to objects (models of causal explanations) as well as for logico-mathematical structures. Subjects follow each step of classification or seriation groupings, and they are aware of their reasons. Subjects can also state, in some fashion, the relevant properties of more complex structures, like those dealing with propositions, for example.

To summarize, the dialectical process that takes place between structures is a fundamental characteristic of cognition. Procedures do not possess—or do not generally possess—this fundamental characteristic. When a structure expands into a more sophisticated one that derives from it, the "older" structure is integrated into the "newer" one. By contrast, on a biological level, "newer" structures generally replace "older" structures, either totally or partially.

Another difference between procedures and structures springs from the preceding ones. Diversification is the rule for procedures, whereas unification is the rule for structures. Procedures become varied because practical problems and/or goals are so large in number: the subject has to discover appropriate means for solving each problem. By contrast, progress in structural knowledge implies unification processes because structures extract internal composition laws and transformations that have their own justification inside the system, in connection with those of other systems. This difference between procedures and structures naturally does not exclude the advantage to be gained in certain cases by generalizing successful procedures, nor does it prevent the discovery of new structures. The subject's capacities are enriched by enlarging the number of distinct procedures. However, constructing new structures leads to effective progress only if they can be related one to the other in an integrative system, as described above. Secondly, being able to reach a goal by a variety of means is an obvious advantage: applying several structures to one content is a cause of structural progress only if the structures are tightly linked. This is the case, for example, for the role played by cardinality and ordinality in the comprehension of natural number. Young subjects do not immediately understand that an ordinal rank such as "fifth in the series" implies that this element is preceded by a cardinal number of four. In short, the richness of procedures depends on their variety and number, and the richness of structures depends on the coherence and complexity of the integrative links between them— not on their number. The more complex they are, the more stable they are: for procedures, this relationship is inversed.

To conclude, despite the considerable differences between them, procedures and structures are the two inseparable poles of all cognitive activities. Procedures and structures are the most general pair discussed in this paper: their opposition, rather than excluding interdependence, promotes it. Every structure is the result of a procedural construction, and every procedure makes use of some of the aspects of structures. Let us point out—for those who do not believe in structures—that structures elaborated in childhood are finally integrated into those of adult scientific thinking. Classification groupings are simple and acquired early, and are also the fundamental structures of zoology and botany. The group of displacements is the basis of geometry. Algebra comprises primitive operations of correspondence, inversion, and reciprocity. In short, science could not exist without the structural instruments that characterize psychological development from early childhood on. Technology derives from procedures. The relationship, however, between technology and science is extremely complex, and technology is not merely an offshoot of science—nor is it the root of science.

References

Ackermann-Valladao, E. Analyse des procédures de résolution d'un problème de composition de hauteurs. *Archives de Psychologie*, 1977, 45, 101–125.

Berthoud-Papandropoulou, I. Children's constructions of correspondences in double seriation tasks. In Frank B. Murray (Ed.), *The impact of Piagetian theory*. Baltimore: University Park Press, 1979, 29–30.

Blanchet, A. La construction et l'équilibre du mobile: Problèmes méthodologiques. *Archives de Psychologie*, 1977, 45, 29–52.

Boder, A. Etude de la composition d'un ordre inverse: Hypothèse sur la coordination de deux sources de contrôle du raisonnement. *Archives de Psychologie*, 1978, 46, 87–113.

Inhelder, B., Ackermann-Valladao, E., Blanchet, A., Karmiloff-Smith, A., Kilcher-Hagedorn, H., Montangero, J., et Robert, M. Des structures cognitives aux procédures de découverte. *Archives de Psychologie*, 1976, 44, 57–72.

Inhelder, B. et Piaget, J. De l'itération des actions à la récurrence élémentaire. In P. Greco et al., *La formation des raisonnements récurrentiels*. Etudes d'épistémologie génétique XVII. Paris: PUF, 1963, 47–106.

Karmiloff-Smith, A. Problem-solving procedures in children's construction and representations of closed railway circuits. *Archives de Psychologie*, 1979, 47, 37–59.

Karmiloff-Smith, A. and Inhelder, B. If you want to get ahead, get a theory. *Cognition*, 1974, 3, 195–212.

Kilcher, H. et Robert, M. Procédures d'actions lors de constructions de ponts et d'escaliers. *Archives de Psychologie*, 1977, 45, 53–83.

Montangero, J. Expérimentation, réussite et compréhension chez l'enfant dans trois tâches d'élévation d'un niveau d'eau par immersion d'objets. *Archives de Psychologie*, 1977, 45, 127–148.

Piaget, J. Le possible, l'impossible et le nécessaire. *Archives de Psychologie*, 1976, 44, 281–299.

Polya, G. *How to solve it*, Princeton, N.J.: Princeton University Press, 1945.

Sinclair, H. et Piaget, J. Sondage sur l'identité, les formes d'équivalence et la conservation lors de la rotation d'un carré. In J. Piaget et al., *Epistémologie et psychologie de l'identité*, Etudes d'épistémologie génétique XXIV. Paris: PUF, 1968, 47–107,

2

The Verification Task and Beyond

Peter C. Wason

*"Given that we know 'p', both what is involved in
believing 'p' and what would make 'p' true or false,
what can we say about 'not-p'?"*

—B. Russell

In 1957 I devised the precursor of the verification task and presented a preliminary account of it (by invitation) to polite but indifferent ears at a meeting of the Experimental Psychology Group on March 25, 1958. The chairman said afterwards that it was always interesting to hear from young research workers even if their work was not yet ripe for publication. The paper based on that talk, "The processing of positive and negative information," was published at inordinate length in the May, 1959, issue of the *Quarterly Journal of Experimental Psychology*.

The verification task has since become a paradigm in the United States, and a large number of studies in the information-processing tradition have ensued from its use. I shall argue that this has not been wholly beneficial because this task is not representative of the way in which negation is used in everyday discourse. In particular I shall attack the spurious status of a "true negative" (hereafter TN). But first I want to tell the story of how it all happened. To do this is to court disaster. Not only does it seem to inflate the importance of the research, but to dwell on the past when so much remains to be done is to risk the charge of self-indulgence. It is a risk I am prepared to run. Published accounts of research, whether in books or learned journals, necessarily omit, in the interests of the pseudo-objectivity of science, questions about how and why the research was done in the first place. As Medawar (1964) has pointed out, the scientific paper gives a total misleading narrative of the thought processes that go into the making of scientific discoveries. To remedy this I have written two general articles on negation, an interim report (Wason, 1962) and a "final" one (Wason, 1972). But even these omit the social context of the research. Hence apart from grinding my own special axe, I shall attempt to recapture conceptual innocence (which Bruner has said is impossible) and tell a personal story for three reasons. First, I think it may be of more than marginal interest to relate how fortuitous factors made me turn one way rather than another. Second, it seems to me quite extraordinary that it took all of us so many years—about fifteen—to reveal facts and assemble theories which, as it turns out, the layman already knows and does not find surprising. Third, I should like to remind the student that papers in learned journals do not reflect all those doubts, mistakes, perplexities, and seconds thoughts which beset everyone who has done research. In order to achieve this aim I shall quote liberally from my notes, which go back to 1957, even if this causes me some embarrassment.

Nowadays, of course, everybody seems to have a theory, but when I began my study I had only a robust phenomenon. Why did I want to investigate it? Two factors made me interested in negation. First, as a postgraduate student in the 1950s, I was inspired by a lecture by Bruner on the ideal strategies involved in his concept attainment task which were to loom so large in the classic *A Study of Thinking* (Bruner, Goodnow, and Austin, 1956). The subtle interplay between positive and negative information intrigued me, and I remember that immediately after the lecture I went to a café and worked over the strategies with my wife. The second factor may sound a little incongruous. In 1953 I had been appointed to the Medical Research Council Industrial Psychology Research Group and (together with A.R. Jonckheere and Sheila Jones) became interested in the incomprehensibility of official leaflets issued by the government to enlighten the individual about how he stood in relation to various benefits. (As a matter of fact I am still interested in these publications.) One pronounced cause of difficulty was the concatenation of negatives: "A Class 1 contribution is not payable for employment by any one employer for not more than 8 hours in any week—but if you normally work for more than 8 hours in any week for any one employer, a Class 1 contribution is payable except for any week when you do not do more than 4 hours work for the employer."

(Incidentally, the Civil Services are inclined to say that the presentation of such leaflets has been improved. If so, the reader should pay close attention to the following sentence from a contemporary leaflet: "Death grant is a sum payable on the death of a man who has paid contributions, his wife, child or widow or on the death of a woman who has paid contributions, her husband, child or widower.")

As a substitute for continuous prose, we devised an algorithmic procedure which eliminated any use of negatives. The principle behind the elimination was the trivial fact that a true negative is logically equivalent to a false affirmative. The people at the treasury were benevolent but not particularly thrilled. More important to me than this official reaction was the cognitive processing which might be involved in understanding affirmative and negative sentences. I should like to think that this development of a pure problem from an applied one owes something to the British tradition of psychological research, epitomized by the work of men such as Bartlett, Craik, Mackworth, and Broadbent at the MRC Applied Psychology Unit.

My notes reveal only a crude and tenuous amalgam inspired by applied and theoretical interests. They contain no mention of the semantic concepts of truth and falsity; in mitigation of my blindness, none of my colleagues with whom I discussed these ideas saw this connection which today is patently obvious. I saw the problem as one of interrelating a "situation" (corresponding to a state of affairs), a sentence (affirmative or negative), and a response (acceptance or rejection). Accordingly, I made a large wooden board divided into four numbered quadrants and considered the different ways in which one might describe the disposition of a number of colored counters arranged on it. (Here one can see the obvious links with Bruner's concept attainment task.) As always before doing a new experiment I seemed to be fumbling in the dark. Would a greater degree of conceptual clarity have enhanced my progress? Put more bluntly—would considered thinking have enabled me to clarify a problem more than crude experimentation?

Outline of problem, 1957. Certain types of discourse such as rules, regulations, and legal documents have in common the fact that they may both explicitly include and explicitly exclude different contingencies. They assert what has to be the case and what has not to be the case in order for the condition to be satisfied. A fundamental distinction between two classes of things can accordingly be drawn.

1. On the one hand, there is the situation (state of affairs) which has to be tested against the conditions. It may represent the facts or existing characteristics which may, or may not, all be relevant. In the experiment the situation might consist of the physical presence of a red, blue, green, or black counter.

2. On the other hand, there are the conditions which describe those aspects of the situation which are necessary for their fulfillment. They consist of names, assertions, negative terms, conjunctions, etc. "Both Black and Red," "Not both Black and Red," "It is not the case that Blue, Green, and Red," etc.

The situation, then, consists in the presence of certain things; the conditions consist in possible descriptions of the situation. When these two classes are considered together it is evident that four possibilities can occur.

a. A condition expressed positively can be fulfilled by the situation, e.g., "Both Red and Black," and the fact that there is a red and a black object present.

b. A condition expressed positively can be unfulfilled by the situation, e.g., "Both Red and Black," and the fact that there is a red and a green object present.

c. A condition expressed negatively can be fulfilled by the situation, e.g., "Not both Red and Black," and the fact that there is a red and a green object present.

d. A condition expressed negatively can be unfulfilled by the situation, e.g., "Not both Red and Black," and the fact that there is a red and a black object present.

Is it easier to discriminate negative information which is fulfilled by the facts, or positive information which is not fulfilled by the facts? [In contemporary terms: is a true negative easier than a false affirmative?]

When the negative information is to be fulfilled by the situation, the subject is directed immediately to the situation which ought to obtain, but when the positive information is to be unfulfilled, the subject is directed to (a) a situation expressed in positive terms which (b) must not obtain. In the former case the exclusion is expressed in the condition itself; in the latter it is expressed in the "mental set" of the subject. And yet accepting the fulfillment of information expressed negatively may be more difficult. Primitive commerce with the environment is in terms of things rather than "not things," and "no" has a different emotional connotation from "yes." Yet at the perceptual rather than the cognitive level, response to the cessation of a stimulus is evidently just as rapid as response to its onset.

It may also be interesting to examine the possibilities of having the subject (a) adjust the condition to fit a given situation, and (b) adjust the situation to fit a given condition. This allows the variation of another factor: the response itself, which can be of a positive or a negative kind. The response could be either one of selection (acceptance) of appropriate conditions (or objects). In either case acceptance or rejection could lead to the same results.

Alas, not all these gloriously complex ideas were investigated; the "direction of response" was forgotten about; the board and counters were never used. I now think this was rather a pity. The unconscious (or conscious) pressures to design a clean, quantifiable experiment predominated over a more playful urge. As Kubie (1958) might have said, the obsessional elements in my thinking overcame the hysterical ones. All that remained was an exploratory experiment in which affirmative and negative conjunctive sentences had to be adjusted (by selecting one out of a pair of adjectives) in accordance with an instruction to make them agree or conflict with a given situation (an array of colored discs). Each of the four conditions—true affirmatives (TA), false affirmatives (FA), true negatives (TN), and false negatives (FN)—was presented six times. The time taken to adjust each statement was recorded by a stopwatch. The most surprising result was that these times were differentiated in the same order at each of the six presentations. The mean times with errors in parentheses were: TA — 8.99 sec. (4), FA = 11.09 sec. (6), TN = 12.58 sec. (8), FN = 15.17 sec. (29).

I interpreted these results in terms of (a) the assumption of a "positive set" established through a long learning process, (b) the inferential nature of negatives in relation to experience, and (c) the emotional connotations of negative terms. There was no difficulty in accounting for the fact that TA was much easier than FN, but the consistent difference between a logically equivalent FA and TN involved a more subtle analysis of the interaction between positive and negative "mental sets." The whole discussion has a curiously dated air about it. My journal entry continues, "It seems plausible to suggest that the nervous system does not behave like the Kalin-Burkhart

Logical-Truth Calculator but, as far as speed goes at any rate, responds in a one-sided way in favor of positive information, just because that kind of information is of such practical importance. In other words, it is assumed that there is an habitual (and unnoticed) positive set to the environment which makes adjustment to negative information inherently slower."

Such an argument hardly provides the basis of a scientific hypothesis because it appears untestable. But then I doubt whether, in 1958, any psychologists, in the United Kingdom at any rate, had heard of transformations in the sense in which the term is used in linguistics. I found it ironical to read in a book published much later (Schlesinger, 1968) "The first experiments with transformations were carried out by Wason and by Eifermann." And apart from transformations there did not seem any solid basis for explanation. My critics pointed out, however, that the affirmative and negative sentences which I had used did not convey the same amount of information, and hence any comparison of the responses made to them is vitiated. (Information Theory still exerted a powerful hold on the thinking of psychologists in the 1950s.) After leaving the problem aside to work on a generative reasoning task (Wason, 1960), I decided to take account of this criticism by using as my material the mutually exclusive classes of odd and even numbers: to assert that a whole number is not odd is to assert that it is even; to assert that it is not even is to assert that it is odd (Wason, 1961). One aim was to see if I could replicate the findings of the exploratory experiment within this more tightly controlled framework. In this "construction task" the subject had to name a digit to make an incomplete affirmative or negative sentence either true or false in accordance with an instruction. A second aim was to investigate a "verification task" in which the subject had to judge whether affirmative or negative sentences were true or false, for example, "Seven is not an even number," "Five is an even number."

The results from the construction task strikingly confirmed those obtained in the 1959 study: at each of the six presentations of the types of sentence the reaction times were such that TA < FA < TN < FN. This particular task has not been at all influential; the only subsequent reference I can find to it is Lazerson and Irving (1977). The results from the verification task suggested a differentiation between the responses to affirmatives and negatives regardless of their truth or falsity. Both the error pattern and the subjects' introspections, however, suggested an interaction between the form of a sentence and its truth value such that TA < FA < FN < TN. (Nearly twice as many errors occurred to TN compared to FN.) The introspections, however, were the most surprising. Confronted by a negative sentence, the subjects contrived to eliminate its negativity. One way of doing this was an artifactual consequence of the binary predicates: "not even" was read as "odd"; and "not odd," as "even." This strategy spoils the basis of a negative sentence and shows that my critics' demand to equate the information from affirmatives and negatives was misplaced. Much more interesting was another strategy in which subjects claimed they mentally deleted the negative, then verified the resulting sentence as true or false, and finally changed their answer to take account of the deletion. It is apparent that the procedure makes TN the most complicated type of sentence: "Seven is not an even number" → "Seven is an even number" → "false" → "true." These processes, which have been axiomatized in terms of the number of steps involved, form the core of the "verification models" which will be considered subsequently.

At the time I failed to appreciate the interest of this result. On the contrary, I (wrongly) attributed the removal of the negative to a distaste for coping with its emotional connotations. There was putative evidence for this strong dislike in the spontaneous comments of the subjects in the 1959 study. With the help of Sheila Jones I resolved to try to separate the denotation of the negative from its connotations. My colleague, Rivka Eifermann (1961) had already tried to exploit this distinction in an ingenious experiment. In Hebrew there are two words for "not"; *lo*, which is used in all contexts including the prohibitive, and *éyno*, which is used only to make a denial. Eifermann repeated my 1961 experiment, using two groups of subjects at the Hebrew University of Jerusalem. She found significantly longer response times and a greater number of errors in the verification of sentences containing the more general negator (*lo*) in spite of the fact that it evidently has a greater frequency of usage. She pointed out, however, that syntactic factors could also have contributed to the difference.

My reaction was to draw a distinction between (a) the stimulus properties of the negative arising from its association with prohibition, and (b) its purely logical function of denial. We thought we could realize this distinction by conditioning neutral signs (nonsense syllables) to serve the function of assertion and denial in sentences about the evenness of whole numbers (Wason and Jones, 1963). It was predicted that the difference between the response times to such covert affirmatives and negatives would be less than the corresponding difference between ordinary (overt) affirmative and negative sentences. This prediction was highly confirmed. Most of the subjects rapidly developed algorithms for processing the covert affirmatives and negatives, and their response to verifying such sentences was very rapid. On the other hand, the minority who admitted interpreting the signs in terms of assertion and denial revealed a significant difference between affirmatives and negatives. But subsequent reflection revealed a flaw in the whole conception of the experiment. The prediction was confirmed, not by virtue of the intended separation between denotation and connotation, but by extra-linguistic decision procedures which do not necessarily capture the denotation of a denial; for example, "if an even number and DAX, or an odd number and MED, then press TRUE, but otherwise FALSE." Negation is a linguistic concept which has no strict meaning outside language. As the decision procedures reveal, in indicative contexts any sign intended to denote negation can be construed in purely affirmative terms. The most that can be said of the experiment was that the majority of subjects showed no comparable tendency to compute the English sentences in terms of algorithmic decision procedures.

In an ethos which is not dominated by cognitive factors and by information processing I rather like this abortive attempt to bring out the effects of affective variables. I do not think the issue is closed. Some unpublished research by Ben Reich (1970) is relevant. He showed that it took much longer to complete the sentence stem "I hate . . . because . . . " than the stem "I love . . . because . . . ", but no such difference between the stems "He hates . . . because . . . " and "He loves . . . because . . . ."

Our experiment did, however, yield one bonus. It revealed the first chronometric confirmation of the interaction, $TA < FA < FN < TN$, which had been suggested by the error pattern in my 1961 study and which has now been corroborated by so many independent studies. The really instructive and extraordinary thing about it was that its interpretation was not apparent for a long time. It escaped Lee McMahon and the examiners of his Ph.D. thesis at Harvard in 1963. It provides the central organizing feature of the verification models which were elaborated in the 1970s. And yet, as I shall argue, its importance has been wildly exaggerated because its interpretation is rather trivial. But in 1962, having just written a popular report on these studies for the Communication Research Centre at University College London, I became bored by the verification task and engrossed by the role of self-contradiction in reasoning (Wason, 1964).

My interest in chronometric studies would probably have lapsed entirely, but I was invited by Jerome Bruner and George Miller to spend a year at Harvard's Center for Cognitive studies. There I set out to investigate my new line of research, which, however, met with no conspicuous success. My interest in verification was revived by the concerted research being done by George Miller and his associates on the implicit knowledge of rules in the understanding of language. They established that the time taken to carry out grammatical transformations was additive and linear (Miller and McKean, 1964). For example, given the sentence "John liked the small boy," it was found that the time taken to make its negative transform, "John didn't like the small boy" and its passive transform, "The small boy was liked by John," summated for the time taken to make the passive-negative transform, "The small boy wasn't liked by John." It was also shown that other grammatical features such as verb form did not have additive effects. When the subjects were asked to carry out the relevant transformation in order to locate the transformed sentence in a list, it was apparent that the passive took about one second longer than the active, and the negative about 0.4 sec. longer than the affirmative. However, subsequent research by McMahon (1963) and by Slobin (1963) suggested that the estimated time for the passive transformation was an experimental artifact.

When the subject had to determine whether a sentence was true or false, the negative again took about 0.4 sec. longer than the affirmative, but the passive transformation consumed hardly any extra time. Hence Miller and McKean (1964) supposed that the additional times were spent in semantic rather than syntactic operations.

Unfortunately the employment of the verification task, with its misleading emphasis on the TN, distorted and exaggerated the effects of negation although this went unnoticed at the time. McMahon (1963) had pointed out that "Through all the experiments negativity, as such, regardless of grammatical complexity, had effects on behavior." But he failed to explain the interaction ($TA < FA < FN < TN$) which permeated his studies. Since Slobin (1963) had also obtained it I felt compelled to formulate a rough and ready model with which to interpret it. It assumes that a negative in a sentence contributes more difficulty than a mismatch between a sentence and its referent. This was represented numerically by assigning a weight of two to a negative, a weight of unity to a mismatch, with an affirmative and a match weighted as zero. The model (Slobin, 1963) predicts the order of difficulty of the four types of sentence which had now been obtained by all of us in the verification task:

Sentence type	Negativity	+	Mismatch	=	Difficulty
TA	0	+	0	=	0
FA	0	+	1	=	1
FN	2	+	0	=	2
TN	2	+	1	=	3

The model is crude and ad hoc. Its chief value at the time was the heuristic one of revealing that FN, despite its name, is not a double negative; it is TN which is a double negative. Subsequently I formulated an intuitive, verbal representation which brings this out more clearly:

TA = a fact
FA = a falsehood
FN = denial of a fact
TN = denial of a falsehood

During 1963 my time at Harvard was running out, but I became obsessed with the idea that more was entailed in understanding a negative than we had hitherto suspected. We had inferred semantic effects but none of us had mentioned pragmatics. I determined to investigate whether the way in which negative sentences are normally used affects our response to them. My starting point was a memorable quote from Strawson (1952): "The standard and primary use of *not* is specifically to contradict or correct; to cancel a suggestion of one's own or another's." In other words, negation functions within an affirmative context. But how could this be realized experimentally? One obvious idea which originally appealed to me was to build up the affirmative context by a temporal succession of items. The list "A fly is an insect, a moth is an insect, a centipede is an insect, a spider is not an insect" seems to be an appropriate use of negation because it first establishes an interest in a class and then (correctly) denies that a member is an instance of that class. It should be verified more easily than the following list, which establishes no such interest in one class: "A swallow is a bird, a cow is a mammal, an adder is a snake, a spider is not an insect." A scheme of this kind makes quite a good "thought experiment." Compare in your mind the process of verifying the following sentences:

1. Five is not even.
2. Four is even and seven is not even.

Example 1 is frequently accompanied by mental deletion of the negative, but example 2 does not seem to do so because of the affirmative context.

My next experimental attempt was to create an affirmative context, not through a temporal succession of items, but through the perceptual properties of a figure. I still have a draft on this idea prepared for an Annual Report of the Center of Cognitive Studies:

It is assumed that an unexceptional fact is analogous to the symmetrical properties of a figure, and that an exceptional fact is analogous to its asymmetrical properties. For example, a red square constitutes an unexceptional fact, but a blue strip on its left edge constitutes an exceptional fact which qualifies the description "red square." It is predicted that the response latencies to negative statements will be relatively fast when such statements refer to exceptional facts ("the left edge of the square is not red"), relatively slow when the statements refer to unexceptional facts ("the right edge of the square is not blue"), and intermediate when a fact appears neither exceptional nor unexceptional (when a figure is half red and half blue). On the other hand, it is predicted that affirmative reference to either unexceptional, or exceptional, facts will not affect the response latencies to such statements.

A pilot study failed to show these effects, but I felt it was a near miss. On a public holiday my family left for Vermont, and I finally evolved a scheme which was ultimately reported in "The contexts of plausible denial" (Wason, 1965). One of my colleagues assured me it wouldn't work, and of course afterwards everyone said it was rather obvious. I was sufficiently pleased with the idea to sketch it on my blackboard. The next event struck me as interesting. Bruner visited my office, and I outlined the new idea which I told him I intended to carry out in London on my return. Without making any comment he went to the telephone and arranged an extension for me to stay on at Harvard for a month or so. At the same time he acquired the services of a new assistant, Susan Carey (now Susan Carey Block), to help me conduct the experiment and shortly afterwards arranged all the technical facilities which I needed. Such a series of events would hardly have happened in the United Kingdom, and I do not think the difference is solely attributable to financial considerations. It struck me as the first of many cases in which Americans seem to possess a wider "horizon of possibilities."

It would be a mistake to suppose that the rationale of the experiment was completely clear at this stage. Only the basic idea was articulated: the distinction between exceptional and unexceptional facts. Basically, I predicted that it would be easier to negate an exceptional fact in terms of the property which makes it an exception than to deny one of the unexceptional facts in terms of the exceptional fact. But (conceptually) I had conflated this idea with the notion that it was more appropriate to deny the property of a smaller classes in terms of the property of a larger class (e.g., "a quarter of the square is not red") than to deny the converse (e.g., "three quarters of the square is not blue"). In my Harvard notes the distinction between the two conditions lay in the difference between "(a) the coding of the facts in terms of differing generality, and (b) explicit reference in the statements to a smaller (exceptional), or a larger (unexceptional) class of interest." Experimentally this produced two conditions—Group A and Group B, both of which I (wrongly) assumed were connected with exceptional and unexceptional facts at different levels.

In Group A the subjects were exposed to a series of cards on each of which appeared eight numbered circles. These were always either seven blue circles and one red one, or seven red circles and one blue one, the position of the one circle in a different color varying in position from card to card. As each card was exposed, the subjects had to describe it aloud so that it could be remembered. These descriptions were always naturally in the form "Circle No. 3 in blue and the rest are red" or "All the circles are red except for No. 3 which is blue." The card was then removed, and one of four types of statement exposed at each trial. The subjects' task was to complete the sentence by pressing a key marked RED or a key marked BLUE, which terminated a timing device. The incomplete types of sentence were:

"Circle number 3 is _____."

(an affirmative statement about the "odd man out," i.e., a "different affirmative," DA).

"Circle number 3 is not _____."

(a negative statement about the "odd man out," i.e., a "different negative," DN).

"Circle number 6 (say) is _____."

(an affirmative statement about any circle in the majority color, i.e., a "similar affirmative," SA).

"Circle number 2 (say) is not _____."

(a negative statement about any circle in the majority color, i.e., a "similar negative," SN).

It was predicted that the difference in response times to complete negative and affirmative statements about the "odd man out" would be less than the corresponding difference for sentences in the majority color, i.e., $(DN - DA) < (SN - SA)$.

In Group B the difference was that the circles were unnumbered, and the incomplete sentences were:

> "Exactly one circle is _____." (DA)
> "Exactly one circle is not _____." (DN)
> "Exactly seven circles are _____." (SA)
> "Exactly seven circles are not _____." (SN)

The same interaction prediction was made for this group.

The prediction was decisively confirmed in Group A and not confirmed in Group B. I accounted for this by comparing the response times to the "odd man out" in the two experimental conditions. These times were strikingly different for the negatives—something which was first pointed out to me by Bruner by superimposing two graphs on my last day at Harvard. Over the entire task of twenty-four trials the affirmative response time to the one circle in a different color was identical in both groups with a mean of 1.60 sec. But the negative response times to the same item were sharply distinguished: 1.96 sec. in Group A and 2.51 sec. in Group B. Clearly the intrinsic relatedness between the "odd man out" and the residual class in terms of which it is negated must account for the facilitation of the negative in Group A compared with Group B. But I was still slow in relinquishing the notion of exceptional and unexceptional facts in both groups. The introduction to the first draft of the paper, entitled "response to negation: The effect of a pragmatic rule," started as follows:

"A formal expression of the implicit rule which governs the use of negation is as follows—'An assertion that x is not the case is generally only useful, hence generally only occurs, when it is assumed that another person might suppose that x is the case.' A negative statement thus removes a possible misconception by stating that an *exceptional fact* is not what it might be supposed to be, e.g., 'the train was not late this morning' (said when it is invariably late and known to be so), 'a spider is not an insect.' On the other hand, negative reference to an *unexceptional fact* may be equally true, but it will be either vacuous or absurd, e.g., 'the train was not late this morning' (said when it is invariably punctual and known to be so), 'a pig is not an insect.' "

George Miller wrote from Oxford (November 4, 1963) to point out that exceptionality and unexceptionality only apply to Group A:

". . . Somehow, I feel the way you have written the paper is more autobiographical (the reader recapitulates the development of your own thinking) than logical. I now think I would argue backwards—let me try. The way you code the information determines whether or not you will regard it as exceptional. If you say 'No. 3 is _____ and the *rest* are _____,' the *rest* means No. 3 is exceptional and has been singled out for attention—so negating it comes easily. But if you say 'one is _____ and seven are _____,' *there is nothing exceptional about either one*, and negating unexceptional statements takes 2.5 sec. wherever you measure it. Whether or not an event is regarded as exceptional depends on how you have coded it—which is another plausible rule you can add to your pragmatic one."

Only now did I seem to become liberated from an obvious conceptual confusion. Why did I live so long with it? Perhaps because I was wedded to my own notes. The idea behind Group A was accordingly called the *exceptionality hypothesis*, and the idea behind Group B was called the *ratio hypothesis*. And it turned out fortuitously, in a kind of *post hoc* way, that the ratio condition became a beautiful control group for the exceptionality condition. What affects the negative (but not the affirmative) response times to the "odd man out" is the initial coding of it as an exception to a residual class.

But other methodological problems still confronted me. Miller and I were invited to give individual papers to the Experimental Psychology Society (January 8, 1964) on syntactic and pragmatic aspects of negation (respectively). In sharp contrast to my 1958 paper, this one led to an animated discussion as if all experimental psychologists had been thinking about negation for years. Davis Howes of MIT said that my results showed nothing whatsoever because I had not carried out a logarithmic transformation on my raw data. (He also mentioned some mysterious article of faith called the "irreducible minimum" which I had evidently ignored, but as I have never been able to track down this arcane concept I did not lose much sleep over it.) His intervention, however, was welcome, and I duly carried out the logarithmic transformation obtaining the same results. He politely told me afterwards that he was not responsible for my education but disapproved of this kind of thing (subtraction of reaction times) being tolerated at the Center for Cognitive Studies. After further crises in which I received opposite statistical advice from two eminent psychologists the paper duly found its way into print.

Margaret Donaldson (1970) failed to replicate the experiment with five- and six-year-old children, but a remarkable replication was achieved by Jill de Villiers and Helen Tager Flusberg ("Some Facts One Simply Cannot Deny," 1975) with two-, three-, and four-year-od children in a radically improved version of my task. Given an array of seven flowers and one shoe, it is easier to deny that a shoe is a flower than that a flower is a shoe. An additional plausibility effect was also observed. When the exceptional item in the array belonged to the same general category a further facilitation occurred. Given seven cats and one duck, it is easier still to deny that a duck is a cat than that a cat is a duck. Particularly remarkable in this experiment was the difference in error rates between the two kinds of negative.

Of the total errors made to negatives (50), 76 percent were made to "unexceptional negatives" compared with 24 percent to "exceptional negatives."

Under Bruner's supervision, the development of negation in children has very recently been further investigated by Roy Pea (1978). Both longitudinal studies and a liberalized adaptation of the verification task enabled him to confirm two hypotheses: (a) that the logical operation of negation to deny statements becomes evident near the onset of syntax in the language of the two-year-old child, and (b) that the developmental sequence for the emergence of semantic functions which negation serves progresses from the expression of internal states (rejection), to comments on external states (object disappearance), to comments on correspondences between external states and language use (truth functional negation). It is not feasible to summarize these rich findings in this context. Instead we shall consider a prototypical *verification model* constructed on evidence elicited from adults in the standard verification task paradigm.

Models of verification (see Chase and Clark, 1972; Clark, 1974; Trabasso, Rollins, and Shaughnessy, 1971; Carpenter and Just, 1975) have been very influential within the information-processing tradition. They have succeeded in axiomatizing the interaction between the truth value and polarity of sentences, and conferred a kind of privileged status on all four types of sentences. Although I shall criticize them as representing an incorrect account of negation in communicative discourse, I do not wish to deny their heuristic value for doing experiments on the way in which sentences and pictures representing "facts" are encoded. The differences between the models are rather technical and need not concern us. They depend, for instance, on such issues as whether the picture or the sentence is presented first and whether the predicates are binary. Carpenter and Just's (1975) model is concerned with the internal representation of a sentence and the operations applied to that representation in order to verify it. In the same spirit, Kruger (1972) is concerned with the additivity of processing times for feature matching and negation coding. For similar papers the interested reader is referred to Tannenhaus, Carrol, and Bever (1976) and Singer (1977). We shall briefly look at one aspect of Clark's "true" model.

The model is called "true" because it is assumed that when considering the truth of sentences individuals have available a potential response set at "true" in a "truth index." The process of understanding is then assumed to occur in four stages. 1. The subject encodes the sentence in a mental representation. 2. The picture is encoded in the same representation. 3. The representations are compared to see whether they match. 4. An output occurs and is converted into some form of response, usually "true" or "false." There is no need to present the model in formal terms here because Clark and Clark provide a very clear informal account of it.

"Many people have the intuition that they change their answers very much as the verification model suggests. They start by assuming the sentences to be true, change their answer once on false affirmatives and false negatives, and change their answer a second time on true negatives. Take "The dot isn't blue," said of a red dot. People work as if they first set aside the negative and judge the positive supposition "The dot is blue." Since it is false, they change their answer to false. But because they had put aside the negative, they must change their answer back to true again. Changing their answer twice takes a great deal of time, and that is why true negatives take so long to verify" (1977, p. 110).

This analysis, based on very precise empirical research, captures nicely my original observations (Wason, 1961). It is also a more accurate account of a passage I stumbled on in 1962 in Russell's *Human Knowledge: Its Scope and Limits:* "When I say truly 'This is not blue' there is, on the subjective side, consideration of 'This is blue', followed by rejection, while on the objective side there is some colour differing from blue" (1948, p. 139). But is Clark's model, or Russell's introspection, true generally? In everyday discourse sentences do not occur in isolation, and in everyday life we have no intuition of these computerlike serial operations when we utter or comprehend a negative sentence. What is really interesting about the results obtained with the verification task is artifactual. In responding to an isolated TN a person seeks to recover its supposition in order to understand it. As Johnson-Laird and I have pointed out, in everyday life the extra step of recovering the supposition goes unnoticed because it has already been processed as part of the context of the utterance (Wason and Johnson-Laird, 1972, p. 39).

From all that has been said so far it might seem that Clark ignores suppositions. This is not so. Clark and Clark constrain their admirable account of suppositions to fit the verification task paradigm, and they run into difficulties in so doing:

"Denials ought to be verified in accordance with their function. Remember that denials are equivalent to suppositions plus their cancellations—as, for example, 37 is equivalent to 38:

37 It wasn't JOHN who hit Bill.

38 You may believe it was JOHN who hit Bill, but that is false.

If Ann says 37 to Ed, he ought to verify it by checking the supposition first, having retrieved from memory the person who did hit Bill. . . . If he believes it *was* John, then her supposition is true. But since she cancelled it, the denial itself must be 'false'. *On the other hand, if he finds that it was Ian who hit Bill, then her supposition doesn't fit the facts and must therefore be false.* But since Ann cancelled this supposition, her denial must be true anyway" (my italics).

The italicized words are designed to convey a real life exemplification of a TN, but the example is contrived. The sentence "It wasn't JOHN who hit Bill" would not have been uttered unless Ann had believed that Ed thought it was John who hit Bill. The verification task is not a communicative situation. The supposition of "x is not y" is "x is y." But when the experimenter presents the TN sentence "The circle is not yellow" the subject does not believe that he is supposed to think the circle is yellow and is correct in his belief. No questions of belief arise—there is no reason to deny the circle is yellow. The supposition is only such in a formal sense.

Roger Brown (personal communication to Roy Pea), however, provides a succinct analysis of TN by making the assumption that the verification task can be construed as a communicative situation:

"Brown's framework is based on a consideration of two correspondences. The first is between the FACT or objective situation to which the statement refers and the utterance which the speaker makes to the listener. FACT and UTTERANCE must correspond for the utterance to be true. The other correspondence to be checked for is the one between UTTERANCE (p) and its PRESUPPOSITION (q). The presupposition in the case of the true negative statement is that listener "o" believes p, which is the presupposition that the 'true negative' then denies. On Brown's account, for there to be 'reason to communicate,' and hence for the negative to be 'plausible,' the UTTERANCE and the PRESUPPOSITION *must not* correspond. It is in this second correspondence, between UTTERANCE and PRESUPPOSITION, rather than the first, between FACT and UTTERANCE, where the 'true negative' statement 'fails' because listener "o" does not believe that p is the case, and the 'true negative' statement presupposes that "o" does believe this. The presupposition (q)—that "o" believes p—matches the speaker's 'true negative,' which results in the 'true negative' being 'wrong' in the sense that 'there was no disagreement between presupposition and fact and so no occasion to talk [negate] at all" (Pea, 1978).

This account agrees with mine, but it goes further in its consequences. Brown argues that the very high frequency of errors in the four- to five-year-old children's responses to TN, as noted by deVilliers in an unpublished study, is due to the fact that the children are commenting on the *appropriateness* rather than the *truth* of TN statements. According to Pea, Brown concludes by stating his view is that children have two very general lessons to learn about language and about negation: 'when there is any reason to speak at all and to speak the truth.'

One wonders, of course, whether such a bold conjecture applies also to adults' responses to TN which are also distinguished by a high error rate. The complexity of the information processing involved, as delineated for instance in Clark's "true" model, seems sufficient to account for error. Since the two explanations are framed at different levels, they are not incompatible.

In spite of my attempts to clarify the issues involved in the verification task, in spite of Brown's elegant analysis, I suspect the task will continue to mislead people about the nature of negation. And for this, the verification models, which reify the processes of comprehension, must take some share of the blame. "If you want to be understood quickly, do not waste time by using negatives. A true negative takes about 48 percent longer to understand." This is the editorial blurb on an excellent popular article by Clark (1974b). It shows how the magical power of a label can influence the understanding of the layman. It accounts for the puzzled frowns of incomprehension which sometimes meet my lectures on the topic; it is hard to appreciate that a *true* negative without a realistic supposition is absurd.

After this interlude on the verification models and criticism of them, I shall pick up the main thread of the narrative. From about 1965 onward my associates in London sought to develop a wider variety of experimental tasks to investigate contextual effects. For instance, Judith Greene (1970) was the first to have the insight that negation signals a change of meaning and that its effects should be investigated—not between a picture (state of affairs) and a sentence, but between two sentences which can agree or differ in meaning. When a negative is used to change meaning its understanding is facilitated compared with when it maintains meaning. We also examined such effects in reasoning tasks rather than with the aid of mental chronometry. Reasoning tasks nicely illustrate that negatives are easier when they exert their 'natural function' of denial. Jonathan Evans (1972) showed that the *modus tollens* inference is about three times as difficult when a contradiction is used to deny a statement which is already negated:

1. If the letter is not A, then the number is 3.
2. The number is not 3.
∴ The letter is A.

The most common response was to say that nothing followed from the premises.

Johnson-Laird and Tridgell (1972) showed that the force of a denial is most clearly appreciated when the negative appears in a categorical rather than an hypothetical premise. It is relatively easy to draw the correct conclusion from the following argument:

1. Either John is intelligent or he is rich.
2. John is not rich.
3. ?

Exactly the same information is conveyed by this argument:

1. Either John is intelligent or he is not rich.
2. John is rich.
3. ?

With the latter argument it is about twice as difficult to draw the same conclusion: "John is intelligent." It was also shown that in the first argument the explicit negative ("Not rich") was responded to *faster* than when the implicit negative, "poor," was substituted for it. On the basis of this result the assumption underlying the verification models were criticized: "In order to grasp that one sentence denies another, the aim should be to establish *not* a one-to-one correspondence between them but a mutual inconsistency." I think this extension of the range of tasks with which to study negation can only be beneficial in the long run. All too often research workers, especially in the USA, have become "hooked" on one paradigm, like the verification task, and this has led to a certain sterility. It has blinded them to issues which cannot be captured by the paradigm.

This essay has aimed to give a report of what I take to be the most important findings in considering the conditions under which a negative sentence is more difficult to understand than an affirmative sentence. In addition, I hope the coarseness of the narrative does something to reveal the process of scientific research in which vaguely apprehended puzzles and clues slowly become articulated, and lead to blind alleys or to minor discoveries, and in which individuals collaborate to help clarify inchoate ideas. After I had completed the second draft of the present article a strange event occurred. I have always supposed that my memory for every instant in my own research was both accurate and vividly clear. I picked up Russell's *Human Knowledge: Its Scope and Limits* to check the quote which I had taken from chapter 9 ("Logical words and falsehood"). My eye fell on another paragraph on the preceding page:

"Perception only gives rise to a negative judgment when the correlative positive judgment had already been made or considered. When you look for something lost, you say 'no it's not there'; after a flash of lightning you may say 'I have not heard the thunder'. If you saw an avenue of beeches with one elm along them, you might say 'that's not a beech'. If someone says the whole sky is blue, and you descry a cloud on the horizon, you may say 'that is not blue'. All these are very obvious negative judgments resulting, fairly directly, from perception. Yet, if I see that a buttercup is yellow, I hardly seem to be adding to my knowledge by remarking that it is not blue and not red?" (1948, p. 138).

I had bought that book in 1951, and I had put a pencil mark against the first sentence: "Perception only gives rise to a negative judgment when the correlative positive judgment had already been made or considered." And yet I had no conscious recollection of this remark, nor of the rest of the paragraph, at any stage of the negation research. The first sentence, which had been marked, is the epitome of "The context of plausible denial," and (even more striking) the example of the single elm is an avenue of beeches might be taken as representative of the task used in that experiment. Similarly, the remark about a buttercup is as good an illustration as any of the emptiness of a TN statement. It is highly plausible to suggest that my research has been unconsciously motivated by Russell's words.

Finally, I owe a word about the apparent waywardness of much of the research. A lot has been written lately about the neglect of theory in psychology (e.g., Newell, 1973). But individual research workers have their own approach to psychological problems—very often it seems as if one does not "find" a problem, but one becomes "possessed" by a problem, and whatever else happens one cannot rest until one has attempted to solve it. And in these cases I think experimentation and theoretical cogitation go hand in hand in a dialectical fashion. It is by actually experimenting, especially with one's own hands (rather than thinking), that theoretical points become clarified. The advances and retreats made in the negation research may not, in retrospect, seem momentous. They are epitomized by the difference between two statements: "Perhaps negatives are more complicated than affirmatives simply because they are negatives" (Fodor and Garrett, 1966, p. 168), and "Perhaps it should not surprise us that the proper function of affirmatives is to make assertions, and of negatives to make denials" (Johnson-Laird and Tridgell, 1972, p. 91). Nobody would have dreamed how much work was needed to bridge the gap between these two simple statements. We do talk about these things differently now.

References

Bruner, J. S., Goodnow, J. J. and Austin, G. A. *A study of thinking*. New York: Wiley, 1956.

Carpenter, P. A. and Just, M. A. Sentence comprehension: A psycholinguistic processing model of verification. *Psychological Review*, 1975, 82, 45–73.

Chase, W. G. and Clark, H. H. Mental operations in the comparison of sentences and pictures. In L. W. Gregg (Ed.), *Cognition in learning and memory*. New York: Wiley, 1972.

Clark, H. H. Semantics and comprehension. In T. A. Sebeok (Ed.), *Current trends in linguistics* vol. 12. The Hague: Mouton, 1974a.

———. The power of positive speaking. *Psychology Today*, September 1974b, 102–111.

Clark, H. H. and Clark, E. V. *Psychology and language: An introduction to psycholinguistics*. New York: Harcourt Brace Jovanovich, 1977.

De Villiers, J. G. and Flusberg, H. B. T. Some facts one simply cannot deny. *Journal of Child Language*, 1975, 2, 279–286.

Donaldson, M. Development aspects of performance with negatives. In G. B. Flores D'Arcais and W. J. M. Levelt (Eds.), *Advances in psycholinguistics*. Amsterdam: North-Holland, 1970.

Eifermann, R. R. Negation: A linguistic variable. *Acta Psychologica*, 1961, 18, 258–273.

Evans, J. St., B. T. Reasoning with negatives. *British Journal of Psychology*, 1972, 63, 213–219.

Fodor, J. and Garrett, M. Some reflections on competence and performance. In J. Lyons and R. J. Wales (Eds.), *Psycholinguistics Papers*. Edinburgh: University Press, 1966.

Greene, J. M. Syntactic form and semantic function. *Quarterly Journal of Experimental Psychology*, 1970, 22, 14–27.

Johnson-Laird, P. N. and Tridgell, J. When negation is easier than affirmation. *Quarterly Journal of Experimental Psychology*, 1972, 23, 87–91.

Kruger, L. E. Sentence-picture comparison: A test of additivity of processing time for feature matching and negation coding. *Journal of Experimental Psychology*, 1972, 95, 275–284.

Kubie, L. S. *Neurotic distortion of the creative process*. Kansas: University of Kansas Press, 1958.

Lazerson, B. H. and Irving, E. Completion of binary statements by children at three academic levels. *Memory and Cognition*, 1977, 5, 263–268.

McMahon, L. E. Grammatical analysis as part of understanding a sentence. Unpublished Ph.D. thesis, Harvard University, 1963.

Medawar, P. B. Is the scientific paper a fraud? In D. Edge (Ed.), *Experiment*. London: BBC publications, 1964.

Miller, G. A. and McKean, K. O. A chronometric study of some relations between sentences. *Quarterly Journal of Experimental Psychology*, 1964, 16, 297–308.

Newell, A. You can't play 20 questions with nature and win. In W. G. Chase (Ed.), *Visual information processing*. New York: Academic Press, 1973.

Pea, R. D. The development of negation in early child language. Unpublished D. Phil. thesis, University of Oxford, 1978.

Reich, B. Affective constraints on the generating of speech. Unpublished Ph.D. thesis, University of London, 1970.

Russell, B. *Human knowledge: Its scope and limits*. London: Allen and Unwin, 1948.

Schlesinger, I. M. *Sentence structure and the reading process*. The Hague: Mouton, 1968.

Singer, M. A constituent comparison model of a picture-first verification task. *Memory and Cognition*, 1977, 5, 269–272.

Slobin, D. I. Grammatical transformations in childhood and adulthood. Unpublished Ph.D. thesis, Harvard University, 1963.

Strawson, P. F. *Introduction to logical theory*. London: Methuen, 1952.

Tannenhaus, M. K., Carrol, J. M., and Bever, T. G. Sentence-picture verification models as theories of sentence comprehension: A critique of Carpenter and Just. *Psychological Review*, 1976, 83, 310–317.

Trabasso, T., Rollins, H., and Shaughnessy, E. Storage and Verification stages in processing concepts. *Cognitive Psychology*, 1971, 2, 239–289.

Wason, P. C. The processing of positive and negative information. *Quarterly Journal of Experimental Psychology*, 1959, 11, 92–107.

———. On the failure to eliminate hypotheses in a conceptual task. *Quarterly Journal of Experimental Psychology*, 1960, 12, 129–140.

———. Response to affirmative and negative binary statements. *British Journal of Psychology*, 1961, 52, 133–142.

———. *Psychological aspects of negation*. London: Communication Research Centre, University College London, 1962.

———. The effect of self-contradiction on fallacious reasoning. *Quarterly Journal of Experimental Psychology*, 1964, 16, 30–34.

———. The contexts of plausible denial. *Journal of Verbal Learning and Verbal Behavior*, 1965, 4, 7–11.

———. In real life negatives are false. *Logique et Analyse*, 1972, 57–58, 19–38.

Wason, P. C. and Jones, S. Negatives: Denotation and connotation. *British Journal of Psychology*, 1963, 54, 299–307.

Wason, P. C. and Johnson-Laird, P. N. *Psychology and reasoning: Structure and content*. London: Batsford, 1972.

3

Analyzing the Primary Code: From Empiricism to Apriorism

Jan Smedslund

Bruner's approach to psychology, even though it is uncommonly sensitive to the complexities of human behavior, shares with most contemporary theories a pronounced empiricist bias. By empiricism is here meant the conception that experience rather than reason is the source of all knowledge. The empiricist position in psychology concerns both the psychologist's conception of his subjects' lives and his conception of his own research. In both cases, knowledge is seen as based on particular experiences (data) from which one generalizes (induction). The modern word for induction is learning.

Empiricism has been formulated in many variants (see Hamlyn, 1967). It seems to me that Bruner, at least in his earlier writings, and many other contemporary theorists as well come very close to the position of John Stuart Mill (Schneewind, 1967), who rejected deduction as a source of knowledge and claimed that all knowledge was inductively based. Even logical and mathematical truths were seen by Mill as being merely highly confirmed generalizations from experience. In my view, empiricism cannot alone form an adequate basis for psychological research and must be supplemented with an aprioristic or deductive view of psychological theory and an historical view of psychological data. The purpose of this article is to argue for the necessity of a shift in our conception of psychological theory. For discussions of the historicity of psychological data, which will not be treated here, see Gergen (1973, 1976) and Smedslund (1972, 1979).

I will take my point of departure in Bruner's use of the concept of "code" in an article written in 1957 "Going Beyond the Information Given" (Bruner, 1973, pp. 218–38). His consistently empiricist interpretation of this concept will be documented. Next, a serious limitation of this approach will be pointed out. After a digression to the early history of science, an aprioristic or deductive approach to psychological theory will be exemplified and discussed.

Bruner's Concept of Code

In the article cited above Bruner defines the concept of code as follows: "A coding system may be defined as a set of contingently related, nonspecific categories. It is the person's manner of grouping and relating information about his world, and it is constantly subject to change and reorganization." From this and many other passages it seems clear that Bruner regards coding systems as incorporating the environmental redundancy that the individual has managed to detect. He describes several types of coding systems, notably elementary equivalence classes, probabilistic ways of going beyond the information given, and formal codes such as transitivity and rules of alternation. Even formal codes, he continues, are regarded as learned:

"What it is that one learns when one learns to do the sort of thing just described, whether it be learning to do syllogisms or learning the principle of single alternation, is not easily described. It amounts to the learning of certain formal schemata that may be fitted to or may be used to organize arrays of diverse information." Bruner's heavy reliance on learning is also revealed in his delimitation of common sense: "the result of inductive learning of what is what and what goes with what in the environment. . . ." Similarly, he regards ordinary language and general physical principles as a coding system.

It is entirely in line with the above quotations about coding that Bruner deals with learning as follows: ". . . learning and problem solving may be more profitably viewed as identification of *temporally* and *spatially* extended patterns and that the process of learning or problem solving be viewed as the development of means for isolating such regularities from the flow of irrelevant events that originate either in the environment, in the organism, or are produced by the organism's response to the environment" (Bruner, Wallach, Galanter, 1959, p. 207; italics mine).

This is a consistently empiricist position. Even formal systems such as mathematics and logic are seen as sets of rules that are learned by the individual in the same way as other invariant or probabilistic relationships in the environment. The position is not changed by Bruner's emphasis on the construction and creative activity of the individual in devising new and improved codes. Nor is it changed by Bruner's later emphasis on the social origins of the individual's coding systems (see Cole and Bruner, 1971). These are still only devices for economic interpretation of regularities in the person-environment interaction system.

Bruner provides no distinction between apprehending a 100 percent valid empirical regularity (confirmation) and apprehending a logically necessary relationship (proof). In other words, the domains of induction and deduction are not distinguished and processes traditionally regarded as belonging to the latter are reduced to the former. Necessity appears to be seen as stemming from the experience of regularity. Insofar as Bruner's concept of learning and Mill's concept of induction can be regarded as equivalent, their positions coincide.

Although Bruner is concerned primarily with processes of learning and thinking in human subjects, the analysis offered above can be readily generalized to scientists including psychologists. One may thus assume that Bruner holds a basically empiricist view of science. This inference is supported by his strong emphasis on empirical research.

A Weakness in the Empiricist Position

The extreme empiricist position apparently shared by Mill and Bruner may be criticized from many different directions. Here, I will focus on one aspect only, namely, the role of ordinary language in psychological research. Bruner regards ordinary language as a coding system of intricate complexity and great importance and, as such, as a central topic for psychological investigation. However, he consistently fails to consider one important problem, namely, the influence of ordinary language on psychological research itself.

Ordinary language is an all-purpose system which is used by people, hence, by psychologists as well—not in particular contexts and with respect to particular topics but irrespective of context and topic. It is not particularly true of ordinary language as used by an individual that it is "constantly subject to change and reorganization," which, according to Bruner, is a characteristic feature of coding systems. Normally, the language of an individual at seventy will not differ radically from his language at twenty. This also reflects the social function of language. Any tendencies to develop an idiosyncratic language to fit individual experiences will lead not only to severe practical difficulties and inconveniences, but also to alienation from one's fellow beings, to psychiatric interventions, and so on. Since people mutually support each other's language, it tends to be highly stable in its basic features, and the changes that occur in terminology and syntax are neither fast nor extensive. In summary, ordinary language permeates the entire world of all individuals and that language is stable and resistant to change.

It may be objected that within ordinary language we can still formulate alternative psychological theories and that, therefore, we are not really prisoners of this language. This freedom, however, does not apply to the basic concepts embedded in language. We are restricted to what can be expressed by means of the given concepts and, at least as long as they remain implicit and merely taken for granted, we cannot transcend them.

The preceding also applies to the scientific work of psychologists. The psychologist's descriptions of his data as well as his formulations of hypotheses and theories must be translatable into the relatively invariant common language of the surrounding society. Because the psychologist cannot communicate in a language unintelligible to his colleagues, he remains encapsulated within the conceptual framework of ordinary language. This language must be regarded as essentially constant in the life of the individual researcher as well as over several generations of psychologists. The English of William James, the German of Ebbinghaus, and the French of Binet are essentially the same languages that are currently being used by their psychologically minded countrymen. This means that they took their departure from and lived with approximately the same basic conceptual framework as we have today. Furthermore, these languages are close enough to each other that they create little difficulty in communication about psychology across linguistic borders.

The preceding means that Bruner's empiricist position ignores an important aspect of language. Although we may study how ordinary language is acquired by children and how it functions in adults, *we also have to rely on it while doing this research*. Strictly speaking, we must, therefore, *presuppose* ordinary language in our research and accept it as logically anterior to our data gathering and our theorizing. Hence, the conceptual network of psychological concepts embedded in ordinary language must be given the status of something that for all practical purposes exists a priori.

The implications of a change from viewing language as something given a posteriori to something given a priori are profound. They involve a transition from inductive methods involving inferences from data to regularities and principles to deductive methods involving inquiry into what follows from concepts and premises. Instead of asking what is empirically true in psychology, one must now ask what is necessarily true. At a single stroke, this transition would do away with simple empiricism. In order to do empirical research one must always presuppose a conceptual system, and one precondition for scientific advance may be to make explicit what is presupposed. Once explicit, these conceptual premises can be used to decide which further statements are logically necessary and which statements are open to genuine empirical test. But if left implicit, the research derived from it may be pseudo-empirical, that is, it attempts by empirical means to test propositions which, if the conceptual system was explicit, could be shown to be logically true or logically false. I have discussed this problem in several publications (Smedslund 1972, 1978a, 1978b, and 1979) and shall return to it below.

In order to give the reader an understanding through analogy of the significance of the preceding arguments, I will now turn to a phase in the history of Western science not ordinarily discussed by psychologists.

The Theorems of Thales

It has been generally agreed that the spectacular development of modern natural science is built upon the mathematical foundations laid by the Greek scientists in antiquity. (See, for example, van der Waerden, 1954, p. 4; Hooper, 1949; and Kline, 1953). In recent times, however, it has also become apparent, through the work of Neugebauer (1952) and others on cuneiform texts, that Greek mathematics may have built on a much older Babylonian tradition. Correspondingly, the influence of Egyptian mathematics may not have been so important as was earlier believed.

For the present purpose, I will focus on the most outstanding and novel feature of Greek science—its emphasis on deduction and proof—rather than the practical, empirically based procedures of its Babylonian and Egyptian precursors. I will bring attention to certain features of the extraordinary transition brought about by the Greeks and point to its relevance for understanding the situation in contemporary psychology. In doing this, I also hope to show why Bruner's total reliance on induction (learning) leads to an incomplete picture of scientific progress and also of human beings.

The available evidence from Babylonian cuneiform texts and from Egyptian papyri shows a practically oriented mathematics, concerned with rules of calculation for the solution of various problems such as the distribution of wages among laborers, the amount of grain needed for production of a given quantity of beer or bread, calculation of areas and volumes, and so on. There is no evidence that these earlier cultures were concerned with formulating general principles and logical proofs, even though an implicit working knowledge of, for example, the relationships expressed by the Pythagorean theorem is found in cuneiform texts from a period more than a thousand years before Pythagoras (van der Waerden, 1954, p. 76).

In striking contrast to the early practical and empirical approach are the following geometrical discoveries attributed to Thales, the first of the known Ionian philosophers, as related by Proclus (van der Waerden, 1954, pp. 87–90). My argument does not depend on the historical accuracy of this attribution but rather on the basic attitude revealed by Proclus and by his source Eudemus in their admiration for the alleged contributions of Thales.

According to Proclus, Thales made the following geometrical advances:

1. He was the first to prove that a circle is divided into two equal parts by its diameter.
2. Besides several other theorems, he had obtained the equality of the base angles in an isosceles triangle; in ancient fashion he called these angles not equal, but similar.
3. He discovered that when two straight lines intersect, angles are equal.
4. He proved the congruence of two triangles in which a side and two angles are equal.

Considering these theorems, two conclusions become apparent. First, we may note that these discoveries deal with intuitively obvious truths that a. people normally have not thought about, but unreflectively take for granted, b. people will agree with when they are presented, and c. people will regard as necessary and inescapable truths. These are the three criteria I have formulated as defining "common sense" (Smedslund 1972, p. 78; see also Grave, 1967). Apparently Thales, the first known representative of the Greek scientific tradition, saw great importance in formulating and proving such apparently trivial and self-evident propositions.

Second, the theorems of Thales cannot be regarded as inductively based codes in Bruner's sense. It is not possible to argue that, for example, the first theorem summarizes the environmental regularity that each time there is a circle and a diameter, the two halves turn out to be equal. Actually, there are not two separate empirical facts, since something is a diameter only if there is a circle, if something is a circle it must have a diameter, and if a diameter is drawn there must be halves. Also, it is no solution to say that the theorems are formal rules that children in some societies may be required to learn. This would not differentiate the theorems from some other types of rules, such as the one that a certain class of geometrical figures are called "triangles" in English rather than "fidgeons" or "milk." The important difference is that there is an inherent necessity in Thales' theorems that is lacking in the correspondence rule "class of geometrical figures—triangle." This latter rule is arbitrary in the sense that it could have been otherwise.

Hence, a consistently inductive position such as the one taken by Bruner in his 1957 paper cannot capture the essential feature of Thales' theorems, namely that he focused on the relationships between concepts organizing our experiences of the world. In theorem 1 he points out that the concepts of *diameter*, *circle*, and *area* are related in such a way that it is impossible (contradictory) to say that a diameter divides a circle into two unequal parts, and necessary to say that a diameter divides a circle into two equal parts. This is not a statement capturing an environmental redundancy, but a statement of a relationship between concepts used to describe the environment. It is not an empirical characteristic of our terrestrial spatial environment that circles are divided in half by their diameters, but it follows necessarily from the way in which we use these concepts.

Deduction starts with a priori assumptions, including those embedded in our basic all-purpose coding system, ordinary language. Deductive work requires a clarification and sharpening of our presuppositions. It poses problems outside the realm of "what leads to what" as Bruner characterized common sense and is concerned with "what implies what." It is generally recognized that mathematical thought is consistent with and has its roots in ordinary language and common sense. This recognition is well expressed by

Lord Kelvin (1824–1907): "Do not imagine that mathematics is hard and crabbed and repulsive to common sense. It is merely the etherealization of common sense" (Kline, 1953, p. 13).

The tremendous excitement of the Greek world in realizing the power of the deductive method and of logical proof can easily be imagined. The method of geometric proof, culminating in Euclid's *Elements*, became the norm for scientific argument up to modern time. Moreover, the achievements of the Greeks in explicating and analyzing those parts of ordinary language that concern spatial relations and quantities were a necessary precondition for the development of modern natural science. For instance, Newton's breakthrough could hardly have occurred without Apollonius' work on the conic sections (van der Waerden 1954, p. 4) and Archimedes' work on the beginnings of infinitesimal calculus (Hooper, 1949, pp. 241–49).

It may be objected that Greek science was severely limited precisely because of its overemphasis on deduction. I will not quarrel with this, except to mention that the stagnation of Greek science also seems to have been related to complex societal conditions (Farrington, 1944). My argument here is merely that analytic and deductive work may be a necessary, although clearly not sufficient, condition for scientific advance. The advantages of spelling out the presuppositions of a discipline are at least threefold: a. Observations can be systematically ordered in categories with an explicit rationale; b. empirical and logical relationships and problems can be clearly distinguished; and c. the presuppositions can be changed. An example of the latter is that non-Euclidean geometries could only be formulated after the presuppositions of Euclidean geometry had been explicated.

Two conclusions may be drawn. First, Bruner's approach in his 1957 article must be seen as ignoring the a priori status of ordinary language and, hence, the deductive aspect of science and human functioning. Second, it is suggested that the development that began with Thales may tell us something about the situation in modern psychology. Perhaps advances can only be made when we start systematically to explicate and analyze those parts of the conceptual framework of ordinary language that relate to psychology. In what follows, the beginnings of such an approach will be presented.

Aspects of an Elementary Theory of Action

Here, an attempt will be made to formulate in a preliminary way a minor part of the conceptual framework relevant for psychology, embedded in ordinary language. It is asserted that the concepts involved are necessarily present in psychological analyses of action and that the theorems relating them are, or can be made, analytic. This is meant to be one illustration of what can be meant by "analyzing the primary code," and of an a priori rather than empirical approach to psychology. Much of the substance of what will be presented can also be found in Heider (1958, chapter 4) and in my interpretation (Smedslund, 1978a) of Bandura's theory of self-efficacy (Bandura, 1977).

A central problem in psychology, both for theoretical and practical purposes, is: *Under what conditions will a subject perform a given act in a given situation at a given time?* In order to solve this problem one must attempt to formulate the necessary and sufficient conditions involved. This, again, presupposes that a number of basic concepts have been defined.

DEFINITIONS

In what follows, *P* means a person or subject, *S* means an initial subjective situation, *So* means an initial objective situation, *t* means a moment or period in time, *A* means an act, *R* means a resulting subjective situation, *Ro* means a resulting objective situaiton, *C* means a thing in or a feature or part of the objective situation, and *T* means a task.

Definition 1. *A subject is one who is conscious.*

Comment: To say that someone is conscious means both that he or she is conscious of something now *and* that he or she is disposed to become conscious of certain other things if they should be introduced now.

Definition 1a. *P is conscious of C at t implies that P at t takes C into account in his or her actions.*

Definition 1b. *If a change in C makes a difference to an action of P at t, then P is conscious of C at t.*

Definition 1c. *P is reflectively conscious of C at t if and only if P at t is conscious of C at t, but P is not reflectively conscious of C at t.*

Definition 1d. *P is unreflectively conscious of C at t if and only if P is conscious that he or she is conscious of C.*

Note: The preceding statements do not amount to a complete definition of consciousness. They merely indicate an implication of consciousness (1a), an observation that implies consciousness (1b), and two subgroups of consciousness (1c and 1d). No simple criteria of reflective consciousness are given. Such criteria may be found in verbal behavior expressing awareness than one is aware of something.

Definition 2. *A subjective situation is the totality of what a subject is conscious of as being the case and as not being the case and as being of actual or potential relevance for the execution of given acts and/or for the achievement of given goals.*

Definition 2a. *An initial subjective situation is the subjective situation before the execution of an act.*

Definition 2b. *A resulting subjective situation is that subjective situation after the execution of an act.*

Definition 3. *A social situation is the totality of what a group of subjects jointly are conscious of as being the case and as not being the case and as being of actual or potential relevance for the execution of given acts and/or for the achievement of given goals.*

Note: "Jointly" means that the subjects both are in actual agreement and believe they are. A number of variants and degrees of intersubjectivity exist (see Rommetveit, in press) but will not be treated here.

Definition 3a. *An initial social situation is the social situation before the execution of an act.*

Definition 3b. *A resulting social situation is the social situation after the execution of an act.*

Definition 4. *An objective situation is the totality of what is the case and is not the case and is of actual or potential relevance for the execution of given acts and/or for the achievement of given goals.*

Note: "Objective" obviously refers to the absolutizing of a particular subjective or social situation. This occurs when a subject or group of subjects believe(s) he or she or they has (have) access to completely reliable and accurate information. The situation as defined by the research psychologist is frequently regarded as objective.

Definition 4a. *An initial objective situation is the objective situation before the execution of an act.*

Definition 4b. *A resulting objective situation is the objective situation after the execution of an act.*

Definition 5. *An act is a motivated (intentional) activity or a motivated (intentional) absence of a certain activity of a subject.*

Note: Many acts consist in passivity, silence, inhibition, etc.

Definition 6. *A motive (or an intention) consists of a direction and a strength.*

Definition 6a. *The direction of a motive is toward the desired (sought for) situation (goal).*

Note: The goal may be characterized solely by the absence of something and, as a limiting case, even by the absence of everything (death, nothingness).

Definition 6b. *The strength of a motive is relative to the strength of other motives. If motive X for P in S at t is stronger than motive Y for P in S at t, then X prevails over Y in determining P's actions in S at t, and vice versa if Y is stronger than X.*

Definition 7. *Pleasure is what people are motivated to reach and to maintain.*

Definition 8. *Suffering is what people are motivated to avoid and to escape.*

Note: A masochistic act is an act with a motive to achieve a situation in which most people would suffer, but *not the masochist*. More precisely, the masochist expects the sought-for situations to involve more pleasure than suffering.

Definition 9. *P can do A in S or So at t means that it is possible for P to do A in S or So at t.*

Definition 10. *P tries to do A in S or So at t means that P attempts to or makes an effort to do A in S or So at t.*

The ability of a person may be defined relative to the ability of another person as follows:

Definition 11. *P has greater ability than Q on T in So at t*

if and only if

a. *P succeeds or Q fails on T in So at t*

or

b. *P succeeds on T in So at t with less exertion than Q*

or

c. *when both P and Q fail on T in So at t, it takes less lowering of the difficulty of T in So to make P succeed than it takes to make Q succeed.*

Similarly, the difficulty of a task may be determined relative to the difficulty of another task:

Definition 12. *T in So at t is more difficult than R in So at t*

if and only if

a. *P fails on T in So at t but succeeds on R in So at t*

or

b. *P performs T in So at t with more exertion than R in So at t*

or

c. *when P fails on both tasks, it takes more increment in P's ability for him or her to succeed on T in So at t than it takes for him or her to succeed on R in So at t.*

Note: The concepts of ability and difficulty when formulated absolutely ("she is very gifted," "that task is very difficult") are implicitly referring to a comparison between respectively the person's typical performance on a given task population and the typical performance of a given subject population on the given task population, *and* to a comparison between the typical performance of a given subject population on the task and the typical performance of the same subject population on a given task population. The scaling becomes more refined when ability and difficulty are explicitly linked with the relative frequencies of success and failure and with specific measures of typicality such as averages.

Definition 13. *The degree of exertion of a subject in performing an act is inversely proportional to the difference between the ability of the subject and the difficulty of the task.* Signs of exertion include:

a. signs of physical exertion

b. signs of frustration

c. signs of preoccupation and low tolerance of disturbance

d. slowness of performance

e. frequency of errors and corrections

f. verbal statements referring to the above

These definitions will have to suffice for the present illustrative purpose. In a more complete presentation many further distinctions must be made in order to reach an acceptable level of precision.

THEOREMS AND COROLLARIES

The necessary and sufficient conditions for the occurrence of an act may be expressed as follows:

Theorem 1. *P does A in So at t if and only if P can do A in So at t and P tries to do A in So at t.* Proof: The first part of the theorem states that P does A in So at t only if it is possible for P to do A in So at t, since can refers to what is possible (definition 9). This is self-evident. The second part of the theorem states that P does A in So at t only if P tries to do A in So at t. Since, according to definition 5, an act is motivated, it must involve an effort or attempt to achieve something. But this is what is called trying (definition 10). Therefore, an act must involve trying and, hence, the theorem is proved.

The necessary and sufficient conditions for the nonoccurrence of an act may, then, be expressed in the following corollary:

Corollary 1. *P does not do A in So at t if and only if P cannot do A in So at t and/or P does not try to do A in So at t.* Proof: This follows directly from theorem 1.

Theorem 1 also permits one to formulate the conditions of behavioral change in two corollaries:

Corollary 2. *P changes from doing A in So at t_1 to not doing A in So at t_2 if and only if there is a change from P can do A in So at t_1 to P cannot do A in So at t_2 and/or a change from P tries to do A in So at t_1 to P does not try to A in So at t_2.* Proof: This follows directly from theorem 1 and corollary 1

Corollary 3. *P changes from not doing A in So at t_1 to doing A in So at t_2 if and only if there is a change from P cannot do A in So at t_1 to P can do A in So at t_2 and/or a change from P does not try to do A in So at t_1 to P does try to do A in So at t_2.* Proof: This follows directly from theorem 1 and corollary 1.

The next step is to formulate the necessary and sufficient conditions for the occurrence and nonoccurrence of, respectively, can and trying.

Theorem 2. *P can do A in So at t if and only if P's ability to do A in So at t is greater than the difficulty of A in So at t.* Proof: This theorem follows directly from the meaning of the concepts involved. Difficulty is a characteristic of a task which influences the likelihood that a person can solve it (definition 12). Ability is a characteristic of a person which influences the likelihood that he can solve a task (definition 11). The simplest way of linking the two concepts to each other and to actual behavior is that the pass/fail limit coincides with the point at which ability equals difficulty. Hence, if a person solves a task his ability surpasses the difficulty and if he fails, the difficulty is too great compared with his ability.

Note: The connection between this theorem and definitions 11 and 12 is not obvious since these definitions do not explicitly link degree of ability and degree of difficulty. However, this is the simplest linkage and apparently the one in use. Definition 13 establishes a kind of linkage since, as the difference between ability and difficulty approaches zero, exertion approaches a maximum.

Corollary 1. *P cannot do A in So at t if and only if P's ability to do A in So at t is smaller than the difficulty of A in So at t.* Proof: This follows directly from theorem 2.

Corollary 2. *There is a change from P can do A in So at t_1 to P cannot do A in So at t_2 if and only if (a) there are decrements in P's ability to do A in So from t_1 to t_2 and/or (b) there are increments in the difficulty of A in So from t_1 to t_2, the net effect of which is a change from P's ability to do A in So at t_1 being greater than the difficulty of A in So at t_1 to P's ability to do A in So at t_2 being smaller than the difficulty of A in So at t_2.* Proof: This follows directly from theorem 2.

Corollary 3. *There is a change from P cannot do A in So at t_1 to P can do A in So at t_2 if and only if (a) there are increments in P's ability to do A in So from t_1 to t_2 and/or (b) there are decrements in the difficulty of A in So from t_1 to t_2, the net effect of which is a change from P's ability to do A in So at t_1 being smaller than the difficulty of A in So at t_1 to P's ability to do A in So at t_2 being greater than the difficulty of A in So at t_2.* Proof: This follows directly from theorem 2.

Theorem 3. *The effect of any given increment or decrement in the ability of P to do A in So from t_1 and t_2, can be compensated by a corresponding increment or decrement in difficulty of A in So from t_1 to t_2.* Proof: An increment or decrement in ability corresponds to an increment or decrement in likelihood of success on a given task, and an increment or decrement in difficulty also corresponds to a decrement or increment in likelihood of success on that same task. If the variations in ability, difficulty, and likelihood are continuous and unrestricted, it follows that it should always be, in principle, possible to specify a change in ability which exactly compensates a change in difficulty and vice versa. Hence, the theorem is proved.

Examples: As a child progresses in ability, the tasks given in school are made more difficult in order to maintain an approximately constant level of exertion (see definition 13). Similarly, as an elderly person deteriorates in ability to do the daily chores, the surroundings may be altered in an attempt to compensate for this by making the demands on the person lighter, again in order to maintain an approximately unchanged average level of exertion.

Definition 13 enables one to derive a whole series of statements that are, here, given the status of theorems.

Theorem 4. *If P must exert him/herself very much to perform A in So at t then P's ability to perform A in So at t is only a little greater than the difficulty of A in So at t.* Proof: This follows directly from definition 13.

Theorem 5. *If P must exert him/herself very little to perform A in So at t, then P's ability to perform A in So at t is much greater than the difficulty of A in So at t.* Proof: This follows directly from definition 13.

Theorem 6. *If P performs A in So at t with little exertion and A in So at t is very difficult, than P must have great ability to do A in So at t.* Proof: This follows directly from definition 13c.

Theorem 7. *If P performs A in So at t with great exertion and A in So at t is very easy, then P must have small ability to do A in So at t.* Proof: This follows directly from definition 13.

Theorem 8. *If P performs A in So at t with great exertion and P has great ability, then A in So at t must be very difficult.* Proof: This follows directly from definition 13.

Theorem 9. *If P performs A in So at t with little exertion and P has small ability, the A in So at t must be very easy.* Proof: This follows directly from definition 13.

The necessary and sufficient conditions of trying may be formulated as follows:

Theorem 10. *P tries to do A in So at t in order to reach R if and only if a. P's strongest motive in So at t is to reach R and b. P believes that A in So at t is the act with the highest likelihood of leading to R, and c. P believes with a likelihood of greater than zero that he/she can do A in So at t and no other conditions intervene.* Proof: If no other conditions intervene, one cannot assume that a subject will choose to try to satisfy a weaker motive before a stronger one (definition 6b). Also, when no other conditions intervene, one cannot assume that a subject will choose to try an act with a relatively lower likelihood of success before an act with a relatively higher likelihood of success. Finally, when no other conditions intervene, one cannot assume that a person will try to do something he believes with certainty he cannot do. Hence, each of the three conditions in theorem 10 are necessary. Together they are sufficient only if no other conditions are necessary. But no other conditions are supposed to intervene, hence, the theorem is proved.

Note: The restriction "no other conditions intervene" is introduced to make possible a proof and, hence, secure the status of a theorem. Without a proof, the statement might be given status of an axiom.

Corollary 1. *Given that no other conditions intervene, P does not try to do A in So at t in order to reach R if and only if the motive to reach R is not P's strongest motive in So at t and/or P does not believe that A in So at t is the act with the highest likelihood of leading to R, and/or P believes with certainty that he/she cannot do A in So at t.* Proof: This follows directly from theorem 10.

Corollary 2. *There is a change from P tries to do A in So in order to reach R at t_1 to P does not try to do A in So in order to reach R at t_2.*

if

a. *P's motive in So to reach R changes from t_1 to t_2 from being the strongest to not being the strongest of P's motives in So*

and/or

b. *P's belief that A in So leads to R changes from t_1 to t_2 from having the highest subjective likelihood to not having the highest subjective likelihood of leading to R of all acts in So*

and/or

c. *there is a change from t_1 to t_2 from P believes with a likelihood greater than zero that he/she can do A in So to P believes with certainty that he/she cannot do A in So.*

and

d. *no other changes occur.*

Proof: This follows directly from theorem 10.

Corollary 3. *There is a change from P does not try to do A in So at t_1 in order to reach R to P tries to do A in So at t_2 in order to reach R*

if

a. *P's motive in So to reach T changes from t_1 to t_2 from not being the strongest to being the strongest of P's motives in So*

and/or

b. *P's belief that A in So leads to R changes from t_1 to t_2 from not having the highest subjective likelihood to having the highest subjective likelihood of leading to R of all acts in S*

and/or

c. *there is a change from t_1 to t_2 from P believes with certainty that he/she cannot do A in So to P believes with a likelihood greater than zero that he or she can do A in So* and

d. *no other changes occur.*

Proof: This follows directly from theorem 10.

Some further corollaries of theorem 10 have great practical value.

Corollary 4. *If P tries to do A in So at t, then P must believe that A is the act in So at t with the highest likelihood of leading to the satisfaction of P's strongest motive in So at t.* Proof: This follows directly from theorem 10.

Corollary 5. *If P tries to do A in So at t, then P must believe with a likelihood greater than zero that he or she can do A in So at t.* Proof: This follows directly from theorem 10.

Each of the three conditions of trying may be further analyzed. The conditions of motivation constitute a complex field of inquiry. However, one elementary theorem is as follows:

Theorem 11. *P in So at t has a motive to reach Ro if and only if and to the extent that P in So at t expects increased pleasure (decreased suffering) upon reaching Ro.* Proof: This follows from the definitions of pleasure and suffering (7 and 8).

Note: See Heider's discussion of the connection between desire and pleasure (1958).

Corollary 1. *P in So at t does not have a motive to reach Ro if and only if P in So at t does not expect increased pleasure (decreased suffering upon reaching Ro).* Proof: This follows from theorem 11.

Corollary 2. *P's motive in So at t to reach Ro is strengthened if the expected increment in pleasure (decrement in suffering) upon reaching Ro is increased, and P's motive in So at to to reach Ro is weakened if the expected increment in pleasure (decrement in suffering) is decreased.* Proof: This follows from theorem 11.

Corollary 3. *P's motive in So to reach Ro is strengthened from t_1 to t_2*
if
a. *P's pleasure in So is decreased from t_1 to t_2*
and/or
b. *P's suffering in So is increased from t_1 to t_2*
and/or
c. *P's anticipated pleasure in Ro is increased from t_1 to t_2*
and/or
d. *P's anticipated suffering in Ro is decreased from t_1 to t_2.*
Proof: This follows from corollary 2.

Corollary 4. *P's motive in So to reach Ro is weakened from t_1 to t_2*
if
a. *P's pleasure in So is increased from t_1 to t_2*
and/or
b. *P's suffering in So is decreased from t_1 to t_2*
and/or
c. *P's anticipated pleasure in Ro is decreased from t_1 to t_2*
and/or
d. *P's anticipated suffering in Ro is increased from t_1 to t_2.*
Proof: This follows from corollary 2.

The conditions of likelihood, both with respect to given changes in pleasure/suffering, occurrence of outcomes, and own ability to execute an act, also constitute a complex field of inquiry. Even so, three elementary and related theorems may be formulated:

Theorem 12. *The likelihood for P in So at t that Ro will involve a certain amount of pleasure/suffering is based on an extrapolation from P's retention of previous relevant experience.*

Theorem 13. *The likelihood for P in So at t that A will lead to Ro is based on an extrapolation from P's retention of previous relevant experience.*

Theorem 14. *The likelihood for P in So at t that he/she can do A in So is based on an extrapolation from P's retention of previous relevant experience.*

Proof of the three preceding theorems: Since nothing else can form a basis for estimates of likelihood, these must be based on the previous experience of P. However, since previous experience is not itself present, it can only be relied on in its retained form. Finally, since the future is not accessible, it can only be assumed to be like the retained past (including retained patterns of change, patterns of change of change, patterns of change of change of change, and so on). This is what is referred to as extrapolation. Hence, the theorems are proved.

Note: These theorems are clearly subsumable under the same general principle which ultimately may be given the status of an axiom.

Corollary 1. *If the likelihood for P in So at t of some future event is L, then the retained relevant past experience of P in So at t must imply L.*
Proof: This follows from theorems 12, 13, and 14.

At this point I will, quite arbitrarily, end my presentation of elementary propositions in the theory of action. Most of the work to perfect this theory remains to be done. I hope, however, to have indicated the kind of remote parallel to the contributions of the Greek mathematicians that I have in mind.

APPLICATIONS OF THE THEORY OF ACTION

The theory is formal and has no empirical truth value. An application, therefore, of the theory to the empirical domain simply means that it leads one to manipulate certain conditions that necessarily imply certain outcomes. If the outcome occurs as expected, one may infer that the antecedent conditions were successfully identified and manipulated. If, on the other hand, the expected outcome fails to occur, one knows that the identification and manipulation of the antecedent conditions and/or the identification of the outcome was unsuccessful. This is similar to the application of geometry (trigonometry) to navigation or surveying. If the expected outcomes do not obtain, the correct inference is that the measurements must have been erroneous. The geometrical principles (trigonometrical tables) themselves are not at stake. Thales is said to have applied his congruence theory to develop a method for determining the distance between two ships at sea (van der Waerden, 1954, pp. 87–88). Obviously, this application was not an empirical test of the theorem.

The miniature system of 13 definitions and 14 theorems with corollaries, presented above, admits ten major categories of procedures for inducing behavioral change, namely pairs of opposite operation of each of five conditions. These are the conditions of can (*difficulty* and *ability*) and the conditions of try (*magnitude of expected increment/decrement in pleasure/suffering, subjective likelihood of a given outcome of an act, and subjective likelihood that a person can do an act*). Each of these will be exemplified.

1. *Increasing task difficulty.* This is an operation on the objective situation (So) in order to produce a change from can to cannot, and, hence, to prevent the occurrence of an outcome. It represents an application of part b of corollary 2 of theorem 2.

Examples: When a small child repeatedly scatters the books on a low shelf over the floor, the parents may move the books to a higher shelf, presumed to be out of the child's reach. In order to help addicts abstain from drugs, a treatment institution may introduce controls and screening procedures which make it more difficult for the inmates to obtain drugs. In order to prevent an enemy from recognizing and destroying a military installation, the buildings are camouflaged. In order to prevent burglary, the locks are reinforced and alarms are installed.

This type of operation may be performed without the person knowing about it, and, in that case, it may have no other consequences than the actual nonoccurrence of the given outcome. This may be the case, for example, with the camouflaging of the military installation. If the enemy does not know about the installation and does not discover it, nothing is changed. It may also happen, however, that the person discovers that he/she can no longer reach the books, obtain drugs, or break into a house. This becomes part of the person's past experience and, hence, influences the subjective likelihood of his solving the task in the future and, thereby, his trying (theorems 13 and 14, theorem 10, parts b and c). This will be further described under operations 8 and 10.

Finally, it should be noted that the outcome of operation 1 may be ambiguous from the subject's point of view. It may mean either that there has been a change in the environment (correct) or that there has been a change in the subject's ability (false). The burglar who fails to open a door may either conclude that new sophisticated locks have been introduced (correct) or that his skills have deteriorated during the last long stay in prison (false). Similarly, the pilot who fails to spot a military installation known to exist may conclude that it has been very cleverly camouflaged (true) or that he needs new glasses (false).

2. *Decreasing task difficulty.* This is an operation on the objective situation (So) in order to produce a change from cannot to can, and hence, to permit the occurrence of an outcome. It represents an application of part b of corollary 3 of theorem 2.

Examples: When a small child fails to get hold of some desired toys on a shelf, the parents may move the toys to a lower shelf presumed to be well within the child's reach. At the beginning of a cruise, social hostesses may arrange and conduct special structured get-together sessions in order to facilitate people's getting acquainted. Markers and signposts are erected in order to help people find their way through the wilderness or to the premises of a certain exhibition in an art center. One may design special passageways in order to help people with wheelchairs get in and out of a building.

This type of operation may be performed without the subject knowing about it, but in that case it has no behavioral effects whatsoever.

Examples: The child does not notice that the toys are not on a lower shelf, and the person in a wheelchair does not notice the new specially designed pathway. On the other hand, if the subject does recognize the changes, and, hence, grasps the toys, gets to know attractive others, finds his way through the wilderness, and so forth, this becomes part of his past experience and influences the subjective likelihood of solving these tasks in the future. This also means that the subject's trying is influenced (theorems 13, 14 and 10, parts b and c). This will be further discussed in connection with operations 7 and 9.

The outcome of operation 2 may sometimes be ambiguous to the subject. It may mean either that there has been a change in the environment or that there has been a change in the subject. A teacher may lower the difficulty of the tasks presented to a child and the child may interpret his successes either as stemming from decreased difficulty (true) or from increasing skill (false). A burglar who manages to open a door easily, may either think that someone has made it easy for him (true—the police are waiting inside) or he may think he has become even more skillful in his trade (false).

3. *Increasing ability*. This is an operation on the subject in order to produce a change from cannot to can, and, hence, to permit the occurrence of a given act. It represents an application of corollary 3 part a, theorem 2.

Examples: When a small child fails to get hold of some toys on a shelf, the parents may teach the child how to climb a nearby chair in order to reach the toys. An older person may teach a shy young man or woman some useful ways of approaching someone of the opposite sex. A group of hikers are shown how to use compass and map in order to ensure a safe passage through a stretch of wilderness. In general, this category covers what is usually called teaching in a broad sense but also includes self-directed practice and incidental learning.

The effects of teaching or learning may not always be recognized as such by the subject. This may happen if there is no opportunity to try out one's newly won skill. It may also happen when the subject falsely attributes his successes to decreasing difficulty of the task rather than to increasing ability. A child who starts to be successful may suspect the teacher of having given him easier tasks, rather than attributing the success to his own growing skill. A younger sibling who actually improves in some skill may fail to notice this and even think he or she is deteriorating, simply by comparison with the faster progress of an older sibling. A novice burglar who opens a safe quickly and without much effort may think that this was an unusually easy task rather than realize that his own skill has grown very fast.

Teaching and self-directed practice always involve experiencing logical and/or empirical relationships. This involves applications of corollary 1 of theorems 13 and 14.

4. *Decreasing ability.* This is an operation on the subject in order to produce a change from can to cannot, and, hence, to prevent the occurrence of an act. It represents an application of corollary 2, part a, theorem 2.

Examples: History contains numerous examples of permanently destructive acts such as blinding, castrating, cutting off tongue and hands. There are also temporary debilitation procedures such as the administration of drugs, anaesthetics, and the arrangement of prolonged sensory deprivation. Finally, one may proceed by teaching a subject skills and knowledge more or less incompatible with the given ability. Examples of this would be to train a person originally versed in classical ballet thoroughly in jazz ballet with no opportunity to rehearse and maintain the former skill. Another example would be to teach an athlete a new technique which would soon render him incapable of using his old one. In general, examples of so-called *retroactive inhibition* belong to this category.

All the preceding categories involve either interferences at the organic level, or the acquisition of incompatible skills. Direct unlearning of an ability is peculiarly difficult. We may teach a person to add numbers or to read, but we cannot teach him or her *not* to know addition or *not* to be able to read, once these skills have been acquired. It is also obvious that ethical considerations prohibit many of the variants of this procedure.

The outcome of this category of change may also be ambiguous. The middle-aged person may think that the new edition of the telephone directory has smaller print than the preceding one, rather than recognize that he or she needs reading glasses. The burglar who fails to open a safe, may think that the well-known safe model has changed, rather than recognize that his skill has deteriorated.

5. *Strengthening a motive through increasing the magnitude of expected increment in pleasure or decrement in suffering.* This is an operation on the subject in order to increase the likelihood and strength of trying, and hence, the likelihood of occurrence of a given act. It involves an application of theorem 10, corollary 3, part a and theorem 11, corollary 3.

Examples: A landlord may try to get a stubborn tenant to move to another apartment by lowering the rent on the other apartment or increasing the rent on the present one, or he may promise better furniture in the new apartment and/or remove some of the furniture in the present one. In desperation, he may even cut off the central heating in the apartment he wants to have vacated. A prototype of this procedure are the religious descriptions of Heaven and Hell as likely destinations for those who behave or do not behave appropriately in important matters. At a more earthy level there are bribes and threats, as well as more or less neutral information about the goal situation by more or less reliable sources. In the stick-and-carrot metaphor, this procedure involves increases in the size of the stick and/or the carrot.

6. *Weakening a motive through decreasing the magnitude of expected increment in pleasure or decrement in suffering.* This is an operation on the subject in order to decrease the likelihood and strength of trying, and hence, the likelihood of occurrence of a given act. It represents an application of theorem 10, corollary 2, part a and theorem 11, corollary 4.

Examples: A landlord may try to keep a tenant from leaving a given apartment by lowering the rent, by promising better furniture, but also by promising to sue the tenant for breach of contract if he moves, as well as informing the police about certain shady activities. Heaven and Hell, bribes and threats are illustrative of this procedure too, as well as information about the goal situation provided by more or less reliable persons.

7. *Increasing the subjective likelihood of a given outcome of an act.* This procedure is an application of theorem 13. If the subject is sufficiently motivated and believes he can perform the act, he may be led to perform it, and hence, experience directly that a given outcome follows more regularly than he had initially thought. A student had always avoided a certain teacher because he did not expect the teacher to take time to answer questions. Since he was quite motivated and had no doubt of his own ability to formulate questions, he was persuaded to try to approach that teacher once. The outcome was positive and after a few more tries, a new expectancy had been established. Another possibility is to let the subject watch others achieve an outcome regularly. If the subject does not think that personal ability is relevant and no other circumstances interfere, this procedure should be efficient. When other circumstances do interfere the procedure may be pointless.

Example: A twelve-year-old who wants to see a certain movie does not change his expectancy of not being admitted by watching adults ask for tickets, pay money, and disappear into the cinema. What affects the youngster is solely the advertisement saying "adults only."

Finally, the subject may be told by what he regards as reliable sources that a certain outcome is to be expected with higher regularity than initially assumed. To the extent that the subject regards the sources as disinterested, honest, and knowledgeable, he will be influenced in his expectancies.

It follows from the preceding that two auxiliary procedures are of crucial importance. One is to establish as firmly as possible that ability is not relevant when others are seen performing the act and obtaining a given result. Another is to establish as firmly as possible the credibility of informants about the likely outcome of the act.

8. *Decreasing the subjective likelihood of a given outcome of an act.* This procedure is the opposite of the preceding one and is also an application of theorem 13. It involves influencing the subject's experiences in such a way that he comes to expect that a given outcome follows less regularly upon an

act than he had previously thought. The consequence of this is that the subject will cease performing that act in the given circumstances. In order to stop a child from throwing a temper tantrum each time a request is denied, parents may decide to ignore this firmly, instead of paying attention, getting upset, discussing, giving in, and so on.

Another variant is to get the subject to reinterpret the outcome situation resulting from an act. A father believes that unyielding and persistent enforcement of a particular rule without discussion may, eventually, produce unqualified acceptance and gratitude in his teen-age daughter. Actually, he interprets the daughter's silence as meaning this. A friend whom he respects may point out to him that, under the particular circumstances, where the daughter regards the rule as deeply unjust and also feels treated like a child, the outcome may be hatred, defiance, and rejection of all the values of the father. Her silence may signify exactly this.

A third variant is to have the subject watch others perform an act with an outcome different from the expected one. The subject may have thought that a particular piece of furniture could be squeezed through a door. After watching another person try this in all possible ways without succeeding, the subject may conclude that it cannot be done.

Finally, the subject may be told by informants that the likelihood of a given outcome of an act is less than he/she has assumed. The reliability of the informant is crucial here. Subjects are apt to evaluate this, taking into account both the informant's motivation (disinterestedness), his honesty, and his expert status.

9. *Increasing the subjective likelihood that a person can do an act.* This is a procedure intended to increase trying and should not be confused with procedure 2, intended to decrease difficulty, or with procedure 3, intended to increase ability. The two latter procedures are directed at increasing can, whereas the present one concerns the subject's *belief* that he/she can. It is an application of theorem 14. The goal is to strengthen the subject's belief that he/she can actually perform a given act in a given situation. This can only be done by, somehow, providing the subject with appropriate experiences. These are parallel to the ones mentioned above under 7 and 8, except that they concern the subject's ability to perform an act rather than the outcomes of that act.

If the subject tries to do an act and succeeds, the increment in subjective likelihood follows automatically, provided that he/she does not believe that some other person helped. If help was involved, it becomes important to sort out the subject's own contribution, and to establish that, with repeated trials, the need for help will diminish. Many children entering school have secret doubts as to whether they will be able to learn to read. Frequently, they come home glowing with pride, having mastered the first steps, recognizing and pronouncing some of the capital letters.

The problems of this procedure center around the subjects who are unwilling or do not dare to try to do the act. With these one may proceed stepwise, starting with very easy, minor components of the act, and gradually developing a belief in own ability. The subject may also watch others of comparable or clearly lower ability perform the act. Finally, the subject may be told by informants that he/she thinks are disinterested, honest, and knowledgeable, that he/she can, or can learn to, do the act. Many of the problems involved have been discussed by Bandura (1977) and his formulations have been translated into deductive terms by Smedslund (1978a).

10. *Decreasing the subjective likelihood that a person can do an act.* This procedure is the opposite of the preceding one and is designed to decrease trying. It should not be confused with procedure 4, directed at decreasing ability, or procedure 1, intended to increase task difficulty. The two latter procedures are directed at decreasing can, whereas the present one concerns the subject's *belief* that he or she can. It is an application of theorem 14. The goal is to weaken the subject's belief that he or she can actually perform a given act in a given situation. This can only be done by providing appropriate experiences.

If the subject tries and fails, the decrement in confidence follows directly, provided that the failure is not blamed on interfering circumstances. Even if the subject does not try, that person's confidence may be decreased by letting him or her watch others of allegedly comparable or superior ability fail, or by having disinterested, honest, and knowledgeable others inform the subject that he or she cannot perform the act. Ethical considerations enter strongly when we are to evaluate this kind of procedure. Only in very special circumstances is it defensible to lower a person's self-confidence. An example of a possibly ethically defensible procedure would be attempts to convince a stubborn elderly political candidate with a heart ailment, that he cannot go through with another campaign. The arguments presented by his doctor, his family, and his friends do not aim at influencing his actual ability to go through with the campaign, but only his conception of his own ability, and hence, his trying.

THE SET OF POSSIBLE PROCEDURES FOR CHANGING BEHAVIOR

The five pairs of elementary procedures described above form part of a system of intriguing simplicity. The system can be presented in a 2 x 3 table of conditional likelihoods. The term "likelihood" is used instead of the term "probability" in order to emphasize that we are not dealing with explicit and formalized entities. The table contains all combinations of two modes, *subjective and objective*, and three conditional likelihoods namely of *performance of the act given trying, occurrence of outcome given the act,* and *occurrence of pleasure/suffering given the outcome.* Procedure numbers are given in parentheses.

Likelihood of	Mode	
	Subjective	*Objective*
Act, given trying	Subjective likelihood of being able to perform act when trying (9, 10)	Objective likelihood of being able to perform act when trying (3, 4)
Outcome, given act	Subjective likelihood of outcome given act (7, 8)	Objective likelihood of outcome given act (1, 2)
Pleasure/suffering, given outcome	Subjective likelihood of pleasure/suffering given outcome (5, 6)	Objective likelihood of pleasure/suffering given outcome (=)

It can be seen from the table that one procedure—influencing objective likelihood of pleasure/suffering given outcome—has not been included in the preceding discussion. The procedure does occur, however, in an auxiliary role in the examples of procedures 5 and 6. Obviously, a direct way of influencing the subjective likelihood is to change the objective one and let the subject experience this. Nevertheless, the two must be distinguished since there are ways of changing the subjective likelihood without changing the objective one.

This brings to an end my presentation of a few very elementary fragments of the "primary code." It is my contention that this kind of analysis, even though it may be criticized in details, sets forth concepts and relationships that we tend to presuppose and cannot easily escape. If we want to influence someone to do an act (or refrain from doing it) the choices are limited. We may try to arrange the circumstances in such a way that it becomes easier for him to do the act, and we may also try to teach him what is necessary in order to perform the act. Furthermore, we may try to influence his conception of the likelihood and magnitude of achieving pleasure and/or avoiding suffering by doing the act. This may be done directly by changing the objective likelihood and letting the subject experience this or by various indirect methods. Also, one may try to influence the subject's conception of the likelihood of the act leading to a given outcome. Again this may be done either directly by changing the objective likelihood and letting the subject experience this or by various indirect methods. Finally, one may try to influence the subject's conception of the likelihood that he/she will be able to perform a given act. This influencing, too, may be done directly through changing the objective likelihood or through various indirect methods.

All psychological interventions may, perhaps, be reduced to these six pairs of opposite procedures, including many complicated subcategories and combinations.

Pseudo-Empirical Research

Some arguments for a deductive psychology have been presented and the deductive approach has been exemplified. The starting point has been the a priori status of ordinary language in psychology as well as in every day life. A conservative conclusion is that it is possible to formulate a great many logically necessary statements in psychology and that it may be of some importance to explore the system of such statements. It appears that many well-known procedures for changing behavior can be deduced from this system, and it is possible that more advanced and detailed procedures may eventually be deduced. If this project is pursued systematically, one may perhaps arrive at psychological parallels to Euclid's Elements or at a well-founded understanding of why this is impossible.

At first, it may appear that the deductive approach outlined above is simply an addition to the rest of psychology as it exists today. It means that besides asking the usual question, what is empirically true and false, one may ask the question what is necessarily true and false. However, there can be no peaceful coexistence between these projects simply because a given psychological statement cannot be both necessary and contingent (empirical). If it is necessary, it is not empirical; if it is empirical, it is not necessary. This means that deciding the status of propositions in this respect becomes a crucial and recurrent problem in theoretical psychology. Very frequently this problem has been ignored or treated too lightly. The result has been *pseudo-empirical* research, that is, research which attempts to verify/falsify logically necessary propositions by empirical means. I have attempted to demonstrate the occurrence of pseudo-empirical studies in some areas of psychology (Smedslund, 1972, 1978a, 1978b, 1979).

The formal miniature system presented above contains many examples of theoretical statements intended to be necessarily true. As an example of necessarily false statements we may choose formulations of the principle of reinforcement including only the four elements: initial stimulus situation (S_d), response, contiguity, and reinforcer. It follows from theorem 10 that actual reinforcement, observable with repeated presentations of the initial situation, will occur only when the motive to achieve the outcome remains the person's strongest motive, when the given response continues to be seen as having the highest likelihood of all responses of leading to the outcome, and if the person continues to believe that he/she can perform the response. If you go to a movie and enjoy it, this does not reinforce the act of entering next time you pass the cinema—if seeing the movie has weakened your motive to see it again. If you find a hundred-dollar-bill on a busy downtown street, your expectancy of finding another one in the same place is not strengthened if you assume that your finding of the bill was accidental. Hence, superordinate systems of interpretations determine the changes in expectancy. Finally, you do not try to repeat a successful act, if you firmly believe in the myth that the Gods give strength to a human being to perform this kind of act only once. Again, a superordinate system of interpretation determines what is learned by an experience. Theoretical formulations must incorporate a sufficient number of factors in order not to be necessarily false as general propositions.

Concluding Remarks

I have tried to describe some consequences of recognizing the a priori status of ordinary language in psychology. One is that parts of theoretical psychology become deductive, that is, consist of derivations from the relationships between elementary psychological concepts. This type of theory is formal and, hence, exempt from empirical testing. A second consequence of apriorism is that it becomes important to determine whether a theoretical statement is necessary or contingent. Only contingent statements can be tested empirically. To attempt to test necessary statements empirically is pointless and has been labelled pseudo-empiricism. Finally, it becomes legitimate and respectable to ask not only for what is empirically true and false in psychology, but also for what is necessarily true and false.

The preceding does not mean that ordinary language as such can serve the purposes of scientific psychology. It rather means that we should try to explicate the general concepts relevant for psychology that are built into ordinary language. This system of explicated concepts should be rich enough to incorporate essential aspects of psychological phenomena, yet simple enough to be handled and applied. Ordinary language permits a great flexibility and complexity in formulating conceptions and viewpoints, yet it always retains its basic conceptual framework. We cannot hope to transcend it before this framework has been made explicit. This explication is the project of deductive psychology.

I have found it important to present this point of view as a corrective to the onesided empiricist metatheory evident in Bruner's 1957 article. This is even more meaningful to do, since Bruner himself has not, to my knowledge, criticized his position since that time. It needs to be said clearly that empiricism focuses our attention on data and blinds us to the problem of analyzing the categorical system we use when apprehending these data.

The preceding does not mean that a return to an armchair psychology is advocated. The interplay between observation and theorizing retains its importance. As before, data will serve as examples and reminders of the distinctions, variables and interactions that occur and need to be taken into account, made explicit, and systematized. However, the specific function of data in systematic research is not the same in traditional as in deductive psychology. In traditional research, a main function of data is to test the truth value of an hypothesis about a relationship between variables. In deductive psychology, data serve as indications of the truth value of specific interpretations or the efficiency of specific procedures. The following example may serve to clarify the difference. A traditional research procedure may be to formulate the hypothesis that all individuals who pass test T will also pass test C, and then proceed to give the two tests to a sample of individuals. The data then serve to verify or falsify the hypothesis. A corresponding deductive approach may start with the derivation of a logically necessary theorem stating that all individuals who possess conceptual skill T must also possess conceptual skill C. The interest would now be in devising a reliable way of testing skills T and C. A couple of procedures are devised and tried out on a sample of individuals. The data serve to indicate the validity of the procedures. If all (or almost all) individuals who pass test A also pass test C, the procedures must be considered as promising. However, if the expected results do not occur, the conclusion must be that one or both procedures are invalid. In empirical work from a deductive position the validity of the theoretical statement itself is not at stake.

References

Bandura, A. Self-efficacy. Toward a unifying theory of behavorial change. *Psychological Review*, 1977, 84, 191–215.

Bruner, J. S. *Beyond the information given*. Edited by Jeremy Anglin. New York: Norton, 1973, pp. 218–238.

Bruner, J. S., Wallach, M. A., and Galanter, E. H. The identification of recurrent regularity. In Jeremy Anglin (Ed.), *Beyond the information given: Studies in the psychology of knowing*. New York: Norton, 1973, pp. 198–207.

Cole, M. and Bruner, J. S. Cultural differences and inferences about psychological processes. *American Psychologist*, 1971, 26, 10, 867–876.

Farrington, B. *Greek science*. 2 vols. Harmondsworth: Penguin Books, 1949.

Gergen, K. J. Social psychology as history. *Journal of Personality and Social Psychology*, 1973, 36, 309–320.

———. Social psychology, science and history. *Personality and Social Psychology Bulletin*, 1976, 2, 373–383.

Grave, S. A. Comon sense. In Edwards, P. (Editor-in-chief), *The encyclopedia of philosophy,* New York: Macmillan, 1967.

Hamlyn, D. W. Empiricism. In Edwards, P. (Editor-in-chief), *The encyclopedia of philosophy*. New York: Macmillan, 1967.

Heider, F. *The psychology of interpersonal relations*. New York: Wiley, 1958.

Hooper, A. *Makers of mathematics*. London: Faber & Faber Limited, 1949.

Kline, M. *Mathematics in western culture*. New York: Oxford University, Press, 1953.

Neugebauer, O. *The exact sciences in antiquity*. Princeton, N.J.: Princeton University Press, 1952.

Rommetveit, R. On "meanings" of acts and what is meant and made known by what is said in a pluralistic social world. In Brenner, M. (Ed.), *The structure of action.* Oxford: Basil Blackweil and Mott, in press.

Schneewind, J. B. and Mill, John Stuart. In Edwards, P. (Editor-in-chief), *The encyclopedia of philosophy*. New York: Macmillan, 1967.

Smedslund, J. *Becoming a psychologist*. New York: Halsted Press and Oslo: Universitetsforlaget, 1972.

————. Bandura's theory of self-efficacy: A set of common sense theorems. *Scandinavian Journal of Psychology*, 1978a, 19, 1–14.

————. Some psychological theories are not empirical: Reply to Bandura. *Scandinavian Journal of Psychology*, 1978b, 19, 101–102.

————. Between the analytic and the arbitrary: A case study of psychological research. *Scandinavian Journal of Psychology*, 1979, 20, 129–140.

Waerden, B. L. van der. *Science awakening*. Groningen, Holland: Noordhoff, 1954.

4

The "New Look" and
Social Differentiations:
A Semi-Brunerian Perspective

Henri Tajfel

A Personal Introduction

By the time I started, in the mid-fifties, doing research on some problems of perceptual judgment which followed directly from Jerome Bruner's work on the "New Look" functional views of perception, the crest of the wave had passed. My first publication on the subject had on its title page a footnote expressing "my gratitude to professor J.S. Bruner for encouragement and advice" (Tajfel, 1957). Without that encouragement and advice, freely and personally given to a stumbling and uncertain stranger, my work might well not have continued later in its new directions; but it is also true that, at the time, I was a Johnny-come-lately. Bruner was moving on to new pastures. *A Study of Thinking* appeared one year before I articulated in print my views about what was then known as "perceptual overestimation." Unsurprisingly, Bruner did not abruptly drop his previous preoccupations. In that same year, he returned to them in print in a bold and grand (but somewhat valedictory) statement (Bruner, 1957). But he *did* move on; when a little later, in 1958-59, I spent the academic year with him at Harvard, perching in one of the tiny offices of the exiguous Bow Street cradle of new ideas on the boil, and the subsequent summer in the more spacious environment of the beautiful and then blissfully empty campus of Dartmouth College, there was no doubt that all kinds of new things were happening. First, during that summer, came another valedictory note: I remember attending some meetings between Jerome Bruner and the late George Klein which were the early labor pains preceding the publication of the "New Look Retrospect" (Bruner and Klein, 1960). At the same time, a lot of activity was already apparent which led to *The Process of Education* being published in the

74

same year as the "retrospect." My own work with Bruner at Bow Street was concerned with the cognitive processes which might account for the differences between people who showed themselves to be fairly consistent in making either "broad" or "narrow" categories (Bruner and Tajfel, 1961; and, as an afterthought, Tajfel and Bruner, 1966). One of the results on my return to Oxford was a research project and a few publications on some individual differences in cognition. Paradoxically, this appears to me today as being a bit out of line in an otherwise fairly consistent development of my interests in certain aspects of social psychology. Most of them have very little to do with individual differences.

When many years later I was asked by a journalist who was preparing a book about psychologists (Cohen, 1977) "What were the main influences on you?", the first and instantaneous sentence in the reply was "Early on, Bruner and the kind of approach he represented." But despite this reference to "early on," it would be a mistake to think that I accepted the invitation to write this chapter (and was delighted to receive it) because I felt the need for an exercise in nostalgia, or even because Jerry Bruner is a good friend with credentials which by now stretch back for a quarter of a century or more. The substance of the "approach he represented" in his earlier work on perceptual processes is today clearly visible to me in the development of my work from certain issues in social "perception" through much of what I had to say later on social categorization to the more recent years when I attempted to develop a framework for some new thoughts and research on the social psychology of intergroup behavior and social conflict.

It is this consistent Brunerian or semi-Brunerian thread that I hope to be able to trace in the pages to follow. I hope to show that this influence remains and will continue to be important in *some* approaches to the study of social behavior and experience, including directions with which Bruner was not himself immediately concerned.

I must conclude this personal introduction with a warning to the reader. One of the boringly familiar features of many publications in psychology is in the overweight of references to the author's own work which one encounters in the lists of titles at the end of a text. In the past, I have been no less guilty of this simple and easy form of self-gratification than many of my colleagues. In this chapter, I shall be able to avoid it even less than is usually the case. My purpose is to show: 1. that there is a continuity of ideas in some of the work I have done over a number of years; 2. that this continuity owes a great debt to some of the earlier conceptions of Jerome Bruner; and 3. that these conceptions retain their validity in some contemporary and future developments in social psychology which I consider important and promising. It would not be possible to do all this without continuously referring to one or another piece of writing or research which is a product of the same Brand X. But whatever discretion remains possible will be exercised.

Value, Money, and People

"Value and need as organizing factors in perception" (Bruner and Good-man, 1947) was an impossibly ambitious title for an experimental study which showed (not to everyone's satisfaction) that children overestimated the size of coins as compared with "neutral" discs, and that "poor" children did it a little more than children who were not so poor. The title was over-ambitious for yet another reason. The work on "perceptual overestimation" became in the ten years or so after 1947 one of the three or four consistent and clearly distinguishable trends of research within the New Look func-tional approach to the study of perception of judgment. But it was also true that the initial paper by Bruner and Goodman had very little to say about the detail and the articulation of the processes which might have been responsible for this assumed overestimation. It confined itself, in the main, to pointing to the phenomenon as yet another example of the general princi-ple that perception must be understood as an active interaction between the human organism and its environment, and that therefore "values and needs" could be shown to intervene in this interaction.

But the *Zeitgeist* of the immediate postwar years was ripe for this kind of a bold statement of principle. The "poor" children who overestimated in Bruner and Goodman's study stirred a genuine hornets' nest which kept going well into the time they grew up to become young adults. Was it really true that they had overestimated? Were the experimental controls adequate? Was it "really" perception? In the years following the 1947 study, there was a rapid growth in the number of experiments and discussions which tried to prove or disprove the existence of the original white elephant. The rear-guard action was mainly fought by some of the traditionalists who felt that the proper business of the study of perception is to establish close and invariant relationships between the sensory input and its perceptual out-comes. When a tally was made toward the end of the battle (Tajfel, 1957), it looked as if, at that time, the overestimationists had won by a fairly com-fortable margin.

But in the heat of the controversy, few people noticed that Bruner had meanwhile changed the rules of the game, As early as 1949, Carter and Schooler had gone so far as to suggest that "there is constant error involved in making these size judgments such that small coins are underestimated and large coins are overestimated in size" (p. 205). But as they were mainly concerned to decide whether all this was or was not "memory" rather than "perception," they did not pursue the matter. It was, however, pursued a few years later when Bruner and Rodrigues (1953) introduced the notion of the "relative increase in overestimation." Although the ideas were not fully developed in the text of the paper, the design of the study contained a strong hint in a new direction: the processes responsible for perceptual overestimation had to be sought not in some absolute (and faintly mystical) subjective increase in the size of objects one liked or valued but in the subjective *relativities* of judgment processes.

This led me at the time to two conclusions. The first was that "perceptual overestimation" stopped being an esoteric oddity; and the second, that neither the term "perception" nor the term "overestimation" could really be applied without getting into endless definitional vicious circles. The questions became rather different but still remained solidly rooted within the functionalist perspective. To take a simple example: when a subject in an experiment is asked to judge the size of individually presented coins in a series, would it not be sensible to assume that one of his main concerns, in the laboratory as well as in a shop when he gets his change, is not to mistake one coin for another? If at the same time it so happens that size is one of the main distinguishing features between coins of different values, is it not useful to exaggerate the differences in size between the various coins? And if this is the case, should one not find an accentuation of judged differences between individual stimuli in a series where differences in value are correlated with physical differences as compared with a physically identical "neutral" series?

A review of previous work made from this correlational and relativist perspective (Tajfel, 1957) and some new experiments (Tajfel, 1959a; Tajfel and Cawasjee 1959; Tajfel and Winter, 1963) confirmed the general idea. Some studies within a larger research program conducted later at the laboratory of social psychology in the University of Mannheim (see Lehmann, 1968; Lilli and Winkler, 1972, 1973; Marchand, 1970) provided further confirmations; although the interpretation of the results led to a new controversy and to new experiments conducted by Klaus Holzkamp and his colleagues (see Holzkamp, 1965; Holzkamp and Keller, 1967; Holzkamp and Perlwitz, 1966) who argued that one was dealing here with a genuine increase in the perceived size of individual objects rather than with functional shifts in the judged relationships within a series (see, for example, Eiser and Stroebe, 1972; Irle, 1975, for detailed reviews).

Whatever may be one's views about the outcome of this debate, by the time it developed and flourished it was a bit like a shunting of a long-distance train to a local sideline. Several years earlier, Jerome Bruner and George Klein (1960) wrote in their "retrospect" that it was a misunderstanding of the New Look's aims and preoccupations to think that its concern was with distortions of perception rather than with the fact that certain biases and shifts away from the "veridical" served as examples of an active organism's reconstruction of the environment for its own purposes. Concerning size judgments, they wrote:

The early experiment of Bruner and Goodman and the various repetitions were not only marked by technical flaws, but also were hobbled by a conception of need factors distorting magnitude judgments—size, weight, brightness, and so on. In time, this emphasis was replaced by one that was more relativistic or scalar in nature: that the relevance of a stimulus dimension changes the nature of the scale of judgment imposed on it by the observer; that overestimation and underestimation were matters of relative or comparative judgment, and not a case of distortion of perception from some veridical state. Thus, Bruner and Rodrigues remarked that it was the subjective scalar separation between sizes in a series of objects where size and value were correlated, and not a matter of the absolute subjective sizes of the objects. Tajfel has taken the matter one step further and shown the manner in which imposed value dimensions that correlate or run counter to magnitude changes affect the scale characteristics that develop in judgment (Bruner and Klein, 1960; p. 118 in Bruner, 1973).

It was because of these views, which developed in the years preceding the "retrospect," that I wrote earlier in this text that "perceptual overestimation stopped being an esoteric oddity." Slight shifts in one direction or another in the judged relationships between the stimuli of a physical series were hardly an earthshaking addition to our knowledge about the human organism's adaptation to its physical environment. They would, however, become important if they provided a basis for extrapolations to those aspects of judgment and cognition which were generally characterized by the fluidity and ambiguity of the information received—and where, because of this general ambiguity *and* the context of the judgments, these shifts, in becoming the rule rather than the exception, had a significant part to play in our structuring of the environment.

The potentialities of such a transposition were quite obviously to be found in the study of social judgment and the cognitive structuring of the social environment. The transposition itself required five simple extensions from what we knew already: 1. "value differentials" such as existed in the series of coins and other objects which had been studied, were much more common in the social than in the physical environment; 2. the shifts found in the judged relationships between the individual stimuli of a physical series correlated with "value" should be found *a fortiori* on "dimensions" of judgment applying to characteristics of individual people; 3. returning to the physical environment, what was true of accentuation of differences between individual stimuli differing in their values, could also be true—on the same functional grounds—for *groups* of stimuli which were placed in separate classes or categories, even if these were free of value differentials; 4. collections of people in the social environment are continuously being placed in separate groups or categories; and 5. if these separate human groups or categories were also endowed with value differentials—again a common occurrence in our social world—then accentuation of differences between them on *certain* dimensions of judgment should not only exist but also be more marked than in the case of "neutral" social categories. The "extensions" 1, 3, and 5 above were reformulated as hypotheses (see Tajfel, 1959b). Extension 2 was clearly confirmed in a subsequent experimental study (Tajfel and Wilkes, 1964). But the remaining issues of social categorization seemed more central to the human construction of social reality. It was here perhaps that one could find a social psychological equivalent to what Anglin described as Bruner's "dogged" argument "against the notion of passive reception in perception, concept attainment and reasoning" and his insistence "in each case that the acquisition of knowledge depends upon an active process of construction" (1973, p. xviii).

Cue Utilization and Category Accessibility

As was seen above, the issue of "veridicality" to which Bruner and Klein made reference in their 1960 leave-taking from the New Look was already prominent several years before. The subtitle preceding this paragraph is the title of a section in Jerome Bruner's paper "On perceptual readiness" (1957). Just before the section starts, he summarizes his preceding introduction as follows:

. . . we have proposed that perception is a process of categorization in which organisms move inferentially from cues to categorical identity and that in many cases, as Helmholtz long ago suggested, the process is a silent one. If you will, the inference is often an unconscious one. Moreover, the results of such categorizations are representational in nature: They represent with varying degrees of predictive veridicality the nature of the *physical* world in which the organism operates. By predictive veridicality, I mean simply that perceptual categorization of an object or event permits one to go beyond the properties of the object or event perceived to a prediction of other properties of the object not yet tested. The more adequate the category systems constructed for coding environmental events in this way, the greater the predictive veridicality that results (1957; p. 14 in Bruner, 1973, italics mine).

And again, a few pages later: ". . . veridical perception requires the learning of categories and category systems appropriate to the events and objects with which the person has commerce in the *physical* world" (italics mine).

The "veridicality" with which Bruner was concerned at the time was the result of an inevitable compromise between the adaptive requirements of an organism and the ordering of objects and events in the physical environment, an ordering which could not be too discrepant from what was, in principle, reproducible by an outside observer or method of measurement. Following Bruner again, let us now make a very high jump to the other extreme of the "shape of experience" which is also the result of *some* forms of cognitive functioning. This is the achievement of identity as it relates to social or cultural myths: ". . . one may speak of the corpus of myth as providing a set of possible identities for the individual personality. It would perhaps be more appropriate to say that the mythologically instructed community provides its members with a library of scripts upon which the individual may judge the play of his multiple identities" Bruner, 1962, p. 36).

These two extremes of the process of construction of reality—the humanly ordered "veridicality" of the perception of the physical world and the creation of identity by a choice from amongst the culturally provided "library of scripts"—have been placed here incongruously together, because I hope to move back from the latter to the former, and thus from some forms of achieved "identity" to "cue utilization and category accessibility." The "veridicality" of the social world, as articulated to himself by an individual, is also capable *by definition* of being reproduced by an outside observer. An entirely unshared and uncommunicable individual identity would be "doomed to be a gem, serene, locked in the silence of private experience," as Jerome Bruner once wrote of what would become of a "raw" perceptual experience, "free of categorial identity." The available library of scripts can and does change from society to society, from culture to culture, from one historical period to another, and even from one social or cultural subgroup to another. None of the resulting individual choices can, therefore, originate and exist as an entirely private creation, even if some of each remains deeply hidden, even to the individual himself, and uncommunicable. Our public behavior betrays to others our choice of identities; and the reflection of it, in ourselves and in others, helps to articulate this choice in our private experience. It is in this sense that there is some "veridicality," that is, some measure of consensus from the surrounding social world to the communicable and communicated aspects of individual identity. This is in some ways parallel to the tentative definition of "intentionality" that Rom Harré and I once concocted at the end of a conference during which was discussed, among other things, the issue of "intentional act" in child development. As we then thought, an awareness of the intentionality of an act exists when one attributes to others the attribution to oneself of its intentionality. This was not meant to be a "private" definition of intentionality. It attempted to provide a researchable option for the study of its development in the young child.

The aspects of individual identity with which I shall be concerned here are those which derive from an individual's membership in those social groups which are salient to him. This has been described elsewhere as "social identity"—the restricted meaning of the term aiming to provide, once again, a researchable option for some problems of intergroup relations (see, for example, Tajfel, 1978a) without any ambition to contribute to the elusive issues of identity "as such." The point of using the notion of social identity in this restricted way was to relate some aspects of an individual's self-image or self-concept to certain problems of intergroup differentiation. Three simple propositions formed the basis of this attempt: 1. in many cultures, or perhaps even universally, people prefer a positive to a negative image or concept or view of themselves; 2. membership of certain groups contributes, positively or negatively, to the self-concept; and 3. under certain conditions (specified elsewhere, see Tajfel, 1974, 1978a and b; Tajfel and Turner, 1979; Turner, 1975) individuals who share a social group affiliation *perceived by them as such* will try to preserve, defend, achieve, or create an image or notion of that group which will contribute to their positive view of themselves.

These "social identity" aspects of the self-concept share one important feature with the approach to the effects of values and categorizations on judgment which was previously discussed. The implications of social identity cannot be properly understood or analyzed unless one adopts the same kind of a "comparative" or "relativist" perspective:

"No social group is an island" is no less true than the statement that "no man is an island." The only "reality" tests that matter with regard to group characteristics are tests of social reality. The characteristics of one's group as a whole (such as its status, its richness or poverty, its skin colour, or its ability to reach its aims) achieve most of their significance in relation to perceived differences from other groups and the value connotation of these differences. For example, economic deprivation acquires its importance in social attitudes, intentions, and actions mainly when it becomes "relative deprivation"; easy or difficult access to means of production and consumption of goods, to benefits and opportunities become psychologically salient mainly in relation to comparisons with other groups; the definition of a group (national, racial, or any other) makes no sense unless there are other groups around. A group becomes a group in the sense of being perceived as having common characteristics or a common fate mainly because other groups are present in the environment.

Thus, the psychological aspects and consequences of the membership of a group are capable, apart from some exceptional cases, of any kind of a definition only because of their insertion into a multi-group structure. Consequently, the social identity of an individual conceived as his knowledge that he belongs to certain social groups together with some emotional and value significance to him of his membership can only be defined through the effects of social categorizations segmenting an individual's social environment into his own group and others (Tajfel, 1978a, pp. 66-67).

A frequent result of this process of intergroup social comparison can be found in social myths, group actions, and social movements which aim at the creation or preservation of a "positive distinctiveness" on certain value dimensions of one's own group from others. No one today needs convincing about the importance of "differentials" in a large number of social and industrial conflicts. Their consideration here from a "subjective" point of view is not intended to deny in any way the primary importance of the "objective" socioeconomic factors which are involved; nor does it contradict the simple truth that any form of a positive social differential is deeply enmeshed with direct socioeconomic gains and benefits. We have by now, however, enough evidence, originating from dozens of experimental studies and several studies in "natural" conditions, to indicate that an analysis of the "objective" factors alone does not tell us the whole story (see Brewer,

1979; Tajfel, 1978a; Tajfel, in press (a); Tajfel and Turner, 1979; Turner, in press, for some of the recent reivews and collections of studies).

These are fairly complex issues, and it is not the aim of this chapter to enter into their detailed discussion. It is the aim here to show that a Brunerian or semi-Brunerian thread is woven into the general fabric, and that there is a clear continuity from the previously discussed functional considerations about judgment processes to the "positive group distinctiveness" or positive social differentiation, the achievement of which often emerges as a result of the comparative notion of social identity.

The social identity "library of scripts" does not just "exist" as an immutable fact of life. It is created out of social realities, it changes with them, it always includes views about "others" without which the scripts would lose both their meaning and their function. In their continuous interdependence with the social realities of the group's relations with other groups, the scripts contain dimensions of comparisons and values with which these dimensions are endowed. Both the dimensions and the values are selected, enhanced, created, or preserved as a function of what is possible and serviceable in the construction of myths and images, and of what is feasible in the undertaking of social action. As we have already said, the end result is often in the achievement of certain differentiations from other groups on the principle that, in many ways, "we are what we are because *they* are not what we are." The continuity of these views about social differentiations with some of the earlier work on accentuation of differences in judgment has found an apt two-sentence summary recently proposed by Commins and Lockwood: "These studies have used, as a starting point, a theory of social comparison (e.g., Tajfel, 1972, 1978a; Turner, 1975) which is concerned with the need of individuals to achieve and maintain a positive social identity. The social group is seen to function as a provider of positive social identity for its members through comparing itself and distinguishing itself, from other comparison groups, along salient dimensions which have a clear value differential" (1979, pp. 281–82).

These differentiations have much in common with the findings about the combined functions of categorizations and values (see Tajfel, 1972; Doise, 1978, for reviews) which followed after "perceptual overestimation" had lost its status as an oddity and was reconsidered as an instance of a wider judgmental process. Jerome Bruner's views about "cue utilization and category accessibility" once again become pertinent. This is so because the systematization of the social world in terms of a *selection* of criteria as to what is important and what is not in a complex and overlapping matrix of social categories is not, as was already said, based on some immutable sets of preordained data. This selection involves at least three phases of social construction. One consists of the cultural creation and development in the society at large of a common background of myths, images, perspectives, and interpetations concerning the social system and its organization. The second phase concerns the points of convergence and divergence, within this common background, of the perspectives adopted by various subgroups which differ from each other in their location within the system. The third consists of the choices made by individuals between the perspectives which are available to them. No assumption is made in this "constructional" view that we are dealing here with a collection of autistic departures from "veridicality." The "constructions" result from an interaction between, on the one hand, the social and physical realities of the life of a society, a community, a social group, or an individual and, on the other, the "values and needs," collective or individual, combined with the potentialities and the limitations of the cognitive tools we have at our disposal.

As Doise recently wrote, "The psychological process of category differentiation is one of those general processes of abstraction which enable one to account for the way in which real living men come to perceive reality as they do, and how they manage to adopt a relatively stable position in the face of the ambiguities and uncertainties of any given situation" (1978, p. 125). (Should one add perhaps that "real living women" manage to do just as well?) Some of the outcomes of this "process of category differentiation" have already been described in the preceding section of this chapter. They consist mainly of the effects that social categorizations and their associated value differentials have on accentuating similarities and differences *on certain dimensions of judgment* between people who are assigned to various social categories (see Doise, 1978; Eiser, in press, for recent reviews of empirical studies).

The criteria by which individuals will select or create certain socially relevant differences or similarities and ignore others cannot be understood without taking into account the variety of social influences, subtle or unsubtle, which provide the guiding posts for this selection. If, however, we had to confine ourselves to a purely cognitive analysis conducted in some kind of a social vacuum, we could not hope to achieve an adequate understanding of stereotypes and of the role they sometimes play in contributing to social ideologies, to program for individual or collective actions (see Tajfel, in press (b), for an extensive discussion of this issue).

I shall perhaps be forgiven for resorting to a personal anecdote—not to "prove" anything, but to illustrate a point. The scene was a coffee shop in London very recently. The young waitress who served my coffee was obviously not English and I asked her where she came from. The answer was Poland, which she had left (legally) less than three years ago. I then revealed that I also originally came from Poland although my Polish had become exceedingly rusty after more than forty years of remaining unused and an intervention of several languages in between—a point which was quickly proved when I tried to produce a few sentences. The girl was surprised that one could forget to that extent one's native language. I then suggested that some of it may have had to do with my being a Polish Jew rather than a Pole *tout court*, and that there were several good reaons for a Jew brought up in prewar Poland, who had been lucky enough to get out, to leave behind him as much of it as he could as quickly as possible: in other words, that I had no powerful urge for seeking out situations which would have enabled me to continue practicing my Polish. A brief discussion ensued about the fate of Jews in prewar Poland during which I was informed 1. that there had not been that much anti-Semitism there, and 2. that, if there was some, it was entirely due to the Jewish domination of the economy of the country. When I pointed out that the great majority of more than three million Jews who lived in Poland until 1939 were both poor and discriminated against in every possible way, I was provided with a proof to the contrary: Wadja's recent film which was distributed in the West under the revealing title of *The Land of Promise*. To my agreement that it was indeed a good film, I also added my considered opinion that it was probably the most blatantly anti-semitic film that has been made since the great flourishing of the Nazi film industry between 1933 and 1945. This statement marked the end of our brief encounter. Another waitress dealt with my bill.

This is not the time or place to start speculating why a film of definitely "epic" proportions, and which must therefore have been either allowed or encouraged or supported officially, came out of Poland in the seventies to revive a threadbare but tenacious cultural myth. The three million plus of Jews in the Poland of the thirties represented approximately the same proportion of the total population as do the Blacks today in the United States. Although I have no recent figures at my disposal, it is a very good bet that the total Jewish population of Poland at present is well below fifty thousand, probably much less than that. The young waitress (she must have been in her late twenties) has probably never knowingly seen a Jew in her life, and it would be preposterous to suspect her (and most people of her generation in Poland) of any anti-semitism understood as a "prejudice" against any individual Jew encountered anywhere. But this is not quite the point. The cultural myth is still there, and still powerful. Jews as a category "in the abstract" can easily become "concrete," given a set of propitious social or political circumstances. It is hardly news to social psychologists that, as Horowitz wrote in 1936 about Blacks in the United States, attitudes toward them are "now chiefly determined not by contact with Negroes but by contact with the prevalent attitude toward Negroes" (p. 35).

Thus, the potentially "accessible categories" are part of the pattern of beliefs, myths, traditions, and images of a culture. The cues will be utilized if and when the accessible social categories become activated and "useful" as a function of new and changing social or political conditions. From a more technical point of view, it can be said that one of the more powerful forms of social influence is to direct the individual's search toward the detection of those similarities and differences in the social environment which happen to fit in with the contemporary requirements of social adaptation.

These similarities and differences (for example, between people socially labeled in one way or another) can be considered at one and the same time as, from a Martian point of view, largely arbitrary (since they represent only a few choices amongst a very large number of possible ones) and as largely determined, since they are channelled by common perspectives upon the here-and-now of social reality.

It may be appropriate to insert in this discussion of the availability of social cues and the accessibility of social categories an example of an experimental study, even if it is grossly inadequate by itself in making the point. This is so not only because the experiment presents one of those skeletal simplifications characteristic of so many such studies, but also because the responses requested of the subjects were not directly "social." But as, to my knowledge, none other exists to make precisely the point, it will have to do. I have argued elsewhere (Tajfel et al., 1971; Tajfel, 1978a) that, unsurprisingly, the "experimenter effect" needs to be considered much more as an important theoretical issue in the study of social influence than as a "problem" creating "methodological" difficulties. The socially directed search for similarities or differences, mentioned above, could be one of the forms taken by the experimenter effect. The purpose of the experiment was to show just that.

Each subject was presented with 100 pairs of stimuli consisting of cylindrical blocks of wood. The two stimuli of each pair followed one another at an interval of three seconds. One of the stimuli of each pair was of constant height (16 cm), the other varied in height in five steps of 4mm. from 15.2 cm. to 16.8 cm. The constant stimulus appeared in each pair. The five variable stimuli were paired with it in twenty successive random orders which were identical in all the experiments. Two groups of subjects served in each experiment. In one group, at the presentation of the second stimulus of each pair, the subjects were requested to decide whether it was "the same" or "not the same" in height as the first stimulus. In the other group the subjects were requested to decide whether the second stimulus was "different" or "not different" from the first. In both conditions the subjects were allowed the responses "doubtful." The subjects were tested individually (Tajfel, 1966, p. 51).

The results were clear-cut. While discrimination between the five stimuli was excellent, at each of the five points there were more responses of "same" than "not different" and more responses of "different" than "not same" when these two conditions were compared. The same results were obtained in two replications of this study in which order and reward for providing the correct responses were varied. Part of the explanation may lie in Wason's (this volume) findings of the subject's aversion of negation in ordinary contexts. But that is not incompatible with the argument made herein, and it is perhaps not irrelevant to mention that a hundred correct responses would have earned a subject £2.50 in no more than about twenty minutes of dull but profitable work. This rate of pay represented in the early sixties, long before the oil prices went up, a generous and significant token of appreciation. Although logically equivalent, the designations of the categories subtly influenced subjects' judgments of the compared pairs.

As I wrote at the time: "The concept of "yielding" to social information discrepant from the individual's own view of the events has served as the main methodological prop for studies (on conformity) rather than a simulation of the more fundamental process of learning to view the world from new angles and new points of view. Without such learning to detect new cues and new configurations of cues, no cultural or social convergence in cognitive phenomena could ever occur" (p. 54–55). If one wished to dramatize a little, one could say that a mini-culture was created in each of the two main conditions of the experiments. In one of them, a subtle and insidious (but—on the face of it—unbiased and "objective") voice of social authority hinted that "differences" should be paid attention to; in the other, the same was true of "similarities." The inherent lack of clarity in the situation (the stimuli of each pair, it will be remembered, were presented successively) meant that an increased motivation to be accurate (or unbiased) did not really help the subjects. One might even suspect that in more markedly ambiguous tasks, an attempt to avoid biases would increase still further the influence of the experimenter or, in other situations, of the *vox populi*. Kafka's lost hero is lost not only because no one *explains* anything to him; no one goes even as far as to provide a *hint* as to what the whole thing is about. The dimensions of social reality are supplied to us by their *représentations collectives* in Durkheim's sense of the term (see Lukes, 1973). This does not mean that we have no choices left, as individuals, to select between them, to make some of them more salient than others, and even—in exceptional circumstances—to create new ones. But the framework is all there, the categories which are "accessible" are limited, and the cues which are "utilized" acquire their meaning only in terms of that framework. We are back to Bruner's question about what could become (or remain) of our experience if it were "free of categorial identity." In the case of the experience of the social world, its structuring in terms of a selection and accentuation of salient similarities and differences between categories of people and of social events seems quite fundamental.

A Retrospect

Too many issues were touched upon too briefly in this chapter. But short of returning to each of them in considerable detail, including in each case lengthy descriptions of research which can be found elsewhere, there was no other way to provide a general perspective—almost in the form of a snapshot—upon the continuity of certain ideas which emerged, directly or indirectly, from Bruner's *earlier* work. In terms of chronology and of a widening scope of issues, one would have moved in the following sequence: the findings about perceptual overestimation; their reinterpretation as an outcome of a process of comparative judgment; the application of this process to dimensions of "person perception" concerning the characteristics of *individual* people; another application to judgments on certain dimensions of *classes* of physical stimuli; the contribution that this combination of findings and views about the processes of judgment, affected as they are by an association of categorizations with values, can make to a theory of social stereotyping; the comparative aspects of social stereotyping leading in turn to a comparative perspective upon "social identity"; the implications of this comparative notion of social identity for an active search—both through social actions and in systems of beliefs—to achieve certain differentiations between social groups; a continuous interaction between this construction of social differentiations and their underlying social realities.

In his own work, Jerome Bruner has made other choices of main directions between the early fifties and the seventies. But his earlier conceptions left a legacy for social psychology which is still today not fully exploited or investigated. There exists at present a very large number of recent studies about various aspects of social differentiations as they apply to intergroup behavior and to the psychological aspects of social conflict; there has also been, in the last few years, a revival of interest in the study of the cognitive aspects of social stereotyping. But the notorious lack of continuity in social psychological research leads to ideas being abandoned and rediscovered—without any clear awareness of their origin and historical sequence. This is a wasteful way to work, since so much needs to be laboriously "rediscovered" rather than directly improved upon and integrated at a new level. There is no doubt that much of this wasteful restarting is embedded in the inescapable psychological requirements for "differentiation" without which no scientists, painters, architects, writers, or composers can claim to have contributed something new and of their very own to what has been done before them (see Lemaine, 1978, for a number of pertinent examples). Genuine scientific advance must undoubtedly represent some kind of a balance between acknowledging the past and claiming a new future. It seems to me that, in social psychology, the tilt has been too much toward the latter alternative.

An attempt to re-estabish this balance would lead me to select three notions, explicit or implicit in Bruner's earlier work, as being still in the forefront of new or potential developments in social psychology. I have no doubt that this choice is arbitrary, since it is determined by my own research interests and my beliefs about what is, or should be, important in the subject. The first of these notions concerns the functional nature of social or cultural belief systems and the functional cognitive "mechanics" of the ways they are transposed to the individual level of processing cultural and social information; the second has to do with the use of the concept of "differentiation" which seems to preserve some intriguing common properties all the way from accentuating differences between the size of coins to the large-scale social phenomena of intergroup differentials; and the third—in the promise that is contained in these first two notions of their contribution to certain new developments in social psychology. These consist of attempting to narrow the existing *theoretical* gap between the study of individual or inter-individual social behavior or experience, which dominates the subject at present, and the social context of this behavior or experience which seems to be largely neglected.

References

Anglin, J. M. Introduction to *Beyond the information given: Studies in the psychology of knowing*. New York: Norton, 1973.

Brewer, M. Ingroup bias in the minimal intergroup situation: A cognitive-motivational analysis. *Psychological Bulletin*, 1979, 86, 2, 307–324.

Bruner, J. S. On perceptual readiness. *Psychological Review*, 1957, 64, 123–152.

————. *The process of education*. Cambridge, Mass.: Harvard University Press, 1960.

————. Myth and identity. In *On knowing: Essays for the left hand*. Cambridge, Mass.: Harvard University Press, 1962.

————. *Beyond the information given: Studies in the psychology of knowing*. Edited by J. M. Anglin. New York: Norton, 1973.

Bruner, J. S. and Goodman, C. C. Value and need as organizing factors in perception. *Journal of Abnormal and Social Psychology*, 1947, 42, 33–44.

Bruner, J. S., Goodnow, J. J., and Austin, G. A. *A study of thinking*. New York: Wiley, 1956.

Bruner, J. S. and Klein, G. S. The functions of perceiving: New look retrospect. In B. Kaplan and S. Wapner (eds.), *Perspectives in Psychological theory: Essays in honour of Heinz Werner*. New York: International Universities Press, 1960.

Bruner, J. S. and Rodrigues, J. S. Some determinants of apparent size. *Journal of Abnormal and Social Psychology*, 1953, 48, 585–592.

Bruner, J. S. and Tajfel, H. Cognitive risk and environmental change. *Journal of Abnormal and Social Psychology*, 1961, 61, 231–241.

Carter, L. F. and Schooler, K. Value, need and other factors in perception. *Psychological Review*, 1949, 56, 200–207.

Cohen, D. *Psychologists on psychology*. London: Routledge and Kegan Paul, 1977.

Commins, B. and Lockwood, J. The effects of status differences, favoured treatment and equity on intergroup comparisons. *European Journal of Social Psychology*, 1979, 9, 281–289.

Doise, W. *Groups and individuals: Explanations in social psychology*. Cambridge: University Press, 1978.

Eiser, J. R. *Cognitive social psychology*. London: McGraw-Hill, in press.

Eiser, J. R. and Stroebe, W. *Categorization and social judgement*. European Monographs in Social Psychology, no. 3. London: Academic Press, 1972.

Holzkamp, K. Das Problem der "Akzentuierung" in der sozialen Wahrnehmung. *Zeitschrift für experimentelle und angewandte Psychologie*, 1965, 12, 86–97.

Holzkamp, K. and Keiler, P. Seriale und dimensionale Bedingungen des Lerens der Grössenakzentuierung: Eine experimentelle Studie zur sozialen Wahrnemung. *Zeitschrift für experimentelle und angewandte Psychologie*, 1967, 14, 407–441.

Holzkamp, K. and Perlwitz, E. Absolute oder relative Grössenakzentuierung? Eine experimentelle Studie zur sozialen Wahrnehmung. *Zeitschrift für experimentelle und angewandte Psychologie*, 1966, 13, 390–405.

Horovitz, E. L. The development of attitude toward the Negro. *Archives of Psychology*, N.Y., 1936, No. 194.

Irle, M. *Lehrbuch der Sozialpsychologie.* Göttingen: Hogrefe, 1975.

Lehmann, M. Physikalische Kleinheit als Indikator für den Wert von Objekten, 1968. As reported in M. Irle *Op. cit.*, 1975.

Lemaine, G. Social differentiation. In H. Tajfel (Ed.), *Differentiation between social groups: Studies in the social psychology of intergroup relations. European Monographs in Social Psychology*, no. 14, London: Academic Press, 1978.

Lillie, W. and Winkler, E. Scale usage and accentuation: Perceptual and memory estimations. *European Journal of Social Psychology*, 1972, 2, 323–326.

———. Accentuation under serial and non-serial conditions: Further evidence in favour of the relative concept. *European Journal of Social Psychology*, 1973, 3, 209–212.

Lukes, S. *Emile Durkheim: His life and work.* London: Allen Lane, 1973.

Marchand, B. Auswirkung einer emotional wertvollen und emotional neutralen Klassifikation auf die Schätzung einer Stimulusserie. *Zeitschrift für Sozialpsychologie*, 1970, 1, 264–274.

Tajfel, H. Value and the perceptual judgement of magnitude. *Psychological Review*, 1957, 64, 192–204.

———. The anchoring effects of value in a scale of judgments. *British Journal of Psychology*, 1959a, 50, 294–304.

———. Quantitative judgement in social perception. *British Journal of Psychology*, 1959b, 50, 16–29.

———. The nature of information in social influence: An unexplored methodological problem. In *Methodological problems of social psychology: Proceedings of the XVIIIth International Congress of Psychology*, Moscow, 1966; Symposium 34, 50–57.

———. La catégorisation sociale. In S. Moscovici (Ed.), *Introduction à la psychologie sociale.* Paris: Larousse, 1972.

———. Social identity and integroup behaviour. *Social Science Information*, 1974, 13, 2, 65–93.

———. The psychological structure of intergroup relations. Part I in H. Tajfel (Ed.), *Differentiation between social groups: Studies in the social psychology of intergroup relations.* European Monographs in Social Psychology, no. 14. London: Academic Press, 1978a.

———. *The social psychology of minorities.* London: Minority Rights Group, 1978b.

———. Experimental studies of intergroup behaviour. In M. Jeeves (Ed.), *Survey of psychology*, no. 3. London: George Allen and Unwin, in press (a).

———. Social stereotypes and social groups. In J. C. Turner and H. Giles (Eds.), *Intergroup behaviour.* Oxford: Blackwell, in press (b).

Tajfel, H. and Bruner, J. S. The relation between breadth of category and decision time. *British Journal of Psychology*, 1966, 57, 71–75.

Tajfel, H. and Cawasjee, S. D. Value and the accentuation of judged differences. *Journal of Abnormal and Social Psychology*, 1959, 59, 436–439.

Tajfel, H., Flament, C., Billig, M., and Bundy, R. P. Social categorization and intergroup behaviour. *European Journal of Social Psychology*, 1971, 1, 149–178.

Tajfel, H. and Turner, J. C. An integrative theory of intergroup conflict. In W. G. Austin and S. Worchel (Eds.), *The social psychology of intergroup relations.* Monterey, Calif.: Brooks/Cole, 1979.

Tajfel, H. and Wilkes, A. L. Salience of attributes and commitment to extreme judgement in the perception of people. *British Journal of Social and Clinical Psychology*, 1964, 2, 40–49.

Tajfel, H. and Winter, D. G. The interdependence of size, number and value in young children's estimates of magnitude. *Journal of Genetic Psychology*, 1963, 102, 115–124.

Turner, J. C. Social comparison and social identity: Some prospects for intergroup behaviour. *European Journal of Social Psychology*, 1975, 5, 5–34.

———. The experimental social psychology of intergroup behaviour. In J. C. Turner and H. Giles (Eds), *Intergroup behaviour.* Oxford: Blackwell, in press.

Wason, P. C. Processing of positive and negative information. *Journal of Experimental Psychology*, 1959, 11, 92–107.

5

Some Social Aspects of Meaning in Oral and Written Language

David R. Olson

Cognitive and linguistic structures serve at least two quite different yet fundamental functions. One is that of veridically representing objects and events, the second, that of constructing and maintaining interpersonal relations between people. Some writers, most notably, Buhler (1934), Jakobson (1960), and Halliday (1970) have labeled these the logical and the social functions of language and cognition. At different periods of time and among different groups of scholars, one or another of these functions has been taken as paramount, as the essence of true language; at other times both have been seen as important factors which could be specialized in various ways.

But more recently, particularly with the development of speech act theory, these two dimensions, the logical and the social, have been shown to be intimately related. As long as linguists and language philosophers were concerned primarily with declarative sentences, it was reasonable to argue that the meaning of sentences could be adequately analyzed in terms of truth-conditions, the relation between the symbol and its referent. However, in a paper, first published in 1949, Hare (1971) criticized logicians for confining their attention to the declarative primarily because of his interest in the logic of moral imperatives. Both declaratives and imperatives, he argued, have a kernel proposition with a sense and reference, but they differ

This paper is based in part on two earlier papers: D. R. Olson and A. Hildyard, Assent and compliance in children's comprehension: Knowing vs. doing, to be published in Dixon, P. (Ed.), *Children's oral communication skills*, in press; and D. R. Olson, On the language and authority of textbooks, *Journal of Communication*, 1980, 30, 186–198.

I am indebted to The Spencer Foundation and to the Social Science and Humanities Research Council of Canada for their support of the research reported herein, and to Nancy Nickerson and Angela Hildyard for their helpful comments on the manuscript.

in that they have different "dictors," sometimes explicit and sometimes implicit, which indicate what function that kernel proposition is to play in regard to the speakers, whether making assertions, issuing commands, or making declarations. Utterances, therefore, both express a proposition and indicate how that proposition is to stand vis-à-vis the speaker and listener, that is, to mark a social relationship.

The purpose of this paper is to outline the relation between the social and the logical aspects of meaning and then to trace these relations in the developmental transition from oral to written language competence, from "utterance" to "text."

The relation between the social and the logical aspects of meaning are readily described in the terms advanced by Austin (1962) and further elaborated by Searle (1969) and Searle and Vandervekan.[1] These writers differentiate the locutionary meaning, that is, the propositional content of a sentence, including reference and predication, from the illocutionary force or social purpose of the sentence, such as asserting or commanding. Every sentence represents some propositional content and some illocutionary force; together they make up such illocutionary acts as assertions (I state . : .), commissives (I promise . . .), directives (I command . . .), declaratives (I christen . . .), and expressives (I congratulate . . .). Illocutionary forces are indicated either by explicit performative verbs—state, promise, command . . . —or through grammatical mood, for example, X is . . . , Is X . . . ?, Do X . . . ?

Two further properties of illocutionary acts are important for our purposes. First, each such act has a set of preparatory conditions which are assumed to be satisfied for the successful completion of an illocutionary act. Assertions have as a preparatory condition that the speaker has reasons for the truth of the propositional content; directives have as a preparatory condition that the speaker has the authority required to give a command or to ask a question.

Secondly, grammatical mood is not a reliable indicator of illocutionary force. Under some conditions, for example, an assertion may serve as a form of a directive. Such indirect speech acts are recognized by means of the failure to satisfy the preparatory conditions for the direct speech act (Searle, 1975, p. 76). An assertion such as "The door is closed" may be an indirect request to open the door if 1. the listener already possesses the information represented by the propositional content, and 2. the status relations are those appropriate for the issuing of a directive.

However, even if a particular illocutionary act is recognized as such, there is no guarantee that it will have the intended effect on the listener (Searle and Vandervekan).[2] That is, an assertion made under appropriate

1. Searle, J. and Vandervekan, D. *Foundations of illocutionary logic*. In preparation.
2. Op. Cit., Sec. I, p. 28.

circumstances will not necessarily be taken as true by the listener and a command appropriately uttered by a listener will not necessarily be obeyed. Hare warns that "the word 'pragmatics', which excludes meaning in the narrow sense, but includes illocutionary force and perlocutionary force in a heterogeneous jumble, has caused much confusion" (1971 p. 114). Hence, the use of the appropriate conventional form for the expression of a particular illocutionary act and the satisfaction of the preparatory conditions for its use is not, in itself, any guarantee that the speech act will achieve its goal or "perlocutionary effect" (Dore, 1977). Several other factors may influence the achievement of the perlocutionary effect including not ony the satisfaction of the preparatory conditions but also factors such as the goals and beliefs of the listener and the host of persuasive or rhetorical devices that attempt to adjust those goals and beliefs. Politeness, for example, may consist of the attempt to satisfy the preparatory conditions for an illocutionary act *or* of the attempt to increase the probability of achievement of a perlocutionary effect.

To return to our primary functional considerations, then, a speech act analysis indicates that utterances express both a propositional content, specifying the relation between symbol and reference—what may be called the logical functions of language—and an illocutionary force, specifying a social relation between the speaker, the language, and the listener—what may be called the social functions of language. Any genuine utterance simultaneously serves these two functions. Let us illustrate this dual structure of meaning:

Logical

Propositional Content

Social   Illocutionary Force   Speaker ⟵——— Symbol ———⟶ Speaker

↓

Reference

Other writers have made much the same point in somewhat similar ways. Halliday (1970, 1973), for instance, has described the contribution of the ideational function and the interpersonal function to the "meaning potential" of the language. Clark and Clark (1977) have stated that in arriving at an interpretation of an utterance, a listener uses two general principles, the "reality" principle and the "cooperative principle." Esther Goody (1978) has contrasted report functions with command functions and has shown how they interact in the comprehension and production of questions.

It is this horizontal dimension, the social dimension, which, until recently, has not been given its due in a theory of meaning. Most hypotheses of the Durkheimian/Whorfian sort, which link cognitive structures with social forms, have focused on the vertical dimension of meaning — the relations between symbol and referent. This is, of course, the aspect of meaning which most weakly reflects social relations. Social relations are, rather, directly managed within the horizontal dimension through such things as setting up or dissolving social relations by means of greetings, through coordinating ideas and feelings by means of assertives and expressives, through coordinating actions by means of directives. Moreover, they are differentially managed through such factors as giving orders rather than complying with them, asking questions rather than answering them, and making assertions rather than assenting to them. Let us see, then, how this social dimension of language is managed in some ordinary oral conversations. Later we shall consider some of the ways these social relations are managed in written textbooks.

Social Functions in Oral Language

A large number of recent studies have shown the ways in which social relations influence the comprehension and production of utterances. Some of the first studies simply noted the interdependence of truth and authority. In their study of the classification skills of traditional Wolof children, Greenfield and Bruner (Bruner (1973)) noted that for the Wolof child "the social and the physical (world) constitute a single level of reality" and again, "the facts are true because the teacher says them" (pp. 373–77). More recent studies both with very young children and school-aged children have elaborated on this theme. Bruner (1978) and Bruner, Roy, and Ratner[3] find evidence for four types of communicative function including indicating, requesting, affiliating, and generating possibility in the early language of children as well as in their prespeech communication. Other studies have found that some of these functions appear earlier than others. Bates (1976) and Bates, Camaioni, and Volterra (1975) found that directives are acquired earlier than assertives. Most recently, Roy Pea (present volume) found that young children first use negation for the "don't" function of rejecting an offer; only later did they use negation for the "no" of denial of the truth of an assertion. That is, directives followed by compliance or rejection were acquired before assertions followed by assent or denial and the suggestion is that the latter is somehow derived from the former.

The priority of functions of language directed to the social uses of requesting and commanding has been frequently reported in the language studies with older children. Most of these studies have examined how social relations, particularly status differences, influence the production and comprehension of such speech act forms as directives and assertions. Ervin-

3. Bruner, J. S., Roy, C., and Ratner, N. *The beginnings of request.* Mimeographed, 1979.

Tripp (1977) found that children varied the form of their directives to honor such factors as age, dominance, and familiarity. James (1978) scaled the politeness of request forms and found that children were more polite when they addressed a higher status individual and when they were requesting a favor rather than a right. Mitchell-Kernan and Kernan (1977) found that addressees lower in rank than the speaker received over five times as many directives than those of higher rank. They also observed an interesting reversal as well. Some children would try to command other children simply to see if the listener would comply with their command, thereby establishing a dominant status relation. Sometimes the addressee, recognizing the attempt, would just reply "Do it yourself." In our laboratory, Angela Hildyard, using a story completion task, has shown that children vary the form of their directives to reflect such factors as age, status, rights, and privileges (Hildyard, 1980).

These effects may be summarized in terms of a set of rules of politeness. Lakoff (1977) has set out three such rules: Formality, that is, use conventional forms, don't impose personal whim on your listener; Deference, that is, give your listener options; and Camaraderie, that is, show sympathy, be friendly. Brown and Levinson (1978) have proposed an elaborate set of such rules: ". . . when formulating a small request one will tend to use language that stresses in-group membership and social similarity. . . . When making a request that is somewhat bigger, one uses the language of formal politeness. . . . And finally, when making the sort of request that it is doubtful one should make at all, one tends to use indirect expressions (implicatures)" (1978, p. 62).

Directives are not the only linguistic form conditioned by social factors. Goody in her study of the use of questions among the Gonja, a traditional society in Ghana, found that questions were used primarily for reflecting or for challenging status and only secondarily for securing information. Hence, children asked few questions even if they often needed information. She concludes, "the interpretation of meaning must depend in part on rules governing social relationships" (1978, p. 20). Similar findings have emerged from studies of the language in classrooms in our society. Bellack, Kliebard, Hyman, and Smith (1966) found that a predominant form of language in the classroom was of the question-answer routine known as the "recitation method"—teachers asked the questions and children provided the answers. Furthermore, the questions were not simply requests for information. The teacher already knew the answer—the point of the question was to see if the child knew the answer. The question serves primarily as a means of holding students accountable for the information acquired from reading a text. These asymmetries persist to declarative sentences as well. Sinclair and Coulthard (1975) found that many of the statements as well as questions used by teachers in fact served as indirect commands. For example, the statement "Somebody's talking" or "I see chewing gum" were not intended as true descriptions but as indirect commands to stop talking and so on. Such sentences call for compliance with a directive rather than for assent to an assertion.

Assertives provide the most interesting case for examining the relations between the social and the logical aspects of meaning. As mentioned earlier the propositional content of an assertive consists of a predicating expression plus one or more referring expressions while the illocutionary force of the assertive is the intention to represent as actual the state of affairs described by the proposition. In addition, there are preparatory conditions for assertions, the most important one being that the speaker must presuppose that he has reasons for the truth of the propositional content (Searle and Vandervekan).[4] (The analogous preparatory conditions for a directive are that the speaker has the authority to give the order and that the hearer is capable of obeying that order.) If utterances consisted simply of a propositional content, the meaning could be adequately represented in terms of the truth conditions specified by that proposition. But if, as is actually the case, that propositional content is embedded in an illocutionary act by a person who asserts, claims, suggests, testifies, or whatever that that proposition is true, the truth of that proposition depends upon the validity of his reasons for taking that proposition as true. And of course, in some cases those grounds may be fragile indeed and therefore open to criticism. Furthermore, the speakers' reasons for the truth of the proposition may not be simply a matter of evidence but of authority. In any social order, some members are more entitled to make assertions than others. In a highly specialized society, these persons may be the experts (Putnam, 1975), in a more traditional society, they may be the elders (Gellner, 1973, Horton, 1970). If a person has authority, the validity basis of his assertion is unlikely to be criticized even if the evidence on which it is based is weak. Similarly, if he lacks authority this validity base may be criticized even if the evidence on which it is based is strong. So one may make an assertion and, if it is accepted by a listener, gain the right to make further assertions. This interplay between assertions and criticism will become important in our discussion of written texts.

Let us, then, examine some assertives and some directives in an oral language context. The following are samples from a dialogue which occurred between two nursery school children, Jamie and Lisa, who had some difficulty arriving at an equitable distribution of a limited resource, namely some dominoes. Let us see how they use language to negotiate this social problem.

L: Let's make a domino house out of these.
J: Okay.
First by grabs.
J: Lookit how many I got. . . . You took a couple of mine!
L: Now *you* took a couple. . . .

4. Searle, J. and Vandervekan D. op. cit., Sec. I-17.

Then by commands.

> L: Now you got to give me three back!
>   . . .
> L: Now give me just one more and then we got the same.

And then by requestful assertives.

> J: Now, you got more than me–e.

And denials.

> L: *No!* We got the same.

By fact collecting, assertions, and inferences.

> L: [Begins to count her dominoes] One, two, three, four, . . . twenty-eight, twenty-nine, [Then counts Jamie's dominoes.] One, two, three, four, . . . eighteen, nineteen . . . [short pause] twenty-nine.
> J: I got nineteen and you got twenty-nine. . . . You got more than me.
> L: No–o [shouting] I COUNTED. . . . You have the same as me. . . . We got the same.
> J: NO–O–O!

And when negotiations break down again, by grasping.

> [There is a shuffle of dominoes across the floor and now Jamie has more than Lisa.]

And finally, by appeal to authority.

> L: You got much more than me now.
> J: No we got the same.
>   [Paul, a volunteer teacher, enters the room.]
> L: Does he have much more than me?
> P: Not too many more!

Almost all of these quite different utterances are attempts to alter or preserve the social arrangement of two children. Note first, that the opening invitation-directive "Let's make a dominoe house out of these" is both recognized as such by the listener and, because it is congruent with the beliefs and goals of the listener, actually complied with. That is, it is both a successful illocutionary act—it is recognized as an invitation—and a successful perlocutionary act—it actually initiates cooperative play. A much more tangled set of interactions occurs when subsequent illocutionary acts are contrary to the goals and or the beliefs of the listener (Dore, 1977). Sometimes these may involve the attempt to modify the goals or beliefs of the listener, as is the case in threats and promises an example of which is the following (Esther Geva, personal communication):

> ANAT [6½ years]:   Dorith, can you give me the brush?
> DORITH [3½ years]: I don't want to.
> ANAT: I won't let you sleep with my bear tonight.
>
> DORITH [comes back and gives her the brush]

Note that the illocutionary force of the request was recognized but it failed to have the expected perlocutionary effect until the listener was convinced that compliance was congruent with her own goal, namely, sleeping with the bear. Symmetrically, one could say that the offer of the bear gave a temporary status advantage to the speaker, which then satisfied the preparatory conditions for issuing a request and hence it achieved its perlocutionary effect. Again, we note that the illocutionary act assumes certain preparatory conditions which if met contribute to the achievement of the perlocutionary effect. But whether or not they are satisfied, the illocutionary force of the utterance appears to have been picked up.

Further aspects of the internal structure of speech acts may be obtained from examining speech acts which fail to secure the intended perlocutionary effect. In the course of their argument about the redistribution of dominoes, Jamie and Lisa both used alternative expressions which in some sense carried the same illocutionary force. They use the directive "Now you got to give me three back" and the assertive " . . . you got more than me." The command expresses that illocutionary force directly, while the assertive expresses it indirectly. Alternatively, the assertive prepared the conditions for issuing the command. Three kinds of evidence indicate that both children regarded these assertives as preparatory to or as indirect means of expressing commands. First, they were invariably expressed by the person who hoped to be the recipient of the dominoes. Second, they were rejected by the listener, who would have had to give up some of the dominoes. Thirdly, in a separate study, Angela Hildyard incorporated assertive sentences similar to those in the transcripts just described, into a series of six narrative episodes about two children. The stories were read to children who were subsequently tested for recall. Invariably, the four- and five-year-olds would respond with a directive rather than with the assertive actually presented in the story. By the second grade, at the age of seven and eight years, children tended to recall the assertions.

But the fact that Jamie and Lisa recovered the illocutionary force of these utterances—an illocutionary force that was successfully recalled—was no assurance that the listener would comply with the direct or indirect command. It was the failure to comply which produced evidence as to the underlying assumptions involved in the use of a directive speech act.

Why, then, did the children use assertives rather than directives to express that illocutionary force? When the direct command failed, both children reverted to the assertion "You have more than me." To explain it merely by reference to politeness is to overlook the logical form of the indirect request. This assertion may be considered a directive only in reference to an agreed upon norm, namely, that both children should have the same amount.[5] The assertion, then, expresses a minor premise in a practical syllogism:

We should have the same amount.	(Major premise)
You have more than me.	(Minor premise)
Therefore, you should give me some.	(Inference or conclusion)

5. That these indirect requests were based on an appeal to a socially shared but unexpressed social norm was first suggested to me by Jürgen Habermas.

A practical syllogism is logically identical to an assertive syllogism (Hare, 1971) except that in the place of a conclusion there may be an action. Just as in an assertive syllogism one may deny the validity of the conclusion by denying one of the premises, or the validity of the inference, so too, in practical inferences one may justify non-compliance by denying the major premise, the minor premise, the inference, or perhaps, the import of the conclusion ("Maybe I should, but I won't"). In the Jamie and Lisa episode, the major premise is the norm for the playgroup. Neither child ever expressed this norm nor did either of them deny it by saying, for example, "I'm bigger so I deserve more" or "They're my blocks, so we don't need to share," nor did either child deny the import of the conclusion; to have done so may have caused the playgroup to dissolve. Rather the speaker repeatedly affirmed the minor premise by saying "You have more than me" thereby inviting the practical inference, and the listener repeatedly denied the minor premise by saying "No, we have the same" thereby invalidating that practical inference. In both cases the assertion and the denial have significance only by virtue of their relation to the assumed but unexpressed norm which served as the major premise.

These children's assertions are similar in form to those commonly found in teacher's speech (Sinclair and Coulthard, 1975). The children's assertions must be interpreted in light of the norms for the playgroup, while the teacher's must be interpreted relative to the norms of the classroom. In both cases the statement relative to the norms for the social group call for the practical inference, in one case to turn over some blocks and in the other to stop talking. In both cases, the listener appears to know that in assenting to the truth of the statements he or she will be obliged to abide by the social norm. The teacher is assumed to have met the preparatory conditions for making an assertion, namely, that the speaker has reasons for taking the propositional content of the assertion as true. A playmate on the other hand need not be granted that assumption and hence the listener questions these preparatory conditions in challenging the truth of the assertion. Jamie asserted that the minor premise is true by appeal to the fact that "I have nineteen and you have twenty-nine," Lisa on the other hand denied the truth of that assertion by saying "I counted" even if, in fact, it was Lisa who had counted that she had twenty-nine dominoes while Jamie had only nineteen.

The child's implicit appeal to a norm is further shown by the fact that neither child used genuine requests in their attempt to gain more dominoes. They used only commands and assertions. Requests may be used primarily for favors, that is, exchanges based on personal grounds (Garvey, 1975). Since the exchange of dominoes was based on a generally held norm, requests are inappropriate. Indeed, as mentioned, both commands and assertives can be seen as deriving from the practical syllogism mentioned above: in one case involving the statement of the minor premise, in the other, the statement of its conclusions. It is noteworthy that neither child stated nor challenged the major premise in the course of their argument. The condition under which they come to be expressed and the form they will take remains to be seen. One conjecture is that they first take a pro-verbial form such as "Play fair," "Cheaters never prosper," "Better late than never," and the like.

Note finally that Jamie told the truth in the hope of getting more domi-noes. Lisa, it seems, told a lie in the hope of keeping things as they are. But that may assume a greater differentiation of propositional content and illo-cutionary force than children of this age characteristically manage. If the assertion is perceived as having the illocutionary force of an indirect request, in denying the truth of that assertion she may be simply refusing to comply with a directive. That is, "No, we have the same" may mean simply "No, I don't have to give you any." Truth telling and lying may occur only when assertives are treated as assertives rather than as indirect requests. To lie is to assert as true a false description of a state of affairs or as false, one known to be true. These children give little indication of the ability to eval-uate the truth value of an assertion independently of its indirect meaning in the directive. Paul, the volunteer teacher who intervened at the end of the episode, displays the ability to differentiate the truth of the proposition from its social directive significance. When Lisa appealed to him, "Does he have much more than me?" Paul replies "Not too many more." The presupposi-tion of that reply is that Jamie indeed does have more, so Paul's sentence, unlike Jamie's, contains a proposition which could have been asserted or presupposed as true. But by presupposing it, he can make the focus of attention of the sentence fall on the directive significance of the sentence—that nothing need be done presumably because the current distribution is not too severe a deviation from the norm appealed to by the minor premise.

For the young child, and particularly in oral situations, propositions are offered as true primarily because they have a social or directive significance. They are attempts to manage social interactions. With age and with school-ing, assertions come to be treated in their own right even if they began as premises in practical syllogisms. An illustration of this differentiation comes from a conversation between two children in third grade who were building a house from Leggo blocks. One child was putting blue blocks on the top of the walls, the second said to stop because they would not show because the roof would cover them up. They continue:

JANET: No . . . because it h . . . it won't show . . . because we're putting
a roof on . . . no . . . Anita.
ANITA: The roof'll be blue then.
JANET: [objecting]: Blue?
ANITA: Yes, blue roof! Didn't you hear of a blue roof before?

JANET: No, I've never heard of that. . . . Why don't you take the red off and—and put another color. [Apparently so they could save the red blocks for the roof]

ANITA: No. [continuing to make a blue roof]

JANET: Well I never saw a blue roof.

Originally, the objection is to using blue blocks for the roof. The objection is based upon the norm that houses don't have blue roofs. But in this case, construction continues while the utterance, that was earlier used as the basis of an indirect request, comes to be discussed as an assertion in its own right.

Some further evidence of the gradual differentiation of assertives from directives comes from a study by Beverly Wolfus in which directives and indirect ability-requests were presented to five-and eight-year-old children. Not surprisingly, given the status differential between the experimenter and the children, all of the children both recognized the directives as commands and complied with them. This perlocutionary effect contrasts notably with the lack of effect of directives issues by peers that were mentioned earlier. In both cases however the commands were recognized as such; that is, they were successful illocutionary acts. More importantly, there were significant age differences in response to ambiguous ability-requests such as "Tell me if you can put the penny in the cup" or "Can you turn over the cup?" These utterances are ambiguous in that while they directly request information, they indirectly request an action. The youngest children treated them as indirect commands for action with which they complied. Children, in second grade on the other hand, treated them as requests for information, which they provided (Olson and Hildyard, in press). For the youngest children, then, it appears that the status difference preparatory to a directive leads them to interpret commands, requests, and sometimes even assertions as directives which call for action; hence, they overlook the slight differences in the conventional meanings of the expressions used. Older children begin to attend to the conventional form and as a result differentiate requests for information from requests for action and both of these from simple assertives.

Young children, therefore, recognize that a directive illocutionary act is a conversational means of securing compliance and that it presupposes the authority of its giver. As long as that illocutionary effect is compatible with the goals and beliefs of the listener it will lead to the desired perlocutionary effect. But if it is counter to those goals and beliefs or if the illocutionary effect fails in any way, through its propositional content or through its preparatory conditions, the listener may reject it as not being well formed and refuse to comply with it. Assertive illocutionary acts are first understood by reference to a set of norms, that is, as the minor premise of a practical syllogism which has a directive as its conclusion. The result, as Sinclair and

Coulthard (1975) say, is that assertives are "scanned for their implications for action." Later some of the very assertions used as indirect directives may come to be seen simply as assertives. As such they will be judged in terms of the preparatory conditions for assertives, such as the grounds for the truth of that assertion rather than those appropriate for directives, such as the status of the speaker. If the assertive is recognized as compatible with the child's belief and if he is satisfied that the speaker has ground for the truth of his assertion, it may achieve the perlocutionary effect of the child's actually coming to believe that the propositional content expressed by the assertion is true.

The finding that young children treat ambiguous directives as requests for action before they treat them as requests for information together with the finding that assertives first play the role of indirect requests has a striking parallel to Roy Pea's (this volume) finding that in the course of early language acquisition, children use negation for rejecting a directive before they use it to deny an assertion. Roughly, the illocutionary force has primacy over the propositional content in a speech act. On the basis of somewhat similar evidence Shatz (1978), Gelman and Shatz (1978), and Bates (1976) inferred that children do not first learn the literal meanings of utterances but rather their social or pragmatic meanings. It is this social or pragmatic aspect of meaning which appears to be altered, if not obliterated, when we turn from the oral language of conversations to the written languages of the texts used in schools.

Social Functions in Written Language

As to the social relations expressed and maintained by written texts, we may begin by noting that texts have authority; they are taken as the authorized version of the society's valid knowledge. The students' responsibility is primarily that of mastery of this knowledge. The text as the repository of cultural tradition is closely tied to the teachers use of the "recitation" method, in which children who have studied the text are given a variety of oral questions which serve the function of holding the children responsible for the information "in the text" (Bellack et al., 1966; Sinclair and Coulthard, 1975). Children seem not to have the right to disagree with the authorized texts; they have to master them and be prepared to defend them. There is, in short, a status difference between writer and reader just as there is between teacher and child in the oral language of the classroom. But how is that authority created and maintained through texts?

Consider this sample of a school textbook: "Slate is a name which is used to include many different kinds of rocks. The most common kind is that made up of clay and silex and is generally known as clay slate. Slate is found in layers below the surface of the earth. Geologists call these layers strata. . . ."

Elsewhere I have discussed some of the more general properties of such a text. It is a monologue, it is not clear who the speaker is, or who the intended listener is, or the purpose for which the text is written. Linguistically, it relies on defined terms; the grammatical structure reflects the logical structure; and the text as a whole reflects a logical hierarchical structure (Olson, 1977; Olson and Nickerson, 1978). And it tends to be used in a particular context for a particular purpose, schooling. Written textbooks, therefore, constitute a distinctive register of language in that they involve a form of language particularly appropriate to a particular context of use including schools and universities, a particular linguistic form, explicit logical prose, and a particular form of interpersonal relations between authors and readers (Halliday and Hasan, 1976). It is the last of these properties that is of interest here.

A glance at the sample of text presented above suggests that one of the most obvious interpersonal differences between the conversations we examined earlier and this text is the absence of markers of illocutionary force. All of the sentences are assertives, but nowhere is it indicated who is doing the asserting. It is difficult to even attribute the assertion to the writer of the textbook. Rather he is passing on a tradition, a discipline; the statements apparently originated elsewhere. Unlike the conversation between Jamie and Lisa, it is difficult here to deny the assertion because it is not clear if the person making that assertion has satisfied the preparatory conditions for the assertion. All one can do is assume they have been met and accept the statement as true. It is this separation of speech from the speaker which is critical to any analysis of written text.

But the separation of a speaker from his speech is characteristic of all archival forms of both oral and written language. This separation permits the preservation of language beyond spatio-temporal limits, including the life span of the speaker. It is therefore a means of preserving information intergenerationally. Textbooks are an important literate archival form; we may, therefore, gain some insight into their characteristics by comparing them to oral archival forms. Bloch's (1974, 1975) descriptions of the formal language of religious ritual and political oratory in a traditional society is ideal for this purpose. In his analysis of the circumcision ritual of the Marina of Madagascar, Bloch found several distinctive characteristics of this formalized language. First, such language constitutes a distinctive register in that utterances of ritual can be interpreted only in the light of their context. Indeed, to utter them elsewhere would be viewed as profanity. Secondly, ritual utterances radically restrict the linguistic options at the lexical, syntactic, and intonational levels; the prototypic ritual is chanted or sung over and over. Bloch suggests that what such ritualized language loses in propositional content, it gains in illocutionary force: "Such utterances gain their illocutionary force through the limited options they provide for dissent. You cannot argue with a song" (1974, p. 71). To disagree with the formula is to disrupt the social order as a whole because the formalized speech specifies and determines the permitted range of responses. Mary Douglas (1975) has described such ritualized linguistic forms as "condensed symbols"—symbols which mean a great deal more to the believer than to the nonbeliever.

Thirdly, the formalized language of ritual involves a different relation between the speaker and the message than does ordinary oral conversation. The speaker reciting the ritual is not speaking his own words but the words of the elders; the orator does not simply express his personal views but rather acts as a spokesman or messenger. Furthermore, this indirect content is frequently reflected by the use of a particular "voice." The voice, the context, the relation of speaker to utterance, and the linguistic form together define a distinctive register—a register specialized for serving a particular set of cognitive and social functions.

Although Bloch's description of a specialized register is extremely interesting, there are three questions which may be raised. First, it is not clear that one can talk of the trade off between propositional content and illocutionary force. As we have seen, all sentences have illocutionary force, and it is difficult to see how a sentence can have more or less illocutionary force. A command is a command. Yet some commands obviously carry more weight than others—for example, when they are issued by someone with great authority or for whom one has great respect.

Similarly, it is not clear why the decrease in linguistic options produces an increase in ambiguity or why ambiguity increases what Bloch referred to as illocutionary force. It seems more likely, to me, that the language has great authority not because of its restricted propositional content but because of the prestige of its source. Thus statements with elaborated propositional content, as the laws of *Leviticus*, can have great authority, if they are believed to come from God. The social significance or force of statements, then, derives not from their ambiguity but from the author/authority of those statements, their pedigree so to speak. Statements with authority are those which derive from a more or less transcendental source. Because of that source they cannot be disputed or gainsaid. This point is important because written archival texts have highly elaborate language, and yet they, too, may have great authority. Hence authority cannot be confined to condensed symbols.

What then is the explanation for the decrease in lexical options and the increase in ambiguity that Bloch reports? The predominant *archival* form in an oral, traditional society is that of oral mneumonic devices including verse, song, formulaic expressions, and speech under ritual conditions. And it is, as Havelock (1976) and Ong (1971) first suggested, in the interest of memorability that socially significant information takes a poetic "condensed" form (see Olson, 1977).

Oral archival forms, then, are devices for differentiating speaker from speech and for preserving that speech across time and space. Several writers have pointed out that the separation of speaker from speech tends to give the speech an authority it would not have if it originated in the mind of the current speaker. Durkheim (Lukes, 1973) stressed that through participation in rituals, *représentations collectives* were made to appear as powerful, sacred, and originating somewhere other than with the current speaker. Similarly, as we have seen, Bloch found that in ritual conditions, the speaker speaks not his own words but the "words of the elders" and he signals these sacred words by the adoption of a special "voice." Both of these devices endow the speech and the speaker with an authority they would not have otherwise—especially if the speaker was a well-known peer.

But no one seems to have noted that the same device for managing authority exists in written language. In referring to a text, or in reading a text to a class orally, or in a student's reading of a text, the language originates elsewhere than in the mind of the current speaker. It has a "transcendental" source and is thereby above criticism. Recall that as long as the speech originates with the current speaker, his listeners know that it is just *his* assertion and that as a result it is apt to reflect *his* knowledge, *his* interests, and that he may or may not have satisfied the preparatory conditions for making an assertion. His utterances are then open to criticism. When the same statement originates or appears to originate elsewhere, particularly if that source is sacred or has high status, it will be immune to, or "above," criticism.

Written texts, among other things, are devices which separate speech from speaker and that separation in itself may make the words impersonal, objective, and above criticism. When the language originates elsewhere than in the personal whim and limited experience of the speaker—rather, in the textbook which the parent or teacher consults—the language is assumed to have great authority. Indeed it may be because the child assumes that textbooks have great authority that he is willing to devote serious and prolonged study to the book rather than simply reading it. Furthermore, it is the role of books in our culture that makes them an ultimate authority in matters of dispute (Esther Geva, personal communication):

> MOTHER: Don't spill water on the kitten because they hate water.
> CHILD: How do you know?
> MOTHER: I read it somewhere.
> CHILD: Oh!

The authority attributed to statements which originate elsewhere than with the present speaker may help to explain two interesting observations on teacher's classroom speech. As mentioned earlier Sinclair and Coulthard

(1975) found that teachers frequently use indirect speech acts in regulating children's behavior. Thus rather than saying to a child "Please be quiet," they frequently adopt such indirect forms as "I hear talking." As they point out, given conventions of the classroom, these indirect directives are polite forms of speech. However, we may note in addition that by simply commenting upon the violation of a norm, the teacher attributes the norm not to herself/himself but to a transcendental source; the norm thereby carries greater authority by being above criticism.

The speaker/speech distinction may also help to explain Feldman and Wertsch's (1975) finding that teachers in classrooms rarely used modal auxiliaries such as *may, might, could.* or expressions of uncertainty such as I think, believe, hope, feel. . . . If teachers take themselves to be the exponents of someone else's views, those of the textbook writer, that absence is quite understandable. As the views they express are not their own but those of the textbooks, their personal feelings, perceptions, and so on are irrelevant.

The description offered of the authority of textbooks may appear too Victorian to be a valid description of the attitude of students to textbooks in modern, liberalized schools, and it seems not to characterize the uses of textbooks by the more highly educated—and not at all the approach taken by members of a professional group or academic peer group. As we well know, we disagree with much of what we read even if it does often appear to come from a transcendental source; we attribute it to a writer who, we assume, is much like ourselves. This suggests the operation of an additional factor, a factor which may underlie the development of critical reading as opposed to the study, memorization, and assimilation of such texts as we have been discussing.

As Esther Goody (1978), Lakoff (1977), Brown and Levinson (1978), and many others have shown, to ask a question, to make an assertion, to issue a command, or to make a pronouncement, you must have the right to do so within some relevant social group. The same is true, I suggest, for the right to criticize and to dissent. The social relations required for the free offering of requests and assertions and their equally free criticism/rejection may be called a peer group. Thus children with their peers freely make their own assertions and deny those of others (see McTear, in press, and Klein and Miller, in press), and academics with their colleagues freely advance ideas and criticize the ideas of others because they act as a peer group; they have the right to speak and to be heard as equals. Once admitted to a peer group, the written work of peers is again taken as an expression of the views of the individual who wrote them; the author and his text are reunited, so to speak. And anything that could now be said directly to the author as an equal (perhaps even more) can also be said/written against his text. That is, a peer group both invites the possibility of criticism and reunites the author with his writings. Membership in that peer group comes at least in part from being a participant in that particular form of discourse, that is, through becoming a writer.

It is this peer relationship, I suggest, which invites critical reading and critical thought. The situation, however, is very different for the author's subordinates, students, and audiences, and especially for the author's exponents—teachers who, because the words are neither ther own nor originate with a known member of their own peer group, lack the right to criticize. It is interesting to note that Rousseau (1966) in his *Essay on the Origin of Languages* pointed out that he distrusted script for this very reason; writing and especially print removed the accent and signature of the speaker from his utterance, which therefore took on a spurious life and authority of its own (see Derrida, 1976). This divorce, as suggested above, is a source of the authority of the written word.

There are, therefore, two obvious ways of enhancing the prestige and authority of assertions and thereby of assuring the perlocutionary effect of assent. One is for the assertions to appear to be true and valid and thereby "above" suspicion, the other is for them to originate in a superior source and therefore be "above" suspicion. These two are ordinarily conflated. Even "true" ideas, however, encounter occasional heavy criticism, as Kuhn (1962) and others have shown, especially from superiors—Roentgen from Lord Kelvin, Galileo from Pope Urban VIII, and so on. And partial "truths" originating from authorities, elders, or some more transcendental source, tend to be minimally criticized. Criticism is least likely when ideas have both some validity and a transcendental source. Textbooks, like religious ritual, have both; they are devices for putting ideas and beliefs above criticism.

Like other forms of language, then, texts have both an intellectual function and a normative, social function. When so viewed, ordinary conversational dialogue, ritualized speech in a traditional society, and written texts in a literate society turn out to have more in common than is at first evident. The latter two serve an important archival function in preserving what the society takes to be "true" and "valid" knowledge, knowledge from which rules of thought and action may be derived. They both help to preserve the social order by minimizing dispute. This task is achieved, however, in quite different ways depending upon, as Havelock has pointed out, the form in which knowledge is stored for re-use. If stored in oral form, it appears as memorable, clear examplars, pithy sayings, ritualized speech, and condensed symbols. If stored in written form, it appears as lists and tables and in the detailed, explicit, expository prose of essays, encyclopedias, and textbooks. But in both cases, the knowledge so stored carries great authority because it appears to originate in a transcendental source, at least, in a source other than the present speaker. Textbooks, nonetheless, constitute a distinctive linguistic register involving a particular form of language (archival written texts), a particular social situation (schools), and a particular form of linguistic interaction (reading and study).

Any archival form, being traditionally or historically grounded, calls for comprehension and production strategies somewhat different from those employed in everyday speech—skills which may in fact require sustained "education" for their acquisition. Basic to those strategies is the displacement of that speech from the speaker and the context of its production. That separation, I have suggested, produces an alteration in the illocutionary force and in preparatory conditions of utterance, with the result that the child's role is changed from that of participant to that of a recipient of language. The child's growing competence with this somewhat specialized and distinctive register of language may contribute to the similarly specialized and distinctive mode of thought we usually associate with formal education.

References

Austin, J. L. *How to do things with words.* Edited by J. O. Urmson. New York: Oxford University Press, 1962.

Bates, E. *Language and context: The acquisition of pragmatics.* New York: Academic Press, 1976.

Bates, E., Camaioni, L., and Volterra, V. The acquisition of performatives prior to speech. *Merrill-Palmer Quarterly,* 1975, 21, 205–226.

Bellack, A. A., Kliebard, H. M., Hyman, R. T., and Smith, F. L. *The language of the classroom.* New York: Teacher's College Press, 1966.

Bloch, M. (Ed.). *Political language and oratory in traditional society.* London: Academic Press, 1975.

Bloch, M. Symbols, song, dance and features of articulation. *Archives Europeenues de sociologie,* 1974, 15, 55–81

Brown, P. and Levinson, S. Universals in language usage: Politeness phenomena. In E. Goody (Ed.), *Questions and politeness.* Cambridge: Cambridge University Press, 1978.

Bruner, J. S. *Beyond the information given: Studies in the psychology of knowing.* Edited by J. Anglin. New York: Norton, 1973.

———. Intellectual autobiography. In G. Lindzey (Ed.), *History of psychology in autobiography* vol 7. San Francisco; W. H. Freeman, 1980.

Bruner, J. S., Greenfield, P. M., and Olver, R. R. *Studies in cognitive growth.* New York: Wiley, 1966.

Clark, H. H. and Clark, E. V. *Psychology and language.* New York: Harcourt Brace Jovanich, 1977.

Derrida, J. *Of grammatology.* Translated by G. Spivak. Baltimore: Johns Hopkins University Press, 1976.

Dore, J. Children's illocutionary acts. In R. Freedle (Ed.), *Discourse production and comprehension.* Norwood, N. J.: Ablex, 1977.

Douglas, M. T. *Implicit meanings: Essays in anthropology.* London: Routledge and Kegan Paul, 1975.

Ervin-Tripp, S. Wait for me, roller skate. In S. Ervin-Tripp and C. Mitchell-Kernan (Eds.), *Child discourse.* New York: Academic Press, 1977.

Feldman, C. F. and Wertsch, J. V. Context dependent properties of teachers' speech. Preprint, School of Education, Harvard, 1975.

Garvey, C. Requests and responses in children's speech. *Journal of Child Language,* 1975, 21, 41–60.

Gellner, E. The savage and the modern mind. In R. Horton and R. Finnegan (Eds.), *Modes of thought: Essays on thinking in western and nonwestern societies.* London: Faber and Faber, 1973.

Gelman, R. and Shatz M. Appropriate speech adjustments: The operation of conversational constraints on talk to two-year-olds. In M. Lewis and L. Rosenblum (Eds.), *Interaction conversation and the development of language*. New York: Wiley, 1978.

Goody, E. N. Towards a theory of questions. In E. N. Goody (Ed.), *Questions and politeness: Strategies in social interaction*. Cambridge: Cambridge University Press, 1978.

Halliday, M. A. K. Language structure and language function. In J. Lyons (Ed.), *New horizons in linguistics*. Harmondsworth; Penguin Books, 1970.

————. *Explorations in the functions of language*. London: Edward Arnold Ltd., 1973.

Halliday, M. A. K. and Hasan, R. *Cohesion in English*. London: Longman Group 1976.

Hare, R. E. *Practical inferences*. London: MacMillan, 1971.

Havelock, E. *Preface to Plato*. Cambridge, Mass.: Harvard University Press, 1963.

————. *Prologue to Greek literacy*. Toronto: Ontario Institute for Studies in Education Press, 1976.

Hildyard, A. The recall of appropriate and inappropriate requests. Paper presented AERA, Boston, Mass., 1980.

Horton, R. African traditional thought and Western science. In B. R. Wilson (Ed.), *Rationality*. Oxford: Blackwell, 1970.

Jakobson, R. Linguistics and poetics. In T. A. Sebeok (Ed.), *Style in language*. New York: Wiley, 1960.

James, S. L. Effects of listener age and situation on the politeness of children's directives. *Journal of Psycholinguistic Research*, 1978, 7, 307-317.

Klein, W. and Miller, M. Argumentation. Paper presented at the conference *Beyond description in child language*, Nijmegen, The Netherlands, June, 1979.

Kuhn, T. *The structure of scientific revolutions*. Chicago: University of Chicago Press, 1962.

Lakoff, R. Language and society. In R. Wardaugh and H. Brown (Eds.), *A survey of applied linguistics*. Ann Arbor: University of Michigan Press, 1977.

Lukes, S. *Emile Durkheim: His life and work*. Markham, Ontario: Penguin Books, 1973.

McTear, M. Getting it done. Paper presented at the conference *Beyond description in child language*, Nijmegen, The Netherlands, June, 1979.

Mitchell-Kernan, C. and Kernan, K. T. Pragmatics of directive choice among children. In S. Ervin-Tripp and C. Mitchell-Kernan (Eds.), *Child discourse*. New York: Academic Press, 1977.

Olson, D. R. From utterance to text: The bias of language in speech and writing. *Harvard Educational Review*, 1977, 47, 257–281.

Olson, D. R. and Hildyard, A. Assent and compliance in children's comprehension. In P. Dixon (Ed.), *Children's oral communication skills*. New York: Academic Press, in press.

Olson, D. R. and Nickerson, N. G. Language development through the school years: Learning to confine interpretation to the information in the text. In K. E. Nelson (Ed.), *Children's language*, vol. 1. New York: Gardner Press, 1978.

Ong, W. *Rhetoric, romance and technology: Studies in the interaction of expression and culture*. Ithaca: Cornell University Press, 1971.

Putnam, H. *Mind, language and reality*, vol. 2. New York: Cambridge University Press, 1975.

Rousseau, J. Essay on the origin of languages. In J. H. Moran and A. Gode (Eds.), *On the origin of language*. New York: Ungar, 1966.

Searle, J. R. *Speech acts: An essay in the philosophy of language*. Cambridge: Cambridge Univeristy Press, 1969.

————. Indirect speech acts. In P. Cole and J. Morgan (Eds.), *Syntax and semantics. Speech acts*, vol. 3. New York: Academic Press, 1975.

Shatz, M. Children's comprehension of their mothers' question-directives. *Journal of Child Language*, 1978, 5, 39–46.

Sinclair, J. M. and Coulthard, R. M. *Towards an analysis of discourse: The English used by teachers and pupils*. London: Oxford University Press, 1975.

PART II

Child Language
in Its Social Context

6

Acquiring Linguistic Skills:
A Study of Sentence Construction
in Preschool Children

Jeremy M. Anglin

It is a pleasure to write a chapter for this book in honor of Jerome Bruner, whose contribution to our understanding of the nature and origins of human cognition is immense. In my chapter I would like to discuss the relevance of some aspects of the skill development theory that Bruner, his colleagues, and students formulated at the Center for Cognitive Studies between 1967 and 1973 for an understanding of the preschool child's growing skill in using language effectively. In particular I would like to explore the possibility that some of the concepts advanced by Bruner and his associates (for example, Bruner, 1968, 1969, 1971, 1972, 1973a, 1973b; Bruner and Bruner, 1968; Bruner and Koslowski, 1972; Hillman and Bruner, 1972; Kalnins and Bruner, 1973; Mundy-Castle and Anglin, 1973) to account for the infant's growing capacity to solve sensorimotor problems are of relevance to grammatical development. I will begin by reviewing Bruner's theory of the development of skill. Then, after I have made a few general comments about acquiring linguistic skills as opposed to sensorimotor skills, I will present some results of a recent study of sentence construction in preschool children as a means of exploring concretely one way in which the theory is relevant to grammatical development. In particular I will try to show that the skill of learning to construct sentences can be viewed in terms of the growing capacities of refining and combining sentence constituents, just as the acquisition of sensorimotor skills has been described by Jerry Bruner and his colleagues in terms of the growing capacities of refining and combining the constituent operations required by the sensorimotor problems that confront the infant in his first year and a half.

I am most grateful to Alexis Murray for her help in conducting the study described in this chapter and to Rose Freigang and Maureen Hayvren for their able assistance in analyzing the results.

Bruner's Theory of the Development of Skill

Bruner and his associates, at least initially, studied seemingly simple sensorimotor skills such as feeding, looking, and especially reaching in infants. From this research they generated a theory of the development of skill. Before I try to describe the developmental theory I should first say a word about the model of adult skill that guided the research with infants. This model was clearly in the same spirit as those put forward by Miller, Galanter, and Pribram (1960) and by Bernstein (1967); it was also consistent with some earlier arguments by Lashley (1951). It was just as clearly in opposition to a stimulus-response or chaining conception of skill. For Bruner, "Skilled activity is a program specifying an objective or terminal state to be achieved, and requiring the serial ordering of a set of constituent, modular subroutines" (Bruner, 1971). Thus the successful execution of any given skilled behavior was viewed as requiring the execution of a series of constituent acts in a serial order which would eventuate in the attainment of a goal or the fulfilment of an intention. The execution of the constituents and their arrangement in a serial order were thought to be both initiated and guided by an intention which also provided the criterion for terminating the act. For example the skilled act of bringing a cup of milk to the mouth to drink from could be viewed as a series of constituent acts— reaching, grasping, retrieving, and mouthing—executed in that order. In this case the order and execution of these constituents were thought to be initiated and guided by the intention to drink.

Three crucial concepts in Bruner's account of adult skill which served to distinguish it from a behavioristic or chaining account were: 1. intentionality; 2. the hierarchically organized constituent structure of skilled behavior; and 3. the generativity of skilled behavior. With respect to intentionality any skilled act was thought to involve a "persistent intention that precedes, directs and provides a criterion for terminating [the] act" (Bruner, 1971). The way in which the intention was thought to guide the execution of a given skill was through feedback. Specifically, throughout the execution of any skilled act the results of behavior were thought to be continually compared with the intended state. If there was a match, the act had been completed. If there was a mismatch, intention-guided behavior was thought to continue until the discrepancy had been eliminated.

With respect to the constituent structure of skilled behavior, most cases of the latter could be viewed as being comprised of constituent modular acts whose appearance in serial order implies an organizing program or set of rules which are hierarchically arranged. (The analogy with computer technology was deliberate.) What makes a given skill difficult is not so often the performance of any given constituent but rather more often the adapting and combining of constituents in a serial order to meet the task demands. The hierarchical structure of skilled behavior is most obvious for relatively complicated skills. For example, the adult skill of partaking of a meal at a dinner table involves a number of component skills such as drinking from a cup or glass, eating with a knife and fork, and so. Each of these component skills requires the execution of a set of constituent operations in an appropriate serial order to be effective. For example, bringing a cup to the mouth involves the constituents of reaching, grasping, retrieving, and mouthing as noted above. Thus skilled behavior requires the execution of a series of component skills in an appropriate order; the execution of each of these component skills, at least in complicated tasks, in turn requires the execution of a set of constituents, and so on.

With respect to the generativity of skilled behavior new tasks could be solved by adapting and combining previously learned constituent skills in new ways. It could be argued that virtually every time we perform a skilled act the particular motor movements involved are somewhat different, and one thing making an expert skilled is his ability to adjust his performance to meet the demands of new situations. According to Bruner this was possible because skilled behavior had not been stamped into a passive organism via a conditioning process; rather, it had been actively acquired in ways that allowed the individual to select, adapt, and combine the constituents required by a task and to execute them in an order appropriate to the demands of that task under the guidance of an intention, even if he had never solved that particular task before.

Skilled behavior, viewed in this way, can be seen to have much in common with certain types of cognitive processes. Bruner has emphasized specifically the similarities between skill and problem solving on the one hand and skill and language production on the other. With respect to the former, Bruner argued that skilled behavior can be viewed as a kind of problem solving. Both skills and problems usually require a series of constituent operations. What makes a skill or problem difficult is not so often the execution of a given constituent but rather choosing, adapting, and combining constituent acts or operations in a way that will achieve the objective. With respect to the latter, Bruner argued that skilled behavior and language production are similar in the ways in which they achieve their flexibility and power. Specifically, functionally equivalent but morphologically distinct constituents of action can be substituted for one another in the execution of a given skill, just as semantically equivalent but phonologically distinct words, phrases, and sentences can replace one another to communicate the same message. Of greater importance was the argument that both skilled behavior and language were productive or generative. As noted above, in the execution of a sensorimotor skill constituent acts can be adapted and combined in new ways to achieve different goals, just as words, phrases, and sentences can be combined in new ways to communicate novel messages.

In view of this kind of model of skill, Bruner and his associates set out to study the acquisition of oral, visual, and especially manual skills in children. Several of their studies of skilled behavior in infants suggested that the intention to achieve a goal was there at the outset. "When one observes the early behavior of infants—say at the outset of visually guided reaching at about four months of age—one is struck by the extent to which intentionality precedes skill. Arousal of intention I would urge is the initial reaction to an appropriate stimulus. . . . Often in response to an appropriate stimulus there are evoked preparatory activities that later will make possible the performance of an adaptive act toward an object. Before the infant can reach, the presentation of an object with sharp contours and good binocular and movement parallax will induce antigravitational activity in the arms, opening and closing of the hands and even working of the mouth" (Bruner, 1971). Such an intention, however, though necessary for the execution of a skilled act, is not sufficient. Also necessary is the capacity to perform a series of appropriate constituent acts in a serial order to fulfill the intention. It is this capacity that was found to distinguish the behavior of younger infants who could not execute a given skill and older infants who could. In this view the development of skilled behavior involves the growing capacities of 1. adapting, refining, or differentiating constituent acts as required by a given task and 2. combining, integrating, or intercalating them in an order appropriate to the requirements of the task. (A specific process—*modularization*, the automatization of sequences of constituents —was hypothesized to be an important means by which the integration of component skills became increasingly possible for the child with development. I shall not, however, attempt to describe language development in terms of this specific process in this paper.)

Let me illustrate this view of the development of skill in terms of one illuminating study conducted by Jerry Bruner and his associates Karlen Lyons and Ken Kaye. This was a study of the infant's growing capacity to use both hands in a complementary fashion to achieve a goal (Bruner, 1971). In this study children of 6 to 8 months, 9 to 11 months, 12 to 14 months, and 15 to 17 months were presented with a box which had a transparent lid which revealed a toy inside it. The lid was mounted on sliding ball bearings and tilted 30 degrees from the horizontal so that the most expedient way of retrieving the object was to push the lid up with one hand, reach into the box, grasp, and retrieve the object with the other hand and then let the lid come gently down with the first hand. Each infant was seated on his mother's lap in front of the box and "the temptation invariably succeeded; the infant attempted as best he could to get the toy" (Bruner, 1971), suggesting that the intention to retrieve the toy was present in all children at least initially. However, success in actually getting the object improved dramatically with age such that less than one fifth of the youngest children (6 to 8 months) were successful whereas close to 90 percent of the oldest group (15 to 17 months) managed to get the toy.

More interesting than the success rates of the children in this study were the approaches that children of different ages took to the task. Some of the six-to-eight-month-olds simply clawed and banged at the barrier without pushing the lid up or retrieving the object. A second form of failure prevalent especially among the two youngest groups of children consisted in opening and closing the sliding lid without an intervening reach into the box between the opening and the closing. A somewhat more advanced strategy, which was awkward but did result in success for some of the somewhat older children, involved the use of just a single hand. Specifically children using this strategy were observed to raise the lid with one hand and then insert that hand into the opening before the lid fell against it. The toy was grasped and extricated from the box by yanking it through the space between the edge of the lid and the edge of the box.

More efficient strategies involving the use of both hands were observed to increase after the first year of life. One awkward approach of this sort involved raising the lid with one or both hands, then going for the object with one or both hands but not holding the lid in the open position long enough to get the object out of the box efficiently. Although this particular pattern was not common—a little over one out of six of the twelve-to-fourteen-month-olds manifested this approach—it was an interesting case in which the constituents appeared to be present, if in a somewhat awkward form, but the sequence of their execution was off. For this reason Bruner described this approach as "slightly apraxic." A more advanced strategy still involved the use of both hands to slide the lid, and then while retaining the open position with one hand, the child retrieved the toy with the other after which he let the lid come down. Finally, the most advanced approach to the task was seen to increase sharply after one year of age. In this approach the child raised the lid with one hand and held it open while retrieving the object with the other hand, after which the first hand let the lid come gently down.

Notice that at least initially the intention to retrieve the object appeared to be present in all infants. Also notice that whereas some of the youngest infants did not appear to be able to open and close the lid, others did. We also know that infants between six and eight months are often able to grasp and retrieve an object. This implies that at least some of the youngest children probably were capable of producing each of the major acts required for success in the task, if admittedly in a somewhat awkward form, but they were not able to adapt those constituents and combine them in a way to achieve the goal. Thus this study suggests that the development of skill can be described in terms of the growing capacities of refining constituents and of combining them to achieve a goal. The differentiation or refinement of constituents is illustrated in the study just described by the changes which occurred in the act of pushing up the barrier and letting it go. Whereas the less skilled children pushed the barrier up and then released it before they could put their hand into the box, the older children pushed the barrier up and held it long enough to allow them to grasp the object with the other hand. The holding operation is a refinement of the pushing which allows the task to be solved effectively. The study also illustrates that development of skilled behavior in this situation involves combining constituents in an order appropriate to the goal of retrieving the object. Whereas younger children might be able to push the barrier and let it go or to grasp an object, it is only the older children who are capable of combining or integrating these acts as required by the task by embedding the act of grasping between the acts of pushing the barrier and letting it go.

This was just one of a number of studies of the child's manual skills. There were also studies of sucking (see Bruner and Bruner, 1968) and of looking (see Mundy-Castle and Anglin, 1973), skills which are acquired earlier than the manual skills discussed above, and also of the intercalation of skills such as sucking and looking (see Kalnins and Bruner, 1973) and looking and grasping (indeed most of the manual skills studied required visually guided reaching). Although there were differences from skill to skill, development in each case could be viewed in terms of refining constituents and of integrating them with others from the same or different skill systems.

Acquiring Linguistic Skills

In the study to be presented below I have attempted to analyze the utterances produced by two-to-five-year-old children in an event description task in terms of constituents to see whether or not, and if so how, grammatical development might be characterized in terms of the combination and refinement of constituents. Before presenting the study, however, I would like to stress that, whatever the similarities may be between sensorimotor skills and the skill we call "language," there are important differences as well, three of which I shall mention here. First, language is a social skill learned through interacting with parents and others (for example, Ninio and Bruner, 1978; Bruner, 1978; Zukow, Reilly, and Greenfield, in press) and used to communicate with others. Second, linguistic skills are fundamentally symbolic whereas sensorimotor skills are not (Piaget 1952, 1962). Finally, linguistic skills require to a greater degree than sensorimotor skills relatively advanced cognitive capacities. For example, the commitment to long term memory of a lexicon which is a prerequisite for the effective use of speech requires a greater capacity to process and store information than does sucking, looking, or reaching.

Just how remarkable a cognitive feat the acquisition of vocabulary is in normal children is revealed by studies of the comprehension (*vs.* production) of words by children. For example, in a recent study Helen Benedict

(1979) has shown that, on the average, the children she studied who were between 9 months and 1 year, 8 months had achieved a comprehension vocabulary of 50 words by 1 year, 1 month and that an average of 22.23 new words were comprehended each month by her children. More remarkable still are the results of a careful study by Mildred Templin (1957) on older children (6 to 8 years) whose data have recently been discussed in an illuminating way by George Miller (1977, 1978). According to Templin's results the median total comprehension (or recognition) vocabulary of the 6-year-olds she studied was estimated to be 13,000 words; the corresponding root comprehension vocabulary was estimated to be 7,800 words. For 7-year-olds Templin's estimates were 21,600 and 12,400 for total and root comprehension vocabularies respectively. For 8-year-olds her estimates were 28,300 and 17,600 respectively. As George Miller points out these figures mean that the median child's total comprehension vocabulary increased by about 21 words per day between 6 and 8 years; his root comprehension vocabulary increased by about 14½ words *per day*. The incredible cognitive capacity for storing words in long term memory suggested by these figures does not have an obvious counterpart in the acquisition of the sensorimotor skills discussed above.

Thus it would have been possible in this paper to focus on aspects of the problem of acquiring linguistic skills that might have suggested the differences rather than their similarities between acquiring language and acquiring the sensorimotor skills discussed above. For example it is not obvious that the commitment to long term memory of a lexicon mentioned above—a prerequisite for the effective use of language—can be described in terms of the model of skill which has been summarized. However, in this paper I would like to discuss the child's growing capacity to construct sentences, which I think can be viewed in terms of the theory of the development of skill outlined by Bruner and his associates.

Recall that with respect to the acquisition of skill the argument was made that intentionality precedes the skill and that the growth of skill occurs as the child develops the capacity to combine and differentiate constituents as required by the tasks which confront him. It seems to me that in his recent work on the transition from prelinguistic to linguistic communication Bruner (1975, 1976, 1978) as well as others have shown again that the intention to communicate precedes the acquisition of language per se; this parallels the finding in the earlier work that the intention to achieve a goal preceded the ability to produce a differentiated and integrated set of constituents to achieve it. For example in his recent paper "Acquiring the Uses of Language" (1978) Bruner has argued: "The child knows (in limited form) what he is trying to accomplish by communicating before he begins to use lexico-grammatical speech to implement his efforts. He tries to achieve his communicative ends initially by gesture and vocalization and these become increasingly conventionalized." He continues, ". . . language

is a developed set of communicative procedures for fulfilling certain functions, and that prior to its acquisition many of the same functions were fulfilled (albeit less well) by other communicative procedures." If this is correct and if the theory of skill development discussed above is relevant, what
remains to be shown is how the development of the capacity to produce
sentences can be understood in terms of the differentiation or refinement of
constituents and their integration or combination. In any event this is what
I shall now attempt to show by presenting a recent study of grammatical
development which I conducted with the generous assistance of Alexis
Murray, Rose Freigang, and Maureen Hayvren, all students at the University of Waterloo.

A Study of Sentence Construction in Preschool Children

One of the major issues which I have thus far avoided in this paper concerns the identification of the constituent acts which make up a larger
skilled behavior. This is a thorny problem which was discussed at length by
those of us who were working on skill in infancy at the Center for Cognitive
Studies (though I am not sure we ever fully resolved it) and was discussed
by Bruner in a number of his writings on the subject. I will not confront the
problems of identifying the constituents involved in the sensorimotor skills
of infants here, but must discuss the issue of identifying constituents in the
production of a sentence, if only briefly.

The problem with identifying the constituents of language is partly due to
the fact that there are so many possibilities. For example, consider the following two sentences each of which was used as a "target sentence" in the
study with preschool children to be described below:

The chairs are leaning against the wall.

The lady is eating the apple.

Each sentence can be described at least as a string of morphemes, as a
string of words, as a string of constituent phrases, as a string of immediate
constituents, or as simply an utterance or a sentence. If one were to choose
the morpheme as the unit of analysis (see Brown, 1973) the first sentence
would consist of 9 morphemes (The chair s are lean ing against the wall)
and the second sentence would consist of 7 (The lady is eat ing the apple).
If one were to choose the word as the unit of analysis the first sentence
would consist of 7 words (The chairs are leaning against the wall) and the
second sentence would consist of 6 words (The lady is eating the apple). If
one were to choose the constituent phrase as the unit of analysis (that is,
subject phrase, verb phrase, object phrase, prepositional phrase) the first
sentence would consist of 3 constituents (subject phrase [The chairs], verb
phrase [are leaning], and prepositional phrase [against the wall]) and the

second sentence would also consist of three consituents (subject phrase [The lady], verb phrase [is eating], and object phrase [the apple]. If one were to choose the immediate constituents as the unit of analysis each sentence would consist of two constituents, a subject and a predicate in both cases. Finally, if one were to choose the utterance or the sentence as the unit of analysis each of the examples would count as just one apiece.

This multiplicity of possible constituents poses the question of which level of analysis will be most useful in describing the child's developing skill of sentence construction. My own feeling is that each of these units of analysis and others can be profitably examined in the study of child language and that the study of each will yield valuable information about language development. For the purpose of this paper I will concentrate on three of these levels—the most specific, the most general, and a level intermediate between these. Specifically, results will be presented in which the morpheme, the utterance, and the constituent phrase (hereafter referred to as the sentence constituent) have been used as the unit of analysis. The way in which each of these units of analysis was defined in the present study will become clear below.

The reader will gather correctly from what follows that the present study, though different in many particular respects, has been greatly influenced by the more ambitious pioneering work of Roger Brown (1973) and his colleagues (for example, Villiers and de Villiers, 1973) on grammatical development. The results are also quite consistent in various ways with those of Brown and his associates, where they are comparable, as I will point out in describing them. They also appear to me to be consistent in a general way with the theory of skill developed by Jerry Bruner and his colleagues, and in this paper in honor of Jerry Bruner, I will attempt to show why I think they are.

METHOD

Subjects Seven groups of subjects participated in this study. A group of ten adults was interviewed first for the purpose of selecting appropriate materials for the study with children. Among the adults there were five male and five female undergraduates from the University of Waterloo whose ages ranged between nineteen and twenty-four years.

After materials had been chosen on the basis of adult performance, six groups of children were then interviewed. The age ranges for the six groups of children were 2–2½ years; 2½–3 years; 3–3½ years; 3½–4 years; 4–4½ years; 4½–5 years. There were equal numbers of males and females in the first, second, and sixth of these groups. The third and fourth groups consisted of six males and four females each, while the fifth group consisted of three males and seven females. Thus in total there were thirty male and thirty female children included in this study. Of the sixty children forty-six were interviewed in a quiet room in the preschool or day care center which they attended. Seven children were obtained through the generous help of an undergraduate student (Connie Elliot) and were tested in the student's home. The remaining seven children were interviewed in their own homes.

Materials Twenty-five black-and-white photographs were taken of various events involving both animate and inanimate subjects. A Polaroid Land Camera was used to take the pictures. Some examples of events were of a woman eating an apple, a chair leaning against a wall, a woman looking up at a ceiling, and so on. Interviews were recorded on a Sony tape recorder.

Procedure The ten adult subjects were told that they were participating in a study of the development of sentence construction in children. They were told that they would be asked to describe the events shown in the pictures in fully grammatical sentences, but to remember that their sentences would be used as reference points for the children's utterances and therefore should be simply expressed. The adults then went through two introductory phases to ensure that they understood what was meant by a fully grammatical sentence. In phase 1 the experimenter showed the adult three pictures, one at a time, and described each picture in a simple declarative sentence. The sentences used to describe these pictures were as follows: 1. "The man and the lady are looking up." 2."Three books are on the table." and 3. "The man and the lady are brushing their hair."

In the second introductory phase the adult was shown three more pictures, one at a time. In each case the adult was asked: "How would you describe what is happening in this picture in one sentence?" If the subject's response was not a fully grammatical description of the event in the picture the experimenter would point this out and would describe it for him. The sentences used to describe these pictures were as follows: 1. "The lady is reading the book." 2. "The glass is on the table." and 3. "The man and the lady are reading books." Notice that in phases 1 and 2 whenever an article was required, the definite article "the" was used.

Each adult was then shown the remaining nineteen pictures, one at a time, in random order. As each picture was presented, the experimenter asked the standard question: "How would you describe what is happening in this picture in one sentence?"

Based on the data from the ten adult subjects a modal sentence was determined for each picture. This modal sentence was the sentence which was produced with the highest frequency by the ten adults. There was some flexibility in the modal sentences in that in certain cases articles ("the," "a"), prepositions ("in," "on"), nouns ("lady," "woman"), and verbs ("eat," "bite") were interchangeable as long as the grammatical structure of the sentence and its meaning were not drastically altered. The pictures for twelve of the nineteen modal sentences were chosen to be shown to the preschool children. The criterion used in choosing a picture was that at least 80 percent of the adults tested had produced the modal sentence in their description of the picture. This criterion was chosen to ensure that the pictures were relatively unambiguous, at least to adults. As it turned out twelve pictures satisfied this criterion. Six of the adult modal sentences were subject-verb-object (SVO) sentences and six were subject-verb-prepositional phrase (SVP) sentences. In every case the verb construction involved an auxiliary verb ("is" or "are"), a verb stem (for example, "lean," "eat"), and the progressive inflection ("ing") attached to the verb stem. The modal sentence forms produced by the adults for each picture used with children are shown in table 1. The top sentences in each of the adult modal sentences shown in table 1 will henceforth be called the "target sentences" for each picture.

After the adults had been tested, the sixty children were interviewed one at a time. The experimenter became familiar with the child before testing commenced. When the child appeared to feel comfortable, he was asked if he would like to play a game with pictures. If the child assented he was taken to a quiet room in the day care center, preschool, or home. This room was made as distraction free as possible, and in each case only the experimenter and the child were present during testing.

The child was told that he would be shown some pictures and would be asked to describe what was happening in each of them with one sentence. To show the child what was required and to illustrate what a sentence was the two introductory phases used with adults were used with the children. In phase 1 three pictures (the same ones that had been used in phase 1 with adults) were shown to the child one at a time and the experimenter showed how to describe them in fully grammatical sentences. As she produced each sentence she explained to the child that her words describing the event were a "sentence." Then in phase 2 three different pictures (also the same ones that had been used in phase 2 with adults) were shown to the child and he was asked: "What is happening in this picture? Tell me in one sentence." or, alternatively, "Can you tell me what is happening in this picture in one sentence?" In cases in which the child seemed to have trouble understanding "happening" the experimenter would substitute "going on" for "happening," resulting in the question: "What is going on in this picture? Tell me in one sentence." or "Can you tell me what is going on in this picture in one sentence?" After the child had produced a response to this question, in every case, the experimenter told him the ideal sentence for each picture—both to clarify the procedure to those children who gave incomplete responses and to reinforce those children who used correct sentences. Again whenever an article was required in phases 1 and 2 the definite article "the" was used in the sentences that were modeled for the child.

TABLE 1

The modal sentences produced by adults for the twelve pictures used in the study of sentence construction in preschool children. The top sentence in each case will henceforth be called the target sentence. (The symbol φ represents no attempt at constituent.)

	S	V	P
Picture 1	{The / A} chair	is lean ing	{against / up against} {the / a} wall.
Picture 2	{The / Two} chair s	are lean ing	{against / up against / on} {the / a} wall.
Picture 3	{The / A} {lady / woman / girl}	is stand ing	on {the / a} chair.
Picture 4	{The / A} {man / guy / boy}	is {stand / balance} ing	on {one / his left} {foot. / leg}
Picture 5	{The / A} doll	is sit ting	{on / in} {the / a} chair.
Picture 6	{The / A} {lady / woman / girl}	is look ing up	at {the / a} {ceiling. / sky φ}

Once the experimenter was satisfied that the child understood the instructions, he was presented with twelve pictures one at a time in a different random order for each subject. For each picture the child was asked:

TABLE 1 (Continued)

	S	V	O
Picture 7	{The / A} {lady / woman / girl}	is {eat / bite} ing	{the / an} apple.
Picture 8	{The / A} {lady / woman / lady}	is {brush / comb} ing	her hair.
Picture 9	The man and the woman / The woman and the man / A boy and a girl / A man and a lady / A man and a woman / Two people / The people	are drink ing	milk.
Picture 10	{The / A} {lady / woman / girl}	is drink ing	{milk. / a glass of milk.}
Picture 11	The man and the woman / The woman and the man / A boy and a girl / The boy and the girl / The girl and the guy / The man and lady / Two people	are shak ing	hand s.
Picture 12	{The / A} {lady / woman / girl}	is bit ing	{the / a} {man / boy / guy} 's {hand. / arm / wrist}

"What is happening (going on) in this picture? Tell me in one sentence."
or, alternatively, "Can you tell me what is happening (going on) in this picture?" After the child had produced a response the experimenter acknowl-

edged this by saying "okay" or "all right" and then proceded to the next of the twelve test pictures. During the test phase (unlike phase 2) the child was not given any specific feedback as to the correctness of his responses or the omissions or errors in his utterances. If the child said he did not know what was happening in the picture the experimenter prodded him in a non-threatening way. If there was still no response then the "don't know" was recorded as 'no utterance.' The experimenter wrote down each of the subject's responses, and the interview was tape-recorded.

RESULTS AND DISCUSSION

The interviews with children were transcribed and six criteria were established to define operationally what would be counted as an utterance. These criteria were:

1. The utterance which was counted for a given picture was the response between the experimenter's last question pertinent to the picture and the experimenter's acknowledgment response ("okay" or "all right").
2. References to a previous picture were not counted as part of the utterance, except when a child used the word "another" in place of the article. This occurred only a few times, when a child remarked on the use of the male and female models in ten of the pictures.
3. The utterance had to describe what was happening in the picture. Speculations about the picture including why the event in the picture was happening were not counted as part of the utterance.
4. False starts were not counted as part of the utterance. For example, in "There's, there's a, The lady is looking up." only the underlined portion would be counted as the utterance.
5. If the child corrected himself as he spoke, only the corrected words were counted as part of the utterance. For example, in "The chairs is no are tipping." only the underlined portions would be counted as the utterance.
6. The child's requests for affirmation, for example, "right" or "see," were not included.

With these criteria it was possible to determine the utterance produced by each child for each of the twelve pictures. This set of utterances constituted the raw data upon which all further analyses have been and are being done.

Analyses of these data are currently underway. It is possible, however, to present here some initial findings from this study. We have attempted and are attempting to examine these data using several different units of analysis for different analyses. What I will report on here are a few of our preliminary findings based on three of these units of analysis, specifically the morpheme, the utterance, and finally, at a level intermediate between these, the sentence constituent. It is the last of these which I shall describe in greatest detail since, unlike our other analyses, they were specifically done with the theory of skill outlined in the introduction to this chapter in mind.

BASIC FINDINGS WITH THE MORPHEME AS THE UNIT OF ANALYSIS

For each child we calculated the length of each of his utterances in terms of morphemes and his mean length of utterance (MLU) across all twelve pictures. Each child's MLU was calculated according to two procedures. In both cases Roger Brown's (1973, p. 54) rules were followed except for rules 1 and 9, which were not applicable to this study. MLU_1 was computed by counting the total number of morphemes produced by each child in all of his utterances and dividing the total by 12 (the number of pictures for which an utterance was required). MLU_2 was computed by counting the total number of morphemes produced by each child in all of his utterances and dividing the total by the number of utterances he actually produced. In other words in MLU_2 "no responses" were not included in the calculations. One might argue that MLU_2 is closer to the way in which Brown and his colleagues (for example, Brown, 1973; deVilliers and deVilliers, 1973) have calculated this statistic in that cases of not responding were obviously not used in their calculations of MLU either.

Figure 1 depicts how the average MLU for each measure changes as a function of age group. Figure 1 shows that MLU rises sharply from an average of 2.56 for MLU_2 (2.36 for MLU_1) in the youngest group until 3-to-3½ years and then more gradually over the next three age groups to 6.63 for MLU_2 (6.31 for MLU_1) in the 4½-to-5-year-olds. Although the increase in MLU as a function of age is striking in figure 1 (the average MLU increased by about 4 morphemes as a function of age group), the figure also shows that even the oldest group as a whole has not achieved the MLU value of 8.17, which was the MLU for the target sentences. This suggests (as later results will also) that although sentence construction skills improve remarkably during the preschool years, grammatical development is not over by 5 years of age (see Chomsky, 1969).

Figure 1 gives an impression of the changes with age in MLU as a function of age group, but it is important to consider the MLU values achieved by individual children as well. This I shall do briefly here in terms of the MLU_2 scores since as noted above of our two measures MLU_2 was probably computed in a way that was more similar to the way in which the mean length of the child's utterances has been computed by Brown (1973) and others. The lowest value of MLU_2 was 1.73 for a child who was 2:5:2 at the time he was interviewed. The next lowest value of MLU_2 was 1.75 also for a child from the youngest group aged 2:2:23 at the time of the interview. If stage 1 is defined as including children whose mean length of utterance falls between 1 and 2 (that is, $1 < MLU < 2$) then these were the only two children who would be classified in stage 1 based on MLU_2 (see Brown, 1973). The remaining fifty-eight children were linguistically more advanced. Six children had MLU_2 values which would place them in stage 2 in Roger Brown's classification scheme ($2 < MLU < 2.5$). The MLU_2 values for these six were: 2.00, 2.00, 2.08, 2.30, 2.36, and 2.45. Each of these stage 2 children was from one of the two youngest groups. The remaining fifty-two children had MLU_2 values in excess of 2.5. The MLU_2 values for these fifty-two children varied from 2.56 up to 8.42. Just one

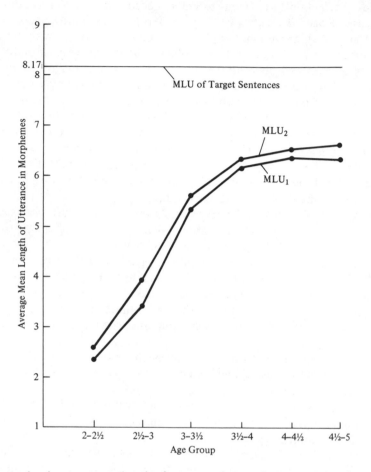

FIGURE 1   Average mean length of utterance in morphemes as a function of age group. Results are shown for two methods of calculating MLU. Aso shown by the horizontal line near the top of the figure is the mean length of the target sentences in morphemes.

child (age 4:7:21; $MLU_2 = 8.42$) achieved an MLU_2 value which was actually higher than the MLU value for the target sentences of 8.17. This was the only child to exceed this figure although three children (aged 3:8:9:, 3:10:28, 4:10:13) achieved an MLU_2 value of 8.00.

This brief discussion of individual MLU values as well as figure 1 (and figure 2 to be presented below) shows that the majority of our children were more advanced linguistically than Adam, Eve, and Sarah were when

Brown (1973) collected the data that were used for *A First Language: The Early Stages*. Only two of our children were in stage 1 (dealt with in the first half of *A First Language*), and only six were in stage 2 (dealt with in the second half). All others were linguistically more mature than that at least as evidenced by their MLU_2 scores.

Brown (1973) had noted that during stage 1 ($1 < MLU < 2$) the speech of the child was composed primarily of content words with few functors or "modulators of meaning" present. That is, it consisted primarily of nouns, verbs, and adjectives and was notably lacking in inflections, auxiliaries, copulas, prepositions, articles, conjunctions, and the like. For this reason the speech of the stage 1 child was characterized as "telegraphic" since his speech omitted the same kinds of speech elements that we might if we were sending a telegram. Brown both acknowledges the possibility of the presence of some functors in the stage 1 child's speech (p. 88) and goes beyond the telegraphic account to a description of the semantic relations expressed by the Stage 1 child. Nonetheless a striking characteristic of the stage 1 child's speech was the predominance of content words over functors. It was not until stage 2 ($2 < MLU < 2.5$) that the child was observed to acquire gradually the grammatical morphemes that modulate the meanings expressed in stage 1 speech. According to Brown these modulators of meaning "like an intricate sort of ivy, begin to grow up between and upon the major construction blocks, the nouns and verbs, to which stage 1 is largely limited" (Brown, 1973, p. 249) during stage 2, although their development in many cases continued well after stage 2.

In view of this interesting finding we decided to examine the degree to which each child's speech in this study was telegraphic in relation to his MLU. The measure of telegraphic speech that was used was the ratio of content words divided by content words plus functors for all the utterances produced by a given child. Content words included nouns, verbs, adjectives, and a few irregular adverbs (for example, "up" in the sentence "The lady is looking up at the ceiling"). There were no regular adverbs ending in the suffix "ly" although if there had been they would have counted as two morphemes, one content word and one functor, apiece. All other kinds of morphemes—inflections, auxiliary verbs, copulas, prepositions, conjunctions, articles, and pronouns—were counted as functors (see Brown, 1973).

Figure 2 is a scattergram which shows this metric of telegraphic speech for each child as a function of his MLU. (MLU_2 was used in this analysis.) Figure 2 shows that no child was totally "telegraphic" in his utterances. The ratio of content words to content words plus functors was less than 1 for every child in this study including the 2 children who would be classified as stage 1 according to MLU_2 (with MLU_2s of 1.73 and 1.75). Nonetheless, figure 2 also shows that the child with the shortest MLU was the most telegraphic of all the children in this study. Seventy-nine percent of the morphemes he uttered in this study were content words as is shown in figure 2. This is almost double the corresponding ratio of content words over content words plus functors for the target sentences which was 41 percent as figure 2 also indicates. The ratio of content words to content words

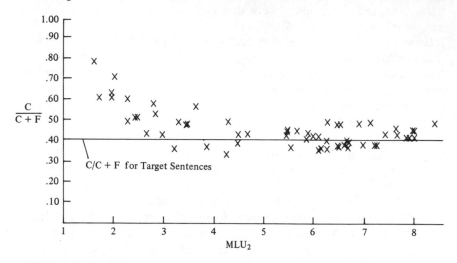

FIGURE 2 Scattergram showing the ratio of content words divided by content words plus functors (C/C + F) for each child as a function of MLU₂. This ratio is a measure of telegraphic speech. Also shown by the horizontal line in the figure is this ratio (C/C + F) for the target sentences.

plus functors does decrease as a function of MLU_2 with the drop occurring as the MLU_2 increases from 1.73 to about 4. Beyond an MLU_2 of 4 there is not much change in the index of telegraphic speech that was used here and indeed, the indices of telegraphic speech for children with MLUs greater than 4 are often close to the index of telegraphic speech calculated for the target sentences (.41).

BASIC FINDINGS WITH THE UTTERANCE AS THE UNIT OF ANALYSIS

We have also analyzed our data using the utterance as the unit of analysis. Two of these analyses will be described briefly here. In the first we classified each of the child's responses for the twelve pictures into one of three categories: 1. grammatical sentence; 2. ungrammatical utterance; and, 3. no utterance. To count as grammatical a sentence had to include a subject and a predicate with all obligatory morphemes expressed. The sentence, however, did not have to be identical to the adult modal sentence to be counted as grammatically correct. For example, if the child said in response to picture 5 "The dolly sitting on the chair" the utterance would be scored as ungrammatical since the child had omitted the obligatory auxiliary "is". On the other hand, if the child said for this picture "The dolly is on the chair." this would be scored as a grammatical sentence since it is composed of a subject and a predicate, both correctly expressed, even though this child used a copula verb ("is") rather than the progressive verb construction ("is sitting") that adults had used.

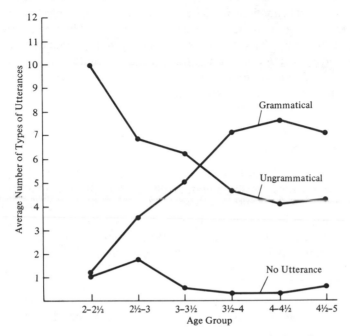

FIGURE 3   Average number of grammatical, ungrammatical, and no utterances as a function of age group.

Figure 3 shows the average number of each type of utterance as a function of age group. Figure 3 reveals that the majority of the utterances produced by the 2-to-2½-year-old group—about 10 out of 12—were ungrammatical whereas only about 1 out of 12 was grammatical. The average number of grammatical sentences increases, and correspondingly the average number of ungrammatical utterances decreases as a function of age group such that the three oldest age groups produced more grammatical sentences (between 7 and 8 out of 12) than ungrammatical utterances (between 4 and 5 out of 12). Figure 3 suggests, as did figure 1, that the child's ability to construct sentences increases dramatically between two and five years of age. It also shows, however, as figure 1 had suggested, that the speech of even our oldest groups was not fully grammatical. Again, it is important to note that group averages are shown in figure 3 and that there were individual differences within groups. An examination of each individual child's performance revealed that there were three children out of sixty who produced no ungrammatical utterances. One child (age = 3:10:28, MLU_2 = 8.00) produced grammatical sentences for all twelve pictures. Another, even younger, child (age $= 3:1:25$, $MLU_2 = 6.5$) produced grammatical sentences for nine of the pictures and "no response" for the remaining three. The third such child (age $= 4:3:29$, $MLU_2 = 7.45$) produced 11 grammatically correct sentences and 1 "no response." Thus three children in this study made no grammatical mistakes. The remaining fifty-seven children did produce some grammatically incorrect utterances. Thirteen of the children (seven of whom were from the youngest group) produced no grammatically correct sentences. All the other children made one or more mistakes but also produced one or more grammatically correct sentences with the proportion of each varying from child to child.

ASSUMPTIONS UNDERLYING THE FOLLOWING ANALYSES

The preceding analyses provide an overall picture of some quantitative aspects of grammatical development, as observed in this study. These analyses were fairly easy (if time consuming) to perform and as we did them we did not feel we were making any potentially controversial assumptions. However, for the analyses presented in the remainder of this chapter certain assumptions were made that may be more controversial. In particular, the major set of analyses to be presented on inter- and intraconstituent development which will be presented shortly is based on the assumption that a "rich interpretation" of the single constituent utterances produced by the children in this study is justified. There is debate in the child language literature about whether or not the child's one-word utterances should be subjected to a "rich" or "holophrastic" interpretation or whether they only allow an "impoverished" or "referential" interpretation (see, for example, Bloom, 1973; Brown, 1973; Greenfield and Smith, 1976; Branigan, 1976a, 1976b). Under the former interpretation the child is viewed as intending to communicate propositions, to describe relations, even though he speaks just one word at a time; under the latter interpretation the child is viewed as simply naming. Although all children in the present study were well beyond the one-word stage (the lowest value of MLU_2 was 1.73), some of their utterances, particularly those of the youngest children, quite often consisted of a single noun construction (for example "The lady"; "Apple") or, far less often, a single verb construction, such as "Bite" or "Drinking". In such cases it could be argued that the child is simply naming and not trying to describe the event in the picture.

Consider, for example, the case of a young child who said "Apple" when shown the picture of the lady biting the apple. If the child had been attempting to describe the event of a lady eating an apple then we could give him credit for having produced the object (without the article) but not for having produced the subject or the verb. However, it is possible that the child in saying "Apple" was simply naming a salient object in the picture, in which case "Apple" should not be counted as "Object" but rather as simply "Name." In this study we clearly were asking children to describe events in sentences rather than simply to name objects (or actions). One might suppose, however, that it was possible that some of our children who produced single constituent utterances redefined the task for themselves as one of naming. Our experimental procedure and our children were such that I think a rich interpretation of single constituent utterances may be justified, and I will explain why I think so in greater detail below, but first I would like to present one analysis of our data which is based on an "impoverished" interpretation of it—or at least one that is less "rich" than the one which was used in analyses of the data to be described subsequently.

AN "IMPOVERISHED" INTERPRETATION OF THE DATA

In the "impoverished" analysis we simply tried to classify each utterance of the child as referential or relational (or as "No utterance" if the child had not responded at all). If the child only expressed the name of one (for example "lady") or more ("a man and a lady") objects in the picture or only the name of an action, such as "eating", that utterance was counted as referential. Sentences with the copula verb like "That's a chair." and "There's a dolly." were also classified as referential [unless they included some statement of a relation of the object indicated to something else (for example, "There's a dolly on a chair.") in which case they were counted as relational]. Utterances in which the child explicitly described a relation between two objects ("The doll is sitting on a chair." "Lady bite apple"), what an object was doing ("A lady's drinking."), an action being performed on an object ("Eat apple"), or an event occurring in a location ("sitting on a chair") were counted as relational. All utterances which contained only a single noun or verb construction and nothing else were counted as referential with one exception. The exception was in the case of prepositional phrases (for example, "on a chair") in which both the preposition and the noun object of the preposition were expressed. Such cases, and there were just a few of them, were counted as relational.

Figure 4 shows the average number of referential, relational, and "no" utterances produced by each of the six age groups. As Figure 4 reveals, the youngest group of children produced more than 7 (out of 12) referential responses according to this analysis, whereas they only produced an average of slightly greater than 3 (out of 12) relational responses. The average number of referential responses decreases with age and the average number of relational responses increases with age noticeably such that the oldest three groups are producing an average of more than 10 relational responses and about 1 or fewer referential responses. Thus under the impoverished interpretation of our data there is a shift between two and five years from

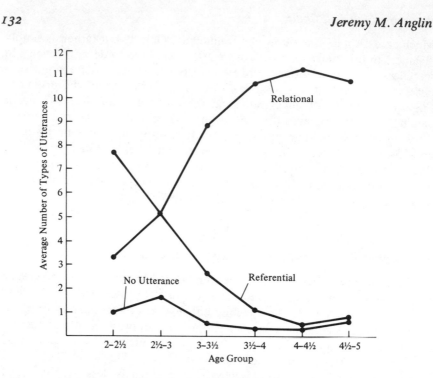

FIGURE 4 Average number of referential, relational, and no utterances as a function of age group.

labeling, naming, or referential responding to relational descriptions of events.

The last set of analyses to be presented are based on the assumption that a rich interpretation of the data is justified. In the analyses described above we used every utterance produced by every child. In the following analyses, however, we excluded utterances in which in our judgment the child was not attempting to describe what the adults had attempted to describe. For example, in response to the picture showing two chairs leaning against a wall one child said: "It's got chairs in it." Since the child did not attempt to describe that the chairs were leaning against the wall but the contents of the picture, this utterance was excluded before the following analyses were undertaken.

For each of the remaining utterances and in view of the adult modal sentences for each picture we attempted to classify them in terms of the sentence constituents [that is, subject (S), verb (V), object (O), prepositional phrase (P)] which the child had attempted to express. For example, if the child said "Lady" for the picture of the lady eating an apple (picture 7) we would classify that utterance as S. If he said "Bite" for that picture we would classify it as V; if he said "Apple" we would classify it as O. Similarly, if he said "Lady eating" we would classify it as SV; "Eating the apple" would be classified as VO, and so on. Each classification was made in view of the picture and the adult modal sentence for that picture. At times the child's words did not match exactly those which appeared in the adult modal sentence. For example, some children said the chair in picture 1 was "tipping" rather than "leaning", and one child called the chair a "bench" rather than a "chair". In such cases we attempted to identify the element in the event depicted that the child was attempting to mention and then classified the utterance accordingly. So for example, "tipping" as described above would be classified as V and "bench" as S for picture 1. As we did this analysis for each utterance we also classified each constituent as grammatically correctly expressed (c) or as grammatically incorrectly expressed (i). Thus for each utterance produced by every child (except those excluded from the analysis as described above) we had a record of the constituents that were attempted, in the order they were attempted, and for each of these constituents whether it had been correctly expressed or not.

Before presenting some of the results from this analysis I would like to discuss the assumption it is based upon and some possible justifications for it. The assumption that we made in doing this analysis was that when the child produced some of the words (or words that were similar in meaning to some of the words) contained within one or more of the sentence constituents of the adult modal sentence, it was fair to give him credit for having attempted that (or those) grammatical constituent(s). It is in this sense that this analysis could be called a rich interpretation of the data.

It might be argued in the case of the single constituent utterances, in particular, that the child may have simply been labeling, in which case he should not be credited with having attempted a sentence constituent like subject (S), verb (V), object (O), or prepositional phrase (P) but rather simply credited for naming (N). A rich interpretation of the two and three constituent utterances seems less questionable. The simple fact that two or three of the three key elements in the adult modal sentence had been expressed makes the likelihood greater that the child was, indeed, attempting to describe the event as adults had rather than simply trying to name things. As will be seen shortly the vast majority of two and three constituent utterances conformed to the adult orders of S before V and V before O; and S before V and V before P which is a sign that the rich interpretation was probably most often justified in such cases. Also the two and three constituent utterances tended to be more fully expressed with grammatical modulators of meaning as well as content words, suggesting again that the child was, indeed, trying to produce a sentence (to describe the event) rather than simply naming.

The assumption may seem more tenuous, however, for the single constituent utterances (for example, "Lady," "The apple," "Biting," "A chair," and so on) since order could not be used to substantiate the assumption, since only one element of the event depicted in the picture had been mentioned, and since often the single constituent utterances were not fully modulated. Nonetheless, in the following analyses (unlike the preceding one) we have subjected single constituent utterances to the rich interpretation described above, and I would like to say briefly why I think we may have been justified in doing so.

The major justifications for a "rich" interpretation concern our procedure and our subjects. With respect to the procedure the child was told that we wanted him to describe what was going on or happening in the pictures in a sentence and *not* to just name the things in the pictures. He was given a total of six examples of how to describe an event in a picture in phases 1 and 2 of our procedure, and at no time were the objects in the pictures ever simply named for him as we communicated the nature of the task to him. Throughout the test session every child was asked to describe what was happening (or going on) in the picture he was shown in a sentence and never a name-eliciting question like "What's that?" In short we felt that our procedure was such that we had communicated to the children that the task was one of sentence construction and not one of naming. Our procedure was designed to communicate this, and the experimenter did not proceed with the test phase if she thought the child did not understand the nature of the task.

The second reason I think our data may allow a rich interpretation concerns the linguistic maturity of the children we interviewed. Recent commentators on the issue of holophrastic speech have suggested that while a rich interpretation may not be justified early in the one-word stage it may be more justified especially toward the end of the one-word stage (Greenfield and Smith; 1976; Branigan, 1976a, 1976b; de Villiers and de Villiers, 1978; Gardner. 1978). Our children were all well beyond the one-word stage (the lowest value of MLU_2 was 1.73), suggesting that all our children should have been using words to describe relations in addition to just naming objects. Indeed, with the possible exception of the state relations signified by the verbs in the SVP adult modal sentences, each of the types of relations occuring in the adult modal sentences (Object, Locative, Agent, Action, Object—and in one case Possessive or Dative—to use Fillmore's [1968] case concepts to describe them) have been observed in the speech of stage 1 children (Brown, 1973). As noted earlier only two children (out of sixty) in this study were in stage 1 and they were well into it with MLU_2s of 1.73 and 1.75. All the remaining fifty-eight children had MLU_2s of 2.00 or greater, which means that they had probably been expressing subjects, verbs, objects, and locative phrases in their speech (regardless of whether or not they were fully grammatically modulated) for some time.

This means that the children in this study were probably capable of attempting to express the kinds of relations expressed by adults for the pictures we used; given our concerted effort to communicate to the child that the task was one of sentence construction (event description) and not one of naming, I feel that the assumption underlying this analysis may be justified.

This kind of analysis was possible because of the use of standard contexts (specifically the pictures) for each of which we had already determined that there was a standard description. Many students of child language (for example, Bloom, 1970; Greenfield and Smith, 1976; Brown, 1973) have pointed out how crucial it is to consider the context in which the child speaks before classifying his utterances as having a given intent. The contexts (that is, pictures) in the present study had been selected on the basis of pretests to be fairly clear cases of a single event and to elicit a standard description from 80 percent of our adults. Thus the context was well defined, for adults at least. And most of our children produced descriptions of the pictures which seemed to be attempts to describe the events depicted, although usually not with a full sentence. As noted above, in cases where the child seemed to be clearly not trying to describe the events that adults had, those utterances have been excluded from the following analyses. All the remaining utterances, including single constituent utterances, were subjected to the analysis in terms of sentence constituents described above, the justification for which has now been presented.

Figure 5 shows the average number of sentence constituents produced by each age group for each picture. Recall that a record was kept for each constituent attempted of whether or not it was correctly expressed. Figure 5 shows both the average number of constituents attempted and the average number of constituents correctly expressed by each age group. As Figure 5 reveals, the average number of constituents attempted (out of 3) increased from a value of just less than 1.30 for the youngest group to a value of 2.59 for the 4-to-4½-year-old group and then dropped slightly to a value of 2.40 in the 4½-to-5-year-olds. The average number of constituents correctly expressed rose from a value of .48 for the youngest group to a value of 2.23 for the 4-to-4½-year-olds and then dropped slightly to a value of 2.03 in the 4½-to-5-year-old group. Thus the average number of constituents attempted nearly doubled during the age range studied; the average number of correctly expressed constituents more than quadrupled. That the development of the ability to construct sentences in this study at least involves the increasing ability to combine sentence constituents is shown by the rising curves in figure 5. Also suggested by figure 5, although perhaps not so obviously, is the fact that the development of the ability to construct sentences in this study also involves the increasing ability to correctly express (that is, fully modulate) the sentence constituents attempted.

This claim is suggested more clearly in figure 6, which shows for each

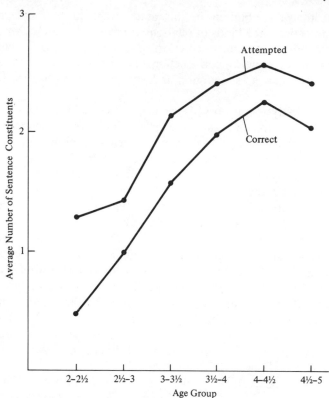

FIGURE 5   Average number of attempted and correctly expressed sentence constituents as a function of age group.

age group the ratio of correctly expressed constituents over all attempted constituents.

Figure 6 shows that only 37 percent of the constituents attempted by the youngest group were correctly expressed, whereas over 80 percent of the constituents attempted were correctly expressed by the three oldest groups. Thus with development, independent of how many constituents they expressed, children increasingly expressed the sentence constituents they attempted in grammatically correct (fully modulated) form.

All of this may seem quite obvious but it does show that the development of sentence construction skills can be viewed in terms of both the combining and the differentiating of constituents, which is the way in which Jerry Bruner and his associates had described the development of sensorimotor skills in infants. Also, figures 5 and 6 provide specific quantitative information about the levels of combination and modulation achieved by children between two and five years of age which would have been difficult to intuit even if the general finding might have been easy to guess.

Another way of expressing the findings revealed in figures 5 and 6 is to say that the development of sentence construction skills involves both interconstituent development and intraconstituent development. But with respect to interconstituent development exactly what is the pattern of combining constituents as a function of age? And with respect to intraconstituent

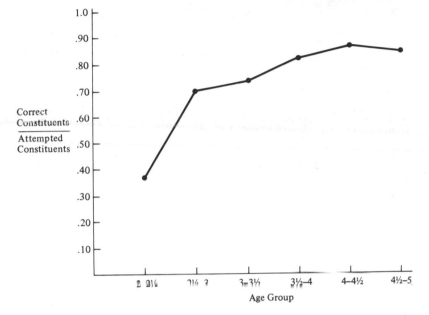

FIGURE 6   The ratio of correctly expressed constituents divided by the number of attempted constituents as a function of age group.

development what is the pattern of refining particular constituents with age? I will attempt to address these questions below.

INTERCONSTITUENT DEVELOPMENT

With respect to interconstituent development table 2 shows the modal type of utterance in terms of sentence constituents attempted by each age group for all twelve pictures (which are identified in terms of their target sentences).

The modal type of utterance for a given age group for each picture was simply the type of utterance which was produced by that age group with the

TABLE 2

Modal type of utterance in terms of sentence constituents attempted for each group for each target sentence. Below each modal utterance type for each age group is shown the percentage of children from that age group that produced it.

Target Sentence	Age	2–2½	2½–3	3–3½	3½–4	4–4½	4½–5
1. (The chair) (is leaning) (against the wall).		S	S	S/SV	SV	SV	SV
	%	60	70	80	60	50	50
2. (The chairs) (are leaning) (against the wall).		S	S	S/SV/SVP	SV	SV	SV
	%	70	50	60	50	50	50
3. (The lady) (is standing) (on the chair).		P	SVP	SVP	SVP	SVP	SVP
	%	70	50	60	70	100	40
4. (The man) (is standing) (on one foot).		S	SV/S	S	SV	SV	SVP
	%	30	40	30	50	40	70
5. (The doll) (is sitting) (on the chair).		S	S	SVP	SVP	SVP	SVP
	%	70	50	50	50	80	50
6. (The lady) (is looking up) (at the ceiling).		S	S/SVP	SVP	SV	SV	SV
	%	50	60	30	40	80	70
7. (The lady) (is eating) (the apple).		O	SVO	SVO	SVO	SVO	SVO
	%	30	30	50	50	100	80
8. (The lady) (is brushing) (her hair).		S	–	SVO	SVO	SVO	SVO
	%	40	30	50	60	80	80
9. (The man and the woman) (are drinking) (milk).		S/SVO	S/VO/SVO	SVO	SVO	SVO	SVO
	%	80	30	50	60	70	80
10. (The lady) (is drinking) (milk).		S	VO	SVO	VO	SVO	SVO
	%	40	60	70	80	90	60
11. (The man and the woman) (are shaking) (hands).		S	V/VO	SVO	SVO	SVO	SVO
	%	40	40	60	60	100	70
12. (The lady) (is biting) (the man's hand).		–	–	SVO	SVO	SVO	SVO
	%	20	40	30	40	60	40

greatest frequency. When two or more utterance types were tied as being the most frequent, each is shown in table 2. Also shown in table 2 below each modal type of utterance is the percentage of children (out of all children including those whose utterances had been excluded) whose utterances conformed to the modal utterance type for that group. In the case of ties, the percentage shown is the total percentage of all of the utterance types which were tied. The results for the six SVP pictures are shown in the top half of the table while the results for the six SVO pictures are shown in the bottom half. A dash (−) in the table means that "no response" was the most frequent type of utterance for that age group for that picture. With the aid of table 2, I shall now attempt to characterize the types of utterances in terms of sentence constituents produced for each picture as a function of age group.

Picture 1. Target sentence: "The chair is leaning against the wall." Table 2 shows that whereas most of the two youngest groups attempted S for picture 1 (for example, "Chair"; "The chair"), the 3-to-3½-year-olds produced SV as often as S with each type of utterance accounting for 40 percent of this age group's responses. The modal response for the three oldest groups was SV ("A chair tipping"; "The chair falling down"). Only six children in this study, four of whom were from the two oldest groups, attempted all three constituents (SVP) in this study.

Picture 2. Target sentence: "The chairs are leaning against the wall." The results for picture 2 show a similar pattern. The modal response type for the two youngest groups was S (for example, "Chair"; "Chairs"). For the 3-to-3½-year-olds S ("Two chairs"), SV ("There's chairs standing up"), and SVP ("The chairs are tipping against the wall.") were tied as being the most frequent utterance type although only two of each type were produced by this age group. The modal response type for each of the three oldest groups was SV ("It's tipping over."; "The chairs are falling."). SVP utterances were again infrequent for this picture with only seven out of sixty children producing this type of response. Two of these were produced by the 3-to-3½-year-olds; two by the 3½-to-4-year olds; one by the 4-to-4½-year-olds; and two by the 4½-to-5-year-olds.

Picture 3. Target sentence: "The lady is standing on the chair." For picture 3 the modal utterance was P (for example, "Chair"; "On a chair") for the youngest group, although only three of these children produced this type of utterance. Nonetheless, this was the most frequent type of response for this age group. The modal utterance type for the 2½-to-3-year-olds for this picture was SVP with 40 percent of this group producing this type of utterance. The modal utterance for this picture for each of the older groups was SVP ("A girl standing up on a chair"; "The lady's standing on a chair.")

with over half of the children in each of these groups producing this type of utterance. Double constituent utterances were infrequent for this picture, although the most common type was VP ("Standing on the chair"). Five of the sixty children produced this type of utterance for this picture.

Picture 4. Target sentence: "The man is standing on one foot." For picture 4 the modal utterance type for the 2-to-2½-year-olds was S (for example, "The daddy"; "Man"; "Guy") with 70 percent of this group producing utterances which were classified as S. In the next older group (the 2½-to-3-year-olds) S ("Man"; "A man") and SV ("He's dancing.") were tied as being the modal response, although only 40 percent of this age group produced either of these types of utterances. In the next oldest group the modal response type is S ("A man"; "The boy"). For the next two groups the modal response type is SV ("The boy is standing like that."). It is only the children in the oldest group who most frequently attempt all three constituents and have SVP as their modal response ("The man's standing on one foot."; "The dad standing on one foot"), with half of this age group attempting all three constituents.

Picture 5. Target sentence: "The doll is sitting on the chair." The modal type of utterance for picture 5 for each of the two youngest age groups was S (for example, "Dolly"; "A dolly"; "A Heather") whereas for each of the four older groups the modal response was SVP ("A dolly sitting on a chair"; "A dolly's sitting on a chair."; "The doll is sitting on the chair."). Double constituent utterances were relatively infrequent for this picture.

Picture 6. Target sentence: "The lady is looking up at the ceiling." For picture 6 the modal utterance type was S (for example, "Lady") for the youngest group. For the 2½-to-3-year-olds two utterance types were tied as being most frequent: S ("a lady") and SVP ("There's a lady looking up in the light.") The modal response for the 3-to-3½-year-olds is actually SVP ("She looking up in the sky"; "The lady's looking up to the sky.") although only 30 percent of this group produced all three constituents. The modal type of utterance for each of the remaining groups is SV ("The lady's looking up."; "She's looking up.") with 80 percent of the two oldest groups producing such utterances.

Picture 7. Target sentence: "The lady is eating the apple." The modal utterance type for this picture for the youngest groups was actually O (for example, "Apple") although only 30 percent of this group produced this type of response. Other types of utterances for this age group for this picture were S (2 cases), V (1 case, "Bite"), SVO (2 cases, for example, "That lady bite that"), one "no response," and one excluded utterance.

SVO ("The lady's eating the apple.") is the modal utterance type for each of the remaining age groups with the two oldest groups producing the greatest percentage of such utterances (100 percent and 80 percent respectively).

Picture 8. Target sentence: "The lady is brushing her hair." The modal utterance type for the youngest group for this picture was S (for example, "Lady"; "The girl") with 40 percent of these children producing this type of utterance for this picture. The modal response for the 2½-to-3-year-old-group was "No response," with 30 percent of the children's utterances from this group being classified in this way. SVO ("A lady's combing her hair."; "A girl combing her hair") was the modal response type for this picture for each of the four oldest age groups, with 80 percent of the oldest two groups' utterances being classified in this way. Double constituent utterances were infrequent for this picture, although the most common type of double constituent response was VO ("Combing her hair"), of which there was a total of seven such responses produced by the sixty children in this study.

Picture 9. Target sentence: "The man and the lady are drinking milk." Two utterance types were tied as being most frequent for this picture for the youngest group: S (for example, "Girl"; "A lady") and SVO ("Man drinking milk"), with four out of ten possible of each of these utterance types. For the next group, the 2½-to-3-year-olds, there was a three-way tie for most frequent utterance type among S ("A lady and a daddy"), VO ("Drinking milk") and SVO ("There's a guy and a lady drinking Pepsi-Cola"), each being produced twice by members of this age group. The modal response for this picture for the four oldest groups was SVO ("Them drinking both milk"; "A man and a girl drinking milk"; "The people are drinking milk."), with the majority of each of these age groups producing this type of response.

Picture 10. Target sentence: "The lady is drinking milk." The modal utterance type for this picture for the youngest group was S (for example, "Lady"; "A lady"), which accounted for 40 percent of the youngest group's responses to this picture. VO ("Drinking milk"; "Drinking juice") was the modal response for the next oldest group for this picture, although only 30 percent of their responses were of this type. This was also the modal response for the 3½-to-4-year-olds, whereas for the remaining three groups the modal response was SVO ("Her drinking milk"; "She's drinking milk."; "The girl's drinking a glass of milk."), with the two oldest groups producing a majority of such responses (90 percent and 70 percent respectively).

Picture 11. Target sentence: "The man and the lady are shaking hands." The modal utterance type for this picture for the youngest group was S (for example, "Lady"; "Man, lady") with 40 percent of their utterances being of this type. There was a tie for the most frequent utterance type in the 2½-to-3-year-olds, with V ("Shaking") and VO ("Shaking hands") each accounting for 20 percent of the utterances in this age group. SVO ("A girl and a man shaking hands"; "They're shaking hands.") was the modal utterance type for each of the four remaining groups; more than half the children in each of these age groups produced this type of utterance.

Picture 12. Target sentence: "The lady is biting the man's hand." "No response" was the modal utterance type for this picture for the youngest age group, although this is more a reflection of the idiosyncratic nature of the responses produced by this group for this picture than anything ese, since only two out of ten children produced no response for this picture. The other utterance types for the youngest group were one of each of the following: O, V, S, SO, VO, and SVO. The remaining two utterances produced by children from this age group were excluded from the analysis as not being attempts by the child to describe what the adults had described. The modal response for the 2½-to-3-year-olds was also "No response," with four out of ten of this group's utterances being classified this way. The remaining utterance types for this group were O, SO, SVO, and 2 SVs, with one child's utterance having been excluded from the analysis. For each of the four oldest age groups SVO ("She's eating his arm."; "A girl biting a man's arm") was the modal utterance type, although only the 4-to-4½-year-olds produced a majority of such responses (60 percent).

This presentation of the performance of the children from each of the age groups for each picture should show that there are differences in the kinds of utterances produced for the different pictures by the various age groups, and for some pictures, such as picture 12, there were considerable individual differences within an age group for the same picture. For eight of the pictures used in this study S was the modal utterance type for the youngest group; whereas for one picture, S and SVO were tied as being most frequent; for one, the modal utterance was "No response"; for one (picture 3 with target sentence "The lady is standing on the chair."), P was the modal response type for the youngest group; and for one (picture 7 with target sentence "The lady is eating the apple."), O was the modal utterance type for this group. P and O were only produced by 30 percent of the youngest groups in these latter two cases, but they were more frequent than any other utterance type including S. This shows that the sentence constituents a child will attempt to express will depend on the particular situation (in this case, picture) which he is attempting to describe. It would be interesting in future research (on these or other data) to see whether the child's attempts to produce the particular constituents that he does can be predicted by certain specific factors. For example, it might be argued that the chair in the picture of the lady standing on the chair and the apple in the picture of the woman biting the apple were quite possibly more salient for the child than the other elements in the pictures, which had been expressed by adults as objects or prepositional phrases in their descriptions of them, and that it is such salience, at least in part, which determines which constituents a child will attempt to express. Various other factors may well be important in determining which particular constituents a given child will attempt in a given situation (see, for example, Greenfield and Zukow, 1978; Olson, 1970). However, since these factors have not yet been studied systematically in this research, I will not discuss them further here.

Another important difference across pictures has to do with the age at which children attempt to express two and three constituents. For some pictures, such as picture 3 (target sentence: "The lady is standing on the chair.") and picture 7 (target sentence: "The lady is eating the apple."), it is only the very youngest group that produces single constituent utterances most frequently. For these two pictures, the modal utterance type includes three constituents (SVP or SVO) for all other age groups. For other pictures (for example, picture 4 with target sentence "The man is standing on one foot."), progress toward a three constituent utterance is more gradual, and in this particular case is achieved as a modal utterance type by only the oldest group, the 4½-to-5-year-olds. In the case of three of the pictures (pictures 1, 2, and 6), all involving prepositional phrases, not even the oldest groups produced as a modal response the three constituent utterance (SVP) that adults had produced but rather the two constituent utterance, SV, in each case. For the remaining nine pictures, the oldest group in their modal utterance type did attempt all three constituents that adults had expressed, although, as noted above, the age group in which a three constituent utterance is first achieved in the modal utterance type varies somewhat from picture to picture.

In spite of the differences in performance across pictures and the differences within age groups for particular pictures, certain general trends are apparent in the data. Specifically, the youngest group (the 2-to-2½-year-olds) produce as their modal utterance type single constituent utterances for most pictures. These single constituent utterances are almost always noun constructions, usually S in the present study, although as has been noted, the modal utterance type for one picture (picture 3) was P and for one (picture 7) it was O. The youngest group rarely produced single constituent verb constructions (V), although such constructions were very occasionally observed in the speech of the youngest children in this study (for example, "Bite" for picture 7). (It should be acknowledged that the notable lack of single V constructions could be partially a function of the use of pictures in this study. It is possible that had videotapes of the events or real life events been used as stimuli for the children to describe, single V constructions may have occurred with greater frequency.) As a function of age group the number of constituents attempted increased. When more than one constituent were attempted in a given modal utterance type the order in which those constituents were expressed conformed to the order in which they were expressed by adults (that is, S before V, V before O; S before V, V before P). There was the occasional individual case of violation of the adult order of expressing the constituents ("Falling down chairs" for picture 2), but such violations were extremely rare in this study, and as can be seen in table 2 every double and triple constituent modal utterance conformed to the adult order.

In this study, although no single constituent modal utterance was a V, every double (and of course every triple) constituent modal utterance did include V. There was the occasional utterance which was categorized as SO or SP, and such two constituent utterances have been reported in the speech of young children (see Bloom, 1970; Brown, 1973); in this study, however, they were relatively infrequent in comparison to the number of SV, VO, and to a lesser extent, VP double constituent utterances that were observed. Thus in this study whereas the single constituent utterances of the youngest children were usually noun constructions, verb constructions were attempted fairly often by the next oldest group and most often by all other groups who infrequently produced single constituent utterances.

As noted above, the rate of developmental progress in expressing all three constituents varies from picture to picture considerably such that the modal utterance type for some pictures had reached the level of three constituents attempted by the 2½-to-3-year-old group (for example, picture 3), whereas for others (pictures 1 and 2) the modal utterance type never reached the level of three constituents in any age group. Nonetheless, it is clear from table 2 and the preceding discussion that generally speaking the older the age group, the greater the number of constituents attempted, although development in this regard is most notable across the first three age groups and less striking across the three oldest groups. (In fact, as figure 5 shows, the 4½-to-5-year-olds did not produce quite as many constituents on average as did the 4-to-4½-year-olds.)

INTRACONSTITUENT DEVELOPMENT

For the next analysis (and the last one to be presented here) we reduced the data even further. We wanted to examine for each constituent for each sentence exactly which grammatical elements were being correctly expressed by each child. Our goal in doing this analysis was to infer the order in which children master the grammatical elements (the obligatory morphemes) in each sentence constituent. We felt that it was important that we base any conclusions about the order of acquisition of the grammatical elements making up a sentence constituent on only those children who had attempted that constituent. Although we had excluded those utterances from the preceding analysis in which the child had clearly not been attempting to describe the event that adults had described, some of the utterances which were included in that analysis contained different types of constructions for some constituents than the ones adults had produced. The two most frequent cases of this involved the use by some children of pronouns instead of the corresponding noun construction (for example, "She is drinking milk." instead of "The lady is drinking milk."), and the use by some children of the copula verb instead of the progressive construction which adults had used ("The doll is on the chair." instead of "The doll is sitting on the chair."). Far less frequent than the use of the copula instead of the progressive verb construction was the occasional case of another type of verb construction such as the past ("The chair fell over." instead of "The chair is falling."). In all such cases those attempted constituents were excluded from the following analysis.

Each remaining constituent attempted by each child was examined to see which of the grammatical elements (obligatory morphemes) had been correctly expressed by that child. It is important to note here that in giving the child credit for having produced a given grammatical element we did not require that the particular words that adults had used also be used by the children. Rather we required that some correctly expressed element be present in the child's attempt at the construction. Thus if a child had produced the utterance "Chairs tipping" for sentence 2, he would have been given credit for a noun stem (ns.) and the plural morpheme (pl.) but not the article (art.) in his attempted S; he also would have been given credit for a verb stem (vs.) and the progressive inflection (pr. infl.) but not for the auxiliary verb (aux.). Notice that credit would have been given in this case for the verb stem (vs.) even though the particular verb stem that adults had used ("lean") was not used by this child, who used "tip" instead. Thus this analysis was done at the level of grammatical categories such as article (art.), noun stem (ns.), and verb stem (vs.) rather than at the level of particular words (for example "The"; "chair"; "lean"). A similar analysis at the level of specific words would yield different patterns of results for some of the constituents for some of the pictures than the analysis into grammatical elements which will be presented here. For example, as the reader will see, for the verb construction "is leaning" for picture 1 the present analysis suggests that more children produced a verb stem than produced the progressive inflection "ing", and more produced the progressive inflection than produced the auxiliary verb. However, fewer children produced the specific word "lean" than produced either the progressive inflection ("ing") or the correct auxiliary ("is"), since these children more often used other types of

TABLE 3

The number of grammatical elements produced by children in their descriptions of the events in the pictures for each target sentence constituent. The data are based on only those children who attempted the target constituent.

	S	V	P
1. Target sentence constituent	The chair	is lean ing	against the wall.
Grammatical element	art. ns.	aux. vs. pr. infl.	prep. art. ns.
Number correctly expressed	44 52	18 26 22	5 6 6
2. Target sentence constituent	The chair s	are lean ing	against the wall.
Grammatical element	art.{adj.} ns. pl.	aux. vs. pr. infl.	prep. art. ns.
Number correctly expressed	31 53 43	13 21 17	8 8 10
3. Target sentence constituent	The lady	is stand ing	on the chair.
Grammatical element	art. ns.	aux. vs. pr. infl.	prep. art. ns.
Number correctly expressed	24 27	30 43 41	43 41 44
4. Target sentence constituent	The man	is stand ing	on one foot.
Grammatical element	art. ns.	aux. vs. pr. infl.	prep. adj. ns.
Number correctly expressed	21 26	19 24 23	11 11 12
5. Target sentence constituent	The doll	is sit ting	on the chair.
Grammatical element	art. ns.	aux. vs. pr. infl.	prep. art. ns.
Number correctly expressed	36 47	18 31 30	32 32 32
6. Target sentence constituent	The lady	is look ing up	at the ceiling.
Grammatical element	art. ns.	aux. vs. pr. infl. adv.	prep. art. ns.
Number correctly expressed	21 25	29 38 37 34	10 10 10

Table columns are grouped under the headings **S**, **V**, and **O**.

	S			V			O			
7. Target sentence constituent	The	lady		is	eat	ing	the	apple.		
Grammatical element	art.	ns.		aux.	vs.	pr. infl.	art.	ns.		
Number correctly expressed	24	27		29	40	36	16	45		
8. Target sentence constituent	The	lady		is	brush	ing	her	hair.		
Grammatical element	art.	ns.		aux.	vs.	pr. infl.	adj.	ns.		
Number correctly expressed	23	26		25	41	35	34	39		
9. Target sentence constituent	The	man and	the lady	are	drink	ing	milk.			
Grammatical element	{ art. / adj. }	ns.	pl.	aux.	vs.	pr. infl.	ns.			
Number correctly expressed	17	22	7	24	51	50	43			
10. Target sentence constituent	The	lady		is	drink	ing	milk.			
Grammatical element	art.	ns.		aux.	vs.	pr. infl.	ns.			
Number correctly expressed	20	24		24	41	40	35			
11. Target sentence constituent	The	man and	the lady	are	shak	ing	hand	s.		
Grammatical element	{ art. / adj. }	ns.	pl.	aux.	vs.	pr. infl.	ns.	pl.		
Number correctly expressed	11	17	15	27	44	42	39	36		
12. Target sentence constituent	The	lady		is	bit	ing	the	man	's	hand.
Grammatical element	art.	ns.		aux.	vs.	pr. infl.	art.	ns_p	poss.	ns_o
Number correctly expressed	16	18		16	25	22	16	7	7	19

NOTE: The abbreviations for grammatical elements should be read as follows: art. = article; ns. = noun stem (or uninflected noun); aux. = auxiliary verb; vs. = verb stem (or uninflected verb); pr. infl. = progressive inflection; prep. = preposition; adj. = adjective; poss. = possessive inflection; ns_p = noun stem (uninflected noun) in possessive case; ns_o = noun stem (uninflected noun) in objective case; pl. = plural inflection (except for S constituents for Pictures 9 and 11 for which any appropriate expression of plurality was accepted as pl.).

verb stems such as "tip" and "fall." In this analysis we wanted to see which grammatical elements for each constituent the children could produce rather than whether they could produce the exact words that adults had used when they expressed those constituents.

Table 3 shows for each picture for each target sentence constituent the grammatical elements expressed by adults and the number of children who had correctly expressed those grammatical elements in the present study. These numbers are based only on those children who attempted the constituent, and, because of the way in which different types of constructions produced by the children were excluded from this analysis as described above, comparisons should be restricted to within constituents rather than across constituents in table 3. For this reason, in discussing intraconstituent development I shall discuss first Subject (S) constituents, then Verb (V) constituents, then Object (O) constituents, and finally Prepositional Phrase (P) constituents.

S Constituents The left-most column of table 3 shows for each picture how often the grammatical elements expressed in the subject (S) of the adult modal sentence were expressed by the children in this study. For example, of children who attempted S for picture 1, all fifty-two produced a noun stem whereas only forty-four produced an article. On the assumption that the number of children who can produce a grammatical element in a given constituent provides a metric of the order in which children are able to produce those elements with development, the order of acquisition of the grammatical elements for the subject of this sentence would be noun stem first and article second. For each of the other S constituents which adults had expressed as an article and a noun stem (for pictures 3, 4, 5, 6, 7, 8, 10, 12) the pattern of results is similar. In each case, more children produced a noun stem than an article. This suggests that the development of each of these S constituents can be depicted as:

$$\text{ns.} \rightarrow \text{art.} + \text{ns.}$$

to indicate that children in attempting to express the subjects of these sentences can generate a noun stem before they can modulate the noun stem with a preceding article.

The three remaining pictures (pictures 2, 9, and 11) involved plural subjects. For picture 2, plurality was always expressed in terms of the plural inflection. Since some adults had expressed the subject for this picture as "Two chairs" as well as "The chairs," we gave the child credit for having produced the first grammatical element in the subject if he produced either an appropriate article (for example "The") or an adjective ("Two"). As table 3 shows, of the children who attempted this construction 53 produced a noun stem, 43 produced the plural inflection, and 31 produced the article or adjective correctly. On the assumption that the number of children producing the grammatical elements provides a metric of the order of acquisition of those elements, the development of this construction can be represented as follows:

$$\text{ns.} \rightarrow \text{ns.} + \text{pl.} \rightarrow \begin{Bmatrix} (\text{art.}) \\ (\text{adj.}) \end{Bmatrix} + \text{ns.} + \text{pl.}$$

to indicate that children in attempting to express the subject of this sentence can first generate a noun stem before they can inflect the noun by appending the plural morpheme to it. In general, however, they do this before they produce an appropriate article or adjective to precede the noun (see Brown. 1973).

The analysis for the other pictures (pictures 9 and 11) involving plural subjects was somewhat more complicated. We gave credit to the child for having expressed plurality if the subject of his utterance indicated plurality in any way. Thus the child was given credit for plurality for such expressions as "Man and lady"; "The man and the lady"; "The people"; and even "Man, lady"; but not for singular subjects such as "Man" or "Lady". Again, since some adults had used an adjective (for example, "Two people") whereas others had used articles ("The people"; "The man and the lady") when they expressed the subjects of these sentences, we gave the child credit for the first element if the child produced either an article or an adjective in his S construction. Credit for the noun stem was given for any noun in the S construction, singular or plural. When the analysis was done in this way of the children who attempted S for picture 9 (and whose data had not been excluded because of the use of pronouns), 22 were given credit for having produced the noun stem, 17 were given credit for having expressed plurality, and 17 were given credit for having expressed an article or adjective. For picture 11, 17 children were given credit for having expressed the noun stem, 15 for having expressed plurality, and 11 for having expressed the article or adjective. Thus there is some, admittedly somewhat weak, support for the hypothesis that in these constructions plurality is mastered earlier than the article or adjective and that the noun stem is acquired first, which is consistent with the finding for picture 2. It should be kept in mind, however, that the analyses were somewhat different for pictures 9 and 11 as compared to that for picture 2.

V Constituents The pattern of performance for elements involved in the present progressive verb construction—the auxiliary verb, the verb stem, and the progressive inflection ("ing")—was clear and consistent across all sentences as table 3 shows. In every case children produced the verb stem more often than the progressive inflection and the auxiliary verb least often of all (see Brown, 1973). If we can assume that the number of children who produce the grammatical elements in the progressive construction provides a metric of the order of acquisition of those elements, the order in which the grammatical elements making up this construction are acquired can be represented as follows:

vs. → vs. + pr. infl. → aux. + vs. + pr. infl.

One verb construction, "is looking up" (for picture 6), contained an adverb as well as the three other grammatical elements. As table 3 shows, of the children who attempted this construction 38 produced the verb stem, 37 the progressive inflection, 34 the adverb, and 29 the auxiliary. Although there was only one such verb construction involving an adverb, on the assumption that the number of children producing a grammatical element provides a metric of the order of acquisition of those elements, the order in which the child acquires the component skills in such a construction would be represented as follows:

vs. → vs. + pr. infl. → vs. + pr. infl. + adv. →
aux. + vs. + pr. infl. + adv.

O Constituents Of the six Object constituents, two (for pictures 9 and 10) involved only a noun stem (that is, "milk") and no other grammatical elements. Each of the four remaining object constructions was slightly different. The O constituent for picture 7 required an article and a noun stem. Of the children who attempted this construction, 45 produced the noun stem, and 16 produced the article correctly. (One reason that only 16 children were credited with having correctly produced an article is that we did not count "a" as a correctly expressed article if it preceded a vowel. A number of children said "a apple" in attempting this constituent and they were not credited with having correctly produced the article.) The O constituent for picture 8 required an adjective, such as "her" and a noun stem, such as "hair". Of the children who attempted this constituent 39 produced the noun stem, whereas 34 produced the adjective. The O constituent for picture 11 required a noun stem ("hand") and a plural morpheme ("s"). Thirty-nine children attempted this construction and produced the noun stem; 36 of them inflected the noun for plurality. Finally, the Object constituent for picture 12 was the most complicated involving an article ("the"), a noun stem in the possessive case ("man"), a possessive inflection ("'s"), and a noun stem in the objective case ("hand"). Of these elements, noun stems in the objective case were produced by the 19 children who attempted this constituent. Sixteen of the noun stems were preceded by an article. Only 7 of these constructions included a noun in the possessive case and all 7 of these were correctly inflected for possession.

Thus for the Object Constituents studied in this investigation it is possible to hypothesize the order in which their component elements are acquired; it should, however, be borne in mind that each hypothesized order is based on only one picture and that the proposed orders are based on the assumption that the number of children who produced a grammatical element in an O construction provides a metric of the order of acquisition of those grammatical elements. The proposed orders for intraconstituent development for the object constituents for pictures 7, 8, 11, and 12 are as follows:

ns. → art. + ns.	(Picture 7)
ns. → adj. + ns.	(Picture 8)
ns. → ns. + pl.	(Picture 11)
ns. → art. + ns. → art. + possessive construction + ns.	(Picture 12)

The proposed order for the O constituent for Picture 12 suggests that the possessive construction is produced after the article, which is produced after the noun object. It does not suggest an order for the elements making up the possessive construction, the noun possessive, and the possessive inflection, since each of the 7 children who produced a noun in the possessive case also inflected it for possession. One might argue that the possessive construction should be treated as a separate constituent in this sentence, in which case the data do not allow us to postulate an order of acquisition of its component parts (although both common sense and Brown's work would suggest that the order for such a construction would be: ns. → ns. + poss. infl.)

P Constituents   This study yielded little information about intraconstituent development for the prepositional phrases. For four of the six prepositional phrases (for pictures 1, 2, 4, and 6) the number of times they were attempted was small (less than 12 out of 60). In the case of all prepositional phrases, when they were attempted they were usually completely unpressed thus not providing information about the order in which their component parts are acquired. For these reasons I will not attempt to infer the order of acquisition of the grammatical elements making up the prepositional phrases on the basis of these data. Brown (1973) and his colleagues (de Villiers and de Villiers, 1973) have found that the preposition "on" is acquired before the articles "the" and "a." And, of course, prior to the use of such functors children have been observed to utter nouns to indicate location in stage 1 speech. These considerations suggest that the way in which the prepositional phrase "on the chair" required by pictures 3 and 5 in the present study develops is:

ns. → prep. + ns. → prep. + art. + ns.

This may well be, and the data from this study are consistent with such a proposed ordering but only weakly so. Most of the attempts to produce the prepositional phrases were uninformative with respect to the issue of the order of acquisition of their component parts since they were completely articulated.

In general our results on intraconstituent development are consistent with the view that the first grammatical element to be mastered by children in the process of learning to produce fully grammatical constituents are content words and specifically nouns in the case of S, O, and probably P constructions and verbs in the case of V constructions. (This, of course, is certainly not to say that the child acquires all content words before any modulators of meaning, or even most of them.) With development these noun and verb bases can be increasingly modulated with the functors adults use when they express such sentence constituents in fully grammatical sentences. When more than one functor is required in a given construction they usually appear to be mastered at different times. For example, our study suggests that in the case of subjects requiring both an article (or an adjective) and a plural inflection, the plural inflection is mastered before the article (or adjective). In the case of the progressive verb construction our data strongly suggest that the progressive inflection is mastered before the auxiliary verb. These findings and others from this analysis of intraconstituent development are quite consistent with those of Roger Brown and his colleagues (Brown, 1973; deVilliers and deVilliers, 1973) in cases where the evidence is comparable. This may mean that the specific factors which determine the order of acquisition of the grammatical elements making up a given type of constituent include semantic complexity, grammatical complexity, perceptual salience, and the like, which Brown and his colleagues have argued are important in determining the order in which modulators of meaning are acquired. However, since we have not yet analyzed our data with respect to the power of various factors to predict the order in which the grammatical elements making up a given constituent are acquired, such factors will not be discussed further here.

One last point is worth making about intraconstituent development based on the results of this study. As was the case for the constituents themselves, when more than one grammatical element making up a given constituent were expressed by a child, the order in which they were expressed was almost always the same as the order in which adults had expressed them. Children at times did not correctly express all the grammatical elements required by a given construction, and table 3 indicates the relative difficulty of the elements for each constituent as observed in this study, but those elements that were expressed were almost always produced in the appropriate order.

Conclusion

The various analyses described above show how dramatically children develop in their ability to construct sentences between two and five years of age. These analyses have shown that the mean length of the child's utterances in morphemes (MLU), that the number of fully grammatical sentences, that the frequency of relational (versus referential) utterances, and that the number of sentence constituents attempted and of sentence constituents correctly expressed each increased strikingly during this age range.

It should be acknowledged, of course, that the various measures of sentence construction skills were highly correlated with one another. For example, the rank order correlation coefficient (Spearman's rho, corrected for ties) between MLU_2 and the number of fully grammatical sentences expressed by each child was .72; between MLU_2 and the average number of constituents correctly expressed per picture by each child was .86; and between the average number of constituents correctly expressed per picture and the number of fully grammatical sentences expressed by each child was .89 ($p < < .001$ for all values of r_s). It is also worth noting that although age was significantly positively correlated with each of these measures, age was not as highly correlated with (predictive of) any of these measures as was another of these measures. For example, the rank order correlation between age and the number of constituents correctly expressed per picture was .72, whereas the correlation between MLU_2 and the number of constituents correctly expressed per picture was .86; similarly, the correlation between age and the number of fully grammatical sentences expressed by each child was .59, whereas the correlation between MLU_2 and the number of fully grammatical sentences expressed by each child was .72 (see Brown, 1973). Thus the various measures of grammatical skill examined in this investigation were highly correlated. Nonetheless, each analysis showed in a different though complementary way the remarkable progress made by children in grammatical development during the preschool years.

The last set of analyses presented shows how grammatical development as observed in this study can be described in terms of the increasing capacity to both combine or integrate and refine or modulate the constituents of language. Thus in this sense grammatical development is like the development of the sensorimotor skills studied by Jerry Bruner and his colleagues, which was also described in terms of the growing capacities of combining and refining constituents. Now that this has been shown, it all seems somewhat obvious. The only trick to showing it was to choose a unit of analysis somewhere between the most molecular (the morpheme) and the most global (the utterance). Once we had chosen the intermediate level of the sentence constituent as our unit of analysis, we were almost bound to show both integration and differentiation of these constituents with development.

Nonetheless, the study does suggest that, whatever the differences are between language development and the acquisition of other kinds of skills, language is definitely a skill, and its acquisition can be described in some respects in ways that are similar to the ways in which the growth of nonlinguistic skills have been described—no matter how obvious this may seem in retrospect. Moreover, it is hoped that the analyses of inter- and intraconstituent development that have been presented, as well as the other analyses, will provide a feeling for the level of grammatical skill achieved by preschool children and for the specific ways in which particular constituents are combined and refined as the child learns to construct sentences.

References

Benedict, H. Early lexical development: Comprehension and production. *J. Child Lang.*, 1979, 6, 183–200.

Bernstein, N. A. *The Coordination and regulation of movement*. London: Pergamon, 1967.

Bloom, L. M. *Language development: Form and function in emerging grammars*. Cambridge, Mass.; MIT Press, 1970.

————. *One word at a time: The use of single word utterances before syntax*. Janua Linguarum, Ser. Minor: No. 154. The Hague: Mouton, 1973.

Branigan, G. Sequences of single words as structured units. Paper presented at the *Eighth annual child language research forum*, Stanford University, 1976a.

————. Organizational constraints during the one-word period. Paper presented at the *First annual Boston university conference on language development*, 1976b.

Brown, R. *A first language: The early stages*. Cambridge, Mass.: Harvard University Press, 1973.

Bruner, J. S. *Processes of cognitive growth: Infancy*. Heinz Werner Lecture Series, vol. 3, Worcester, Mass.; Clark University Press, with Barre, 1968.

————. Eye, hand, and mind. In Elkind, D. and J. H. Flavell (Eds.), *Studies in cognitive development: Essays in honor of Jean Piaget*. Oxford: Oxford University Press, 1969.

————. The growth and structure of skill. In K. J. Connolly (Ed.), *Motor skills in infancy*. London and New York: Academic Press, 1971.

————. The nature and uses of immaturity. *American Psychologist*, 1972, 27, 1–22.

————. Organization of early skilled action. *Child Development*, 1973a, 44, 1–11.

————. *Beyond the information given: Studies in the psychology of knowing*. Edited by Jeremy M. Anglin. New York: Norton, 1973b.

————. The ontogenesis of speech acts. *Journal of Child Language*, 1975, 2, 1–19.

————. From communication to language—a psychological perspective. *Cognition* 1976, 3, 155–287.

————. Acquiring the uses of language. *Canadian Journal of Psychology*, 1978, 32, 4, 204–218.

Bruner, J. S. and Bruner, B. M. On voluntary action and its hierarchical structure. *International Journal of Psychology*, 1968, 3, 239–255.

Bruner, J. S. and Koslowski, B. Visually preadapted constituents of manipulatory action. *Perception*, 1972, 1, 1, 3–14.

Chomsky, C. *The acquisition of syntax in children from 5 to 10*. Cambridge, Mass.: MIT Press, 1969.

de Villiers, J. G. and de Villiers, P. A. A cross-sectional study of the acquisition of grammatical morphemes in child speech. *Journal of Psycholinguistic Research*, 1973, 2, 267–278.

————. *Language acquisition*. Cambridge. Mass.: Harvard University Press, 1978.

Fillmore, C. J. The case for case. In E. Bach and R. T. Harms (Eds.), *Universals of linguistic theory*. New York: Holt, Rinehart and Winston, 1968.

Gardner, H. *Developmental psychology: An introduction*. Boston: Little, Brown, & Co., 1978.

Greenfield, P. M. and Smith, J. H. *The structure of communication in early language development*. New York: Academic Press, 1976.

Greenfield, P. M. and Zukow, P. Why do children say what they say when they say it? An experimental approach to the psychogenesis of presupposition. In K. E. Nelson (Ed.) *Children's Language* vol. 1. New York: Gardner Press, 1978.

Hillman, D. and Bruner, J. S. Infant sucking in response to variations in schedules of feeding reinforcement. *Journal of Experimental Child Psychology*, 1972, 13, 1, 240–247.

Kalnins, I. and Bruner, J. S. The coordination of visual observation and instrumental behavior in early infancy. *Perception*, 1973, 2, 307–314.

Lashley, K. S. The problem of serial order in behavior. In Jeffress, L. A. (Ed.), *Cerebral mechanisms in behavior: The Hixon symposium*. New York: Wiley, 1951.

Miller, G. A. *Spontaneous apprentices: Children and language*. Edited by R. Nanda Anshen. New York: The Seabury Press, 1977.

———. The acquisition of word meaning. *Child Development*. 1978, 49, 999–1004.

Miller, G. A., Galanter, E., and Pribram, K. H. *Plans and the structure of behavior*. New York: Holt, 1960.

Mundy-Castle, A. C. and Anglin, J. M. Looking strategies in infants. In L. J. Stone, H. T. Smith, and L. B. Murphy (Eds.), *The Competent infant: Research and commentary*. New York: Basic Books, 1973.

Ninio, A. and Bruner, J. S. The achievement and antecedents of labelling. *Journal of Child Language*, 1978, 5, 1-16.

Olson, D. Language and thought: Aspects of a cognitive theory of semantics. *Psychological Review*, 1970, 77, 4, 257–273.

Templin, M. C. *Certain language skills in children: Their development and interrelationships*. Minneapolis: University of Minnesota Press, 1957.

Zukow, P., Reilly, J., and Greenfield, P. Making the absent present: Facilitating the transition from sensorimotor to linguistic communication. In K. E. Nelson (Ed.), *Children's Language* vol. 2. New York: Gardner Press, in press

7

The Development of Negation
in Early Child Language
Roy D. Pea

While the child's task of learning words seems relatively straightforward it has always bedeviled language theorists. In fact, in having to construct word meanings from words used in conversational settings replete with actions, gestures, objects, and events, the preverbal child faces one of the most difficult yet critical problems of life. Empiricist accounts of the acquisition of word meaning, such as Quine's (1974), assume the adequacy of an ostension theory, by which words paired with objects provide the child with the referential connection required for language symbolization. Compelling arguments have been given against ostension as the source of word meaning (Bruner, 1974–75; Harrison, 1972), but empirical considerations weigh against it as well. The fact that children use negatives among their earliest words provides direct counter-evidence to such empiricist doctrine. Negation has no referent, unlike nominal terms or adjectives (such as color words), and is inherently relational in nature. It is not even logically possible for the child to be taught the use of negation by ostension, for although there are a finite number of normally used words truly ascribable to a particular object, there are an infinite number of words not truly ascribable to it. In other words, there are far fewer things that an object is, than that it is not. Of course, negation has meanings other than the truth-functional meaning of not-x I have been describing, but for all of the negative meanings to be considered the same point holds—one cannot refer to negation.

Fortunately there are more seductive reasons for studying the development of negation in children's language and thought than to rebut an ostension theory of word learning. Negation is a pervasive and essential conceptual and linguistic device, particularly in its meaning of not-x, where x represents some proposition (Jespersen, 1917; Quine, 1960). There are many reasons for the ubiquity of negation in natural language. A mind limited to describing only what *is* the case, without the power of negating, would be without logic, science, or explicit correction, all of which are reliant on propositional negation (Altmann, 1967; Harrison, 1972; Wilden, 1972). Comparative analyses of communication have shown that negation is central to human language, yet conspicuously absent from the natural communication repertoires of other animals (Altmann, 1967; Sebeok, 1962). Philosophers have taken special note that propositional negation operates on sentences as part of a metalanguage and is, therefore, of a higher logical type than the language it operates upon; they have emphasized that the ability to conceive of propositions as true or false (dependent on the operation of negation by which these values are defined) is one of the central aspects of language comprehension and use (Dummett, 1973; Kant, 1963; Marshall, 1970). It would be naïve to claim that knowledge of the truth-conditions for sentences is all we know as speakers of a natural language, given the rich variety of acts we accomplish in our uses of language (for example, Searle, 1969, 1976), but such rules, integrally tied to the conception of negation, are a major part of our knowledge about language.

The pragmatic conditions of negation use provide yet another motivation for the study of negation development. Negatives in natural language serve to mark a discrepancy from a positive assumption that someone is presumed to believe, whether oneself or another. This social fact about the uses of negation raises a central question in the acquisition of communicative competence. For if the appropriate use of negation requires inferring the belief states of other persons, one might expect the young child to have great difficulties, for the reason that knowledge about the physical properties of objects, social relations, and event contingencies in social and physical interactions has just begun to develop. Whether the differing world views of children lead their uses of negation askew of the pragmatic conditions of adult negation is one problem we must confront.

A major quest in the study of the development of negation and language in general is to explain the emergence of truth-functional negation, used to deny propositions which are not true, from the very early expressions of negation that are affective in nature. The latter uses of negation, as an interpersonal tool for constraining agency by rejection, are vastly different from the use of negation to deny statements. Truth-functional negation is meta linguistic and depends on a knowledge of truth-conditions for predications. In the terminology of early twentieth-century discussions of language development, negation provides a paradigm case of the emergence of the language of "intellect" from the language of "affect."

In this chapter I plan to explore some fundamental aspects of children's acquisition of the semantics of negation, paying particular attention (as one who has worked with Jerry Bruner would) to the transition from prelinguistic to linguistic communication. After examining the range of contexts in which children express negation in their first year of language use, I develop a taxonomy of negative meanings. Results of longitudinal studies of six children are then presented which indicate that different meanings of negation emerge in an invariant sequence, whereas individuals vary as to which lexical items they use to express the same negative meanings and in the negative meanings most prevalent in the language they use. The invariance is explained by developments in cognitive representation which allow for the new meanings, and the variation is viewed as resulting from the specific experiences of different children in mother-child discourse. An account of the formation of negative word meanings is provided which emphasizes the interaction between parental uses of negation in specific types of settings and children's first uses of negative terms. Focusing on the interactions in which early negations get used, by both child and adult, removes some of the mystery from negation semantics and from the process by which children come to know the pragmatic conditions of negation use.

Meanings of Negation in Sentences

In the few systematic studies devoted to the semantic development of negation, several meanings of negation have played central roles. An influential tripartite division was proposed by Bloom (1970, p. 173):

1. *Nonexistence*, where the referent was not manifest in the context, where there was an expectation of its existence, and it was correspondingly negated in the linguistic expression;

2. *Rejection*, where the referent actually existed or was imminent within the contextual space of the speech event and was rejected or opposed by the child; and

3. *Denial*, where the negative utterance asserted that an actual (or supposed) predication was not the case.

Bloom found that the syntactic expression of these different negation meanings proceeded in the order nonexistence, rejection, and denial for all three of the American, English-speaking children she studied.

McNeill and McNeill (1968) also realized the insights which a concentration on negation semantics could provide for negation development, beyond the structural descriptions carefully provided by Bellugi (1967) in earlier syntactic studies. Their study reported data for one child from the age of two years three months learning Japanese as a first language. The McNeills proposed a system of three binary feature contrasts for different meanings of negation: Existence-Truth, External-Internal, and Entailment-Nonentailment. These studies by Bloom and the McNeills are often interpreted as each supporting the emergence of semantic functions of negation in the order nonexistence, rejection, and denial (Bloom, 1970, p. 173; Cromer, 1974; de Villiers and Flusberg, 1975), but there are critical discrepancies between them that have even been noted by McNeill (1970, p. 96). A brief review of the findings will make this clear.

The McNeills thought that the task of tracing the course of semantic development for negation would be considerably simplified by observing the acquisition of Japanese, since the four common forms of simple negation in Japanese have different semantic functions and (+) or (−) feature markers on each of the three binary dimensions mentioned above:

1. *Nai (aux)* is a denial of a previous predication, which I will call "nonentailing denial";

2. *Nai (adj)* is an assertion of nonexistence of X given an expectation, by the speaker or listener, that X was previously present (where X is an object or event);

3. *Iya* is a straightforward rejection, glossed as "I do not want"; and

4. *Iiya* is a denial of a previous proposition plus the implication that something else is true; this may be called "entailing denial."

The McNeills viewed negation development as the acquisition of dimensions that are marked (±) in a semantic feature analysis. A central problem with this view, however, is the oddity of the "Existence-Truth" dimension, which is not a dimension at all, unlike the other two. This dimension, they suggest, concerns the "condition" of negation, the existence or lack of either some thing or the truth of some sentence. But sentences and things are of different types. Only sentences have truth-values, so the existence of things and the truth of sentences are not diametrically opposed as are the ± values of the other two dimensions. Since truth-values involve arbitrary and rule-governed truth-conditions for sentences, the "truth" aspect of the McNeills' dimension is of a higher order and logical type than the "existence" aspect, with the consequence that any ± feature analysis with these two conditions is artificial.

The McNeills concluded that the Japanese child's semantic development of negation proceeded in the order of nonexistence, nonentailing denial, rejection, and entailing denial. The difference between Bloom's and the McNeills' findings is that the Japanese child purportedly "had the idea of linguistically registering the truth of statements before she had the idea of linguistically registering her inner states in relation to outer ones" (1968, p. 61), whereas all of Bloom's subjects expressed denial *after* rejection in syntactic expressions.

The developmental histories of negation semantics offered by Bloom and the McNeills dealt with the expression of negative meanings in *sentences* children produced; they do not really address questions about the development of meanings of negation during the single word utterance period. Yet there are important reasons for studying the origins of negation semantics. One is to determine the adequacy of a single negative word for expressing the three negative meanings Bloom discusses, and the fact that "nonexistence first" may be an artifact of the need for specifying a referent of the nonexistence proclamation (Bloom, 1970, p. 219). Since the communication requirements for effective discourse can differentially affect the complexity of expression for different meanings of negation, the developmental order of expression for negative meanings *in sentences* tells us little about the development of negative meanings per se. A second reason is that children display a rich variety of uses for negative words even in the single word utterance period. From a wider perspective, as Vygotsky's psychogenetic method (1978) has shown, the study of the history of behavior that begins at its source, and traces the dynamic relations between its components, holds the promise of explanatory analyses of processes of development instead of descriptive accounts of developmental products.

Negation in the Single-Word Utterance Period

Before progressing to a description of communicative contexts of single-word negatives, we must confront a problem rarely acknowledged for child semantics in general, and not at all for child negation. What exactly is "negation"? Like many words, "negation" does not have any one central or defining essence, but a number of meanings that partake of family resemblances to one another (Wittgenstein, 1958).

Dictionary definitions tell us that negations express such meanings as denials, refusals, prohibitions, and statements of nonexistence. One critical thread running through these expressions is the likelihood of their being expressed by the words "no" or "not," the primary negative particles in English. The dictionary definitions include the meanings of negation distinguished by Bloom and the McNeills, but the problem of polysemy for a negative word such as "no" or "gone" is a difficult one, not unlike the lexicographer's problems with polysemy in general. And unlike other areas of semantics, such as kinship or spatial terms, we have no standard linguistic studies on negation semantics to refer to. Negation is so fundamental a part of lexical meaning in general (for example, in antonymy) that a "semantic field" for negation would include many of the words in a language (Miller and Johnson-Laird, 1976).

How fine a line should be drawn between different meanings of negation? Conceivably, we could have either one general meaning or a proliferation of meanings, literally one for each distinct occasion of use. At least this sets the limits. The level of generality chosen may be motivated by different concerns. Miller (1978) indicates two potential strategies: a lexicographic approach which proliferates senses of a word in its occupation with making as many conceptual distinctions as possible, specifying discourse and selectional restrictions for each specified sense; and a second approach which only introduces a new sense when combining it with another sense would yield a uselessly overgeneral meaning. The lexicographic approach eventually has its limits, and the latter approach is restricted by how one construes "uselessly overgeneral." We will not settle the problem in this brief discussion, but its consequences for negation semantic development deserve attention.

One striking feature of early verbal negation is the great range of contexts in which the first negative words are used before they are ever combined with other words to form sentences. A problem for the child language investigator analyzing the contexts of use for single-word negation is to delineate psychologically real semantic categories of negation for the child. It would be a great help if the child produced just two different negative words, such as "no" and "gone." each only appearing in set situations, perhaps "no" only to reject objects and "gone" only when people walk out of rooms. But actual negative usage is much more complex than this. Children rapidly generalize negative words to new situations with the same tenacity that they carry over object words to new category exemplars, and the developmental psycholinguist's task requires detailed descriptions of contexts of negation use (both discourse and situational) and the difficult work of trying to detect nuances of meaning that have later consequences in, for instance, later structural differentiation of negation expression. At this time, a complete picture of early negative use is not available, but the following observations provide a sketch for one.

I would like to suggest a tentative resolution of the meaning delineation problem by proposing that certain *families* of negative meanings can be identified in the wide variety of uses of single-word negation, and that several specific questions about the emergence of different meanings for negation in children's speech may then be answered.

As focus for discussion, figure 1 provides an overview of contexts in which negatives were used in the study I will describe or by children followed in previous child language studies.[1] For purposes of exposition, the child's negative utterances are listed separately as to whether they are adjacent to adult utterances or initiated by the child and, hence, nonadjacent.

On the adjacency side of the figure, the types of adult utterances that precede the child negatives are listed. Fuller elaborations of variations of the different contexts are specified in the right-hand side of the figure; these are not presented in the left-hand side purely for reasons of space. The proliferation of distinct contexts in these descriptions will lead us back to the families-of-negative-meanings account already mentioned.

Negation is frequently used to reject parental prohibitions or imperatives, and this negative context frequently recurred in long rounds of turns (that is, iterative loops of adult command-child rejection). Disappearance nega-

1. This literature is reviewed in Pea (1978). The most descriptive published accounts to date are Bloom (1973) and Leopold (1949).

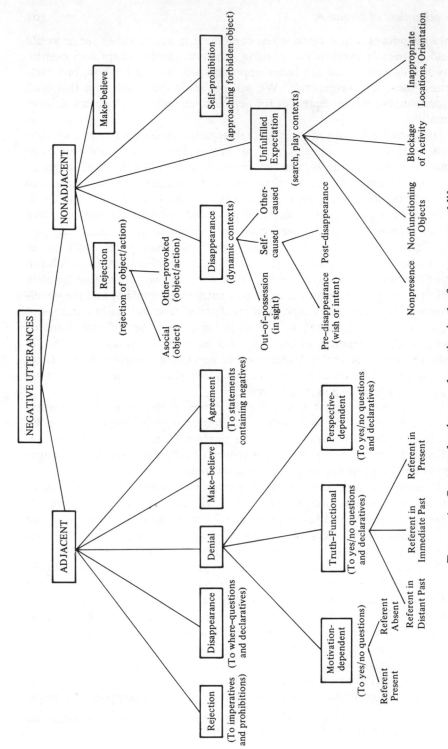

FIGURE 1   Contexts for the use of negation in the first two years of life

tions, such as "gone," were usually coupled with where-questions in discourse, but occasionally with declaratives, each of which often cued a search for a non-present object which, after search, was not found. A variety of disappearance contexts had negative words expressed in them, such as child-caused object disappearance and other-caused object disappearance, and each of these variants may vary along yet other parameters—object in/out of possession of child at the time of disappearance, negative word produced before (as a negative wish) versus after the object disappears, and so on.

Negatives are also often responses to yes/no questions and declaratives and may serve to deny the proposition expressed in the question form. The yes/no questions answered by the child's negatives may be placed in one of at least three categories, requiring different kinds of evidence for an accounting of the truth of the proposition in question. Many questions, such as "Do you want a cookie?", "Can you open it?" or "Can you see the mouse?" depend on the child's desires, abilities, or perspective. Yet another important class of yes/no questions and declaratives express propositions whose truth depends on facts of the world external to the child's viewpoint, such as "Is this Daddy's pipe?" or "Did we go to the fair?" All three classes of yes/no questions may also vary in the dimension of time, so that the proposition in question relates to present, immediately prior, or distant past events.

Other uses of early negation are for make-believe, as in disappearance comments such as the sentence "Roy gone," used with laughter by one child as Roy stood in the child's plain view. Negatives are also sometimes used to agree with prior negative utterances (see Bellugi, 1967, Pea, 1978).

The heuristic diagram presented in figure 1 should not be considered a complete list of early contexts and meanings with which negative words are used, but it captures the diversity of situations in which young children use negatives. One could even proliferate further subcategorizations of the nodes of the figure, differentiating yet more situational variants. But the list of early contexts for "no" and related words used by children is *not* a typology of early meanings for negation, for there is no reason to assume that these "types" (and subtypes, if our diagram delineated more subtle meaning differences) are in any sense distinct in children's conception of their own use of the negative words in these situations. One *could* take a lexicographic approach as an initial guideline for distinguishing different negative meanings that may be psychologically differentiated for the child. The reason, however, why this is a bad first start is that there are certain families of negative word contexts, with many features in common for any given family, that naturally cluster together. Though one still can not conclude that the semantic categories thus obtained match up with distinct negative meanings for the child, the categorization is at least motivated by similarities in the child's behaviors and situational contexts of the different category members.

For example, the child's use of "no" to reject an object offered to her, accompanied by a pushing-away gesture, is very much like the child's use of "no" in rejection of a prohibition constraining her action.

The semantic categories used here for meanings of child negation are a result of such groupings of negative word uses in different contexts, and they resemble in some respects the categories described by Bloom and the McNeills.

Rejection negatives were defined as those action-based negations with which the child rejects an event, person, object, or activity which is in the immediately perceivable context of rejection or imminent in the mother's behavior or utterance (whose truth-value is contingent on the child's current motivations). The "imminent" disjunct of the definition refers to uses of negatives used in contexts in which highly routinized activities provide cues for the child (such as a diaper in the mother's hand) of imminent to-be-rejected actions, and negatives used in response to desire questions such as "Do you want a cookie?"

Disappearance negatives are uses of negatives with reference to the disappearance of something which had been present just prior to the child's utterance but is no longer perceivable to the child. The "something" may be an object or person, an activity, or some form of sensory stimulation (such as the sound of a washer or radio) which disappears or ceases.

Related to the negatives of disappearance but distinct in important ways are negatives of *unfulfilled expectation*. Negatives expressing the meaning of this semantic category are used to comment on constraint on activity, absence other than immediately prior disappearance or cessation, or, more generally speaking, some aspect of the child's continuing line of activity (such as search or play) which does not occur (for example, blockage of movement of bicycle, toys that are malfunctioning) or is not found (a block not in its habitual location).

Truth-functional negation consists of the use of a negative in response to an utterance expressing a proposition that is true or false given the facts of the situation it refers to and, hence, the truth-conditions of language. Such truth-functional negations express logical judgments and constitute a subset of the negatives captured by Bloom's "denial" category defined earlier. This stands in contrast to some rejection negations, which negate a proposition the truth of which depends on the child's own motivations.

Self-prohibition negation is a form of egocentric symbol use in which the child approaches a previously forbidden object or begins to do something which has been prohibited in the past and then expresses a negative. Such negations are not necessarily accompanied by the child's avoidance of the forbidden act.

These five semantic categories of negation will be the central focus in this chapter, with the purpose of investigating general features of the development of different meanings of negation. These categories account for a substantial proportion of all the negatives children produced in the study reported here, unlike the potential meaning categories of negative agreement, negative wish, make-believe negative, and non-truth-functional denial negation. Such negations do occur during the first year of language use, but only infrequently.

The proliferation of different uses for negation by the age of two years deserves special emphasis, especially because it stands in contrast to arguments by Steffensen (1978) that the word "no" during this period is "lacking in semantic content" and only fulfills the conversational requirement of responding to yes/no questions. The richness of early negation semantics becomes apparent when one studies children's spontaneous use of negation and negation in response to parental linguistic forms other than yes/no questions.

Cognitive Representation and Meanings of Negation

One can now ask, given our characterizations of different semantic categories of negation, in what order the first expressions of different negative meanings develop. Longitudinal data from six children indicate that children first convey inner states via rejection negation, then make comments on the disappearance of things in the world, and only later truth-functionally negate false statements about the world. Individual differences occurred in the developmental ordering of unfulfilled expectation negation and self-prohibition negation, although for all children such meanings preceded the expression of truth-functional negation. These findings may be explained by analyses of the progressively higher-order representational requirements, or cognitive bases, of the conception of different meanings for negation. The general "cognitive complexity" of negation has been a standard observation in studies of adult cognition and child language, but this unanalyzed notion deserves reconsideration.

Negation is a semantic domain which readily lends itself to conceptual analyses of representational complexity. The claim is that for the child to conceive the different meanings of negation that I have described, increasingly abstract forms of cognitive representation are required. Whether one advocates the developmental theory of Bruner, Piaget, or Werner, a familiar developmental progression is the emergence of symbolic or abstract representations from more primitive mental activity limited to concrete motor-affective sensorimotor intelligence. This progression places important limits on negation semantic development.

Rejection negations express inner attitudes of rejection toward behaviors, events, or objects that are embedded in the child's very early motor-affective activities; the topic of this type of negation has no need for internal representation because it is immediately present in the context of the rejection. Darwin (1872; also Jakobson, 1972) has emphasized in his comparative studies of emotional expression, over a century ago, that the early negative expressed universally with nasal sounds (Jespersen, 1917) and the headshake, or conventional gesture of negation, are each natural signs which directly express attitudes of aversion.

Disappearance negation, on the other hand, typified by the child's comment of "gone" or "no more" as a ball disappears from sight, requires abstract cognitive representation. Unlike the object of rejection negation, the ball is no longer present, and the negative comment must abstractly denote the vanished object or event of disappearance.

These considerations of the cognitive demands of different meanings for negation lead to the prediction that rejection negation, rooted to concrete motor-affective activities, will be the first meaning of negation that children express, followed by the emergence of disappearance negation, which requires the elaboration of more complex cognitive representation. Though such a prediction may seem intuitively obvious, recall that the account of semantic development proferred by the McNeills' (1968) claims that the "natural order" of emergence of meanings for negation is "from outer to inner," from the negative meanings of not-here and false toward expressions of rejection.

Truth-functional negation also requires abstract cognitive representation, of yet greater complexity and of a different logical order. Negatives with this metalinguistic meaning of not-x consist of comments on the use of abstract language by another person and are by definition of a higher logical type than disappearance negation (Bateson, 1968, Wilden, 1972). From the perspective of development in cognitive representation, truth-functional negatives should not be used by the child prior to the meanings of rejection and disappearance.

It is important to observe that, theoretically, all three functions here may be expressed gesturally, with the negative headshake, as well as in single words. For example, the child could shake her head in rejection, when objects disappear, or in response to yes/no questions or false statements. A much more complex developmental landscape than this is revealed in the course of the children's negation development. We will return to the semantic categories of self-prohibition and unfulfilled expectation negation in a later section.

METHODS

The six children studied lived in the immediate vicinity of Oxford, England, and were acquiring English as a first language. Two boys and two girls (HS, SR; CS, JK) were studied from eight months to one year eight months; and one boy and one girl (RT; CB) from one year to two years.

Each child was visited individually in his or her home once each month for about ninety minutes, and videotaped for a total period of thirty minutes while playing, feeding, bathing, and during other home activities. Mothers were also queried about their child's current uses of the headshake and negative words but were uninformed as to the specific questions of the study.

Transcriptions from the video records included all speech produced by the children and adults present, with additional relevant nonlinguistic behavior, for example, actions, pointing, and context (gaze direction, objects present) noted in temporal relation to the vocalizations.

The data for analysis were headshakes and verbal negations, consisting of single or multiword utterances made up of at least one negative word or a word co-occurring with a headshake. Negative words were such morphemes as "no," "not," "n't," approximations of "no" such as /na/ or /nə/ and words such as "gone," "all gone," "away," and "stop." These negatives were transcribed from the video records and from unfilmed but tape-recorded observations which had been supplemented with context notes at the time of the observations.

RESULTS

All six children first expressed rejection negation, and they expressed this meaning in headshakes before they did in speech. Previous studies by Carter (1974) and Ruke-Dravina (1972) also found a gestural priority. Headshakes were first used around the age of one year to one year one month with an age range for the group of ten months to one year two months. For example, RT did not spontaneously use negation until one year one month, when he shook his head on five different occasions, three different times in response to different questions of the form "Do you want——?" where the referent was visible, once in rejection of a prohibition from his mother, and once to reject bicycle clips offered to him.

Four of the children first used the headshake to reject food, diaper changing, face cleaning, and other ritual maintenance acts. The other two children first used the headshake in response to questions pertaining to ritual functions, such as "Do you want some milk?" or "Want to go to bed?" that were redundant given the objects or actions that were at hand.

Considerable differences were found with respect to the time period between the first uses of nonimitative uses of headshakes to reject and the later nonimitative expression of negatives in speech. This gap ranged from one to nine months for the children studied. Rejection was generally the first negative meaning encoded verbally. Two of the six children first used negative speech to express rejection, one used speech to express rejection and disappearance at the same time, while another child first used negative speech to express rejection and self-prohibition. Two males had still not used verbal negation at the last visit when they were one year, eight months.

Table 1 summarizes the ages of the children at first appearance of the different functions of negation, both in gesture and in speech.

TABLE 1

Age in Months at First Appearance of Negation Meanings

Child	Rejection		Disappearance		Truth-Functional		Unfulfilled Expectation		Self-Prohibition	
	Gesture	Word	Gesture	Word	Gesture	Word	Gesture	Word	Gesture	Word
CB	13	15	—	19	—	23	14	16	—	21
CS	10	13	—	13	—	19	—	18	11	17
JK	14	15	—	16	—	19	—	16	15	15
RT	13	15	—	16	—	22	14	18	14	14
HS	11	—	—	—	—	—	—	—	16	—
SR	13	—	—	—	—	—	—	—	—	—

It is important to note that the cognitive representation analysis does not specify that the communicative function of rejection will be the first meaning to be expressed *verbally*. It may be the case that if the headshake alone is efficacious for the child in communication for expressing rejection then it will not necessarily be the first meaning of negation expressed verbally. The central issue is not the order of verbal expression of these meanings of negation, but the order of expression of negative meanings via conventional forms, whether in gesture or speech.

Four of the six children went on to express negative comments of disappearance with the word "gone," predominantly in contexts where objects or persons had disappeared immediately beforehand. They all also expressed important intermediary forms of negation between the affective negations of rejection and the more abstract negatives of disappearance. In the month prior to the use of disappearance negation for each of these children, "gone" was used in contexts where objects fell out of their possession but remained in their clear line of sight, and were often then picked up by the children immediately after they had made the remark. But at this time the children had not made such comments when things actually disappeared. A fifth child had not used the word "gone" for disappearance negation before the completion of the studies, but like the other children, consistently said "ga" when towers of blocks fell over or objects fell from his hands. This development—from "gone" in the sensorimotor present to "gone" for non-present objects—suggests that constraints in cognitive representation delay the expression of disappearance negation for absent referents. Such a finding would be expected on this cognitive approach. It also provides new support for Werner and Kaplan's (1963) developmental principle of "distancing," which claims developmental continuity between language fused to action and perceptual schemas in the present, and language distant and differentiated from its referential objects.

Truth-functional negation was the last of these three negation functions to appear for the four children expressing this type of negation at all. Bloom's (1970) more general category of "denial" negatives includes, as mentioned earlier, cases where the child denies previous utterances whose truth is contingent on the child's motivations in the situation, rather than inherent truth conditions of the statement involved. An example of denial negation which is not truth-functional negation is Gia's reply "no, now I do it" to the adult question "now can I do it?" Although the child has negated the adult proposition "I can do it," the truth of that proposition was dependent on Gia's *choice*. Truth-functional negatives, by contrast, are negative comments expressing judgments of the falsity of statements about properties, names, or actions. Several examples illustrating this meaning of negation are given in table 2. Negatives with this meaning were not first

TABLE 2
Examples of Truth-Functional Negation Use

Names

1. (CB, age 2;1)
   Experimenter: Is that a biscuit? (E pointing at CB's apple)
   CB: No, apple.

2. (RT, age 1;10)
   RT: Trains.   [RT points to a train he has made with 2 railroad cars; at this point each car is a "train" for him, multiple cars are "trains"]
   Experimenter: Is that a train?
   RT: No. Trains.

Possession

3. (CS, age 1;7)
   CS: Big.   [CS points to a large pair of shoes next to her small pair; the large pair are Ned's]
   Experimenter: Is this big? [E points to CB's small shoe]
   CS: No, mine.
        Ned. Big. [CS points to one of Ned's big shoes]

Presence/Absence

4. (CS, age 1;7)
   Mother: Is the ball gone?   [M shows CS the ball]
   CS: No.

Misinterpretation Correction

5. (CS, age 1;9)
   CS: Womble.   [CS is searching for the Womble doll]
   Experimenter: Ball?   [E intentionally misunderstands CS]
   CS: No.
   Experimenter: Womble?
   CS: Yeh.

expressed by headshakes alone, but in speech within a month of the onset of syntactic constructions for all four children. The experimental study of children's negative corrections of false statements provides further support that this meaning of negation emerges around the age of two years (Pea, 1979).

A typical use of truth-functional negation took place in a conversation about the temperature of a bicycle seat. RT (one year ten months) had just had his diaper removed and sat on a very cold metal bicycle seat. When asked "Is it warm?" he answered "No, cold!" This meaning of negation provides the earliest verbal index of rudimentary logical thought, reflecting the awareness of the propositional operation of negation (Pea, 1979).

Bloom (1973), in her studies of single-word speech, also provides support for the sequence of emergence of meanings of negation found here. "Away" was first used by her subject to reject things as they were thrown away and afterwards when things disappeared. Truth-functional negatives later appeared as correct responses to yes/no questions about names and predicates.

One can also ask whether the first conventional negative symbol was extended to express new negative meanings. Recall that the headshake was first used to express the first negative meaning of rejection. But the first expressions of both disappearance and truth-functional negation were not headshakes, for any of the children studied. Rather, disappearance negation was realized in words such as "gone," "stop," and "byebye," while rejection, when expressed in speech, was predominantly coded with "no," and occasionally "don't." Truth-functional negatives were usually "no" or "not," and only two children ever accompanied the truth-functional negative word with a headshake.

It is intriguing that three children combined the headshake with an affirmative word to convey a negative meaning before they used words together in sentences. For instance, "pussy" with an accompanying headshake was used when a cat disappeared from a television screen, and "mumma" with a headshake functioned as a self-prohibition not to touch mommy's glasses. These very creative dual-channel negatives were never the first appearance of a new negative meaning, as one might expect given the genetic primacy of the headshake, but later developments of only brief use.

The cognitive interpretation of negation semantic development charted here has the virtue of providing systematic predictions of developmental sequence for the emergence of different meanings of negation. The focus is on the developmental map sketched by elaborations in cognitive representation that allow for the emergence of new meanings for negation from the origins of conventional negation in communication. Children first convey negation through headshakes for rejection, then comment on disappearance, and later use truth-functional negation in judgments about language use.

Cross-language research would provide a test of the universality of this sequence of emergence.

Topics of Negation and the Genesis of Negation Pragmatics

Another way of relating these findings is in terms of development in the *range of topics* for negations children use. Since rejection negation is the first meaning that negatives are used for, the first topics of negation are concretely present in the child's immediate field of activity and transcend the here and now only when negative comments come, several months later, to mark disappearance. In disappearance contexts, the topic of negation has just recently gone out of view. One might predict that subsequent developments in the distancing of the topic from the child's negative utterance will grade from these immediately prior disappearances to topics of a more general natural, to rulelike assumptions on the child's part. This is strictly true for only two (CB, RT) of the four children who used verbal negation at all during the course of study, and involves the relation between negations of disappearance and of unfulfilled expectation.

Unfulfilled expectation negatives, one might expect, based on norms constructed through experience, will emerge only after disappearance negations, which are not unlike a verbal "orienting" to a change (presence to absence) in the immediate sensory field. CB and RT met this expectation, as did the child described by Bloom (1973), but CS and JK conveyed unfulfilled expectation negatives *before* disappearance negation. Such variation could reflect individual differences, or the developmental invalidity of the distinction between negative contexts of disappearance and unfulfilled expectation, or an overgeneral definition of unfulfilled expectation negation. Evidence points to the third choice. Since *all* of the uses of unfulfilled expectation negation occurring prior to disappearance negation (for CS and JK) were in *action* contexts (either when toys did not work or when the child's movement was blocked), as opposed to unfulfilled expectation negatives commenting on expected *existence* or *location*, the action uses seem to constitute a primitive precursor of the existence and location uses (which for any given child never occurred before the first expressions of disappearance negation).

The more mature uses of unfulfilled expectation negation provide an important insight into the development of negation pragmatics. The more general assumptions on which existence and location negations of unfulfilled expectation are based are at first local norms, or habitual associations, such as the fact that frequently encountered or acted-upon objects have standard locations or spatial arrangements. This developing knowledge about structure in the physical and social environment is describable in terms of scripts that the child learns, naturally occurring sequences, or configurations of activities, objects, events, and behaviors (Nelson, 1978; Schank and Abelson, 1977). These scripts serve as normative knowledge, so that when differences from them arise, the child marks the discrepancy with negation. This description fits well with the pragmatics of ordinary language negation for adults, with the scripts defining the child's assumed affirmative contexts for negation. They provide the groundwork for continuity in the development of negation pragmatics, since it is also discrepancies from positive assumptions that motivate negation use by adults. Table 3 illustrates the growing range in topics of negation for the four children using verbal negation.

TABLE 3

Developmental Change in Topics of Negation and Number of Negations

Age in months[a]

Child	8	9	10	11	12	13	14	15	16	17	18	19	20	21	22	23	24	25	Total
CS	X[b]	0	1	4	1	7[c]	5[c]	7	40	74	39	78	X	59	X	X	X	X	315
JK	0	0	0	0	0	X	4	21	44	22	22	22	20	X	X	X	X		155
CB	X	X	X	X	X	4	2	9	5	5	5	7	6	17	45	31	X	17	153
RT	X	X	X	X	1	6	8	1	6	15	1	9	7	53	43	38	111	X	299

[a] The underscoring of the numbers of negations produced at each visit indicates the *highest* level of topic abstraction for the negations used. This does not mean that the occurrence of simpler topics ceased, only that the range of topics with regard to "distancing" from the topic (see text) increased. *Key:* single line = topic in the here & now; double line = topic recently disappeared; triple line = topic expected but not found.

[b] Child was not visited at this age.

[c] Only in response to "Where's X?" questions.

The character of unfulfilled expectation negation is best captured by a few examples. When CB (one year ten months) looked into my toybag, for the previous ten months always containing a ball she favored, she said "ball, Mummy," to which her mother answered "I don't know where it is," to which CB replied *"no* ball, Mummy." Nothing had disappeared; the ball just did not appear where she expected it. During the same visit, CB found a teapot lid, usually on top of a teapot that was now missing, and as she held up the lid, she remarked "no teapot." Similar negative comments were made by CB when:

1. only half an apple, or part of a button was shown in a picture (hence, incompletely);
2. her coat, pot, toys, and other objects were not in their proper places;
3. objects were used unconventionally, as when her mother cut a string with a vegetable knife; and
4. puzzle pieces were placed in the wrong slots.

These cases show that CB's habitual norms, like the other children's, were quite idiosyncratic to her household, yet of great importance to her. So when RT (one year nine months) looked at an empty chair where his cat usually sat, he said, "pussy gone." Or when CS (one year nine months) was asked where Auntie Sonya was (she was in the garden, where CS saw her earlier), she replied, "gone get dinner," probably because Sonya frequently went out to pick up fish and chips. Since CS was in the single-word utterance period at the time and was using "gone" productively, this was very likely a ritual phrase.

One may expect, since negatives in the adult language are used to mark deviations from expectations or norms, that the major development from negative comments based on such local norms as the habitual location of objects would consist of moves toward a more general level of agreement or conventionality. Such a view is hard to support on close inspection.

Potential examples of negations with topics of general knowledge may be heard from the mouths of two-year-olds, but a fuzzy area of indeterminacy exists between cases of habitual location and ones based on what (on first view) seem to be general conventions. JK (one year six months) pulls down the trousers of her G.I. Joe doll and, upon discovering he has on no underpants, says, "no pants." Now is this negation based on general knowledge, a convention adults would share of a form such as "under trousers, one wears underwear"? Or is it one based on the local, habitual association of co-occurrence of pants beneath trousers? The distinction, particularly in common cases like this one, is shaky, yet it is at the heart of one account of negation pragmatic development (Volterra and Antinucci, 1978).

To carry the breakdown of the distinction further, one need only reflect on how the assumptions denied in the negative speech of adults are also often based on local, idiosyncratic norms or expectations, such as "there's no beer in the fridge" when one's spouse was supposed to buy some at the store, or "there's no fire left" after waking up cold from a nap near the hearth. The habitual locations of objects, such as clothes, keys, and furniture, are of great importance for our everyday affairs, just as they are for children.

Many apparent differences between the topics of adults' and children's negations are only illusory. But when the child's topics of negation move beyond the here and now, are they always similar to those of adults? No. Volterra and Antinucci (1978) have characterized the differences that occur as "pragmatic misfires," cases where the presuppositions (or topics, in my terminology) of the adult and child just do not match up. They describe an example where a child looks at a hospital tower and says "Look there is no bell." Yet adults know it is church towers which have bells and are not surprised to see hospital towers without them. The child's task, according to Volterra and Antinucci's approach, is to "pull his own presuppositions into line with the listener's." But how does such an alignment take place?

In their analysis of negation development for Italian and American children, Volterra and Antinucci (1978) stress that the determining factor in the emergence of presuppositions for negation based on "normative classes" shared by adult and child is the developing ability to represent cognitively such abstract general knowledge.

But developments in cognition alone cannot explain such presuppositional changes, which must come from the sociocultural conventions of the child's language community. The process of aligning child-adult language knowledge is accomplished largely through dialogue, and the older child, when such pragmatic misfires occur, is better able to repair the breakdown of understanding with the listener. The few studies of children's responses to clarification requests, though not addressing negative speech per se, indicate the complexity of identifying the source of the misunderstanding (Cherry, 1979; Garvey, 1978; Stokes, 1976).

In adult conversations using negation, too, our knowledge frequently does not match up with our listener's expectations. If it did, as Brown (1973, personal communication), Givon (1978), Labov and Fanshel (1977), Wason (1965, this volume), and others have pointed out, there would be no conversational point to negative utterances. But adults are very adept at clarifying knowledge differences when pragmatic misfires occur and at making explicit their assumptions and background when engaging in discourse. The ability to synchronize assumptions through clarification moves in a conversation when misfires do occur is thus a critical component in the emergence of pragmatically successful negation, once the topic becomes abstracted from the present.

Volterra and Antinucci (1978) describe general developmental patterns in distancing the topic of negation beyond the present similar to those described in this chapter (table 3). There is, however, one other critical difference between the formal linguistic analysis proposed by Volterra and Antinucci and this account of negation topic development. They formally characterize what I have called the "topic" of negation as a "presupposition." The presupposition is then attributed to the child's listener, so that the listener is held to believe p, where p is the presupposition negated by the child.

One of Volterra and Antinucci's examples will make their approach clear. A sixteen-month-old child says "gone" after a flame is blown out from a match. Their interpretation of this utterance is that the child negates the presupposition "the flame is present" which he infers that the listener believes. Two developmental facts argue against the appropriateness of this formal analysis, applied across the board to negative utterances produced by children fifteen to thirty-five months old. Such "presuppositional" structures are taken to be an integral part of the child's cognitive representation of the speech context and the knowledge state of his listener, yet inferring the beliefs of another person is certainly not a requirement of making such an utterance, since children use many negatives without addressing another person, particularly when objects disappear. Such inferences of beliefs would also require more sophisticated social cognition than two-year-olds seem to have available (Gearhart, 1979; Shantz, 1977). Independent evidence from experimentation is necessary before claiming that children in this period have the ability to infer specific beliefs of another person.

Discourse Contexts of Negation and Lexical Variation in Negation Expression

The development of meanings of negation for children from one to two years old has been explicitly related to the growth of representational abilities. Cognition alone, while allowing more abstract topics of negation, can provide neither the meanings of negation nor the specific words children use to express them. The meanings and forms of negation are conveyed by speakers of the language by virtue of the child's engagement in a sociocultural and linguistic community. This transmission becomes clear from the striking individual differences in negation expression for the children studied longitudinally. Discourse contexts varied across mother-child dyads, and variations in the words children used to express negative meanings occurred.

Topic initiation provides a useful focus for a look at discourse contexts for negation. Adult-initiated negatives are those which the child produces after an immediately preceding adult utterance. Self-initiated negations are those which are not adjacent to adult speech but are spontaneously used.

The central finding from an overall analysis of self-versus-adult-initiated negation is somewhat surprising: 40 percent (or 367/922) of the total negatives produced by the four children who spoke during the period of study were initiated by the child. This means that children were making negative comments on their own a considerable amount of the time, when things and people disappeared, when toys would not work as they should, when things were not found in their habitual locations, and in self-prohibition.

Negation topic initiation for any given mother-child dyad is not, unfortunately, very informative if one seeks out developmental trends. One might suspect that children would at first produce negatives predominantly in response to adult utterances and, with development, come to be able to introduce negations spontaneously which before required maternal conversational support. This suspicion is consistent with recent data indicating that propositions are first constructed across utterances produced by mother and child and that this discourse experience supports the child's later expression of propositions on her own (Keenan, Schieffelin, and Platt 1976; Ninio and Bruner 1978). But topic initiation for negation does not seem to follow such a pattern. The picture is one of great interindividual variability and substantial up and down fluctuations across sessions in the proportion of self-initiated negations for any individual child.

Large individual differences occurred in the overall predominance of self or adult initiated negation. For example, CS, whose mother was extremely prohibitive and constraining in her child-rearing, produced only 20 percent (or 64/315) of her overall negatives spontaneously, since most of them were in emotionally charged negative retorts to her mother's commands and prohibitions. JK produced 72 percent (or, 111/155) of her negatives spontaneously; this was largely a consequence of her mother's fostering of independent play, often accompanied by what might be described as egocentric speech. The other two children are near the 40 percent average (CB: 49 percent, or 75/153; PT: 39 percent, or 117/299).

One consequence of such differences is that the different children produce radically divergent overall proportions of different meanings of negation; 58 percent of JK's negatives were comments on disappearance, whereas only 7 percent expressed rejection. Recall that it was JK's mother who fostered independence and solitary play. CS's language environment, however, was characterized by constraint and commands, and 37 percent of her negations expressed rejection, while only 26 percent were comments on disappearance. So in one important sense, the predominant types of discourse contexts for negation provided by mothers can affect the predominant meanings of negation children choose to express. It is in this light that the agreement in developmental ordering of negative meanings for the different children is all the more striking.

Specific negative meanings were sometimes expressed by words idiosyncratic to the conversations of particular mother-child dyads. JK and CS, for example, unlike CB and RT, shook their heads as they named the possessor of prohibited objects in expressing self-prohibition negation, a reflection of the parents' prohibitions in statements such as "that's *Mommy's*" modeled with headshaking. Specific prohibitive formats between mother and child yielded other special self-prohibition negatives, such as JK's "don't eat it" for soap bars, and CS's "mustn't bite" when playing with her sister, each of which were used during the single-word utterance period.

Such lexical variation was not limited to expressions of self-prohibition negation. Only JK used "done" in rejection of objects she was tired of, only CS used "I 'nt" to reject commands (it is an Oxford working class slang contraction for "I won't"), and only CB used "alldone" for disappearance negation when machines stopped. More examples could be adduced, and in each case uses of the specific lexical expression of the negative meaning are to be found in the child's previous language environment in similar situations.

Lexical variation was not the rule, however, in the words used to express a specific negative meaning. All of the children used headshakes and "no" for rejection, "gone" and "allgone" for disappearance, and "no" for truth-functional negation. But the existence of such clear cases of lexical variation provides proof that the forms of negation are a result of the conversational environments provided by the child's language peers.

An Interactionist Perspective on the Origins of Negation Semantics

The emergence of negation semantics may be framed in terms of three major phases. In the first, the child's task is to discover the meaning of negatives in the speech of the adult, to form an initial basis or core to the meaning of "no" and related negatives. In the second, the child first uses negation and begins to generalize negation to novel situations. In the third phase, discourse contexts for negation shape the elaboration of negative meanings conveyed by the child, a phase where the child enters a dialectic of language interaction and apprenticeship in which her negatives get responded to and in which negatives that are heard in discourse addressed to the child are assimilated to the child's current (and accommodating) conceptions of negation. The processes by which conventions of adult negation get stored and adapted as the child's lexicon for negation changes in both lexical forms and meanings are the ultimate aim of explanatory accounts of such developments, but for now our analyses are confined to descriptions of maternal speech, the child's speech, and probable inferences as to how the dialectic of communicative exchange contributes to language development. The key to such processes is ultimately to be found in careful studies of the conversational contexts in which early word meanings are negotiated. The first two of these phases are the focus of the following section, which describes the origins of negation in interactional contexts and the child's earliest reactions to and uses of negation.

The Genesis of Negation Comprehension

The predominant meaning of negation in the life of the child during the first year of life is prohibition. Prohibitions from the parent, usually expressed with "No!" and headshake, are addressed to children as they become increasingly ambulatory in the period between nine months and one year. Such prohibitions interrupt and constrain the child's actions, some of which, if carried to completion, would harm the child, for example, handling electrical sockets, hot or sharp objects, or damage property deemed valuable (books, records, glasses).

Spitz (1957) sees the child's uncompleted act in conjunction with the parent's negative word or gesture as a major source of the first meaning of "no" for the child. His account assumes that the child's frustrated *id* drives thereby endow the negative word and gesture with a specific affective cathexis that ensures the child's remembrance of the negative symbols. The child's first use of negation, on this view, is a result of identification with the prohibiting parent, and refusal or rejection is the first meaning since the symbol is imbued with aggressive cathexis in the unpleasurable experiences associated with its memory traces. Apart from the status of the psychoanalytic components of this theory, it is certainly consistent with observations that "no" is one of the first words children learn (Gopnik, 1978; Leopold, 1949; Nelson, 1973) and one of the most consistently used words throughout the single-word utterance period (Bloom, 1973), the finding that rejection is the first meaning of negation children express, and the prevalence of prohibition negation in the language of parents to children for my case studies. The case for prohibition and constraint as the context for children's first learning of a meaning for negation is best put in a genetic description of prohibition comprehension.

For child safety, the parent must establish an effective verbal means of constraining child exploration. Child language diarists often note the early comprehension of "no" in prohibition at nine months to ten months (Leopold, 1939, p. 112; Lewis, 1963, p. 43), and the claim is made that the child halts actions more as a result of the loudness, pitch, duration, and suddenness of onset of "no" than by virtue of its conventional meaning.

Such prominent attitudinal characteristics of the negative speech signal may provide some substantive ground to Spitz's claim that negative word and gesture become endowed with a "specific affective cathexis" as a result of the adult's prohibitions. But how exactly do parents get children to comply with verbal prohibitions? A general framework for this accomplishment may be charted from observations made during the period from eight months to eleven months for four English children; it also provides insights into the child's formation of a concept of negation as constraint.

Parents at first physically constrain children when they issue verbal prohibitions. Just as in early command situations, where the mother says "Give me the ball" as she gently pries it from the hand of the child and later accomplishes the same act with an open palm and ultimately the verbal command alone, the prohibiting mother says "no" and shakes her head as she pulls or lifts the child away from the forbidden act. Soon the adult wishes prohibition compliance at a distance by language and gesture alone, and within a month of physical constraints, children manifest signs of understanding "no" and the headshake in a prohibition situation. The child withdraws from objects, or impedes action (even if only temporarily) before renewing progress to the forbidden act. The child also demonstrates forms of inhibition with regard to the prohibited object or act, which are action analogues of later self-prohibitions. Intentionally disobeying is yet another sign of understanding.

Several distinctive levels of prohibition reaction reflect increasing understanding and approach what the adult counts as prohibition negation comprehension.

It is first important to note that the child brings well-developed (if primitive) means for rejection to the task of prohibition comprehension. Displeasure is displayed by physical means; the child rejects objects or actions by turning her head aside, pushing or throwing the aversive thing away, or flailing her arms (see Bühler and Hetzer, 1935). The means for communicating rejection here are as strikingly direct as were the parent's initial prohibitions of forced compliance by physical means. Parents also frequently interpret these behaviors as expressive of negation and expand them with lexical negatives: "no, no, don't want it." Ryan (1974) has emphasized the importance of such intent interpretations for the eventual linguistic expression of intention.

The child does not, however, initially use behaviors from the physical rejection repertoire to respond to parental prohibitions. Cries are used at first, and it is a month or more before the onset of physical rejection of prohibition. The children's prohibition reactions quickly change form. When the parent first uses verbal prohibition without physical constraint, the child ignores the prohibition in nonunderstanding. Then if the prohibition is made persistent, by repetition, louder voice, or physical constraint, it may be effectively heeded by the child. A standard part of this last scenario is the look from the child to the prohibiting parent, generally with body aligned in the direction of the prohibited object, or even still touching it. The child looks to the prohibitor but does not immediately withdraw. Prohibition sequences while the child continues to touch the prohibited object are marked by numerous replays of touch-prohibition-look rounds. The child's withdrawals, if they occur at all, are very short-term.

Two of the four children at nine months presented striking inhibitory behavior when such repeated prohibition cycles were prevalent. After an initial string of prohibitions and withdrawals, the child begins to approach the forbidden object and spontaneously inhibits a repetition of the prohibited action; the child looks at the prohibited object, arm aims out toward it, is self-impeded in midstream, then slung back and forth several times in approach-avoidance fashion, and withdrawn (CS was prone to touch a radiator that was often hot, and SR had a favorite rubber tree leaf).

For each of the children there next occurred what adults often describe (Lewis, 1963) as guilty, "permission requesting" looks to the parent, at first immediately after a prohibition the child has complied with in the middle of a renewed approach toward the object. Such looks were later used in anticipation of prohibition. Looks would be made in the parent's direction before any prohibition had been made in the immediate context, as the child prepared to touch what the parent felt he or she "knew" should not be touched. Concurrent with these anticipatory "permission requesting" looks were instances where the children reacted against prohibitions by using primitive physical means of rejection (arm waving, fretting sounds) which were at a distance for the first time from their "object"—the parental prohibition. Werner and Kaplan (1963) note that such progressive distancing between the child and the object of reference results in a shift from ego-bound things of action to ego-distance objects of contemplation. The primitive means of rejection once directly affecting the rejected thing (the child pushed things away) now represents that same pushing away or rejecting at a distance.

One other feature of prohibition reactions in this period is the "sneaky smile," where the child's actions superficially resemble earlier times when the prohibition was ignored out of nonunderstanding, except that now the child smiles at the parent in defiance and continues with the forbidden action after demonstrating prohibition compliance on earlier occasions. The children at this point, from ten months to eleven months, have begun to use primitive rejection and open defiance to reject constraint and prohibition.

Apart from the later development of the headshake, already described, this completes the major changes in the development of children's prohibition reactions and eventual comprehension. A noteworthy feature of this development is the progressive growth of the dyadic nature of prohibition. The child learns to react to the prohibition in two quite divergent ways: *compliance*, a measure of which, from the adult viewpoint, is nonrebellious withdrawal (passivity), and *defiance*, where the child comes to display an autonomy from the parent's wishes and exerts a control over his or her own behavior (activity). In learning the constraining nature of prohibitive acts vis-à-vis the prohibitive communication relationship, the child is learning to inhibit actions in the socially prescribed way. The child is also, however, learning how to inhibit others by constraining them via negative reactions to prohibitions. Prohibition is thus an area of early language comprehension where the realization of role reversibility so central to language becomes naturally emergent as the child attains active agency.

These observations complement those of Lewis (1963) and Spitz (1957) in marking out several intermediate steps of "understanding" the adults' negative prohibitions before the child ever begins to use negative symbols. Children first reject parental prohibitions at a distance by unconventional (nonsymbolic) physical means which they had previously utilized to physically, or directly, reject things. Spontaneous inhibitions of frequently forbidden acts by several children suggest the advent of an internalization of prohibition constraints that need not be current to be effective. This internalization is most obvious in the oft-observed phenomenon of gestural and verbal self-prohibition, a subsequent development of great importance for understanding the development of negation semantics.

The First Uses of Negation

We have already seen that the first meaning of conventional negation conveyed by children is rejection. Spitz (1957) claims that prohibition refusal is invariably the first use of negation, but the longitudinal studies of negation here do not support this claim. Several children first used negation to reject food at feeding, while others first used rejection negation in response to actions such as diaper changing, or in response to ritual questions such as "Do you want a drink?" Children's initial extensions of negative symbols to new contexts were confined to these variants of rejection—of action, object, prohibition, or question (also see Carter, 1974).

Soon after the establishment of rejection negation, the use of negation in self-prohibition appeared for all but one of the six children studied. Many careful observers of child development have noted early instances of negation, whether in gestural or verbal form, which occur when the child is about to touch or is touching a "forbidden object" (Bloom, 1973; Bruner, Caudill, and Ninio, 1976; Edwards, 1978; Escalona and Corman, 1971; Greenfield and Smith, 1976; Piaget, 1962; Spitz, 1957). Such a development is typically brief in duration.

All of the examples of "self-prohibition" cited in this literature involve acts which the child has been forbidden to do in the past, and what appears to occur is that the child issues a self-command to not do what he or she is about to do or is in the course of doing. As an operational definition, "self-prohibition" is somewhat of a misnomer for this behavior, because the child often touches the object anyway. The situation might be more accurately depicted by saying that the child is saying to self what the parent has said when the same thing has been done in the past. But what is the import of this observation?

Past interpretations of this phenomenon have been psychoanalytic in nature. Escalona and Corman (1971) remark that self-prohibition demonstrates that the child has "internalized something like a conscience." Spitz's (1957) interpretation of this type of negation follows that of Anna Freud (1952) in her discussion of preliminary phases of superego development. He suggests that the child has assumed the role of prohibitor and is engaged in the make-believe game of carrying out the forbidden action playing ego against self. Whether one accepts the "conscience" or "self-awareness" interpretation or neither, the use of "no-no" or headshake when in the midst of a forbidden action is a significant step on the way to the development of truth-functional negation. Whereas before, symbolic negation for the child has been a means of rejection, it has not involved *norms* of any sort but only the child's internal decisions of "I want this; I don't want this." By externally rehearsing the two roles of the prohibited, socially constrained act, the child is in sequence playing out the roles of self-as-action-proposer and other-as-action-constrainer. The awareness of this contrast is most striking when the child actually stops the action as if the parent had been the one to say "no" rather than self, as several observers have noted (see Greenfield and Smith, 1976).

Knowledge of this contrast between affirmative and negative messages is thus displayed; the child both initiates and negates the initiation. So whereas in the past the affirmative and negative were conveyed in the relationship between parent and child, it has now become transmuted to within the self.

Such transmutation has several important consequences. One is the internalization of conventional norms for permissible-nonpermissible acts, the other is the fact that this contrast of affirmation-negation is internally represented with the linguistic "no" as negative form. This may be compared with the cognitive interpretation of "egocentric speech" in preschoolers by Vygotsky (1962), who argues that such speech serves an external planning function which, when it diminishes in frequency and finally disappears, has in fact become internalized and mediates thought processes. The development of all higher mental functions, including concept and word meaning formation, is in Vygotsky's (1978) theory a result of the transmutation of the interpsychological, or, socially accomplished process to the intrapsychological, or, internally regulated process. In this theory, we view "self-prohibition" as a turning "inward" of the externally accomplished interpersonal negation of prohibition. "Self-prohibition" provides an external index, soon to disappear, of the child's conceptualization of an affirmative-negative contrast that incorporates external social norms extrinsic to the child's immediate need satisfaction. This internal binary contrast provides one of the conceptual bases for later negations of judgment involving truth-conditions for utterances.

The child later comes to use such truth-functional negation to express judgments on the use of language by others to predicate properties and existence of things. Edwards (1978) and Bateson (1968) have also presented proposals relevant to the phenomenon of self-prohibition and consonant with this Vygotskian orientation.

Edwards (1978) suggests that one important source of early word meanings for the child are the constraints that the adult imposes on the child's actions by social prohibition, as well as those imposed by the natural constraints of the physical world. He discusses cases where the child comes to use words in contexts which seem to derive from the use of the same words by the adult to impose constraints on the child's freedom of action. Several of these words are then extended to situations of constraint imposed by the physical world, such as when the child could not put building blocks together.

Edwards focuses on three realms of meaning: negation, possession, and several words "which in the adult grammar would be classified as Verbs and Adjectives." He shows the close connection between prohibitions and the child's use of rejection negation and of possession. "No," "no touch," "mummy's," and "don't," among other words and phrases, are all used by one of the children in what appear to be self-prohibitive contexts. The child proceeds to touch objects that have been prohibited by the parent in the past, such as her parents' books, glasses, pencil, and watch. When the child denotes "ownership" of the prohibited objects in her vocalizations, Edwards suggests that this is due to a primitive ownership notion based upon previous impositions that have conveyed the idea of "privileged access" to certain objects by others. One example clearly shows that these social constraints are basic to the child's conception of possession at this point (A is the child, S is the mother, E is the experimenter):

Language	*Context*
A: No touch.	[A looking at E's tape recorder]
S: No touch.	
No.	
That's correct.	
A: Mummy's tape.	[A pointing and looking at the tape recorder]

The tape recorder, A has been told many times before, is not to be touched. Alice's mother had never been to a recording session before and did not own a tape recorder, yet the child assimilated the forbidden object to her general schema of objects her mother possesses which are not to be touched.

Similar constraints are involved in A's use of the word "leave" in self-prohibitive contexts, which seems to derive from her parents' phrase "leave it" or "leave it alone," rather than being a Verb. In addition, words one might view out of context as Adjectives convey quite different meanings in context, such as "big" when two objects will not fit together (i.e., one of them is "too big"), "sharp" for a kitchen knife that is a forbidden object, and "stuck" when two objects will not go together as a child wishes. Most of these words involve physical constraints imposed on the child's actions.

So from a radically different perspective than the psychoanalytic account of Spitz (1957), Edwards (1978) draws the similar conclusion that constraints on the child's actions provide an early source of word meaning and that such a notion of contraint is psychologically real as a component of the child's early word meanings for negation stemming, ultimately, from the communicational contexts of social constraints on the child's actions.

Edwards' data highlight one area of early word meaning where the effect of social mores is pristine in form, since not all cultural subgroups prohibit children from touching the objects from which this child was restrained. With regard to the development of negation pragmatics, the child is learning sociocultural conventions for negation use. Obeying negation prohibition is a salient early affirmative context for negation.

The second proposal is Bateson's (1968), where, in tracing a speculative evolution of arbitrary denotative "naming" and truth-functional negation from an earlier iconic signal code, he suggests that "It appears likely that the evolution of the simple negative arose by introjection or imitation of the vis-à-vis, so that 'not' was somehow derived from 'don't' " (1968, p. 626).

Bateson does not mention self-prohibition, but the "don't" negation he describes as accomplished in interaction patterns when one organism proposes a pattern of action that another forbids with "don't" is what we we have called prohibition. Bateson proposes, following the passage cited above, that we "look for the evolutionary roots of the simple negative among the paradigms of interaction."

Though Bateson's hypothesis refers to processes of phylogenesis, we are clearly dealing with an analogous problem in tracing the ontogenetic sequence from the "no" that serves the "don't" function of rejecting, to the use of "no" and "not" for expressing truth-functional judgments. I have suggested that the constraint on actions serving as a source of early negation meaning becomes internally represented and that "no" as constraint provides the cognitive index, or, root negative conception necessary for the later use and understanding of truth-functional negation. The child's progress in establishing the metalinguistic nature of such mature negation is reflected in the progressive severing of the temporal link between topic and utterance of negation, which is accomplished through development in cognitive representation. Constraints on children's behavior provide the seeds for the semantics and pragmatics of negation.

References

Altmann, S. A. The structure of primate social communication. In S. A. Altmann (Ed.), *Social Communication Among Primates.* Chicago: University of Chicago Press, 1967, 325–362.

Bateson, G. Redundancy and coding. In T. A. Sebeok (Ed.), *Animal communication: Techniques of study and results of research.* Bloomington, Indiana: Indiana University Press, 1968, 614–626.

Bellugi, U. *The acquisition of the system of negation in children's speech.* Unpublished doctoral dissertation, Harvard University, 1967.

Bloom, L. *Language development: Form and function in emerging grammars.* Cambridge, Mass.: MIT Press, 1970.

———. *One word at a time: The use of single-word utterances before syntax.* Janua Linguarum, Ser. Minor: No. 154. The Hague: Mouton, 1973.

Brown, R. *A first language: The early stages.* Cambridge, Mass.: Harvard University Press, 1973.

Bruner, J. S. From communication to language—A psychological perspective. *Cognition*, 1974-75, 3, 255–287.

Bruner, J. S., Caudill, E., and Ninio, A. Language and experience: The John Dewey lecture. Paper presented at the University of London, October 29, 1975.

Bühler, C. and Hetzer, H. *Testing children's development from birth to school age.* Translated by H. Beaumont. London: Allen & Unwin, 1935.

Carter, A. L. *The development of communication in the presensorimotor period.* Unpublished doctoral dissertation, University of California, Berkeley, 1974.

Cherry, L. The role of adults' requests for clarifications in the language development of children. In R. O. Freedle (Ed.), *Discourse processing: Multidisciplinary perspectives* vol. 2. Hillsdale, N.J.: Abex Publishing Co., 1979.

Cromer, R. F. The development of language and cognition: The cognition hypothesis. In B. Foss (Ed.), *New perspectives in child development.* London: Penguin Books, 1974, 184–252.

Darwin, C. *The expression of the emotions in man and animals.* New York: The Philosophical Library, 1955, originally published 1872.

De Villiers, J. G. and Flusberg, H. B. T. Some facts one simply cannot deny. *Journal of Child Language,* 1975, 2, 279–286.

Dummett, M. *Frege: Philosophy of language.* New York: Harper & Row, 1973.

Edwards, D. Constraints on actions: A source of early meanings in child language. In I. Markova (Ed.), *The social context of language.* New York: Wiley, 1978.

Escalona, S. K. and Corman, H. H. The impact of mother's presence upon behavior: The first year. *Human Development,* 1971, 14, 2–15.

Freud, A. A connection between the states of negativism and of emotional surrender. *International Journal of Psychoanalysis,* 1952, 33.

Garvey, C. Contingent queries and their relations in discourse. In E. O. Keenan (Ed.), *Studies in developmental pragmatics.* New York: Academic Press, 1978.

Gearhart, M. *The cooperative construction of social episodes: A developmental analysis of role play in peer dyads.* Unpublished doctoral dissertation, Graduate Center, City University of New York, 1979.

Givon, T. Negation in language: Pragmatics, Function, Ontology. In Cole, P. (Ed.), *Syntax and semantics. Pragnatics* vol. 9, New York: Academic Press, 1978.

Gopnik, A. The development of non-nominal expressions in 1-2 year-olds: Why the first words aren't about things. Paper presented at the *First International Congress for the Study of Child Language.* Tokyo, August 7-12, 1978.

Greenfield, P. M. and Smith, J. H *The structure of communication in early language development.* New York: Academic Press, 1976.

Harrison, B. *Meaning and structure: An essay in the philosophy of language.* New York: Harper & Row, 1972.

Jakobson, R. Motor signs for 'yes' and 'no.' *Language in Society,* 1972, 1, 91–96.

Jespersen, O. *Negation in English and other languages.* Copenhagen, 1917.

Kant, I. *Immanuel Kant's critique of pure reason.* Translated by N. K. Smith. London: MacMillan, 1963, originally published 1787.

Keenan, E. O., Schieffelin, B. and Platt, M. Prospositions across speakers and utterances. *Paper and Reports on Child Language Development,* 1976, 12, 127–143.

Labov, W. and Fanshel, D. *Therapeutic discourse: Psychotherapy as conservation.* New York: Academic Press, 1977.

Leopold, W. F. *Speech development of a bilingual child: A linguist's record. Vocabulary growth in the first two years,* vol. 1. Evanston, Ill.: Northwestern University Press, 1939.

———. *Speech development of a bilingual child: A linguist's record. Grammar and general problems in the first two years,* vol. 3. Evanston, Ill.; Northwestern University Press, 1949.

Lewis, M. M. *Language, thought and personality in infancy and childhood.* New York: Basic Books, 1963.

Marshall, J. C. Can humans talk? In J. Morton (Ed.), *Biological and social factors in psycholinguistics.* London: Logos Press, 1970, 24–52.

McNeill, D. *The acquisition of language.* New York: Harper & Row, 1970.

McNeill, D. and McNeill, N. B. What does a child mean when he says "no"? In E. Zale (Ed.), *Proceedings of the conference on language and language behavior.* New York: Appleton-Century, 1968.

Miller, G. A. Lexical meaning. In J. F. Kavanagh and W. Strange (Eds.), *Speech and language in the laboratory, school and clinic.* Cambridge, Mass.: MIT Press, 1978, 394–428.

Miller, G. A. and Johnson-Laird, P. N. *Language and perception.* Cambridge, Mass.: Harvard University Press, 1976.

Nelson, K. Structure and strategy in learning to talk. *Monog. Soc. Res. Child Dev.* 1–2, Serial No. 149, 1973, 38.

————. Cognitive development and the acquisition of concepts. In R. C. Anderson, R. J. Spiro, and W. E. Montague (Eds.), *Schooling and the acquisition of knowledge.* Hillsdale, N.J.: Lawrence Erlbaum Associates, 1977, 215–239.

Ninio, A. and Bruner, J. S. The achievement and antecedents of labelling. *Journal of Child Language,* 1978, 5, 1–15.

Pea, R. D. *The development of negation in early child language.* Unpublished doctoral dissertation, University of Oxford, England, 1978.

————. Logic in early child language. *Ann. N.Y. Acad. Science,* forthcoming.

Piaget, J. *Play, dreams, and imitation in childhood.* Translated by C. Gattegno and F. M. Hodgson. New York: Norton, 1962.

Quine, W. V. O. *Word and object:* Cambridge, Mass.: MIT Press, 1960.

————. *The roots of reference.* New York: Open Court, 1974.

Ruke-Dravina, V. The emergence of affirmation and negation in child language: some universal and language-restricted characteristics. In K. Ohnesorg (Ed.), *Colloquium Paedolinguisticum.* The Hague: Mouton, 1972, 221–241.

Ryan, J. Early language development: Towards a communicational analysis. In M. P. M. Richards (Ed.), *The integration of a child into a social world.* London: Cambridge University Press, 1974, 185–213.

Schank, R. C. and Abelson, R. P. *Scripts, plans, goals, and understanding.* Hillsdale, N.J.: Lawrence Earlbaum Associate, 1977.

Searle, J. R. *Speech acts: An essay in the philosophy of language.* Cambridge: Cambridge University Press, 1969.

————. A classification of illocutionary acts. *Language in Society,* 1976, 5, 1–23.

Sebeok, T. A. Coding in the evolution of signalling behavior. *Behavioral Science,* 1962, 7, 430–442.

Shantz, C. V. The development of social cognition. In E. M. Hetherington (Ed.), *Review of child development research* vol. 5. Chicago: University of Chicago Press, 1977.

Spitz, R. A. *No and yes: On the genesis of human communication.* New York: International Universities Press, 1957.

Steffenson, M. S. Satisfying inquisitive adults: Some simple methods of answering *yes/no* questions. *Journal of Child Languages,* 1978, 5, 221–236.

Stokes, W. Children's replies to requests for clarification: An opportunity for hypothesis testing. Paper presented at the *First annual Boston University conference on language development,* October, 1976.

Volterra, V. and Antinucci, F. Negation in child language: A pragmatic study. In E. O. Keenan (Ed.), *Studies in developmental pragmatics.* New York: Academic Press, 1978.

Vygotsky, L. S. *Mind in society: The development of higher psychological processes.* Edited by M. Cole, V. John-Steiner, S. Scribner, and E. Souberman. Cambridge, Mass.: Harvard University Press, 1978.

————. *Thought and language.* Translated and edited by E. Hanfmann and G. Vakar. Cambridge, Mass.: MIT Press, 1962, originally published 1934.

Wason, P. C. The contexts of plausible denial. *Journal of Verbal Learning & Verbal Behavior,* 1965, 4, 7–11.

Werner, H. and Kaplan, B. *Symbol formation: An organismic-developmental approach to language and the expression of thought.* New York: Wiley, 1963.

Wilden, A. *Structure and function: Essays in communication and exchange.* London: Tavistock, 1972.

Wittgenstein, L. *Philosophical investigations* 3rd ed. Translated by G. E. M. Anscombe. Oxford: Blackwell & Mott, 1958.

8

The Maintenance of Conversation
Roger Brown

Jerome Bruner's work in developmental psycholinguistics (see Bruner, 1974, 1975; Ninio and Bruner, 1978; Ratner and Bruner, 1978) has concentrated on what had largely been disregarded in earlier work: preverbal behavior; preverbal behavior in structured games; preverbal behavior construed in an illocutionary way, as "speech acts" of a sort (Searle, 1969). No one can gainsay the intrinsic interest of his analyses. Of course, the subject matter itself is banal just as child speech is banal, but he has taught us to see the finely articulated patterns, thereby making childwatching interesting in still one more period of the total span.

From his analyses, it has always been clear that some aspects of adult speech are practiced before speech itself: turn taking, role switching, attention holding, and so on. For the most part, however, what is practiced in infancy has seemed most indubitably relevant to the conversational skills of adulthood, which skills they quite precisely parallel. Interesting arguments have been made that the games of infancy are, in various ways, also necessary preparation for the learning of semantics and grammar. But, perhaps because this latter learning is still largely mysterious, the case for preverbal propaedeutics has not been very convincing. Ratner and Bruner themselves say: "But, in fact, there have been virtually no studies done to explore in detail how such rule-learning (in game-like play) affects the child's mastery of language" (1978, p. 591).

Partly as a result of Bruner's stimulus, the last few years have seen many inquiries into the conversational or discourse aspects of developmental psycholinguistics. Some of us breast-fed on transformational grammar and weaned to Melba toast semantics have not been convinced that the study of pragmatics and presuppositions and the parental "register" would help much with the central problems of language learning. Indeed some, more cynical than anyone we know, have suggested that discourse problems were

The research for this paper was supported by National Science Foundation Grant No. GSOC-7309150.

a kind of diversion to keep everybody occupied until greater insights were granted into grammar and semantics. Working, in a rather discontinuous way, on early childhood conversation, I have come to believe that what is learned from a study of conversation may help us to learn how some aspects of semantics and grammar are learned. But all I can offer are a few hypotheses and these, I am afraid, suggest a process of greater complexity in psycholinguistic learning than we are accustomed to or know much about.

Let me take up the descriptive process at about the point where Jerome Bruner most usually drops it and see what clarification can be gained. The age I have picked is thirty months—because we[1] have two-hour audio transcriptions of twenty-one children when each was approximately that age. The transcriptions were all made in closely comparable circumstances: the child and his or her mother in a large playroom together with Professors Jill and Peter de Villiers and an assortment of picture books; small toy animals, persons, and furniture; puppets and cans of colored playdough. Nothing to do but play, with observers under glass and audio equipment concealed. The transcribed records are the kind we usually make: every grammatical jot and title carefully recorded, with actions and objects loosely described insofar as they are relevant to the title. It was almost a figure-ground flip flop of the, primarily video and incidentally audio, records of the Bruner team.

We created, of course, a particular kind of social situation. The mother knows that the object is to get the child to talk, and the child probably knows it too. Furthermore, the mother is very experienced at doing just this, and Jill and Peter de Villiers are not just experienced at it; they are wizards at it. Mother and the de Villiers constituted an "adult committee" with the common goal of engaging the child in conversation—using toy props.

The children were taped at thirty months primarily because that was the point at which our colleague, Professor Jerome Kagan, was prepared to make them available to us. Thirty months may seem a little too old to make connection with Bruner's studies, which often focus on the six-month to fifteen-month span. I judge that there is an overlap, however, between his most rapidly developing children and our least rapidly developing children, since he cites utterances of one and two words and our baseline boy, CC, had a mean-length-of-utterance (MLU) of exactly 1.01: scarcely ever more than one morpheme-per-utterance from CC.

1. The twenty-one children of this study were selected from Boston-area middle-class male and female children by Professor Jerome Kagan, whose interests centered on the first thirty months. Of course, my interest and that of Professors Jill and Peter de Villiers were very high in children of thirty months, and so we agreed with Professor Kagan to make standardized two-hour transcripts at the thirty month age. Eventually, we plan to put together what we have learned with what he has learned. I wish to express my appreciation to Professor Kagan and to Professors Jill and Peter de Villiers, who did the hard work of making the transcriptions.

An incidental goal of our data collection was to demonstrate, once and for all, that chronological age is no good as an index of general psycholinguistic development. With age constant at thirty months, the twenty-one youngsters, studied in closely comparable circumstances, registered MLUs (calculated by the de Villiers and checked for reliability) that ranged from 1.0 to 3.78. In Brown's (1973) stage terms—that is, a range from stage I to stage IV—a psycholinguistic climb accomplished by Eve between 18 and 28 months, by Adam between 27 and 34 months, and by Sarah between 27 and 35 months. In short, as the twenty-one transcripts make dramatically clear, individual differences in rate of psycholinguistic development are, in the early years, enormous. But to believe that, you must first believe that MLU is an index of interesting psycholinguistic abilities. To lend credibility to this view, we have tables 1 and 2 which constitute the first six statements of, respectively CC, whose MLU was 1.01, and AR, whose MLU was 3.78.

TABLE 1

The First Six Utterances of CC (MLU = 1.01)
Together with Accompanying Adult Speech

CC	Adult
	"Do you want me to shoot you?" (Mother) [with C's toy gun]
"Yeah."	
	"Shall I shoot them?" (Mother) "No, not me. Not me." (Jill)
"Yeah."	
"Gun." [looking for other gun]	
	"What?" (Mother)
"Gun."	
	"Your gun is right over here." (Mother)
"Ah."	
	"Ah. You ought to put your hat on. Do you want to put it on?" (Mother)
"No."	

Probably you feel that there is a substantial difference between the sequences of table 1 and 2? Of course AR says a bit more than CC, but not so very much; her Adult Committee says a great deal more, but I think the strong impression that AR is developed far beyond CC in basic psycholinguistic knowledge does not, in these brief samples, derive from anybody's length-of-utterance. The difference that is physiognomically most evident is

TABLE 2

The First Six Utterances of AR (MLU = 3.68)
Together with Accompanying Adult Speech

AR	Adult
	"What's this one, Anna?" (Mother)
"A rabbit."	
	"That's a nice doll. What's she got on, Anna?" (Mother)
"Boots."	
	"Boots, Anna. That's right." (Mother) "Think we can make him stand up? Think he stands up? Shall we try?" (Peter) "Is he gonna stand up, Anna?" (Mother) "See if you can make him stand up." (Peter)
"Me see if he can stand up." [daddy doll falls]	
	"Oh! Kaboom! Can you tell Peter who's coming to see you today?" (Mother)
"Momma and Poppa."	
	"Momma and Poppa. Where they coming from, Anna?" (Mother)
"Birmingham."	
	"Let's pay hide-and-seek with this peanut. Now I'll keep my eyes closed. Can you tell me where it is?" (Peter)
"They're open." [his eyes]	

in the level of communication. CC answers explicit Yes/No questions with "Yeah" or "No," and that is about all that passes between him and his Adult Committee. AR's Committee asserts a good deal and presupposes far more, and in doing so, they shape six multi-faceted slots for her contributions. Each one that she makes is a key well-fitted to its slot and so suggests that she understands all that went into the shaping of it. One has the impression that a great deal passes back and forth; and AR gives evidence of understanding complex matters.

Above all, perhaps, one feels the continuity of the conversation is preserved across AR's sequence. There are no jarring *nonsequiturs* of the sort found in CC's record between his "Yeah" and "Gun" and between his mother's "Your gun is right over here" and his "Ah" followed by her "Ah." Please excuse my lock-and-key metaphor for communication and the others

I am still to use. The metaphor is a useful tool when what is eventually to be asserted can make little sense without preliminary familiar approximations, and that is the case for the not very usual sense I want shortly to give to "communication."

Grammar and Semantics as Evidence of Communication

If you were to read sample pages from our twenty-one transcripts in the order of increasing child MLU, and so presumed psycholinguistic development, I believe that the change you would find most salient is in the average length of the episodes that seem to maintain conversational continuity. In CC's records, most of the child's utterances seem to arise either from independent impulses or, at most, from a single immediately prior *Yes/No* question or a direct imperative. At the other extreme, continuous episodes often run to twenty or more child utterances, and when a complex construction task is undertaken with the playdough, one often has the impression of unbroken conversational continuity across many pages of transcript.

Impressions of the data were the starting point, but I have gone well beyond that to the point of writing an explicit manual for scoring the mean-length-of-episode in each transcript and have myself scored all twenty-one, using that manual. The manual, though sixty pages long and very boring, is not yet sufficiently redundant or precise to teach a naïve judge to score reliably. Professor Jill de Villiers has used it with her undergraduate course "Psycholinguistic Methods" and found the reliabilities to be quite low. I am confident that they can be elevated to respectable levels by the usual methods of discussing differences and multiplying examples, but it has not been the thing I was most interested in doing so far. It is the conception more than the potential research tool that interests me. Nevertheless, having done many months of work, I would like to report the twenty-one MLEs and their relations to corresponding MLUs (*rho* is .73 with $p < .001$) since any reader of this paper will be sophisticated enough to withhold some credence until the MLE scoring system has been further developed.

The conception of an unbroken episode is distinct from several related ideas in the analysis of discourse or conversation and so needs to be clearly explained as well as accounted for. Only a child utterance can initiate an episode, in my scoring, and only a child utterance can terminate one. A single child utterance defines a minimal episode and it is always scored dichotomously as relevant or not-relevant with reference to prior, contemporaneous, and subsequent speech by either a member of the Adult Committee or of the child as well as reference to all recorded aspects of the nonverbal situation. An unbroken succession of relevant child utterances, however much adult speech or action intervenes between, constitutes an epi-

TABLE 3

The Relation between MLU and MLE for Twenty-one Children
and for Adam, Eve, and Sarah at Stages I and IV

Child	MLU	MLE	Child	MLU	MLE
CC	1.01	.49	Eve I	1.68	.66
JG	2.18	3.66	Sarah I	1.73	.90
EO	2.18	3.68	Adam I	2.06	.94
JM	2.28	4.31			
SB	2.43	13.00			
MR	2.51	9.16			
JA	2.61	12.33			
MG	2.74	11.22			
JE	2.88	10.44			
LB	2.90	9.50			
TO	2.93	5.52			
JN	3.05	7.77			
ME	3.08	9.80			
AL	3.14	22.60			
RS	3.26	11.37			
AT	3.33	12.00			
KL	3.48	10.85			
ML	3.51	17.25			
TM	3.53	16.50	Eve IV	4.06	26.75
EW	3.58	24.40	Adam IV	4.06	15.91
AR	3.78	20.50	Sarah IV	4.10	20.70

sode, and the episode's length is the number of such utterances. The number can be less than one because even a single child utterance may be scored as non-relevant. With the first child utterance scored as non-relevant, an episode ends and a new one begins with the next child utterance. And so if all this is intelligently done, the MLE of a transcript is an index of the stretch of conversation across which the child may be said to *hold up his end*.

Adult utterances are meticulously studied because they provide the most important data by which to judge the relevance of the child's contribution, but adult utterances are not themselves scored and that is why an adult can neither initiate nor terminate an episode. I treated the adult speech in this way because it seemed clear that these adults never were and never would be at a loss to pick up the thread of a conversation with a thirty-month-old child. It was essential to define a discontinuity independently of the adults so that we shall eventually be able to see how they respond when the child "drops the ball." A major goal of the research is to learn what adults do to repair a break in conversational continuity.

We have long known quite a bit about immediate adult responses to telegraphic sentences (Brown and Bellugi, 1964) and ungrammatical sentences (Brown and Hanlon, 1970), and these seem to be quite automatic and lawful, though their instructional value is in doubt. When a child snaps a thread in discourse, the adult experience is different. The break, if it is a clear one, is experienced consciously and efforts are made to do something about it. This is especially clear in the kinds of situations we set up where the whole purpose of three skilled adults was to manufacture verbal and nonverbal situations in which a thirty-month-old child would find it possible fully to participate. I wanted, in short, to define interruptions solely in terms of the child's speech so that adult reactions to the breaks should be independent data. While the research is not sufficiently advanced to make a full report here of these reactions, I will use them as a source of hypotheses since they are, of course, data quite directly related to the problem of the possible effects of conversational skills on grammar and semantics.

Some students of discourse have been interested in what might be called "staying with the topic" (see, Keenan and Schieffelin, 1976) and that does sound very much like maintaining conversational continuity. Operationally, however, the two are quite distinct. My scoring permits a change of topic without an interruption of continuity. In the exchanges of table 2, the first topic concerns a doll, the second an impending visit from grandma and grandpa ("Momma and Poppa"), and the third initiates a game of hide-and-seek. All three changes are made by the adults, but there is no sign in AR's responses that she fails to follow them and very positive signs that she perfectly understands the shifts. As in more complex conversations, if the new topic is duly announced and within the range of shared understandings, there is no lapse of communication. At a later point, we shall have a set of examples of communication lapses and it will be clear that they are a very different thing.

THE SCORING OF ONE RESPONSE

My definition of "communication," in the kind of conversation under consideration, derives directly from the kinds of data one uses in judging whether a child utterance is relevant or not. Allow me still to defer a general definition until I explain the scoring of one utterance: AR's "A rabbit" in table 2. The single immediately antecedent adult utterance is included because it is the most important source of data on the relevance of the response. In talking about the scoring of this and later utterances, I shall invoke ideas identical to or similar to ideas used by Ervin-Tripp and Mitchell-Kernan (1977), Dore (1978), Garvey (1975), Gordon and Lakoff (1971), Labov and Fanshel (1975). I arrived at the rules of my scoring

manual by studying the work of these and other authors and then by a
detailed analysis of five records from our total of twenty-one (AR, JM,
ELK, LB, and CC). What I sought to do was first to identify intuitively
points where communication (in some vague sense) seemed clearly to
break down. And then I used everything I know about grammar, semantics,
and pragmatics to identify the conditions of such breaks so that they might
be identified without recourse to intuition. The examples I will use in this
paper can be so scored and are not among those cases where reliability is
hard to establish.

My notion of relevance begins with the concept of presupposition.
It can be said at once that the maximally clear sense of "presupposition,"
according to which presupposition (p) must be true if the proposition presupposing it is to have any truth-value at all, can almost never be invoked
in our materials and so must regrettably be set to one side. We shall instead
be concerned with pragmatic presuppositions which describe the contexts in
which a sentence can be "felicitously" uttered. Most linguists when they discuss pragmatic presuppositions still talk about semantic relations between
sentences or propositions. I shall not want to do that (nor, indeed, do most
nonlinguists who have written about presuppositions) but will instead
understand presuppositions in a psychological sense which is close to that of
Stalnaker (1977). In general, a child's utterance will be scored as relevant
if it gives some evidence that he presupposes or takes for granted the existence of felicitous conditions which are also presupposed by his adult interlocutors.

We must begin with the mother's "What's this one, Anna?" The sentence
is a question, and a question like this presupposes certain felicity conditions
which are roughly but clearly enough set down in table 4. It may be
assumed that the mother knows when to invoke a simple question of this
type and so, perhaps, that the four conditions listed under "a" in table 4 are
believed by her to obtain. Since we can be sure that the mother already
knows that the reference is a rabbit, condition "2" under "a" is violated.
We must suppose, then, that this is no true question at all, but rather a kind
of quiz or what Labov and Fanshel (1977) label a "request for display."
The mother is not asking for information she lacks, but asking that AR display knowledge the mother almost surely knows that AR has.

The crucial point in my definition of communication in exchanges like
this is that a relevant response from the child will inform or reassure the
adult that the child shares with the adult certain background beliefs, the
felicity conditions of the adult sentence. AR does so, but how does she do
so? By bringing into play her knowledge of rules of grammar and a rule of
reference. The mother's question is a Wh question which calls for a specific
noun phrase (NP), and that is what AR delivers: not a sentence, not a
command or a question or "yes" or "no," but a NP. Furthermore, we may
guess from the mother's unperturbed reaction, a NP that correctly names
the indicated referent.

TABLE 4

Felicity Conditions for A Wh Question (a) and
A Parallel Request for Display (b)

a. Felicity conditions for the question: "What is this one, Anna?"
   1. The question-raising referent is in the focus of attention of both the questioner and the respondent.
   2. The questioner does not know the answer.
   3. The questioner has reason to want the answer.
   4. The questioner believes the respondent can supply the answer.

b. Felicity conditions for a parallel request for display item.
   1. The question-raising referent is in the focus of attention of both the questioner and the respondent.
   2. The questioner already knows the answer.
   3. The questioner is not sure that the respondent knows the answer.
   4. The questioner wants to display the fact that the respondent knows the answer.

We are, of course, thoroughly accustomed to think of grammar and semantics as accomplishing communication in the sense of the content of an assertion, a question, or a command. We are, I think, less accustomed to think of semantics and grammar as responsible also for communication of the impression that the speaker shares with his interlocutor a mass of background information. This sharing, which can usually be taken for granted between adults, cannot between adult and child, and its communication is a matter of great importance.

What of the fact that "What's this one, Anna?" is not, pragmatically, a question but rather a quiz masquerading as a question as quizzes do all our lives long? AR could show that she knows that she is being quizzed, and some of our twenty-one children sometimes did. She need only have said: "*You* know!" If she had done so, that would not have interrupted the continuity of the episode but would only make more specific for her mother just what beliefs, or felicity conditions, it is that the two share. However, the mother seems to feel no need for reassurance on this specific point, and a NP is a satisfactorily comprehending response from a compliant child who consents to be put on display—as most do.

This is not the end of the evidence given by AR's response that she shares certain background understandings with her mother. From the grammatical point of view, the particular question asked by specifying "this one" calls for a NP that is a count noun and not a mass noun. The NP that AR provides is marked as a count noun by the indefinite article "a." And there is more to the semantics that is reassuring than the fact that the name given suits the referent. We all participate in an understanding about questions of this sort which probably would never have occurred to me had not one of our twenty-one children often violated it (JM). The name requested is expected to be on the level of abstraction that Rosch and her colleagues

(Rosch et al., 1976) have called the "basic object" level. Had AR responded: "A toy" or "An animal," as JM sometimes did, I think we may confidently guess that her mother would have come back, as did JM's mother, with: "What *kind* of a toy?" in a somewhat irritated tone. Violation of this semantic presupposition seems to be rare and conveys either a strong sense of resistance or a rather alarming kind of incomprehension.

It is my belief that we have created in our twenty-one two-hour sessions a kind of conversation in which the least part of communication is the content of what is explicitly said. In the present concrete case, no adult really needed to be told that the referent was a rabbit. What might the adults, and the mother in particular, have been interested in? In the information, or probably simply the confirmation, that she and her daughter shared certain important background beliefs, that they were in respect of the beliefs tested by this exchange "of one mind." The conversational situation we have created does not seem to me to be rare or artificial. Between adults and small children it is a very usual thing, only slightly exaggerated here. Most parents are motivated to interact with their children from infancy on in order to initiate and maintain communication. This communication, both non-verbal and verbal, seems always to have the same two functions. It serves as a running check on the child's progress in building an apperceptive mass shared with his family—his psycholinguistic socialization as it were. At the same time, the adult tries to add a pebble to the pile. Grammar, semantics, and pragmatics relate to conversation, in the first place, in that the state of a child's competence or knowledge in all these areas is continually tested in conversation by his or her ability to make relevant contributions. It must be from the child's performance in "conversations" (which may be non-verbal as well as verbal) that the adult is enabled to form an approximate conception of what the child shares with adults in the culture.

ANALYSIS OF COMPLIANCE WITH AN INDIRECT REQUEST

There would not be enough space in a single paper to explicate even all of one page of one transcript. Nevertheless, I should like to provide enough samples to give a rough sense of the scope of the scoring manual. Let us, to that end, move from AR's first response in table 2 to her fourth. The full exchange reads:

"Can you tell Peter who's coming to see you today?"   (Mother)

AR: "Momma and Poppa."

"Momma" and "Poppa" are to be understood as "Grandma" and "Grandpa." At first glance one might take the mother's question to be a Yes-No question since it has that form. However, we are in this exchange involved with a sentence that has a pragmatic intent very different from its grammatical form. I think Labov and Fanshel (1977) have analyzed such cases with a special elegance that I would like to appropriate. Let us, therefore, admit at once that the sentence: "Can you tell Peter who's coming to see you today?" is not a Yes-No question at all but rather an indirect request. As an indirect request, it can be derived, in a way that Labov and Fanshel have shown us, from the felicity conditions of a direct request.

The derivation of indirect requests begins with the felicity conditions for direct requests, of which a crude but easily understood version appears in table 5. There are always alternative indirect forms, but the following are reasonable derivations from the four conditions listed.

1. I don't think Peter knows who's coming to see you today. (need)
2. I'll bet you have not told Peter who's coming to see you today. (need for the request)
3. Can you tell Peter who's coming to see you today? (ability)
4. Would you tell Peter who's coming to see you today? (willingness)

TABLE 5

Felicity Conditions for a Direct Request Such as
"Tell Peter Who's Coming to See You Today."

1. There should be some reason or point to the action. (need)
2. The child should be unlikely to perform the action unless requested. (need for the request)
3. The child should be able to perform the action. (ability)
4. The child should be willing to perform the action. (willingness)

The mature speaker of English knows that none of the above has the intended significance suggested by its grammatical form. It would be a rude joke to answer number one above. "No, in fact, he doesn't"; or number two, "Quite right, I haven't." It would be resistance or unaccountable ignorance to answer number three, "No, I can't"; and rank insubordination to answer number four, "No, I won't." AR, of course, does none of these but understands perfectly, as do almost all of the twenty-one children almost always, that the pragmatic force of the seeming question is directive or imperative. The matrix sentence is a Yes-No question, but it contains an embedded Wh question which dictates grammatically that the answer ought to be a NP and that is what AR provides.

The word "who" in the question and the VP "coming to see you" indicate that the NP should be "+ animate" and probably "+ human." From AR's mother's quiet satisfaction with the answer "Momma and Poppa," we gather that AR has got it right semantically. There is no possibility of enumerating all of the background information that AR's answer attests to— but it includes knowledge of the grammar of embedded sentences, the felicity conditions for direct requests, and the nature of indirect requests as well as, of course, such nonlinguistic things as memory for recent information. Her answer is not a diagnostically specific index that she shares any particular belief with her mother, however, but is rather consistent with the entire assemblage and in violation of nothing. It is generally the case that a child's utterance is relevant to all of the immediate conversational background or else is quite totally in contravention of everything. In this latter case, it is usually difficult for an adult to pinpoint the problem and difficult, therefore, to make useful repairs.

THE IRRELEVANT UTTERANCE

Irrelevant utterances are, of course, produced by thirty-month-old children, and it is time to look at a collection of them. In table 6 we have a set of child responses that were scored as irrelevant, and you can probably see that they are, even though I have only reviewed a few of the scoring rules contained in the manual. In advance of a close study of data, one would reasonably think that the breaks in episode continuity, by providing parents with an opportunity to make instant repairs, would constitute the most important link between discourse and the basic psycholinguistic competencies. Presented with a child utterance which reveals that some essential belief or knowledge is not shared, that the apperceptive mass is in some respect defective, why should not the parent make good the defect? Close study of relevant data reveals a range of possibilities.

Some Errors Can be Diagnosed and Corrected In table 6, we have the adult question "What's that?" asked about a toy sink, and the answer

TABLE 6

Examples of Irrelevant Responses Which Break Episode Continuity

Adult	Child
"Jason, would you like to put a pampers on?"	"Dat?" [doll's shoe]
"What must I make you with that?"	"Yeah."
"Ask the man if he wants some raisins."	"Some raisins."
"What's that?"	"Dishwasher." [actually a sink]
"Who do you think I can see in the box?	"Mirror."
"Which is your ball?"	"Drink copee."
"Why don't you put the cars up there and then make them go down again?"	"What?"
"Oh you don't have to be shy."	"Hi, Mommy."
"What color's that?"	"Still doggy."

"Dishwasher." In fact, these modern-day privileged children almost all called the toy sink a dishwasher. A few adults corrected the children with "No, it's a sink," and the correction may or may not have had its intended effect. However, surprisingly few parents bothered to make even this correction. The mistake seemed understandable and who knows whether in the World of Tomorrow it may not be the case that all kitchen sinks have dishwashers. Irrelevancies with so clear a cause were, in any case, rare.

The Cause of Irrelevancy May be Diagnosed but Correction May Be Difficult   This is a common case. Jason probably did not want to put a Pampers on because he was otherwise engaged. Inattention, boredom, whimsy are ever-present as possible explanations of irrelevancy. In such cases, our twenty-one mothers and, of course, the de Villiers knew better than to persist. A young child will not be pushed. He has not learned to see the need of it.

The question "Who do you think I see in the box?" elicited the response "Mirror" whereas it ought to have elicited "Yourself" or "Yourself in the

TABLE 7

An Extended Effort to Understand SB's Problem with the Mirror in the Box

SB	Adult
	"Come and see this box. This is a mystery box. Who do you see?" (Peter)
"Nothing." [box contains mirror]	
	"Nothing? Who do you see in the box?" (Peter)
"Nothing."	
	"Isn't that a funny box? What's in there?" (Peter)
"There's nothing."	
	"Who do I see in the box? Who do you think I can see in the box?" (Peter)
"What?"	
	"Who do you think I can see?" (Peter)
"Mirror's in it."	
	"Who can I see?" (Peter)
"Mirror's in it."	
	"Mommy in there? Come over here and see if you can see who's in the box. Who do you see?" (Peter)
"Mirror." "Where's raisins?"	

12-sentence interlude on raisins

"Who does the doggy see in the box?
Who do you think the doggy sees?"
(Peter)

"Mirror."

"Who does the kitty see?" (Peter)

"A mirror."

"Who does the bunny see?" (Peter)

"A mirror."

"Who does the man see?" (Peter)

"A mirror."

"Who do you see in the box?" (Peter)

"Mirror."

"I think you can see yourself, right?"
(Peter)

"Yeah."

"What's that? What's in there?" (Peter)

"A mirror dere."

General exhaustion

mirror." In a miscalculation rare for him, Peter de Villiers seems to have thought that this little misunderstanding might be cleared up then and there. Table 7 records the long, sad record of his efforts and ultimate failure. An adult less experienced than Dr. de Villiers might have tried a similar inquiry and correction when the question "What color's that?" elicited "Still doggy." No notion of color apparently. Why not try a few lessons? You are not advised to try unless you have a lot of time and a compliant child.

The Cause of Irrelevancy Can Usually Not Be Diagnosed or Easily Set Right   Four of the utterances in table 6 are grammatically or semantically or pragmatically complex and elicit responses that indicate lack of understanding somewhere in these boundless domains:

Adult	Child
"What must I make you with that?"	"Yeah."
"Ask the man if he wants some raisins."	"Some raisins."
"Which is your ball?"	"Drink copee."
"Why don't you put the cars up there and then make them go down again?"	"What?"

In none of the above cases is it exactly clear, usually not even roughly clear, what the child does not understand. And in no case has anyone, whether parent or psycholinguist, any clear idea of a useful response to make.

Episodic breaks of this most difficult kind were in the vast majority in our transcripts. There were several kinds of reaction that our Adult Committee made to such drastic *non sequiturs*. The most common was in the interest of resuming mental contact as quickly as possible. The child's utterance, whatever it might be, was unquestioningly accepted and the responding adult then made an effort at weaving a context around it which might be what the child had in mind or might, in any case, appeal. The attitude reminds one of a benevolent professor who accepts any student question or comment and then tries to make sense of it. At any cost, one does not wound but keeps things going.

In some ways, the adult confronted with an unintelligible child response is in a situation like that of a psychiatrist speaking with a thought-disordered schizophrenic patient. Everything the patient says is, in strictly linguistic non-semantic respects, in good order, but the utterance in context is unintelligible. My impression is that there are three difficulties: 1. Patient and doctor do not share the background information that would render the patient's utterance comprehensible; 2. The patient is not aware that this problem exists and will usually deny it; and 3. Neither participant knows exactly what background is critical, but unshared. In such circumstances, wise psychiatrists do not push the patient to make himself clear then and there. However, devoted psychiatrists who are also gifted at cryptanalysis work in a necessarily discontinuous and indirect fashion at gaining the background they need, and occasionally they become able to decode a given patient's speech.

Children are not schizophrenics, and maturation and general experience no doubt do much to fill in what is lacking in background. Nevertheless, my impression is that parents do learn quite a lot from conversational breakdowns with their children and that they endeavor to fill in the knowledge gaps that are suggested, but I think they do it discontinuously with small efforts dispersed over long periods of time; this makes it very difficult to isolate what they do and to study its effects. One thing I am sure of, from these twenty-one transcripts and my longitudinal records of Adam, Eve, and Sarah, is that just as children will not be pushed, parents will not be discouraged. Put off for the moment by an undiagnosably irrelevant response, they retreat only to return to the attack at a better time. Again and again in the twenty-one transcripts a particular sentence type elicits a *non sequitur* or a blank stare, and the adult gives it up—for the time being. But, even in the two hours' time, the adult will try that kind of construction or meaning a second time and a third. One can see little progress in two hours, but if you read the twenty-one developmentally ordered transcripts as if they were the longitudinal records of a single child, one sees in the later transcripts comprehending responses to sentences that elicited blank looks in earlier transcripts, and one sees the child himself employing the quondam opaque constructions.

We have, I think, conceived of the whole psycholinguistic learning process much too simply and mechanically. Psycholinguistic learning is probably not a matter of parents responding correctively to particular utterances in a way that somehow leads to general rules. It is more a matter of keeping a rough running account of a child's total psycholinguistic competence. This, one does in conversation by making innumerable efforts that are usually rather nonspecific in outcome. Still, amazing as it seems, parents have an approximate sense at any given time of what their child knows and can do, and I think they get this from regular tapping of the apperceptive mass.

In fact, a memory capacity of this order is not at all out of line with other things that humans clearly manage. Each of us keeps a running account on some number of good friends—of what things one has shared with each, disclosed to each, and dissembled with each. We also keep categorical kinds of accounts with students, colleagues, remote relatives, and the like. Women sometimes remember what they have worn in what company on what occasion. So do men sometimes. When we are young, we are able to remember who has heard each comical story, banal opinion, and felicitous phrase. I believe that the psycholinguistic learning between parent and child must be on this level of complexity, and if it is, most of our methods at present are some degrees of magnitude too simple.

The Difference a Game Makes

Even at thirty months not every child utterance, by any means, can be scored for relevance with reference only to the adult utterance immediately preceeding it. Nor is every child utterance responsive to a question or a directive or even responsive at all; many are initiatory. In the simple conversations recorded in our protocols, it was possible to identify six simple turn-taking games: Name the Referent; Locate the Named Referent; Hide-and-Seek; Name the Possessor; Name the Color; Talk on the Toy Telephone. A game in progress, or rather a single "round" of a game (to use Bruner's term), is ordinarily easily identified since commencement of a round may even be announced and, in any case, recurrent identifiable structures have been made explicit in the manual. For children of this age, the roles in the games are all interchangeable.

At the bottom of the first page of AR's transcript, a round of Hide-and-Seek occurs. A peekaboo antecedent may be learned, as Ratner and Bruner (1978) have shown, by the second year of life. All of the verbalization in the game as played at that age originates with the mother, but in our age group the children also do a lot of talking. In table 8, we have the transcript of two rounds of Hide-and-Seek involving AR, and I will discuss the considerations that enter into the determination of relevance in a case like this —though not in such great detail as with the preceding examples.

TABLE 8
Two Rounds of Hide-and-Seek

AR	Adult
	"Now I'll close my eyes and you hide it [a peanut]. Okay? You hide it. Now I'll keep my eyes closed. Can you tell me where it is?" (Peter)
"They're open." [his eyes]	
"In my cup."	
	"Oh, that's good! We found it. Okay, now let's put another one in." (Peter)
"Now you close your eyes."	
	"Okay. I'll close my eyes. Hide it somewhere else this time." (Peter)
"It under their cup."	
	"Their cup. That's right, so it is!" (Peter)

FINDING RELEVANCE IN SEEMING IRRELEVANCE

AR's first utterance is "They're open," and it follows directly upon the adult utterance "Can you tell me where it is?" This latter, we recognize as an indirect question (querying the ability condition of the direct request), and we and the adults already have evidence even on this same first page that AR understands such indirect request and knows how she is expected to respond to them. However, if we ignored the game in progress and limited our attention to the immediate adult-child exchange, we should judge that a communication breakdown had occurred since "They're open" is a declarative sentence, not a locative NP, which is the nature of the slot the indirect request creates.

Looking to the next adult utterance above, we see that Peter had promised to keep his eyes closed as the rules of the game require, and it is clear that AR is pointing out his violation of the rules. We can be quite sure of this since the pronoun "they" agrees with "eyes" in number and since the record specifies that Peter neglected to close his eyes. In the present case, AR gives us two utterances in succession without adult intercession. She proceeds to deliver a locative NP as required by the indirect request, and we may judge that it is semantically accurate from the enthusiastic reception that follows. Clearly, she had understood both adult utterances and all that lies behind them and has proceeded to respond to them in serial order, holding the more recent adult utterance in storage until its turn came. Both utterances would be scored as episode breaks if we thought communication were a sentence-by-sentence "pushme-pullyou" affair. Within the familiar structure of a game, it is clear that they are not, as clear to the interacting adults as it is to us as we read the transcript.

AR's next utterance "Now you close your eyes" is once again an utterance that does not follow from its immediate adult antecedent: "OK, now let's put another one in." In spite of the softening incorporative "let's," this is a simple direct request, and one might think it impertinent of AR to come back with a still more direct request of her own. Especially impertinent in that AR presumes to use the word "Now" which, as Ervin-Tripp and Mitchell Kernan (1977) have shown, is the very hallmark of the teacher, the pacesetter, the mistress-of-the-revels. Notice that Peter has used it some thrice even in this brief section. Once again, knowledge that a game is in progress prevents us from supposing that communication has broken down; AR is reminding Peter of the next structured step which shows, among other things, that she has all the background information on how this game is played.

In the final utterance of table 8, AR announces: "It under their cup." This is a not very clearly relevant response to the adult antecedent; "Hide it somewhere else this time." Not very clear until we notice that "else" of the instruction and look some seven utterances up to find that AR has previously hidden the peanut in her own cup ("In my cup"). She cannot restrain herself from pointing out that she had indeed done as asked. How much that is quite precise can be learned from what AR says in the context of a familiar game: Not only is her response relevant, she understands the word "else" and can hold another location in mind across at least half-a-dozen exchanges.

THE PLAYDOUGH CONSTRUCTION GAME

This is a game of very complex structure (only suggested by figure 1) which would be beyond the capacity of Bruner's infants. Still, though one is expected to graduate eventually from Hide-and-Seek to Playdough Construction to Debate or Spelling Bees or Football, certain elements of structure appear in all: Turn-Taking, Successive Rounds, Role Interchangeability, and so on. And talk, within the frame of a well-defined game, is judged relevant or not by new criteria, and the cases of failures of relevance can sometimes be diagnosed with precision. Finally, the game, like an incipient art form, creates structure in terms of which innovation can be recognized as a creative act.

FINDING IRRELEVANCE IN SEEMING RELEVANCE

JG had an MLU of only 2.18, which placed him just above our baseline boy, CC. Nevertheless, he, like all the children, was invited to construct

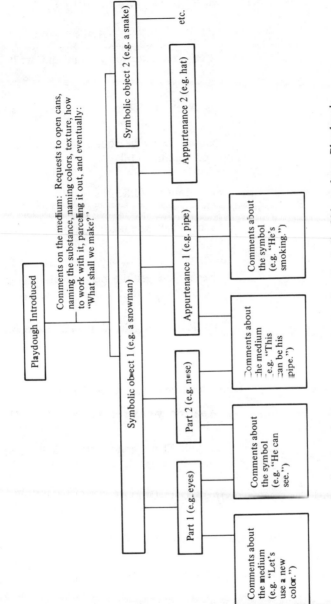

FIGURE 1   The Complex Game of Creating Symbolic Objects from Playdough

TABLE 9

A Game of Playdough Construction in Which
Seemingly Relevant Responses Prove Irrelevant

JG	Adult
	"Let's get some playdough and we'll fix it." (Jill)
"Okay."	
	"Stick it on. There, is he fixed?" (Jill)
"Yeah."	
	"Good. Don't be rough with it or it'll come off again." (Jill)
"That?"*	
	"Playdough." (Jill)
"Yeah."	
	"What shall we make?" (Jill)
"Dat big one." [piece of playdough]*	
	"Yeah, you get the big one and I'll get this little bit. Is that a doggie?" (Jill)
"You like a doggie?"	
	"I'd love a doggie. Can you make me one? (Jill)
"Yeah."	

Long sequence of uninformative exchanges but no doggie

JG	Adult
	"What do you want me to make?" (Jill)
"Ball."	
	"A ball. That's good. Let's pick it all up then we won't get it on your feet." (Jill)
"That?"*	
	"It's my shoe." (Jill)
"Yeah."	

More uninformative exchanges and then

JG	Adult
"Eatin" dat."*	
	"What is that? He's eating all the playdough." (Jill)
"Eatin' playdough."*	

*Utterance suggests incomprehension of the game.

symbolic objects from cans of variously colored playdough. For three full pages of transcript, JG and Jill played with the playdough, and for almost that entire stretch, I initially scored JG's responses as relevant. Table 9 presents a large part of this interaction over playdough with only some repetitions and uninformative stretches omitted.

Scoring one response after another, I had the impression of an unbroken episode, a long communicative conversation. In retrospect, I see that JG was able to give this impression with just two very "local" rules: 1. Respond to Yes-No questions with "yeah" and 2. Express compliance with every directive. To be sure, there were several very awkward points (marked with astericks in table 9). Why did he ask what unformed playdough was when he and Jill had already been playing with it for some time? Why, when asked "What shall we make?" did he respond with the nonsymbolic awkward NP "Dat big one?" And why, after long stretches of seemingly symbolic play did he intrude the irrelevance "That?" with respect to Jill's real shoe? The dramatic finale finds JG happily eating the playdough (which is, they say, pleasantly flavored).

In sum, a very limited local comprehension of a few kinds of utterance was all that was actually manifest. From this game, we all learned that JG did not understand the process of constructing symbolic objects. Nor did the one child less mature than he. CC threw it about and, at length, also had a taste of it. Both children could, of course, "make believe" or "pretend" with toys, as children can from a very early age. But the process of symbol-construction was still beyond them. In general, the complexity of the uses made of playdough could be scored and would correlate with both MLU and MLE. It seems to be an index of advanced symbolic function. In this game, all referents have vanished and require to be imagined and then given substance. With AR at the other extreme of psycholinguistic competence, but at the same chronological age, we will learn something of what may be done at thirty months.

CREATIVITY IN TALK AND ACTION

When AR played the Playdough game, she proved especially inventive. The discontinuous quotations of table 10 are, I think, especially instructive as to the role played by a rule-structure in creating conditions for creativity. Making a snake out of variously colored playdough is a game calling for simulacra of body parts. Played literally, the parts will have flesh-parallels of similar color in real snakes.

The uses of the color white in a snake are not obvious, but Peter thinks, quite reasonably, of a stripe down the back. In opting for a nose, Anna thinks of an animal body part and so stays within the confines of the game, but it is not a body part generally attributed to snakes and so her answer is inventive and yet within the rules. The two considerations together make it possible to understand her response, not as nonsense or an episode break, but as a contribution that is more than relevant. It can be, and was appreciated as, creative.

Perhaps AR's "underarm" for the snowman is even more strikingly creative. The color is fine and an underarm is undoubtedly part of a body, but it

TABLE 10

Some Creative Moves by A.R. in the Playdough Construction Game

AR	Adult
	"What are we gonna do with it?" (Peter)
"We're gonna put white on da snake."	
	"Put white on the snake, okay. Shall we make it into a long thin line like this? . . . See? Now the snake has a white stripe down his back." (Peter)
"Put it on a face."	
	"Put it on his face?" (Peter)
"A nose."	
	"A nose? Wow." (Peter)
	"I've never heard of a snake with a nose." (Jill)
	. . .
"We can use pink."	
	"Okay. What are we gonna use pink for?" (Peter)
"We gonna use it underarm."	
	"What?" (Peter) [surprised]
"Underarm."	
	"Oh! An underarm!" (Jill)
	"That's good, Anna!" (Peter)
	. . .
"We can make a lion out of it. Let me make food for him."	
	"What kind of food does he eat?" (Peter)
"He eats some of this food."	
	"Okay. What's that?" (Peter)
"Some broccoli for him."	

is not a perceptual segregate, not an entity, and so all the more inventive. Broccoli, in the role of fodder for lions, becomes, for the first time in my experience, "delicious." The response is relevant, a NP naming an edible. But a vegetable for a carnivore and, intended or not, a particularly humorous one since nothing could so deprive a lion of his roar as this drab, generally overcooked, foul-tasting green. I believe that the rudiments of artistic creation appear in these answers, and it is only their occurrence in a rule-structured context that makes them such.

Conclusions

These have been embarrassingly imprecise thoughts about how the games and conversations of infancy on which Jerome Bruner has lavished his talents are clearly early training for discourse and how discourse competence may interact with basic competencies of a semantic, grammatical, and pragmatic sort. The hypotheses are these:

1. A young child's discourse competence defined as the length of a conversation to which he or she can make continually relevant contributions grows in high positive correlation with non-discourse indices of psycholinguistic competence.

2. A young child's contributions to discourse that is designed to elicit contributions from him or her can serve to indicate to parents how much psycholinguistic knowledge he shares with them and so serve as the primary source for the parents' rough conception of the child's present state of knowledge and ability.

3. Irrelevant contributions from a young child can infrequently be traced to an item of knowlege that is easily corrected then and there. More usually, a single irrelevant contribution is only a clue to a general difficulty, but may be put together with other clues and used to motivate continued efforts at building the total apperceptive mass toward an adult state.

4. When child contributions are made in the course of a well-structured game, both relevance and irrelevance may be scored more confidently, deeply, and diagnostically.

5. Games, because they have molar rules or structures, create the opportunity for lawful and happy inventions which we think of as creative.

References

Brown, R. *A first language.* Cambridge, Mass.: Harvard University Press, 1973.
Brown, R. and U. Bellugi. Three processes in the acquisition of syntax. *Harvard Educational Review,* 1964, 34, 133–151.

Brown, R. and C. Hanlon. Derivational complexity and order of acquisition in child speech. In J. R. Hayes (Ed.), *Cognition and the Development of Language*. New York: Wiley, 1970, 155–207.

Bruner, J. S. From communication to language—a psychological perspective. *Cognition*, 1974/1975, 3/3, 255–287.

Dore, J. Variation in preschool children's conversational performance. In K. E. Nelson (Ed.), *Children's Language* Vol. I. New York: Halsted Press, 1978.

Ervin-Tripp, S. and C. Mitchell-Kernan (Eds.). *Child discourse*. New York: Academic Press, 1977.

Garvey, C. Requests and responses in children's speech. *Journal of Child Language*, 1975, 2, 41–63.

Gordon, D. and G. Lakoff. Conversational postulates. In D. Adams et al. (Eds.), *Papers from the seventh regional meeting of the Chicago linguistic society*. Chicago: Chicago Linguistic Society, 1971.

Keenan, E. O. and B. Schieffelin. Topic as a discourse notion: A study of topic in the conversations of children and adults. In C. Li (Ed.), *Subject and topic*. New York: Academic Press, 1976.

Labov, W. and D. Fanshel. *Therapeutic discourse psychotherapy as conversation*. New York: Academic Press, 1977.

Ninio, A. and J. Bruner. The achievement and antecedents of labelling. *Journal of Child Language*, 1978, 5, 1–15.

Ratner, N. and J. Bruner. Games, social exchange and the acquisition of language. *Journal of Child Language*, 1978, 5, 391–401.

Rosch, E., Mervis, C. B., Gray, W., Johnson, D., and Boyes-Braem, P. Basic objects in natural categories. *Cognitive Psychology*, 1976, 8, 382–439.

Searle, J. R. *Speech acts*. Cambridge, England: Cambridge University Press, 1969.

Stalnaker, R. C. Pragmatic presuppositions. In A. Rogers, B. Wall, and J. P. Murphy (Eds.), *Proceedings of the Texas conference on performatives, presuppositions, and implicatures*. Arlington, Va.: Center for Applied Linguistics, 1977.

9

How Mothers Maintain "Dialogue" with Two-Year-Olds

Kenneth Kaye and Rosalind Charney

Our work crosses two fields: early language development and the earlier social interaction between infants and adults. Since about 1970, many authors have proposed that mother-infant interaction somehow lays a groundwork for the structure of language. There are, however, at least two different versions of this hypothesis. First is the notion that certain universals of *linguistic* structure are prefigured in infants' joint action with mothers and fathers upon the object world. For example, Bruner (1975) has argued most coherently that mutual gestural reference is a precursor of deixis; that there is a topic-comment and presuppositional structure in sensorimotor interaction, leading to predication; and that basic grammatical cases—Agent, Action, Object, Instrument—are clearly marked in mother-infant interaction before the onset of speech proper.

A compatible but somewhat different form of the hypothesis holds that the early interactions of mother and infant are particularly suited to prepare the way for those later interactions in which language is learned. This is our view (Kaye, 1979): The structure developed in infancy is *social* structure, which then enables the child to interact with adults in ways that optimize learning. The main features of social interaction and cognition in infancy —joint reference to objects, turn-taking, mutual imitation, the signalling of intention—are not necessarily directly internalized by the child in language, but at least provide a discourse structure without which the rules of language in the narrower sense could not be learned.

Both versions of the general hypothesis assume that the fine points of a particular language are elaborations of a basic set of speech acts that depend upon social contexts and make use of those contexts in conveying

This research was funded by the Spencer Foundation. We are grateful to Patricia Benda, Solveig Dahlstrom, and Richard Pearse for transcribing and coding, and to Susan Goldin-Meadow for kindly reading and discussing the manuscript.

meaning (Austin, 1962; Searle, 1969; Dore, 1975). Stated in the way we prefer, the hypothesis suggests that the young child is able to learn the informative features, the obligatory transformations, and the optional forms of speech acts because of the ongoing discourse in which they are embedded. Mead (1934), Brown (1968), and Macnamara (1972) among others have pointed out that the back-and-forth cycles of discourse provide great redundancy for the child, so that he is very often in the position of hearing a proposition expressed when he already knows its intended meaning, and of hearing variant forms for his own propositions.

The rules for successful dialogue constrain each speaker not to interrupt the other and not to change the subject abruptly: to wait for the other to finish and then to continue the topic of the other's turn (Fillmore, 1973). There are also rules for signalling to the other when one is completing one's own turn (Duncan, 1972). Sometimes (but not always) a speaker will end his turn with a question, request, or gesture to which the other is expected to respond directly.

All these rules have analogies in mother-infant interaction, but mainly on the mother's side. She produces the turn-taking even in the earliest feeding of her newborn, by inserting responses into gaps in the baby's activity (Kaye and Wells, in press; Kaye, 1977). The biological mechanisms of sucking, of attention, and of arousal all take the form of on-off cycles, to which mothers and other caretakers respond. In face-to-face play with infants, as well as in feeding and bathing and dressing them, mothers' speech and facial expressions simulate (and exaggerate) conversations with full-fledged interlocutors (Brazelton, Koslowski, and Main, 1974; Stern, 1974; Trevarthen, 1977; Newson, 1977; Snow, 1977). The dialogue consists in the mothers adjusting their behavior to the infants', eliciting responses from them whenever possible. Furthermore, mothers maintain continuity of topic by responding to infants' "meanings." We see a clear and continuous progression from attaching meaning to the newborn's burp or involuntary twitch ("Oh! You don't say!"), to acknowledging the arousal inherent in a burst of arm and leg movements ("You're excited, aren't you?"), to interpreting a babbling noise as intentional signification ("What? You want your nana?"), to glossing a poorly articulated word ("Okay, here's some juice.") The mother's behavior barely changes: What changes is that the turn-taking becomes more symmetrical, the baby's turns become real speech acts.

In fact even when the child begins to verbalize, the adult-child exchanges should not be equated with true dialogues. The asymmetry—the leadership role of the mother in creating and maintaining a semblance of dialogue—is not restricted to the infancy period. It continues at least another two years. Conversational asymmetry (and not just linguistic asymmetry) extends well into the time when the child himself is a language user. The intention of the present study was to describe the nature of that asymmetry at twenty-six months and again at thirty months of age.

We shall define a communicative unit, which can be called a "turnabout" —a turn which unequivocally *both* responds to the other and expects a response from the other—and we shall then trace these units in the conversations of our subjects. Our research strategy is to use a few of the subjects for an exploratory analysis and then to analyze individual differences in the sample as a whole. We are concerned with the behavior of mothers and children in general, but we also seek variables in the early discourse which will predict the individual child's subsequent progress as a language learner and conversationalist.

Method

Our subjects were drawn from a cross-section of white, English-speaking families in the city of Chicago. Originally, fifty-two mothers were recruited in late pregnancy or a few hours after delivery for a study of "infant development" in the first six months of life. They were aware that we were observing their interaction with the infants, but we played down the extent to which their own behavior was to be analyzed: The mothers' behavior was observed, we explained, just because we wanted to know "what babies react to." The initial study involved five interviews and six observation sessions, mostly in the subjects' homes. Shortly after the children's second birthdays, twenty-nine of the mothers were contacted (all except those who had dropped from the previous study before six months; had moved away from Chicago or to an unknown address; or had no telephone, which made it too difficult for us to schedule visits). We expressed an interest in their children's language development and asked if we could make three home visits, at 26, 30, and 34 months. Two of the mothers declined due to family problems. The remaining 28 children (one mother had a pair of male fraternal twins) included 15 boys and 13 girls.*

The twenty-six- and thirty-month visits each consisted of six five-minute videotaped play periods, mother and child sitting adjacent to one another at a corner of the kitchen table. Different materials were presented during the six periods so as to provide a variety of contexts for conversation (in this order): a wooden puzzle, a picture book (Scarry, 1971), a set of blocks, a toy tea set (two cups, two saucers, two plates, and so on), a book containing six illustrated sentences which the mothers were asked to get their children to imitate, and a Fisher-Price "Play Family" consisting of father, mother, children, dog, and furniture. The categories for coding were derived

---

* Throughout this paper N is the number of infants, but statistical significance is based on one less degree of freedom because of the one mother with twins. In general, her behavior with the two boys differed—but less than the difference between one mother and another in our sample. These results will be included in a subsequent report on the twins.

from consideration of all six situations; however, our quantitative analysis
in this paper will be restricted to the picture book and tea set sessions.

At thirty-four months we administered the Peabody Picture Vocabulary
Test and videotaped a thirty-minute interaction between the child and the
first author, who presented a fixed series of puzzles, sorting tasks, and configurations of blocks to be imitated. Only the test of language comprehension (PPVT) will be of concern to this paper.

It was quite easy to segment the mother-child exchanges into units
referred to as "turns" in the child discourse literature, defined by a pronounced pause in which the partner might or might not take the floor:

Child[1]	Mother
1. [Flipping pages]	
	2. What is that? [Points]
3. A fish.	
	4. That's a boat.
5. [Nods]	
	6. Does it look like a fish?

The entire five-minute session was transcribed as illustrated in the example above. A "turn" might consist of a single utterance with accompanying
gestures, two or more utterances strung together without a definite full stop
between them, or certain well-defined nonverbal acts (for example,
"Nods"). The acts or utterances constituted a turn if they had a potential
connection to the other person (whether or not that connection was actually
met by the other) or if they were a salient independent act to which the
other *might* have responded. Reliability (percent agreement) between the
two coders as to the segmentation of turns was 83 percent over eight sessions which they each transcribed independently at various times throughout the two-month coding process. In addition to the words uttered, all
pointing, nodding, or shaking of the head, questioning intonation, significant
gestures, significant gazes, and visual orienting to where the other had
pointed were included in the transcripts. Percent agreement between the
coders on these features was 81 percent. Only 11 percent of the children's
and 1 percent of the mothers' turns contained any inaudible words, and
these turns were always codable on the basis of their audible portions plus
nonverbal features.

The coding scheme was based on our observation that not all turns took
notice of the partner's preceding turn (even implicitly), and not all turns
solicited a response (even implicitly). For example, turn 1 above is what
we call an *unlinked* turn, not because it is nonverbal (which it also hap-

1. S38, 30 month, picture book

pens to be) but because it has no explicit or implicit connection to the mother's behavior. Turns 2 and 6 are *mands;* 3, 4, 5, and 6 are *responses.* So 6 is both a response and a mand, which we call a *turnabout:* Using Fillmore's (1973) analogy, the mother catches the ball (in this case, the fish) and throws it back to the child.

Immediately after transcribing each session (while the videotape was still mounted in case it proved necessary to review it), the coder labeled each turn as a response or not, and as a mand or not. Thus all turns fell into four mutually exclusive types: those which were only responses, only mands, turnabouts, and unlinked turns. A turn was considered a response if any part of it met one of the following criteria:

1. answering a question, correctly or incorrectly.
2. self-repetition when solicited by the other (for example, by the other's "Huh?").
3. repetition or paraphrase of the other's most recent turn.
4. requests for clarification ("What?" or "Huh?" and so on).
5. substantive continuation of topic. This could take many forms, including: one pointed to an object (mand) and the other named it (response); one said "Soup" and the other said, "What kind?" (both response and mand); or one said "Bear," the other said "Yeah" (response) and the first said "He's running" (response because the referent of "He" was a topic acknowledged by the other).
6. certain intrinsically responsive expressions ("Yeah," "Uh-huh") and gestures (looking where other has pointed, accepting an offered object).
7. any turn beginning with "And," "But," or "Because" (the syntax inherently continues a topic either introduced or acknowledged by the other). We did not require in this case that the topic actually have been acknowledged: If a mother said "A bear" (pause) "And a dog," she was behaving as if her topic had been acknowledged.
8. any act or utterance continuing a cadence, as when the two participants engaged in naming pictures for one another in rhythmic alternation.
9. commenting on the other person's behavior ("Take your finger out of your mouth"—a response as well as a mand). However, referring to something the other was *not* doing ("You're not listening"—a mand) was not considered a response.

In summary, we accepted any concrete evidence that a turn was responsive to the other person in its content or in its nonverbal accompaniment. Inter-coder agreement on responses (number coded as responses by both divided by the mean number coded as responses by each) was 85 percent.

A turn was considered a *mand* if it met any of the following criteria, regardless of whether or not it was also a response:

1. question syntax or intonation (unless blatantly to oneself, as in "What do we have here?" said under one's breath).
2. command or request, explicit or implicit, verbal or by manipulation (for example, pushing the other's hand off page).

3. pointing or calling attention to something not already the current topic.
4. offering an object.
5. a very expectant look, as if to say "Well?" or "Am I right?"

In summary, anything to which it would be rude not to respond in normal adult discourse was a mand. Reliability of coding mands was 84 percent. Agreement as to *turnabouts* (turns coded as both response and mand) was also 84 percent.

We typed the codes into the computer in sequence—a total of 7664 turns in the picture-book situation and 7192 with the tea set. The analysis was done by a system called CRESCAT, designed for the anlysis of complex behavioral events in sequence (Kaye, 1978).

General Comparisons

Turn taking almost always went smoothly, as other authors have reported for this age group (Bloom, Rocissano, and Hood, 1976): Only 2.7 percent of the mothers' turns and 4.8 percent of the chidren's were interruptions (a turn starting while the other continued a nonverbal turn was not considered an interruption). Another 11 percent of their turns started simultaneously. In 70 percent of the interruptions, the person who was interrupted yielded to the other (responding to the interruptor instead of attempting to continue with his or her own turn). In 80 percent of the cases of simultaneous starting, one partner yielded at once and the other continued. Interruptions and simultaneous starts were included as turns in the results reported in this section but were excluded from the analysis of chains of turns, contingent responses to mands, and so on.

The results for the picture-book were quite similar to those in the tea-set situation as table 1 shows. Three-way repeated measures (age x situation x person) ANOVAs indicated significant differences between mothers and children in the proportions of unlinked turns ($F(1,22) = 52.5$, $p < .001$), responses other than turnabouts ($F(1,22) = 43.2$, $p < .001$), and turnabouts ($F(1,22) = 119.9$, $p < .001$). Mothers had more turnabouts as a proportion of all turns (T) and as a proportion of all responses ($T/(R+T)$. There were no age differences in these variables, and only one difference between the two situations: more turnabouts by both partners with a tea set than with the picture book ($F(1,22) = 8.8$, $p < .01$). There were no significant interaction effects.

Although unlinked turns were more frequent among the children than among the mothers, they were still less than 13 percent. In other words, seven out of eight of the children's turns took cognizance of the mother either by responding to her or by manding.

TABLE 1

Mean Percentage of Different Types of Turns

	Picture Book		Tea Set	
	Child[1]	Mother[2]	Child	Mother
U UNLINKED TURNS				
26 mo	12.6	2.7	12.9	5.5
30 mo	10.1	2.8	12.9	4.3
R RESPONSES (excluding turnabouts)				
26 mo	43.9	27.8	43.8	23.7
30 mo	46.5	25.2	41.3	26.2
M MANDS (excluding turnabouts)				
26 mo	22.0	20.1	16.0	13.7
30 mo	16.8	20.7	15.5	13.5
T TURNABOUTS				
26 mo	21.5	49.4	27.3	57.2
30 mo	26.6	51.3	30.3	56.1

The major difference between mothers and children was in turnabouts, roughly twice as frequent among the mothers' turns as among the children's. Their total proportions of mands (M + T) was, of course, also greater. Despite the fact that our definition of mands included even implicit ones such as pointing to a picture, only about 44 percent of the children's turns were mands, and only about 26 percent were turnabouts, or turns in the full sense of "catching the ball and throwing it back."

The expected proportion of turnabouts by a chance compounding of responses and mands can be found by the formula (R + T) x (M + T). The turnabouts T would exceed this expected proportion if responses and mands were positively associated, or would fall below it if there were a tendency for responses and mands to be mutually exclusive. For both tasks and both ages, the children combined responses and mands less frequently than would be expected on the basis of chance ($p < .001$ by binomial sign test). Their observed proportions of turnabouts averaged about 85 percent of the expected values. Thus the children tended to produce either a response or a mand rather than both. The mothers produced many responses and many mands, and their turnabouts were about as frequent as would be expected from a chance combination of responses and mands (observed/expected = .96).

1. N = 27 at 26 months and 26 at 30 months. One family moved from the city prior to 30 months and two videotapes were uncodable.
2. N = 26 at 26 months and 25 at 30 months. One mother had twins.

The conversational asymmetry of the two partners is perhaps best summarized by the fact that, at both ages in both tasks, about 70 percent of all turnabouts in our transcripts were due to the mothers.

Length of Turns

To some extent, the children's relative lack of turnabouts may have been a consequence of their limited abilities to use many words in each turn. As table 2 shows, the longer turns were more often turnabouts. The mothers of

TABLE 2

Percent of Linked Turns Which Are Turnabouts[1]

Length of Turn

	0-word	1-word	2-word	3-word	Regardless of length[2]
Mother[3]	11	40	46	57	50
Child[3]	3	30	41	46	24

course had more words per turn, all averaging between 4.0 and 6.0, while the children averaged between 1.0 and 3.0 words per turn. Only 7 percent of the mothers' turns with the picture book and 6 percent with the tea set were nonverbal, compared with 25 percent and 42 percent, respectively, of the children's turns.

Table 2 also shows, however, that even when the number of words in a turn was controlled for, mothers' turns were more often turnabouts than were children's turns. (These data came from eight subject pairs selected at random, at both ages.) The children did produce some nonverbal turnabouts (for example, silently handing the mother a requested object); as well as one-word ("Huh?" or "There"), two-word ("And piggies!") and so on. But the mothers produced more turnabouts of any given length. In other words even when a child's turn contained several words it was more likely to be *either* a response or a mand than to be both. So we conclude that the mothers' greater tendency for turnabouts resulted only partly from their ability to produce longer utterances.

1. Figured as percent of all those turns containing a given number of words, excluding unlinked turns.
2. From table 9:1.
3. Picture-book situation only, both ages, eight subject pairs selected at random.

Chains of Responses

Continuity of topic is maintained between speakers so long as each of their turns is a *response* in the sense we have defined in this study. A chain of turns can be defined as an unbroken series of responses without regard to the question of mands:

Child[1]	Mother
	1. [Points to a picture] What is that one?
2. Kitty cat.	
	3. Well what is it?
4. Kitty cat.	
	5. Well, I know there's a kitty in it, what's he in?
6. Huh?	
	7. What's he riding in?
8. Airplane.	
	9. Right.
10. [Turns page]	

Items 2 through 9 in this example are all responses. What was actually responsible for maintaining a chain, however, was more than just the high frequency of responses from both partners. One of the partners, the child, was far less likely to respond unless the mother's turn was a mand (in the context of a chain, a turnabout as in items 3, 5, and 7). This is shown in table 3. The child could ignore the mother's turn by taking an unlinked turn

TABLE 3

Next Turn, After Mands and Non-Mands
(Two Ages and Two Situations Combined: Shown in Percentage of Distribution)

	Child Turn Following Mother Non-Mand	Child Turn Following Mother Mand	Mother Turn Following Child Non-Mand	Mother Turn Following Child Mand
No turn	22.3	9.8	8.4	4.8
Unlinked turn	15.1	9.9	1.4	0.5
Response only	18.4	48.9	21.9	35.3
Mand only	20.9	8.8	12.5	4.7
Turnabout	23.5	22.5	55.8	54.7
TOTAL	100.0	100.0	100.0	100.0

1. S44, 30 month, picture book

(number 10), or producing a mand of his own, or simply by doing nothing. When the mother's turn was not a mand, children took one of these options 58 percent of the time (table 3). If the mother's turn was a mand, they failed to respond 29 percent of the time. This means that a mother could increase the likelihood of a response, and thus of the child's continuing the chain, by turnabouts following his mere responses. As long as she kept manding, he was likely to keep responding; so if she responded-and-manded, she could keep the chain going. Table 3 reveals two ways mothers initiated and maintained chains of turns: by many mands (68 percent after a child's turn which was not a mand and 59 percent after one which was) and by responding to 78 percent of the children's turns which were not mands as well as to 90 percent of those which were.

In short, the dialogue is largely due to the mother. By faithful linkage to the child's turns she creates a continuous cycle and can carry the child along with her, turn after turn, like a cork on the waves.

A precise measure of the effect of the mothers' mands in constructing chains of mutual responses takes the form of a conditional probability: How much more likely was a child's response after a mother's turnabout than after her simple response? (This is different from table 3, which examined the likelihoods after a turn which was a mand *vs.* a non-mand, regardless of whether or not it was also a response.) The answer is that a turnabout had a 71.3 percent likelihood of eliciting a response from the child—that is, of his continuing the chain—while if a mother simply responded to her child (#9 above), she had only a 46.5 percent likelihood of his continuing the chain.

There was another way mothers could continue chains. When one partner failed to take his or her turn, the other could add another link by repeating or paraphrasing his or her own turn, or by responding to the other's previous turn in another way. This example comes from an unusually long chain of twenty-five turns:

Child[1]	Mother
	18. Ok. Here you go (T)
19. [Puts knife on plate and smiles at mother]	
	20. Well what about me? (T)
	21. Give me a knife, I have to have one, too. (T)
22. [Inaudible response]	
	23. Please? (T)
24. [Gives to Mother] (T)	
	25. Thank-you.

1. S1, 30-month, tea set

We have marked the turnabouts (T) in this example (item 23 is one because the topic—knife—is considered to have been acknowledged in item 19). The mother's turn number 21 is a restatement of number 20, which the child ignored. Mothers took two turns in a row in this way more often than children did: 59 percent of the turns in chains were mothers' turns (at both ages).

Despite these efforts by the mothers to maintain continuity, the average chain was only 4.2 responses long in the picture-book situation, 4.8 responses with the tea set. As tables 1 and 3 indicate, the children were almost as reliable at *responding* as their mothers were (see also Bloom, Rocissano, and Hood, 1976), but they still tended not to mand responses from their mothers and not to respond to non-mands.

It is possible to compute how long the average chain of responses would have been if mother and child had both behaved as the children behaved. To make this projection we use the proportions of responses and turnabouts in the first two columns of table 3 as transitional probabilities, computing the expected frequency of chains of one, two, three responses, and so forth. The result is that the average chain would have been about 1.7 responses long if the mothers had responded as the children did. On the other hand, if the children had responded as the mothers did in the last two columns of table 3, the average chain would have reached about 7.0 responses.

Types of Turnabouts

The category "turnabout" can be subdivided into a great many types on the basis of various criteria including the number of words involved (table 2), degree of explicitness of the links, direct or indirect questions, and others. After examining the transcripts we settled on four subcategories which were mutually exclusive, exhaustive, and reliably codable; they seemed to us quite different though they shared the characteristic of being both response and mand:

Two-part turnabouts were turns in which the response component was separate from the mand component:

1. "Yeah, what's this?" was one turn because there was no pause, but it was really response + mand.
2. "You like that, huh?" without the tag question on the end would merely have been a response.

Requests for clarification or verification—"What did you say?" or "You're putting it in the cup?"—were listed under our coding definitions as both responses and mands. That is, they inherently both responded to the other and asked for a response from the other. However, they did not ask for a *new* response.

Answering mands were mands elicited by a question or command. Suppose one asked "What did you say?" and the other responded "Give me the fork." The repetition was a response to a request for clarification. It also happened to be a mand. Similarly, if in answer to "Can I have a fork?" the child offered a fork, it would be both a response and (by definition) a mand.

Finally, there were *follow-up* turnabouts, mands which were a direct outgrowth of the other's remark or behavior. These were the turns which gave the clearest impression of attempts to sustain the conversation: "What does the other hippo say?", "Can I have one, too?", and so on. We also included in this category various kinds of corrections of the other's utterance ("No, it's a frog!"—with expectant tone) or of the other's behavior ("Get your thumb out of my coffee.")

When turnabouts were broken down into these types further differences appeared between the children and the mothers. The word "Huh?" alone (a request for clarification) accounted for more than 7 percent of the children's turnabouts and less than 2 percent of the mothers'. About 75 percent of the mothers' turnabouts, or 40 percent of all their turns in either situation, were turnabouts of the "follow-up or correction" variety, building on what the child had just done or said and attempting to elicit something more on the same topic. These were rare among the children, accounting for only about a third of their turnabouts, or, 9 percent of all turns. (These results are based on an analysis of four subjects at both ages in both situations.)

Individual Differences

Although every mother produced more turnabouts than did her own child, the range of differences among children and among mothers in the frequency of turnabouts was almost as great as that between children and mothers. The size of our sample made it possible to investigate the reliability of these differences across situations and over time, as well as the similarity of individual children to their mothers.

Tables 1 and 3 presented the proportions of responses and mands exclusive of turnabouts, so that the columns would sum to 100 percent for purposes of clarity. As variables characterizing the individual subjects, however, we used the *total* proportions of responses (R + T) and of mands (M + T), the measures most directly based upon our coding categories.

Our measures of individual differences showed some stability across the two situations (table 4), but among the children this was only true at twenty-six months and among the mothers it was only true of mands and turnabouts. We believe that the reason the children's individual discourse styles

TABLE 4

Correlation between Picture-Book and Tea-Set Situations

	26 months		30 months	
	C	M	C	M
% Unlinked	.51**	.12	.01	—.33
% Responses (total)	.37	—.02	.24	.15
% Mands (total)	.47*	.51**	—.02	.64***
% Turnabouts	.51**	.15	—.03	.57**

  * p < .05
 ** p < .01
*** p < .001

were inconsistent across the two situations at thirty months, despite the similar patterns for the group means (table 1), was the fact that by thirty months their play with the tea set had developed considerably. At twenty-six months the tea-set situation was not so different from that of the picture book—a set of objects for naming and showing—and so the two brought out similar behavior in any given child. This interpretation, however, depends on additional analysis of the children's play outside the scope of this paper.

When we look at the stability in our measures over time (table 5), we find highly reliable individual differences among the mothers in both mands and turnabouts while the correlations over time among the children were not significant. The children changed over this period, in comparison with

TABLE 5

Correlation between 26 and 30 Months (Tea-Set and Picture-Book Combined)

	C	M
% Unlinked	.34	.37
% Responses (total)	.18	.30
% Mands (total)	.15	.62**
% Turnabouts	.25	.65***

  * p < .05
 ** p < .01
*** p < .001

one another—while the mothers' individual styles remained constant. It should be noted that these styles were not related to the mothers' education; they distinguished individuals reliably even when years of schooling (our best measure of socioeconomic status) was controlled.

Finally, we asked to what extent individual mothers' styles predicted their children's, or vice versa. In table 6, the picture-book and tea-set situations are reported separately because the results were not the same. There were

TABLE 6
Relation Between Mothers' and Children's Frequencies of Different Types of Turns

| | Picture Book | | | Tea Set | | |
	Mother 26 MO	*Mother* 30 MO	*Child* 26 MO	*Mother* 26 MO	*Mother* 30 MO	*Child* 26 MO
UNLINKED						
Mother—30	.41*			.32		
Child—26	—.28	—.08		.59**	.37	
Child—30	.05	.27	.36	.27	.02	.18
RESPONSES						
Mother—30	.32			.09		
Child—26	.14	.03		.44*	.30	
Child—30	.31	.39*	.42*	.42*	.15	.09
MANDS						
Mother—30	.43*			.74***		
Child—26	—.27	.05		—.53**	—.13	
Child—30	.43*	.01	.19	—.37	—.55**	.27
TURNABOUTS						
Mother—30	—.39*			.50*		
Child—26	—.03	.02		—.30	—.24	
Child—30	.53**	.39*	.37	—.03	—.18	.35

* $p < .05$
** $p < .01$
*** $p < .001$

no variables, for either task, on which the children's score at twenty-six months predicted the mother's at thirty months. With the picture book, it was the case that the mother's earlier frequencies of mands and turnabouts predicted the children's later scores. In the case of turnabouts, the mothers and children were uncorrelated with each other at twenty-six months but became correlated at thirty months. This certainly suggests a maternal effect upon the extent to which individual children increased in their use of turn-abouts.

However, the tea-set situation produced a different picture. At both ages there was a strong negative correlation between mothers and children in mands: If a child's mother made many mands, the child made few. Again there appears to be a maternal effect (since the mother's behavior was stable over time while the child's was not), but the effect was a negative one in this situation—and extending to mands in general, not to the special set of mands we call turnabouts. Our impression from the videotapes was that in the play with the cups and saucers, which prompted role play and encouraged children to reverse roles with their mothers, some did so more than others. Some children directed the play by telling their mothers what to arrange or serve, when to drink, and so forth, while in other pairs the mother did most of the directing. Thus some pairs were high in maternal mands and low in child mands and others were low in maternal mands and high in child mands.

Effect on Language Measures

One would like to be able to trace the effects of differences among mothers in mands and turnabouts, upon the children's eventual progress in conversational skill as well as in other measures of language development such as, for example, vocabulary growth and increase in grammatical complexity. Unfortunately the present study does not offer an answer to that question.

Our best assessment of the children's language growth was the PPVT (Form B) administered at thirty-four months. The median score of 32, mean 30.9, and S.D. 9.4 were all very close to the published American norms for the test (Dunn, 1965), a reflection of the fact that our sample was deliberately selected to be a representative one. Since all of our subjects were the same age when tested we simply used their rank on the test as our outcome variable. This score was predicted .70 (p < .001) by a composite score from the two earlier visits, based on the children's words per utterance, their number of distinct lexical "types" (different words) produced per minute, and their second longest utterance. Once this predictor based on the children's early productions was partialed out of the PPVT rank, no further variance could be explained by any aspect of the mothers' behavior which we measured at twenty-six and thirty months. There were no sex differences in our sample, for either the production measures or the comprehension (PPVT).

On the other hand, the PPVT rank was predictable by the mother's number of years of schooling (our mothers ranged from several high-school dropouts to one with a master's degree), r = .43, p < .05, or by the mother's words per utterance, r = .40, p < .05. It is of course well known that children's language development is related to their mother's education, but the present data do nothing to resolve the nature-nurture issue inherent in such a finding.

It remains possible that the differences among mothers in these aspects of discourse style produce differences in their children's conversational skills without affecting comprehension or production measures *per se.* We are currently exploring this hypothesis using the children's conversations with the investigator at 34 months.

Discussion

We would summarize our findings thus: It is true that conventions of waiting for the other person to stop talking, and of signalling by intonation, gesture, or gaze that one expects a reply are well established by the third year of life after eighteen months or so of verbal exchanges. But such exchanges are still managed very largely by the adult partner. Turnabouts, the kind of turn in discourse which both responds to the other (verbally or nonverbally) and implies an expectation of response from the other, are much more characteristic of the mother than the two-year-old when they interact with one another. The children by this age are capable of turnabouts in all the varieties we have listed (for they produce some), but they do not produce many. The majority of their turns are either responses or mands but not both; when they are both, they are rarely of the type most frequent on the mothers' side of the discourse, which follow up or expand upon a topic. The latter type accounts for about 40 percent of all the turns taken by mothers in our two situations and only 9 percent of the turns taken by the children.

In fact, there is some evidence that the mother, in an effort to maintain the conversation, produces more turnabouts than she would if she were talking to another adult. We videotaped two adults for five minutes with our picture book. Their interaction was completely symmetrical, and 39 percent of their turns were turnabouts: more than our average child but fewer than our average mother. As Snow (1977) notes, the main goal in adult-adult conversations is getting one's turn; the main goal of an adult in an adult-child conversation is getting the child to take his turn.

We found, however, substantial individual differences among the subjects. During the period from twenty-six to thirty months the differences among the children were fairly unstable, while those among the mothers— in the proportion of their turns which were full turnabouts and in the proportion which were mands (including turnabouts)—were highly stable.

What is needed for a proper test of the outcomes (if any) of maternal differences in the management of early dialogues is a sample in which a sufficient number of children are matched for social class and early indices of their language development. Our data indicate that the mothers in such a sample would still differ considerably with respect to mands, turnabouts, and the like; the possible effects of these differences upon their individual children should then be explored.

Beginnings

Most striking to us is the fact that "turnabouts" on the part of mothers is much the same as they have been doing since the infants' birth. It is not an instructional process unique to the development of language. It is, on the one hand, a basic part of adult language. The mothers are merely treating the child as if he were already a full participant in dialogue, and at the same time they are modeling his role for him. On the other hand, it is a basic aspect of mother-infant nonverbal interaction. Across a good many studies of face-to-face play in the early months (Richards, 1974; Brazelton, Koslowski, and Main, 1974; Stern, 1974; Trevarthen, 1977) the rule seems to be that if an infant gives his mother any behavior which can be interpreted as if he has taken a turn in a conversation, it will be; if he does not, she will pretend he has. Newson (1977) has illustrated and discussed this "as if" character of mothers' early play with their infants. Snow (1977) observes how the process continues into the second year:

Mother	Child
(3 months)	
Are you finished?	
Yes? [removing bottle]	
Well, was that nice?	
(7 months)	
Look, what's that?	
What's that?	[Looks at object]
Well, you thought it'd gone away,	
didn't you?	
(18 months)	
Who's that?	Daddy.
That's not Daddy, that's Dougall.	
Say Dougall.	

[Snow, 1977, pp. 14–18]

We hope the reader can spot the four turnabouts in these examples (the first is a "verification," the others are all of the "follow-up or correction" type). Our purpose is to point out that a mother's discourse does not change much when her infant begins to talk: It is not a strategy specifically for language training. It is a basic mode of interaction with infants, highlighted even in the very first feedings. Kaye and Wells (in press; Kaye,

1977) found that mothers use their newborn infants' pauses in sucking as occasions for jiggling the infant, creating a turn-taking structure. Mothers quickly learn to keep their jiggling brief so that it fits into the pauses and receives an "answer" in the form of the next burst of sucks. Jiggling is a turnabout.

Elsewhere we have discussed the many different manifestations of turn taking through the first two years, emphasizing the extent to which it is managed by the mother, making use of biological rhythms in the infant: the on-off cycles underlying sucking, attention, arousal (Kaye, 1979). Our view is that the infant's rhythms provide a structure to which parents can respond—indeed, cannot help responding—and in so responding the parents create a semblance of a dialogue involving the infant at a level well beyond his actual capacities for intentional discourse. The data presented to the infant from which he is to develop a language are much richer than simply a corpus of overhead speech, or a series of discriminative stimuli plus reinforcers. He is presented with ongoing discourse in which he is already a participant, on topics very largely selected by his own interests. His meanings are interpreted, expressed, and expatiated upon before he even knows what meaning is.

The structure in which such expansion and clarification of the child's meanings takes place is the dialogue. Thus thought as well as language grows from the communication of the meaning of gestures, as Mead (1934) and Vygotsky (1962) reasoned half a century ago, and as Bruner (1975) has so forcefully argued from recent data.

A similar point can be made with respect to the learning of specific linguistic rules, once language development is underway. Deictic shifters like *I-you* and *here-there* would be extremely difficult for children if language were learned by observation, because they are not associated with any particular person, place, or thing. The reason they are learned early and with few errors is that the child acquires their meaning as a participant in discourse, not as an observer (Charney, 1978, 1979). The shifting back and forth of perspectives that such words encode is a basic part of the child's experience of language. From the first, language is learned in relation to speech roles.

The present study shows that the child can find himself taking speech roles without quite intending to do so. Even in the third year mothers continue to behave "as if" their children were full participants in dialogues, while the children only gradually become so. We tapped an age period when all twenty-eight children had already begun to take the kind of turns which best characterize true discourse, but when the major responsibility for creating and maintaining the dialogues still rested with their mothers. That responsibility continues (and comes to be shared with other teachers) as the development and coordination of language and thought continue. Vygotsky (1962) and Bruner (1972) have both described the adult role as one which meets the child more than halfway, amplifying primitive understandings in the direction of the patterns of thought and interaction particular to a given culture.

The development of conversational pragmatics begins early—at birth—and continues late. It is a stream of language development parallel to those of semantics and syntax, intertwined with them. The infant's assumption of full partnership in dialogues is a process recapitulated on each new plane. It is completed within a few weeks for feeding, a few months later for play with objects, later still for simple naming of objects. The adult's role, which comes quite naturally to mothers and fathers, is to use each new plane of mastery as a springboard for the next challenge.

References

Austin, J. L. *How to do things with words.* Oxford: Oxford University Press, 1962.

Bloom, L., Rocissano, L., and Hood, L. Adult-child discourse: Developmental interaction between information processing and linguistic knowledge. *Cognitive Psychology,* 1976, 8, 521–552.

Brazelton, T. B., Koslowski, B., and Main, M. The origins of reciprocity: The early mother-infant interaction. In M. Lewis and L. Rosenblum (Eds.), *Origins of behavior,* vol. 1. New York: Wiley, 1974.

Brown, R. The development of WH questions in child speech. *Journal of Verbal Learning and Behavior,* 1968, 7 279–290.

Bruner, J. S. The nature and uses of immaturity. *American Psychologist,* 1972, 27, 688–704.

———. From communication to language—a psychological perspective. *Cognition,* 1975, 255–287.

Charney, R. *The development of personal pronouns.* Unpublished doctoral dissertation, University of Chicago, 1978.

———. The comprehension of *here* and *there. Journal of Child Language,* 1979, 6, 69–80.

Dore, J. Holophrases, speech acts, and language universals. *Journal of Child Language,* 1975, 2, 20–40.

Duncan, S. Some signals and rules for taking speaking turns in conversation. *Journal of Personality and Social Psychology,* 1972, 23, 283–292.

Dunn, L. *Peabody picture vocabulary test.* Circle Pines, Minnesota: American Guidance Service, 1965.

Fillmore, C. *Deixis II.* Unpublished lectures, University of California, Santa Cruz, 1973.

Kaye, K. Toward the origin of dialogue. In H. R. Schaffer (Ed.), *Studies in mother-infant interaction.* London: Academic Press, 1977.

———. *CRESCAT: Software system for analysis of sequential or real-time data.* Chicago: University of Chicago Computation Center, 1978.

———. Thickening thin data: The maternal role in developing communication and language. In M. Bullowa (Ed.), *Before speech.* Cambridge: Cambridge University Press, 1979.

Kaye, K. and Wells, A. J. Mothers' jiggling and the burst-pause pattern in neonatal feeding. *Infant behavior and development,* in press.

Macnamara, J. Cognitive basis of language learning in infants. *Psychological Review,* 1972, 79, 1–13.

Mead, G. H. *Mind, self, and society.* Chicago: University of Chicago Press, 1934.

Newson, H. An intersubjective approach to the systematic description of mother-infant interaction. In H. R. Schaffer (Ed.), *Studies in mother-infant interaction.* London: Academic Press, 1977.

Richards, M. P. M. The development of psychological communication in the first year of life. In K. J. Connolly and J. S. Bruner (Eds.), *The growth of competence.* London and New York: Academic Press, 1974.

Scarry, R. *Richard Scarry's ABC word book.* New York: Random House, 1971.

Searle, J. R. *Speech acts: An essay in the philosophy of language.* Cambridge: Cambridge University Press, 1969.

Snow, C. E. The development of conversation between mothers and babies. *Journal of Child Language,* 1977, 4, 1–22.

Stern, D. Mother and infant at play: The dyadic interaction involving facial, vocal, and gaze behaviors. In M. Lewis and L. Rosenblum (Eds.), *The effect of the infant on its caregiver.* New York: Wiley, 1974.

Trevarthen, C. Descriptive analyses of infant communicative behavior. In H. R. Schaffer (Ed.), *Studies in mother-infant interaction.* London: Academic Press, 1977.

Vygotsky, L. *Language and thought.* Cambridge, Massachusetts: MIT. Press, 1962.

10

Perception and Communication in Infancy: A Cross-Cultural Study

Alastair Mundy-Castle

Our assumption is that we are born with a disposition to distinguish objects and persons and to react to each in a different manner. When a young baby is in the "object mode," his whole being is one of intense, focused concentration on the object concerned. If he is in the "person mode," his behavior is manifestly communicative, showing animated varieties of expression and gesture directed toward the other person, who usually responds in like manner. My interest in this theme was inspired by movies of babies; the movies were made by Richards, Trevarthen, and Brazelton and shown at the Center for Cognitive Studies in 1968 (see Trevarthen, 1977). They observed distinct behavior patterns, which were colloquialized around the Center as "communicating" and "doing"—the former occurring during interpersonal exchanges; the latter, during baby-object interaction.

In the present paper the theoretical orientation is phenomenological. That is, we believe that mind is central in the regulation of behavior, furthermore, that mental experience is irreducible to sense or other elemental

Many people contributed to this paper, in various ways. My greatest debt is to Jerome Bruner, with whom I first began research on infancy; his interest and encouragement are a continuing source of inspiration. The research itself was supported by grants from the Nuffield Foundation in London and the Spencer Foundation in Chicago. Collaborators included the late Prof. M. O. Okonji, Dr. C. Trevarthen, Dr. (Mrs.) O. Odiakosa, Mr. R. P. Bundy, Mrs. E. Akinsola, Mr. O. B. Kayode, Mrs. N. Darnton, Mrs. R. Jaiyesimi, Mr. E. Akinade, Mrs. A. F. Oshun, Mrs. R. I. Agbarakwe, Mrs. C. O. Udoh, Miss J. B. Sawyerr, Dr. J. and Mrs. P. Hubley, Mr. K. Bundell and Mr. K. Onyendi. The research would of course have been impossible without the help of our subjects, to whom we are greatly indebted.

I would like to express my appreciation to the Spencer Foundation of Chicago for their grant to Colwyn Trevarthen and myself in support of the cross-cultural research. Pictures were provided by John and Penelope Hubley.

structure (cf, Turner, 1967). We agree with Husserl (1973) that thoughts and feelings are purposive and personal, that they reach out toward what they are about, and are intentional.

We do not concern ourselves here with the existentialist dilemma of "being" and "essence," nor with the search for what an object really is (cf. Sartre, 1957). What we do accept is that our subjective experience of the world is crucial in the determination of our behavior—and a corollary of this, that each of us perceives the world in unique fashion, although there may be common features experienced by different people (cf. Strongman, 1979).

The approach is both nativist and empiricist. The major difference from conventional scientific psychology is its acceptance of experience as the central subject for study. Thus, in considering interactions between babies and mothers we assume that each is a person and that each is influenced by what he or she is experiencing at any given moment. We find ourselves sympathetic to notions such as "primary" and "secondary" intersubjectivity, and are in fact currently collaborating with Trevarthen on cross-cultural studies of mother-infant communication during early life. Some Nigerian data from this research are presented below.

Empiricist adherence to the principle of Occam's razor led many behavioral scientists to exclude mind as operative in human psychology. We reject this conclusion as a fallacious outcome of reductionist thinking. We also dismiss the naïve conception of experimentation as a one-way system, where everything is controlled except for the independent variable and its effect on the dependent variable (cf. Mundy-Castle 1970). We agree with Sears (1951), Bronfenbrenner (1977), Cairns (1979), and others that psychological experimentation demands interactional methods, particularly when social exchange phenomena are studied.

In Husserl's phenomenology, an objective world can only exist through intersubjectivity, by the association of individual subjectivities (see also Merleau-Ponty, 1962; Thines, 1977). Although it is evident we have an intuitive appreciation of key principles governing our objective universe (Bower, 1974; 1979), our adaptation to physical reality is a function of interactions with other people, particularly "significant others" such as mother, father, and family members (cf. Mead, 1934). It is this kind of reasoning that led Trevarthen (1975, 1979) to propose intersubjectivity as an innate pattern of communicating, and the author to postulate culturally mediated variations in patterning of social and technical skills (Mundy-Castle, 1968, 1974).

The paper has three sections. The first considers cultural influences on infant and child rearing and the question of "African Personality." The second is concerned with the development in infancy of perception of objects separated by space and time; the third with perception of people, exemplified in mother-infant and stranger-infant interaction sequences and identified as a communication process. The term "cross-cultural" in the title refers to African and Euroamerican cultures, with an emphasis on the former.

Cultural Influences

It is reasonable to ask whether one can legitimately speak of Euroamerican or African culture. In Nigeria alone there are many different language groups and culturally diversified patterns of living, broadly demarcated by ethnic and religious affiliations. Much the same could be said of the United States. Nevertheless, the established nationhood of these two groups provides a unifying blanket, as it were, asserting the reality of their respective cultures. But in the absence of a "United States of Africa," is it legitimate to talk of African culture? The continent is vast, with a wide variety of people and living patterns. Are there any general cultural features permitting the ascription "African" without distortion of fact?

Pertinent is the concept of African personality. According to the late Ogbolu Okonji (unpublished manuscript), the term was introduced into the vocabulary of black movements by Edward Blyden at the close of the last century. It became popular in the fifties and sixties, during the civil rights movement in the United States, and the decolonization period of black Africa. A foremost proponent of the concept was Kwame Nkrumah, who used the term as a slogan and anchor for the Pan-Africanist movement. The allied concept of negritude was simultaneously advanced in Francophone Africa, notably by Aimé Césaire, Hioune Diop, and Leopold Senghor. There is no doubt that these ideas of blackness and African personality served a powerful unifying function with profound social and political effects. The question remains, however, whether there is any psychological validity in the concept of African personality.

Here the author agrees with Okonji, who, in effect, answered "yes—at least as a testable hypothesis." This conclusion is predicated on certain cultural beliefs and practices that cut across African cultures—ones which seem likely to affect personality development. Important among these is the African approach to infant rearing, which includes:

1. protracted breast feeding;
2. demand feeding;
3. demand sleeping;
4. extensive and frequent communion with significant others, especially mothers, aunts, grandmothers, and siblings;
5. frequent body contact, especially by backing, caressing, and fondling;
6. instant caretaking in response to distress;

7. frequent involvement in rhythm, dance, music, and singing;
8. early participation in household duties;
9. encouragement of motor development, particularly sitting, standing, and walking; and
10. emphasis on obedience and respect for elders.

Of relevance to the question of an African personality is the African attitude toward the having of children, epitomized in the statement: "the most serious misfortune that can befall a woman is to be childless" (cf. Kaye, 1962). The African woman is traditionally happy and eager to be pregnant, and during the first year of life at least, the African baby is given total security, emotional warmth, and nurturance to a point that can be described as indulgent (Okonji, unpublished manuscript).

Another important source of likely influence on personality development is exerted by the extended family system and the values that go with it. These include a profound respect for ancestors and ancestral ways and for promotion of solidarity and survival of the family (de Graaft-Johnson, 1965). Ancestors are revered not only because they are elders but because through death they are imbued with supernatural powers (Okonji, 1975). The African is primarily an animist, and the world he knows is the soul world. The distinction between mind or spirit and matter which has been apparent in western philosophy is inapparent (Odhiambo, 1967). There is belief in reincarnation and immortality of the soul, together with widespread acceptance of witchcraft and an associated fear that misfortune is the result thereof (Ampofo, 1967).

There is another important aspect of African culture which distinguishes it from Euroamerican. It resides in the extent to which different modes are used for culture transmission. In Western culture great attention is paid to "second order" media, in the form of printed words and pictures and television, whereas in the traditional African context much more attention is paid to first order "in-context" cultural communication, through music, dance, drama, and ritual. The character of this influence on thought has been examined from philosophical and psychological viewpoints, notably by Innes (1950), McLuhan (1962), Horton (1967), Cole and Scribner (1974), and Goody (1977). Here we may refer to observations by the Ghanaian artist, the late Kofi Antubam (1963), that "the real disease of the Western world is a perverse over-sophistication" (p. 20) and that "spontaneous self-expression, so highly valued in African cultures, constitutes the greatest weakness of modern Western diplomacy" (p. 28).

Whether for good or ill, it seems that modernization is beginning to exert an eroding effect on some of the foregoing traditional beliefs and practices. This is suggested by a questionnaire interview survey conducted among the three major ethnic groups in Nigeria, namely Hausa, Igbo, and Yoruba (Mundy-Castle and Okonji, 1976). The study was made by Lagos University psychology undergraduates from each of these groups, under supervision by the author and Okonji. The localities for the study were Kano City in the north, Enugu in the east, and Ibadan in the west. We included both urban and rural samples from each of these areas; in the Ibadan survey both middle- and upper-class samples were studied. None of the rural parents had any secondary schooling and many, particularly in the north, were without any formal education. In contrast, the urban samples were much more educated, especially the men. The northern (Hausa) samples were almost all Islamic by religion, which means among other things that they knew how to read the Koran and write Arabic script. The Eastern (Igbo) samples were mainly Christian, apart from 50 percent of the rural fathers, who were pagan. The Western (Yoruba) samples comprised both Muslim and Christian followers, the former predominant in the rural sample, the latter in the urban samples. The socioeconomic status of urban and rural samples was sharply distinguished by their respective dwelling-places, water and lighting facilities, and material possessions. All the upper class Ibadan group and varying proportions of the other urban samples had cars, television sets, refrigerators, and electric fans, whereas these items were nonexistent in the rural samples. Similarly the water for the urban areas came through pipes and taps, whereas the source for the rural areas was either rain or river or well water. The main form of transport among the Kano rural group was the donkey; among the rural Igbo, the bicycle; and in the Ibadan rural group, the feet.

Our questionnaire was modelled on one developed by A. Taylor in Ghana which in turn was based on an earlier one proposed by Ruth Benedict (Kaye, 1962) In addition to the demographic aspects already mentioned, it contains prefixed answer scales and open questions relating to child bearing and child rearing: for example, attitudes toward family size, prenatal and neonatal behavior, feeding, crying, exploration, play, toys, hygiene, speech, toilet training, psychomotor development, sleeping arrangements, sex roles, sibling rivalry, discipline, moral upbringing, children's responsibilities, and intelligence.

The questionnaire was administered individually to parents from the three regions and took about three hours in all. This usually required two separate sessions. Since our student from the north was male, he was not allowed to interview any mothers, this being contrary to Islamic rules.

In the present context there is no need to go through all the results of the survey and we will simply comment on certain important features. In general it is clear that there is a shift from a traditional orientation among the rural samples, especially in the north, to more modern attitudes among the urban samples. Thus, in regard to the having of children, whereas 100 percent of the Kano and Ibadan rural samples agreed that there is no limit to the number of children one should have, only 7 percent of the Ibadan upper-class parents agreed with this statement. Similar differences were observed with many other items in the questionnaire, as shown in table 1.

TABLE 1

Sample Data from Interview Survey

Statement	Percentage Agreement[1]						
	KR	ER	IR	KU	EU	IUM	IUU
It is wicked to limit the number of children one has.	95	75	100	83	40	31	7
Very young children are fondled and caressed by everybody in the house.	100	85	100	100	73	80	60
No baby is allowed to cry for more than a few minutes without being picked up and comforted.	100	80	100	100	92	59	46
Children are warned not to wander outside the house by stories of bogey men and so on.	100	75	100	100	53	75	33
Children who are seen sitting still of their own accord are suspected of some illness.	100	90	100	100	69	92	53
Good mothers have no fixed time for feeding but feed their children whenever they cry or look hungry.	100	80	53	100	33	36	6
Babies love their mothers more if the mother breast feeds them.	100	90	100	100	75	89	53
Bottle feeding is harmful for children and prevents their proper growth.	100	20	90	0	15	3	0
Nobody worries about children wetting or soiling their clothes before the age of one year.	95	90	100	95	90	97	80
Good mothers never make a fuss when babies urinate or stool on them even when the mother is well dressed.	100	85	100	95	70	66	26

Parents think it is important that a child should learn to sit and walk at an early age.	100	95	87	100	81	86	40
Good children sit quietly in the house when adults are present.	100	90	100	100	88	86	33
Children who do not carry out their household work are punished.	100	90	100	100	78	80	40

[1] K = Kano, E = Enugu, I = Ibadan, R = Rural, U = Urban, UM = Middle-Class Urban, UU = Upper-Class Urban

Note the statement: "No baby is allowed to cry for more than a few minutes without being picked up and comforted." This was agreed with by 80 to 100 percent of parents from all but two of the localities. The exceptions were Enugu urban (59 percent) and Ibandan upper urban (46 percent). According to Whiten (1975) this instant response to an upset baby is not characteristic of English mothers from Oxford, who provide less overall body-contact to their babies than African mothers.

Parental expectations of rapid psychomotor development appeared in all of the areas surveyed, a finding similar to that described, for example, by Durojaiye (1975) in his studies of Yoruba and Baganda infants. However, as he and others, especially Super (1979), proposed, the accelerated development may be a function of the greater physical exercise afforded to the African baby. The Igbo mothers observed by Whiten made very frequent changes in the position of the infant, including supporting them in a standing position. The same happens among the other ethnic groups in Nigeria, according to our survey. Apart from the Ibadan upper-class sample, all others gave 80 to 100 percent agreement with the statement: "Parents think it is important that a child should sit and walk at an early age." This emphasis on encouragement of psychomotor development among Nigerian parents, taken with the postural changes afforded their infants during carriage—on back or hip—is in contrast to the relatively static experience of, for example, English babies, who move around in perambulators and have much less experience of shifting posture.

Generally speaking, the results of this survey support our claim of a set of beliefs, attitudes, and practices toward child rearing that are characteristically African, although further comparative studies are needed. We would however question the claim by Whiten (1975) that rural Igbo mothers did not seem to play object games with their babies, in contrast to urban English mothers from Oxford. Instead we would look for a different form of object game with different rules. Although we shall return to this question later, we should note the strong social component in the play of African children (see Kaye, 1962). A game like "solitaire," common in England when the author grew up, is inconceivable in the African collective family.

Games are educational, and in this respect Kaye notes that in southern Ghana make-believe games were widely practiced and encouraged, in the belief that they teach children how to fulfill adult roles. Another common form of traditional African social training is storytelling, usually done in the evenings and incorporating folktales, riddles, and proverbs. These are then discussed, helping children learn correct expression and style as well as right from wrong. The present author's experience in rural Ashanti, Brong Ahafo, Ewe, Fanti, Guang, Igbo, and Yoruba communities corroborates the foregoing observations on child rearing.

Toys in a traditional African household are rarely bought by their parents. Even if they are, as likely as not they are taken away from the child as punishment, if not damaged at the hands of many. Children often make toys out of waste and natural materials, like tins, bottles, lids, nails, wood, wire, paper, boxes, tubes, stoppers, and so on. Whereas they exercise originality and ingenuity in such creations—which is undoubtedly to their advantage—they have relatively little direct practical experience of the technological and scientific concepts that are built into Western "reactive playthings" and technological toys. As technology is an integral part of modern life, these children may encounter problems in technological adaptations. Pertinent here is one of our student's undergraduate honors thesis, the results of which are neatly subsumed in the title "Familiarity Breeds Conservation" (Nuga, 1973).

There are other notable differences in the environmental experience of African and Euroamerican children. The latter as babies may spend considerable time in cots, pens, and perambulators, often as not surrounded by gadgets designed to enhance visual and visual-motor attentiveness. These babies are often static, perhaps watching mobile objects or playing with them, and are often alone, although mother or caretaker is usually within earshot. By contrast, the African baby is much more mobile and almost always in the company of others. His life is a part of ongoing family action and, in consequence, exhibits more spontaneity than that of the Euroamerican child, whose activities tend to be regulated by clocks and programs.

Western children spend a lot of their time reading, looking at picture books, writing, drawing, watching and operating TV, and playing with sophisticated logical models and puzzles. Such activities are antisocial in the sense that they are either solitary or socially exclusive and tend to focus people's attention on the object involved or the task in hand. In the traditional African family context, games have a pronounced collective, intersocial bias, frequently incorporating rhythms, music, song, and dance. The difference in childhood activity of Africans and Euroamericans is likely to produce differences in their approaches to life. Solution of problems will be sought in reality itself among the former, on models of reality among the latter (cf. Nadel, 1939). In the traditional African society, what one does is far more important than what one knows (Fajana, 1968). Furthermore, there is greater social consciousness in both thought and body movement than in Western society (see also Okanji, 1975).

Development of Perception

An awareness of these cultural differences in child rearing practices led the author, in cooperation with Jeremy Anglin at the Center for Cognitive Studies, to begin a research program on the development of visual attention in infancy. We were interested in examining the genesis of visual anticipation and the role of early experience in this process. Our long-term aim was to conduct the study in several cultures, so as to identify culturally universal patterns. The original study was conducted in Cambridge, Massachusetts, and the second study has now been done in Nigeria.

Our Harvard sample was confined to middle-class white American families, virtually all of whom had at least one mobile suspended over their baby's cot, together with a variety of other visually exciting objects and patterns. It was a time in America (1967–70) when ideas of 'visual enrichment' were in vogue, and the mothers took keen interest in their babies' visual development. The comparison sample, studied in Lagos between 1975–79, comprised mainly working- and lower middle-class Yoruba and Igbo babies, drawn from a radius of about five miles around our laboratory in the Lagos University Teaching Hospital, Idi Araba, Lagos. These babies were never in cots or perambulators and there is little regulated visual or visual-motor experience of the kind described for the Cambridge sample. The babies are moved about on their mothers' backs, are rarely left alone, and are present during home and work activities. There are usually many other children around as well as adults, and there is a strong sense of sound and vibration, whether by voice, music, or traffic, often all together. The photograph in figure 1, taken from one of our subject's windows, is a fair reflection of the environment of our Lagos research sample. It is an environment which brings into focus the basic vital demands which must be met on a day-to-day basis: how to acquire food and water, dispose of wastes, get from one place to another, combat floods, avoid theft, and the like.

In the original Cambridge study, babies were seated in a Harvard chair, a modified infancy chair, facing a large cream-colored wooden box, in the front of which were cut two rectangular windows (Mundy-Castle and Anglin, 1974). Behind and above each of these windows was suspended a glittering ball on elastic and nylon thread. As soon as the baby was settled the experiment began: a ball was lowered into each window in alternating succession. A ball appeared in one window for 6 seconds, was raised, and

FIGURE 1   PHOTO © BY JOHN AND PENELOPE HUBLEY

then, following an interval of 3½ seconds, a ball appeared in the other
window for 6 seconds. The regular side-to-side alternation of stimuli was
violated at trials 15 and 28, when the ball was exposed for 2 trials in the
same window. Normally, 30 trials were given, although if the baby was
happy, 60 or more might be presented, sometimes with variations in exposure pattern. Behind the windows were two observers whose task was to
press a signal button whenever the baby looked into their window. These
signals were recorded on a polygraph, together with stimulus presentations
and the output of a 1/sec. timer. One of the observers gave a low voice
running commentary on the baby's behavior, and this was recorded on tape.
The experiment was conducted in a quiet laboratory without interruptions.
The American sample consisted of 135 children, ranging in age from 10 to
230 days. The Nigerian sample consisted of 90 children, ranging in age
from 5 to 297 days. The Lagos replication study was similar to the one in
Cambridge, with an important difference; there were no violation trials.
This was because of technical problems in stimulus programing, which we
could not overcome. Otherwise the two studies were experimentally comparable. Figures 2 through 4 show some of our subjects.

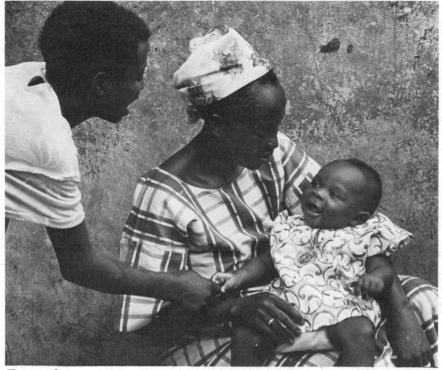

FIGURE 2　　　　　　　　　　PHOTO © BY JOHN AND PENELOPE HUBLEY

Our major finding is that both samples revealed the same sequence of perceptual development, evidenced in cross-sectional and longitudinal studies. The sequence involves the emergence of three looking strategies (see also Mundy-Castle, 1970). Strategy 1 appears between five and fifty-five or so days but there is considerable individual variation. Initially it involves prolonged looks at one window only, usually the lower edge or corner. As the baby grows older these looks are directed at the ball itself, and occasionally may be given briefly to the other ball when it appears in the second window. A baby using strategy 1 does not like having his gaze removed from where he is looking; he will oppose the mother if she is requested to force his head in another direction, and may cry if she succeeds.

The second strategy appears between twenty-five-to-eighty-five or so days, again with individual variations. It is characterized by looks that match the side-to-side alternation of balls. At first this pattern may be unilaterally biased, following from a window preference usually seen with strategy 1. With full development of the second strategy, shifts to attention from one window to the next become closely correlated with stimulus-presentations, and frequently incorporate anticipations. Thus as soon as the ball in one window is withdrawn, the eyes are shifted over to the other window and

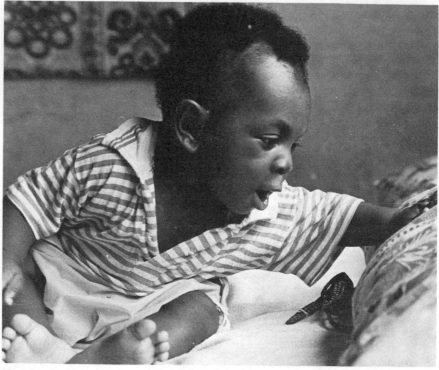

FIGURE 3

remain there until after that ball is withdrawn, when they return to the first window, and so on.

Strategy 3 occurs between 50 and 100 or more days and incorporates two new components. First, there is the appearance and intensification of window-to-window "cross looking," especially during intertrial intervals. Second, usually rather later, there appears what we call "trajectory tracking"; that is, the baby's eyes follow the upward path of the ball as it is withdrawn behind the upper edge of the window frame and continue the trajectory on up to the ceiling. In later trials this upward trajectory may sweep across and down to the top of the other window, thus anticipating a ball at the top of a window rather than the side, as occurs with the second strategy. It is worth noting that such trajectory tracking is seen even if the objects exposed in the two windows are not the same. Another important feature of this third "search and extrapolate" strategy is its reference to any outstanding details that are available in the baby's visual field, such as patterns on the ceiling, pictures on the walls, or anything else that has about it some visual significance. In our Harvard studies the experimenters were not aware of the protruding edge of an otherwise obscured picture on one wall, until babies using this strategy drew their attention to it.

FIGURE 4   PHOTO © BY JOHN AND PENELOPE HUBLEY

Evaluation of these three strategies suggest that the first is a form of undifferentiated looking, while the second and third allow for progressively expanded differentiation of the available visual field. It should be noted that a baby using strategy 3 may revert to the earlier ones, particularly if he becomes drowsy: indeed, all of us from time to time may use the locking pattern of strategy 1. It is experienced as a state of dreamy abstraction, comparable to that of thoughtfully gazing into the glowing embers of a fire. It seems to fuse awareness of self into perceptual context and has about it a hypnotic quality. But it appears to provide the young infant with a contextual base for the development of referential search, elaborated in the development of strategies 2 and 3.

The second of these suggests the use of a rule; "Look at ball until it disappears, then shift eyes to other window and wait." Clearly it incorporates the notion of two places rather than one. Experiments in Cambridge using prolonged and variable intertrial intervals showed babies using strategy 2 waiting up to twenty seconds for a ball to appear. As soon as it was withdrawn, they would switch their eyes to the other window and wait again. Under these circumstances, babies sometimes missed the violation trials altogether, oblivious of the ball that had repeated itself in the other window. Babies using strategy 3 would never miss such irregularities in stimulus presentation, since their looking repertoire monitors both windows more or less at once and incorporates extrapolatory search as well. Sometimes a baby using this strategy may adopt a picture on the wall as his "base," darting glances from there to the windows to pick up ball presentations whenever they occur, possibly looking to the top of the window rather than the side. It is clear from these studies, as Bower (1974) observed, that babies using strategy 3 have mentally coordinated place and movement. Babies using strategy 2 are aware of the existence and location of two significant places but not of movement between them. Babies using strategy 1 are perceptually absorbed in a unitary place and resist being pulled away from it.

The results presented here suggest a universal sequence in the emergence of these three looking strategies. Despite profound cultural differences between the Cambridge and Lagos samples, we see the same patterns of looking occurring at similar ages.

Some minor differences between the two samples are emerging in our ongoing, more finegrain, statistical analysis. These differences are in the number of looks and crosslooks made by babies using strategies 2 and 3; more were made by the American sample. This could be an effect of "visual enrichment," but could also be attributable to differential arousal effects consequent on the violation trials used in the Cambridge study. These matters will be subjected to further analysis and discussed in a later paper (with R.P. Bundy).

If it is established that there are within-strategy differences in visual exploration between Nigerian and white American babies, the finding would be the opposite of that found in motor development. Here there is evidence of faster advance among African than Euroamerican babies, perhaps because of the cultural differences in handling and motor encouragement (for example, Durojaiye, 1976; Hopkins, 1976; Super, 1979).

Communication

Words are abstractive. A term like "perception"—as James, Dewey, Whitehead, Bartlett, Bruner, and others have cautioned—refers to but a part of a process. It draws attention away from the totality of an experienced event. Perception is only a slice of a much larger system in the sense that what we perceive is a function of present, past, and future; it incorporates context, motives, needs, appetites, goals, and other psychological conditions; and it takes account of other people and the necessity to communicate with them.

The process of perceiving is inextricably linked with that of communicating. Babies express the nature of their perceptions through their ongoing behavior. We spoke earlier of babies responding differently to objects than to persons. Babies in the two-ball alternation experiment generally assumed the object mode, showing rapt attention to ongoing action and its setting. Only rarely did they display the animated, gesticulative, communicative behavior that characterizes the person mode. Not that this never happened. In the Lagos experiment, we were puzzled when communicative behavior was occasionally seen in babies of two months and older. Later other judges including Trevarthen agreed that the babies were, indeed, indulging in pre-speech toward the ball-window apparatus. This unusual response to objects obviously needs more study. To us it seemed the babies were showing their enjoyment, regardless of our concealment.

There is an important implication in the foregoing sentence. It incorporates our perceptual evaluation of the baby's subjective condition. It points to the essence of communication. Just as the experimenter, or any other sensitive person, continuously makes perceptual inferences about a baby's state of mind, the baby makes such inferences in his perceptions of others. Perception is an interaction process, between person and object in the object mode, and person and person in the person mode. Of especial interest is the combinatory interaction of person-person-object, where, for example, a mother guides the attention of her baby in handling a toy, or a baby wordlessly requests his mother to hold an object steady so that he might grasp it. In such situations baby and mother show rapid shifts between object and person modes and exhibit the intersubjective principles of cooperative endeavor.

Our methods of studying Yoruba mother-infant communication were developed with Trevarthen as part of a cross-cultural project conducted in Lagos and Edinburgh. Our laboratory procedure involved black and white video-records of a series of mother-infant interactions. Two cameras were used, one focused on the mother from behind the baby on the left, the other on the baby from our operations room through a hole in the curtaining of a glass screen. A mixer system gave a simultaneous splitscreen display of mother and baby, with operator control of lateral and vertical image dimensions. An advantage of this technique, compared with the cheaper mirror-reflection system, is its allowance for close-up observations by zoom control, useful for detailed analysis of face, eye, and mouth expressions.

Twenty-one babies and their mothers participated in the study, making from two to five visits each to the laboratory, usually at monthly intervals. Three age-groups were sampled: 1–4 months, 4–8 months, and 8–12 months. Home visits were conducted for sociological, observational, and photographic purposes (the latter by J. and P. Hubley). Mothers' homes were within five or so miles of Idi Araba, and none had more than two years of primary schooling. Socioeconomic level was generally low. The research data were collected between December, 1977, and June, 1978.

Babies sat in the Harvard chair on a table, mothers on an ordinary chair facing their baby. Interactional instructions were given in Yoruba (for the mother) and in English (for the record), and were approximately as follows:

1. Make your baby smile.
2. Talk with your baby.
3. Make your baby put out his tongue.
4. Make your baby clap his hands.
5. Make your baby track with his eyes a ball suspended from a thread held in your hand while you move it from one side of your head to the other.
6. Make your baby look at a person seated on your right.
7. Sing for your baby.
8. Make your baby put an object (toy person) in one of the three holes in this toy car.
9. Make your baby smile again.
10. Immobilize your face (for about 1 minute) then resume normal face.
11. Leave your chair and go out of sight of the baby. (Mothers were replaced by a stranger for 1–2 minutes, then requested to return.)

The whole series took about fifteen to twenty minutes. Mothers with babies in the youngest age group were not requested to do item 8.

Consider the general hypothesis of our studies: that babies are innately disposed to act purposively toward objects and persons, the latter eliciting communicative expressions of affect and intent, the former provoking object-directed attention. This differential purposiveness provides the material basis of intention. Whether with persons or objects, such interactions are formally and temporally regulated and give evidence of coherent subjectivity. Intersubjectivity is revealed in the early patterning of person-person interaction. It transforms individual subjectivities and provides the basis of human communication. (Trevarthen, 1979).

Our first results from the Lagos study confirm the above hypothesis. A video-analysis conducted by the author with Kevan Bundell at Edinburgh (1978) showed babies aged two months and under, engaged in looking, alternated looking, visual tracking, pointing, reaching, and attempted grasping in relation to objects; and smiling, imitating (of mouth, tongue, and arm movements, and vocalization), prespeech, game playing (incorporating rhythm, voice, hand, arm, body, and head) and proto-conversations—in relation to persons. Notable in these interactions was the part played by the mothers, who frequently imitated and constructively developed their babies' actions.

These observations are indications of early intentionality and expressive communicative behavior, and support Trevarthen's conception of primary intersubjectivity. Patterns suggestive of secondary intersubjectivity were seen in babies aged from two months onward; they included the "shared intent" relation of joint action on an object and the reciprocal interaction of person-person relations. These cooperative patterns were evidenced in rhythmic singing, clapping, body-dance, laughter, game-playing, and conversational exchanges; they included examples of babies requesting, offering, and rejecting. They constitute the use by the baby of intersubjectivity to regulate a mother's behavior (cf. Trevarthen and Hubley, 1978). The process fosters the development of a deep emotional bond between mother and baby, which if broken, may elicit anxiety and distress (Ainsworth, 1967). This was observed in the stranger situation in three of the babies aged between eight to twelve months. Similarly, although the immobilization procedure rarely elicited overt distress reactions, smiling on remobilization was sometimes seen. There were also several instances of babies trying to get their immobile mothers to respond, by increased activity, vocalization, and expressive orientations toward the mother. Sometimes these efforts had the desired effect, the mothers involuntarily breaking their forced composure and smiling or vocalizing in return.

Earliest ages at which some of the foregoing signs were observed are as follows:
Pointing at, reaching for, and grasping mother's tongue, visual tracking, imitation of smiling and tongue protrusion—22 days. Imitation of mouth shape into "O"—30 days. Proto-conversations using one-syllable vocalizations—40 days. Prespeech, imitation of vocalization and mouth movements—42 days. Person-person games, imitation of hand-clapping, head-nodding, and laughter—90 days. Person-person-object relations—105 days. Imitation of eye-widening and eyebrow-lift—120 days. Rejection of mother's guiding of hand to object—150 days. Person-person-object games—180 days.

Our observations of early imitation in infancy confirm reports by other workers (for example, Zazzo, 1957; Meltzoff and Moore, 1977; Dunkeld, 1978). We agree with the view of imitation as communication, the imitator showing his appreciation of what the imitated person is doing by doing likewise. That a young baby can do this is evidence of awareness of self and others as alike, not only in form and structure of action, but also in quality of experience. The mutual laughter and other signs of pleasure associated with push-pull and comparable interpersonal games cannot meaningfully be divorced from the state of mind that goes with them. Game playing in infancy is above all an intersubjective exercise, serving to introduce the child to rules, roles, and sequencing in communication, to agent-action-object and associated case relationships, as well as to the structure of the acts in which communication is embedded (cf. Bruner, 1975).

The results adduced in this paper suggest the presence in human infancy of three key developmental features, namely:

1. intentionality, or purposiveness exhibited differentially toward objects and persons;
2. subjectivity, or existential experience; and
3. intersubjectivity, or capacity to exchange experience with others.

Implications for Language Acquisition

Although our analysis of results from the Lagos mother-infant interaction study is incomplete, particularly in their relation to the comparative data collected by Trevarthen and his colleagues in Scotland, we are in a position to make some observations on their implications for language acquisition.

It is axiomatic of our phenomenological approach that personality, thought, and self are the outcome of mutual interactions in a social matrix. But, as MacMurray (1961) pointed out, use of the term "social" to describe this process is ambiguous, since many animals are social. The distinguishing feature in the human being is the extensive involvement from birth onward of communication in the patterning of human life. It has long been recognized that the possession of language sets man apart from other animals, but only recently has it become evident that language is acquired through a process that begins with birth. As Bruner (1975, 1978) argues, it is not linguistic innateness that is innate about language acquisition, but some special fundamental features of human action and attention. The child's recognition of the grammatical rules of language derives from their correspondence with the operative structure regulating joint endeavor. Our finding of a similar pattern of joint action and attention among the Yoruba as elsewhere supports Bruner's suggestion that the conceptual structure underlying it is a crosscultural universal. The nature of this structure is a set of semiotic relations that are closely paralleled in the primitive categories of case grammar, and these are found in all languages. In Halliday's (1975) terms, a child learns to mean long before he speaks. He does it by manipulating the contextual structure of his actions, according to rules acquired in joint activities with others, particularly the mother (see also Greenfield and Smith, 1976). These rules are universal to human society. and are culturally encoded into all languages. The reader is invited to try abstracting some of them from the Nigerian examples that follow (cf. Bruner, 1974, 1975, 1977, 1978; and Greenfield and Smith, 1976).

1. Mother (M) has been requested to talk with her baby (B), a girl (f) aged 42 days (d). Both are looking intently at one another and smiling. B's left hand is in M's right. M, though Yoruba-speaking, chooses to use English.

M: How are you? How are you?
B: Unh!
M: Fine.
B: Unh! Unh!
M: Fine. How are you?
B: Eh! Eh! Eh! Unh!
M: How are you?

Suddenly B begins the typical prespeech mouth movements described by Trevarthen (1977). M responds instantly with tongue protrusions, mouth movements, and vocalization. Both are still looking intently at each other. Then, while B continues with her prespeech, M yawns and looks away from B. B stops prespeech and begins to withdraw her left hand from M. M shakes B's hand a little, looking back at B. B looks first at their linked hands then elsewhere, no longer in the person mode. The engagement, which lasted some twenty seconds, is thus ended, although another is soon to begin.

2. M, in talking with B (m, 40d), chooses to put herself into her baby's mind, as it were. Both are looking intently at each other, frequently smiling.

M: Nibo ni iya yi gbemi wa lataro? Kini mo nse n'ibibayi?
[Where did this woman bring me since morning? What am I doing here?]
B: Unh!
M: En! [a common Yoruba exclamation]
D: En!
M: En! Kini? Kini? Kini? Kini mo noo mbi bayi?
[What? What? What? What am I doing here?]
B: En!
M: En!
B: En!
M: En!
B: En!
M: En-En!
B: O!
M: En En!

M is now requested to immobilize her face. She does so, continuing to look at B, who does likewise. Neither is smiling. After 9 seconds, B says: "En!" M immediately responds but does not move her face, saying "Mm!" B smiles, continuing to look at her. Again he vocalizes and again she responds. So, the interaction continues. . . .

3. In this illustration M seems to reveal an appreciation of both the encoding and segmentary nature of language. She is trying to get B (f, 60d) to talk with her, doing so by simultaneous speech and touch. When B responds in the way M wants, M replies by speech alone. B's name is "Bibo"; both are smiling and looking at each other intently.

M: Bibo! [Touches cheek] Bibo! [Touch]
B: Aah!
M: Aah!
B: Aah! Aah!
M: Aah! Aah! Bibo! [Touch] Bibo! [Touch]
   Hoolloo! [Touch]
B: Aah!
M: Hallo [Touch]
B: Aah!
M: Hallo [Touch]
B: Aaho!
M: Ha!
B: Haa!
M: Hayoyo!
B: Haalyo!
M: Yes!
B: Hallyo!
M: Yes! Yes! Hallo!
B: Uh! Aah!
M: Yes! How are you?

In presenting this printed version, the author regrets his inability at conventional phonetic rendering. The reader is assured however that the several Nigerian audiences who have viewed this section of our edited videotapes agreed that a two-month-old baby can say something very much like 'Hallo'!

The remaining examples are presented in less detail, and are chosen to emphasize the incorporation of action, attention, and gestural expression in prelinguistic communication. They also show how the looking strategies discussed earlier are built into social interactions.

4. M is trying to get B (f, 30d) to track visually a ball on thread held in M's hand. B reaches for ball with both hands, looks from ball to M, smiles briefly, and looks back to moving ball.

5. M is talking with B (f, 90d) who opens mouth and protrudes tongue. M smiles, grasps tongue, and tries to push it into B's mouth, saying: "Pa nu de. Pa nu de. Gba hon wole. Onijeku je!" (Close your mouth. Close your mouth. Put in your tongue. You like eating anything!) B smiles and sticks her tongue out again. M continues smiling, pushing B's tongue in again, as well as touching her chin and cheeks. The interaction quickly turns into a game, involving tongue-pushing, face-prodding, smiling, laughter, and vocalizing.

6. M is requested to make B (m, 90d) clap his hands. After some exhilarating demonstrations by M, B brings his hands together in imitation, while showing delight and vocalizing. A laughing-clapping game ensues. M is requested to leave and is replaced by a white male stranger (S). After studying S intently, B tries out the clapping action. S responds by leaning forward and adjusting B's position. B repeats the clap action a few times. S smiles but does not play the

game. B does not smile. When S leaves and M returns, B immediately smiles and claps, M does the same, and the happy laughing-clapping game is resumed.

7. B (m, 100d) tracks ball held by M, glances sideways at onlooker on right, continues to track ball, looks sideways and back for onlooker (who has moved to the back out of B's sight). M calls B's name and shakes ball to attract his attention to it. B smiles at M, vocalizes, and looks back at ball. Every now and then he looks round for the missing onlooker, also at M's face.

8. M is instructed to get her son (180d) to put the boy person into the truck. She pushes the truck toward B, who smiles and vocalizes, his eyes on the truck. M repeats the action a few times, to B's enjoyment, then stops. B looks up at M, then pushes the truck toward her. A two-way pushing game ensues, with much mutual enjoyment.

9. B (m, 260d) is not happy with the way M is handling the ball-tracking situation, showing this by facial expression and vocalization. M offers him the ball. B declines the offer by withdrawing, averting his gaze, and not grasping the ball. A minute later, M repeats the offer. B accepts the ball but immediately, with serious face, throws it to the ground, ripping it off the string as he does so. During a repeat visit forty days later, a similar episode occurred. M offers ball, B reaches for it as if to grasp it, then quickly withdraws his hand and averts his gaze.

10. In the ball-tracking situation, B (m, 300d) wants to take hold of the ball, showing this by crying and gesticulating when M laughingly makes it impossible: M: "Ole mu! Gba! Gba!" (You cannot catch it! Have it! Have it!) B reaches and grasps ball. M pulls it away. B cries out and looks at M in irritated protest.

11. B (m, 360d) is crying. M gives him the ball. He takes it and throws it down, looking disgruntled. He looks up at M, then at the ball again. She returns it to him, smiling. He repeats his previous action, this time looking up at M and smiling. Very quickly a happy ball game is being played, with mutual vocalization and laughter.

On this happy note the author ends the article but not the game. In respectfully offering it to Jerry Bruner, he looks forward to the next move.

References

Ainsworth, M. D. S. *Infancy in Uganda: Infant care and growth of love.* Baltimore: Johns Hopkins, 1967.

Ampofo, O. The traditional concept of disease, health and healing. *Ghana Bull. Theol.,* 1967, 3; 2, 609.

Antubam, K. *Ghana's heritage of culture.* Leipzig: Koehler and Amelang, 1963.

Bower, T. G. R. *Development in infancy.* San Francisco: Freeman, 1974.

Bower, T. G. R. *A primer of infant development.* San Francisco: Freeman, 1977.

Bronfenbrenner, U. Toward an experimental ecology of human development. *American Psychologist,* 1977, 32, 513–531.

Bruner, J. S. Child's play. *New Scientist,* 1974, 62, 126–128.

————. The ontogenesis of speech acts. *Journal of Child Language.* 1975, 2, 1–19.

————. Early social interaction and language acquisition. In H. H. Schaffer (Ed.), *Studies in Mother-Infant Interaction.* London: Academic Press, 1977.

————. Learning how to do things with words. In J. Bruner and A. Garton (Eds.), *Human growth and development.* Oxford: Clarendon, 1978.

————. Acquiring the uses of language. Berlyne Memorial Lecture, Toronto, 1978.

Cairns, R. B. *Social development: The origins and plasticity of interchanges.* San Francisco: Freeman, 1979.

Cole, M. and Scribner, S. *Culture and thought.* New York: Wiley, 1974.

de Graaft-Johnson, K. E. Social control in a changing society, *Ghana Journal of Sociology,* 1965, 1; 2, 47–55.

Dunkeld, J. *The function of imitation in infancy,* Ph.D. thesis, Univ. Edinburgh, 1978.

Durojaiye, M. *Psychomotor achievements of African babies.* Kampala: Makerere Univ. Psychol. Monog, no. 1, 1976.

Fajana, A. Some aspects of Yoruba traditional education. *Odu: University Ife Journal of African Studies,* 1966, 3:1, 1, 16–28.

Goody, J. *The domestication of the savage mind.* Cambridge: University Press, 1977.

Greenfield, P. M. and Smith, J. H. *The structure of communication in early language development.* New York: Academic Press, 1976.

Halliday, M. A. K. *Learning how to mean—explorations in the development of language.* London: Arnold, 1975.

Hopkins, B. Culturally determined patterns of handling the human infant. *Journal of Human Movement Studies,* 1976, 2, 1–27.

Horton, R. Philosophy and African studies. In D. Brokensha and M. Crowder (Eds.), *Africa in the wider world.* Oxford: Pergamon, 1967.

Husserl, E. *Ideas.* New York: Collier, 1913 (1962 Ed.).

Innis, H. A. *Empire and communications.* Oxford: Clarendon, 1950.

Kaye, B. *Bringing up children in Ghana.* London: Allen and Unwin, 1962.

MacMurray, J. *Persons in relation.* London: Faber and Faber, 1961.

McLuhan, M. *The Gutenburg galaxy: The making of typographic man.* London: Routledge, 1962.

Mead, G. H. *Mind, self and society.* Chicago; University Press, 1934.

Meltzoff, A. N. and Moore, M. K. Imitation of social and manual gestures. *Science,* 1977, 198, 75–80.

Merleau-Ponty, M. *Phenomenology of perception.* New York: Humanities, 1962.

Mundy-Castle, A. C. Paper presented at Makerere-Syracuse Workshop in Social Psychology. New York, 1968.

————. The descent of meaning. *Soc. Sci. Inform.,* 1970, 9, 125–142.

————. Social and technological intelligence in western and nonwestern cultures. In S. Pilowsky (Ed.), *Cultures in collison.* Adelaide: Australian National Association. Mental Health, 1975.

Mundy-Castle, A. C. and Anglin, J. Looking strategies in infants. In L. J. Stone, H. T. Smith, and L. B. Murphy (Eds.), *The competent infant.* London: Tavistock, 1974.

Mundy-Castle, A. C. and Okonji, M. O. Mother-infant interaction in Nigeria. Tilburg, 3rd IACCP Congress, 1976.

Nadel, S. F. The application of intelligence tests in the anthropological field. In F. C. Bartlett, et al. (Eds.), *The study of society.* London: Kegan Paul, Trench and Trubner, 1939.

Nuga, G. O. *Familiarity breeds conservation.* B. Sc. Hons. Thesis, Univ. Lagos, 1973.

Odhiambo, T. R. East African science for development. *Science,* 1967, 158, 876–881.

Okonji, M. O. The decolonialization of the social sciences in Africa and traditional African psychology. *Thought and Practice: J. Phil. Assn. Kenya,* 1975, 2, 101–113.

————. The african personality. Unpublished manuscript. Dept. of Psychology, Univ. Lagos.

Sartre, J. P. *Being and nothingness.* London: Methuen, 1967.

Sears, R. R. A theoretical framework for personality and social behaviour. *American Psychologist,* 1951, 6, 476–483.

Strongman, K. T. *The Psychology of Emotion,* second edition. Chichester: Wiley, 1979.

Super, C. M. Behavioural development in infancy. In Monroe, R. L., Monroe, R. H., and Whiting, B. B. (Eds.), *Handbook on Cross-Cultural Human Development.* Garland, 1979.

Thines, G. *Phenomenology and the science of behaviour.* London: Allen and Unwin, 1977.

Trevarthen, C. T. Descriptive analyses of infant communicative behaviour. In H. R. Schaffer (Ed.), *Studies in mother-infant interaction.* London: Academic Press, 1977.

———. Basic patterns of psychogenetic change in infancy. In T. Bever (Ed.), *Proceedings of the O.E.C.D. conference on "dips in learning".* St. Paul de Vance, March, 1975.

———. Communication and cooperation in early infancy. A description of primary intersubjectivity. In M. Bullowa (Ed.), *Before speech: The beginnings of human communication.* London: Cambridge University Press, 1979.

Trevarthen, C. T. and Hubley, P. Secondary intersubjectivity: confidence, confiding and acts of meaning in the first year. In A. Lock (Ed.), *Action, gesture and symbol: The emergence of language.* London: Academic Press, 1978.

Turner, M. B. *Philosophy and the science of human behaviour.* New York: Appleton-Century-Crofts, 1967.

Whiten, A. Mother-infant interaction in Nigeria and Oxford: a pilot study. Preliminary Report, Univ. St. Andrews, 1975.

Zazzo, P. La problème de l'imitation chez le nouveau-ne, *Enfance,* 1957, 2, 135–142.

11

Toward an Operational and Logical Analysis of Intentionality: The Use of Discourse in Early Child Language

Patricia M. Greenfield

The more deeply I have gone into the psychology of language, the more impressed I have become with the absence in psychology of certain forms of psychological analysis that are needed in the study of language acquisition and language use generally. One such is the role of intention and the perception of intention in others. Language use is premised in a massive way upon presuppositions about intentions and about the reasons why people do or say things. Yet psychology, or at least positivistic "causal" psychology, ignores the role of intention and assigns no interpretation to reasons in the regulation of behavior. Such matters are most often treated as epiphenomena.

—J. S. Bruner

This chapter is about the possibility of operationalizing intention through the analysis of conversational discourse and, more generally, the sequential aspect of interaction behavior. My attempt to realize this possibility is based upon the belief 1. that the logic of teleological analysis has been a

Preparation of this chapter was supported by a grant from the Spencer Foundation. Special thanks to Diane Fujitani for typing most of the manuscript on a Sunday. The final version benefited immeasurably from the careful reading and comments of David Olson, Emmanuel Schegloff, and Patricia Zukow.

major barrier causing intention to be ignored in psychology preventing its integration of intention into the causal paradigm of experimental psychology; and 2. that the analysis of short, discrete units in isolation (utterances or sentences, in the area of language and language acquisition) rather than more extended streams of behavior has, up to now, prevented the problem of operational definition from being approached in a systematic fashion.

Margaret Boden, a philosopher-psychologist, points out the essential connection between these two points in her book, *Purposive Explanation in Psychology* (1972). "The first logical criterion of teleological explanation is the necessity of prospective reference. In 'formally mechanistic' contexts by definition, no reference to the future need be made in explaining the occurrence of a present phenomenon" (p. 40). This logic of prospective reference means that current behavior can be understood only in relation to its future course, and this implies the necessity for studying extended behavioral sequences, rather than the discrete behavioral "atoms" required by positivistic "causal" theories. Thus, "purposive" explanation is not "atomistic." Atomistic explanations connect independently identifiable units. Future units may be predictable from the prior occurrence of other units, granted certain general postulates of correlation. But the future units need not be appealed to in any way for the initial identification of the prior units and thus are logically isolable from them (Boden, 1972, p. 41).

Teleological analysis was out during the reign of behaviorism. For example, in the operant paradigm, the reinforcer follows a response. The reinforcer was not considered to be a goal which "causes" behavior; rather behavior produces the reinforcer (Greenfield, 1971). How could something that occurred later (the goal) cause something prior (the means)? The answer is that a goal can have mental or cognitive existence not only before its attainment in the outside world, but before the response itself. This psychological existence is called an intention.

The emergence of cybernetic concepts in the fifties made this formulation of an intention as some type of cognitive model seem like a serious possibility for the first time. The appearance of *Plans and the Structure of Behavior*, by Miller, Galanter, and Pribram (1960), was an important step in the application of cybernetic concepts to the analysis of intentional behavior. For these authors, intention refers to a plan, and the basic unit of a plan is the freedback loop. Their feedback loop consists of four sequential phases: Test, Operate, Test, Exit (hence the acronym TOTE). The Test constitutes an internal model of a set of conditions discrepant from current conditions. This discrepancy sets off the Operate phase, consisting of behavior directed toward the elimination of the discrepancy. Repeated Tests assess whether the discrepancy has been eliminated. When a Test results in a match between the model and actual conditions, a stop order results and the activity terminates (Exit). Thus, the Test really consists of a model of an end state or goal that antedates behavior itself (the Operating phase). Thus, the TOTE has an intentional structure. The fact that Totes could perfectly well be concretized as elements in a computrer program brought up the possibility of a cognitive model without necessary recourse to the elusive concept of consciousness.

The reality of such a model as more than just a useful metaphor for human behavior was enhanced by Pribram, Spinelli, and Kamback's (1967) neurophysiological findings that intention—the internal representation of a goal—can be electrically recorded in the projection areas of the macaque monkey's brain, a phenomenon labeled feed-forward or corollary discharge. It was found that this mechanism, formally parallel to the initial Test in a TOTE unit, facilitates the intended behavior which follows. However, we cannot observe corollary discharge behaviorally any more easily than we can observe the test phase in a cybernetic loop, and so we are often in a position of making inferences about the intentionality of behavior from subsequent attempts at goal attainment. Can such inferences be logically justified? And what would be the behavioral bases for such inferences? Let us approach the second question first.

Making Intention Observable: Toward Operational Definition

Bruner suggests some citeria for the operational definition of intention: "Intention, viewed behaviorally, has several measurable features: anticipation of the outcome of an act, selection among appropriate means for achievement of an end state, sustained direction of behavior during deployment of means, a stop order defined by an end state, and finally some form of substitution rule whereby alternative means can be deployed for correction of deviation or to fit idiosyncratic conditions" (1974, pp. 168-169).[1] This approach has an honorable history in American psychology going back to McDougall, who made a list of what he called "objective marks of purpose" (Boden, 1972).

However, not all these behavioral characteristics are defining attributes in the sense of Bruner, Goodnow, and Austin (1956). Searle's analysis of intentionality selects two from among this list as having definitional status: 1. directedness, roughly equivalent to Bruner's "sustained direction of behavior during deployment of means"; and 2. presentation or representation of conditions of satisfaction, roughly equivalent to Bruner's "stop order defined by an end state."[2] These criteria must now be inserted into a logical

1. Golinkoff, R. drawing on Bruner is currently utilizing these criteria as a basis for identifying intentionally communicative vocalizations in prelinguistic infants. This paper was presented at the meeting of the Society for Research in Child Development Interdisciplinary Workshop on the Development of Communication, University of Delaware, 1979.

2. Searle, J. R. Intention and action. Paper was presented at the meeting of the LaJolla Conference on Cognitive Psychology, LaJolla, California, August, 1979.

framework in order to find a home within the province of experimental psychology. This framework constitutes a positive response to the first question, above, as to whether inferences about intentionality can be logically justified. After presenting the logical framework, I shall propose ways of concretizing these criteria so that they may be observed in the stream of communicative interaction.

A Logical Analysis of Intention

The specific logical operations used to study an intention are different from those used in standard experiments, *although it is important to realize that they are but different operations within one and the same, unified logical system.* What follows is an attempt to formalize Searle's basic definition of intention. In this formalization, D is the directionality of behavior toward a specifiable goal G contained in the intention I. The condition T is the termination of the directed behavior upon attainment of G, the goal. Goal is a more common term corresponding to Searle's conditions of satisfaction. The logic of operationally establishing an intention goes as follows: if intention I exists, D and, under condition G, T follow; if intention I does not exist, neither does D or T, under condition G. From this, it follows that the presence of D and T under condition G implies I. This situation can be summarized as follows: (Key to symbols: $\rightarrow$ = implies; Λ = and; $\sim$ = not)

$$I \rightarrow D \wedge (G \rightarrow T)$$
$$\sim I \rightarrow \sim (D \wedge (G \rightarrow T))$$

Intention implies Directedness and (if Goal, Termination)

$$\therefore D \wedge (G \rightarrow T) \rightarrow I$$

This conclusion means that if we can establish directedness and termination in the presence of the goal, we have established a particular intention.[3] What differs from the usual experimental situation is that the necessary and sufficient conditions of the Intention follow it in time. In the classical paradigm involving independent and dependent variables (Iv and Dv), the hypothesis to be proved is typically Iv→Dv. Generally there is no reason to

3. Schegloff (personal communication, 1980) points out that a given goal can be described in different ways. Operationalization of intentions does not, however, depend on a unique or common description of a particular goal; rather it requires a description such that, under similar circumstances, another observer could identify the same goal in the ongoing stream of behavior.

Schegloff also points out that a given, observable goal can result from different internal intentions. The operational definition cannot select the operative intention in a given case. Therefore, insofar as an observable goal has multiple possible intentions behind it, it seems more accurate to claim that, in a particular instance, we have operationally identified not a *particular, specific* intention, but a class of intentions defined by the goal that has been observed.

assume or attempt to prove $\sim Iv \rightarrow \sim Dv$ and therefore it does not follow that $Dv \rightarrow Iv$. (Indeed, every introductory psychology student is taught that to go from $Iv \rightarrow Dv$ to $Dv \rightarrow Iv$ is to commit the logical fallacy of affirming the consequent.) However, in talking about the logic of an intention we are talking about interdependencies of parts in a complex intraindividual structure, in contrast to independent and dependent variables, which are by definition logically independent. In the latter case, it follows that other stimuli besides the one in question could produce a given response. However, it is not the case that directional behavior and its termination upon attainment of a goal can exist without a corresponding intention. Therefore, $\sim I \rightarrow \sim (D \wedge (G \rightarrow T))$. This relationship must be true because, without an intention, how would a direction be set or a goal be recognized as such? That is to say, there is a structural interdependence among the various parts of an intention that does not exist between an independent and dependent variable in the classical paradigm of experimental psychology. Pursuing the analogy with the TOTE units of Miller, Galanter, and Pribram (1960), we can say that a feedback or cybernetic loop cannot exist without setting conditions for the initial test. This structural interdependence produces the mutual implication that does not exist in an $Iv \rightarrow Dv$ paradigm. It is this situation of mutual implication that makes it logical to identify a particular intention by events which follow it in time.

Note, too, how much more complex the logic of an intention is in comparison with the logic of a standard experiment. Unlike the later, the logic of intention contains an embedded conditional component $(G \rightarrow T)$, that is, (if G, then T). This conditional component produces an indeterminacy in interpreting certain behavioral phenomena. That is, if Termination occurs in the absence of Goal attainment, there might or might not be an intention. This formal consequence mirrors the situation in life: an extensive effort to realize a goal may be abandoned before it is attained if the effort is too difficult. Or the absence of goal attainment may mean that an intention was not present in the first place.

In conclusion, the logical complexity and partial indeterminacy of intentionality may well have been barriers to its acceptance in experimental psychology, especially in the absence of an explicit formal analysis to aid in the interpretation of concrete phenomena.

Analysis of Intention within an Interactional Framework

The key to an interactional approach to intention is the negotiated interpretation of intention. Considering the period in which children are making the transition to language, researchers have often raised the question as to how we know the mother's interpretation corresponds to the child's actual intention, something actually going on within the child (Howe, 1977; Rodgon, 1977; Ryan, 1974). People do not generally ask how we know whether the child's interpretation of the mother's intention is correct at this stage. One reason is that the question has not been looked at interactively from the child's point of view. That is, no one worries about what the child's interpretation of the situation is. One only wants an "objective" description of behavior and the child's interpretation (if it could be known) is considered superfluous to this end. This is so because language is given privileged status as behavior and the mother's intentions, occurring in linguistic form, are taken at face value as "objective" facts. In contrast, the child's interpretations, occurring on the level of action and visual behavior (that is, the sensorimotor level) are not valued and generally not even noticed.

The processes of mutual interpretation that go on in communicative interaction, as manifest through microanalytic techniques, can, however, reveal observable signs of the two major features of intentionality: directionality and terminal requirements (Bruner, 1974) and go beyond the solipcism of each participant's interpretation of the other participant's intention. This interactional approach draws heavily on conversational analysis in sociology as developed by Schegloff and Sacks (1973), but does not necessarily stay within it bounds.

My example will draw from the analysis my students and I have made of the comprehension of offers, both both verbal and nonverbal, by young children just starting to talk (Reilly, Zukow, and Greenfield, 1978; Zukow, Reilly, and Greenfield, 1979). From viewing and reviewing videotapes of naturally occurring communication in the home, the following interactional model of the general structure of an offer sequence was developed:

I. Offer establishment
    a. Offer presentation: Within an ongoing interaction the caregiver establishes the topic of the offer as well as the fact that an offer is in progress, that is, the communicative force (offer) and propositional content (object or activity) are presented.
    b. Offer acknowledgment: The child's behavior not only is appropriate as a response to the offer presentation (Ia) but also establishes the offer presentation interactionally, i.e., shows that is was taken to be an offer. Further, the acknowledgment elicits either realization or nullification (IIa).

II. Offer consummation
    a. Offer realization or nullification: The caregiver displays that she has assessed that the child's prior behavior constitutes an offer acknowledgment (Ib). This display facilitates the enactment (IIb) of the offer in the case of positive acknowledgment (Ib) or terminates the offer in the case of a negative acknowledgment (Ib).

b. Offer enactment: In the case of positive acknowledgment (Ib) followed by an offer realization (IIa), the child consumates the offer by taking the object, performing the activity, or refusing to do so.

The breaking down of the offer into these minute components allows intentionality to become observable and therefore operationally identifiable. That is, we may now observe directionality of behavior and termination of directional behavior in the presence of the goal. Here is an example from our data laid out in this interactional framework:

I. Offer establishment
   a. Offer presentation: "Do you want a cookie, Jim?"
   b. Offer acknowledgment: Jim begins to reach for the cookie.
II. Offer consummation
   a. Offer realization: Mother finishes bringing cookie to child.
   b. Offer enactment: Child grasps cookie.

The first part of the offer establishment, Ia, "Do you want a cookie, Jim?" is hypothesized to represent the intentional offer of a cookie on the part of the mother. As a speech act, the offer implies a communicative intention to be acknowledged as an offer. This implies a particular intention: the commitment to give the object of the offer to the other person if the other person shows evidence of positive feeling toward it. (This definition of the offer as a particular sort of intentional structure is based on Searle's [1975] analysis of commissives.) To confirm our hypothesis concerning the existence of these intentions, we must establish conditions D and $(G \rightarrow T)$. With respect to this intention, evidence for D (directionality) in the mother's behavior is provided at IIa where mother finishes her movement of bringing the cookie to the child, following the child's demonstration at Ib of positive feeling toward the offer by beginning to reach for the cookie. Two ordered points are needed to establish a direction. Item IIa establishes directionality because it follows Ia and therefore constitutes the second point. Evidence of termination (T) of directional behavior in the presence of G is also implied by IIb: For the child to grasp the cookie, the mother must *stop* doing or terminate what she was doing at IIa, holding onto the cookie while passing it to the child; that is, mother lets go of the cookie.

Directionality in fulfilling the communicative intention to have the offer acknowledged can be demonstrated only where there is not immediate acknowledgment, where, unlike the offer under discussion, Ib did not, in fact, follow directly after Ia. We must look at offers where immediate acknowledgment does not occur in order to find at least two behavioral points going in the direction of obtaining acknowledgment. In this offer, for example, after the initial offer presentation at Ia, the mother gets an actual cookie (absent until now) and re-offers, on the sensorimotor level rather than linguistically, extending the cookie to Jim. Re-offers such as this one establish directionality of behavior vis-à-vis the intention to have the offer acknowledged. Once acknowledgment occurs, the phase of offer presentation ends, its termination condition fulfilled. Thus, it is just where the intended consequences do not immediately occur that the intentional structure becomes most visible. One of Bruner's criteria of intention is apparent in this example: the re-offer of the sensorimotor level manifests the mother's ability *to substitute alternative means* where necessary.

On the child's side, we can also find evidence of directional behavior and its termination in the presence of the goal. In the case of the child, our hypothesis is that he has the intention to accept his mother's offer. His behavior of starting to reach to the cookie at Ib establishes the first point in a particular direction. Grasping the cookie at IIb constitutes a second point in the direction, as well as the termination of the activity of getting the cookie.

The interactively negotiated nature of intention is demonstrated in this example. The child's acknowledgment at Ib (beginning to reach) constitutes an interpretation of the caregiver's intention to offer. Schegloff and Sacks generalize about the usefulness of pairs such as Ia and Ib: What two utterances produced by different speakers can do is: by an adjacently positioned second, a speaker can show that he understood what a prior aimed at, and that he is willing to go along with that. Also, by virtue of the occurrence of an adjacently produced second, the doer of a first can see that what he intended was indeed understood, and that it was or was not accepted (1973, pp. 297-298). This described the situation perfectly, except that we include nonverbal components as possible members of a pair. Schegloff and Sacks restrict their analysis to the linguistic parts of communicative interaction, but there is no theoretical barrier to extending it to the nonverbal components of dialogue. Note, in fact, that the analysis applies as well to the child who reaches toward what has been offered as to the child who says, "Yes."

The caregiver's enactment of the offer at IIa (bringing cookie to child) constitutes an acceptance of the child's previous interpretation of the interaction as an offer by establishing the directionality of her own behavior. This move also constitutes an interpretation of the child's intention to receive. The next move of the child, taking the cookie at IIb, manifests his own directionality and thus constitutes an acceptance of the caregiver's interpretation of his intention. In this way person B's collaboration with person A's intended plan provides behavioral evidence for person B's perception of person A's intention. Consequently an interactive analysis not only throws each participant's own intentions into relief, it also illuminates how each perceives the intentions of the other.

At both IIa and IIb, the acceptance of the other participant's interpretation of one's own intention does not necessarily mean that the interpretation was accurate and that we know the first person's original intention. It does mean that this interpretation is currently acceptable as a basis for further action. Hence the interaction displays a mutually negotiated interpretation of the intention of each participant. Because each interpretation may influence the other's next move, there is really no way of knowing the original intention of either participant.[4] However, the agreed upon interpretation of each person's intention in the dyad is an important phenomenon in its own right. Note, too, that complementary intentions are necessary between the parties for either party's intention to be carried out. For instance, the child's intention to accept an object cannot be carried out without the mother's intention to give it to him.

Intent and Consciousness: Searle's Distinction between Prior Intention and Intention in Action

. . . intent in communication is difficult to deal with for a variety of reasons, not the least demanding of which is the morass into which it leads when one tries to establish whether something was *really*, or *consciously* intended. Does a prelinguistic infant consciously intend to signal his displeasure or express his delight? (Bruner, 1974–1975, p. 262).

Searle has most recently made a distinction which seems to obviate the need to decide on consciousness.[5] This is the distinction between intention-in-action and prior intent. The latter involves *representation* of conditions of satisfaction, whereas the former involves mere *presentation*. That is, in prior intention there is some mental model of the conditions of satisfaction *before* the action begins. In intention-in-action the conditions of satisfaction are implicitly present *during* the intentional action. There need not be an explicit representation, such as a visual image or a linguistic formulation. Prior intentions include intentions in action, but not vice versa. For example, "I intended to raise my arm," followed by the act of doing so constitutes a prior intention followed by an intention-in-action; this intention-in-action is actually a component of the prior intention. If I raise my arm without saying anything in advance, it then becomes simply an intention-in-action. Searle goes on to answer Wittgenstein's (1953) question: If I raise my arm, what is left over if I subtract the fact that my arm went up? His answer: intentionality, and, more specifically, intention-in-action.[6] This

---

4. The possibility of shifting goals causes difficulties for the formalized operationalization put forth earlier in the chapter, as Schegloff (personal communication, 1980) pointed out to me. In such a sequence, only the last goal is consummated. It has been pointed out earlier in the chapter that, in any case, the interpretation of an intention is logically indeterminate whenever a goal is not consummated. It follows that the operational analysis being proposed would successfully identify the last in a sequence of shifting intentions, but could not identify the original intention nor any earlier intention in the sequence.

5. Searle, op. cit.

6. Searle, op. cit.

distinction between prior intention and intention-in-action allows us to clarify the sensorimotor infant and the representational linguistically competent adult: the former is capable of intention-in-action, but not prior intention, whereas the latter is capable of both.[7] At the same time the distinction makes clear the commonality in intentional structures at different developmental levels: from infancy through adulthood human beings manifest behavior directed toward the fulfillment of specific conditions of satisfaction. Unlike the notion of *conscious* intention, that of *prior* intention is susceptible to operationalization, through the indices of 1. overt representation and 2. the timing of such representation before action takes place. This is not to say that prior intention cannot be internally represented, but only that the potential for external representation renders it observable upon at least certain occasions. Yet Searle's notion of prior intention seems to capture much of what we understand, in everyday usage, by conscious intention.

Our study of adult-initiated offers provides many interesting examples of sensitive interfacing between a prior communicative intention expressed linguistically (representation) by an adult and intention-in-action manifested enactively (presentation) by a young child. Take, for example, the offer transcribed in table 1. The mother initially represents her offer overtly by means of the linguistic form: "(Do ya) wanna comb the baby's hair?" This sentence linguistically represents both intentional components of a speech act identified by Searle (1979): the illocutionary force—here, the intention to offer, marked by "(Do ya) wanna"—and the propositional content or intentional object—here, combing the baby's hair. The mother proceeds to carry out an intention-in-action by holding out the doll (2.24.00), presenting the comb (2.24.66), and showing Alice how to comb hair (2.26.12). This intention-in-action is thus part of and subordinated to the linguistically expressed prior intention ["(Do ya) wanna comb the baby's hair?"] Alice, for her part, acknowledges the offer (Ib) in action by taking the doll (2.29.93). Her mother's act of giving her the comb (IIa Ia' at 2.30.51) indicates her interpretation of taking the doll as signifying Alice's intention to comb the doll's hair. Alice confirms this interpretation by taking further steps in the same direction at Ib' (2.30.70) and IIb' (2.31.20), where she reaches toward and grasps the comb. Finally, at IIb she combs the doll's hair (2.31.90). The point here is that the mother expresses a prior intention which, because it is a communicative intention, involves a complementary intention on the part of the listener in order to be realized. Alice

7. Olson (personal communication, 1980) responded to this section by noting that the tide or a thermostat also fulfill the basic conditions for intention-in-action. This seems true for the simplest intentions-in-action typical of early infancy. However, extended sequences of action later in the sensorimotor period, especially when they involve substitution of alternative means in the face of barriers, manifest intention-in-action that goes beyond the capacities of waves or thermostats, limited as they are to a single, direct means of action.

TABLE 1

Toybox
A ⊂
L ⊐

Living Room

min	sec	frac	LILA (L) Mother non-verbal	verbal	eye gaze	ALICE (A) Child eye gaze	verbal	non-verbal	
2	21	56	seated, holding doll		< A	▽		seated	
	22	58	reaches into box		> ↓ box	> ↓ doll			Ia
		90	counter-clockwise turn,						
	23	23		(Do ya) wanna comb the baby's hair?/					
		46				> L's hand		stands up, holding hat	
		90	clockwise turn holding out doll						
	24	00		Here's a co:mb/	< A	> (comb)			
		66	arm in box, pulls out comb						
		90						smiles	
	25	26	smiling, combs doll's hair		▽ comb				
		50							
	26	12		A::h(m)/		> ↓ L			
		61							
	27	43			< ↓ A				
		73				> ↓			
		93							
	28	70	reaches up, combs A's hair					arm extended, steps toward L: A ⊂ ⊐ L	

Time	Child	Utterance	Mother	Offer
73		Comb A:lice's hair /		
88			leans forward toward doll	Ib
2 29			takes doll,	IIa
30			drops hat	Ia'
93	sits up			IIa
06	holds out comb			Ib'
16			reaches toward comb	IIa
51				IIa'
70				
90	extends hand closer to A			
31 15		(Here) comb Mommy's hair?		
20			grasps comb	IIa
40				IIb'
80	> ↓ doll			
88	drops hand			
90			combs doll's hair	IIb

The end of an utterance is represented by an oblique (/). The length of an utterance is depicted by a column of vertical obliques to the right of the time code. Contextual notes are enclosed in double parentheses; uncertain transcriptions in single parentheses. Underlining indicates increased loudness. Overlap is indicated by brackets ([ ]). Colons (: :) indicate syllable lengthening. A lexical item that is cut-off before completion is indicated by an upper-case dash, e.g., *wha⁻*. When the termination of one utterance or word is nearly simultaneous with the beginning of the next utterance or word, this rapid offset/onset or latching is indicated as follows, *In↓==Out↑/*. Pauses are specified in seconds and tenths of seconds, e.g., (1.7), while pauses of undetermined length are indicated as follows, (.). Brackets indicate duration of mothers' utterances. The direction of eye gaze is represented vis-a-vis the TV monitor screen horizontally as follows: >, facing right; <, facing left; △, facing away from the camera; ▽, facing toward the camera. Eye gaze direction on a vertical axis is represented in this way: ↑, up; ↓, down. Body orientation, in the upper left hand corner of the transcript, is schematized as follows ⊂, body facing to the right; ⊃, body facing to the left, and so on. The offer constituents Ia, Ib, etc., are also entered to the right of the transcript.

responds with a complementary intention but it is an intention-in-action, there being no indication in her overt behavior of any symbolic representation of a prior intention. Searle's distinction brings into clear relief the intentional quality of each participant's role, while highlighting developmental differences in form.

Displaying Directionality and Conditions of Satisfaction through Selective Repetition

Is the negotiated process of interpretation occurring in interaction a meaningful index of intention? Or is acceptance of the other participant's interpretation of one's own intention so automatic that it provides no information at all? This question is particularly important in studying early language acquisition where the child's linguistic means to overtly reject an interpretation are limited or nonexistent. But our basic criteria of intentionality reveal instances in which the child rejects the mother's interpretation of the intended content of communication. Here is an example from *Early Words* (Greenfield, Bruner, and May, 1972), a film made to illustrate phenomena in the late one-word period. The child in the film is Matthew (my son) at twenty-two months of age:

> Matthew is stringing Playskool wooden beads. The beads are different shapes, but the same basic size. He says "Big" as he threads one on the tip of the string. I ask "Is that a big bead?" and he repeats "Big," adding a second bead to the tip. I say "What's big? Oh, you want to put two beads on, is that big?" and he responds, "Yeah."

Here we see what Bruner calls "sustained direction of behavior" in the form of repetition. Termination of the communication does not occur until a specific interpretation occurs: that two beads make his construction big. This example is interesting because Matthew seems to be making a very subtle discrimination between two possible meanings of the word "big."[8] The initial misinterpretation as big bead elicits a repetition of "big"; the repetition in turn becomes evidence of sustained directionality.[9] Thus, this example also illustrates the point made earlier that intentional strucure is most visible where the intended consequences do not immediately occur.

8. G. W. Shugar, University of Warsaw (personal communication, 1977) suggested that we could get a fuller idea of the structure of adult-child communication were we to record what happens after the adult's interpretive expansion; this idea is exploited in the present analysis to reveal the intentional structure of such communication.

9. Schegloff (personal communication, 1980) points out that the repetition may also have the additional purpose of correction and that this addition might be operationally revealed through intonation changes.

Another point about the example is the presence of explicit confirmation of the "conditions of satisfaction" by the word "yeah," a topic to which I shall return later.

The question can arise, as always, as to whether Matthew changes his intended message in midstream. Although always possible, as mentioned earlier, it seems unlikely with this particular example because the interpretation finally accepted by Matthew also agrees more closely with the state of affairs in the referential situation than the earlier one which he rejected. That is, the beads were all basically the same size, but he did in fact make a two-bead tower. Indeed, *big* turned out to mark a prior intention on Matthew's part. After saying the word, he proceeded to add the second bead.

The logic of prior intention means that its identification depends on knowing what happens *after* the intention is expressed. This runs counter to the behavioral and experimental tradition in psychology, according to which it is customary to understand behavior in terms of what has *preceded*, rather than followed it. It is important to make this difference clear. Otherwise adherence to the old paradigm will constitute an unacknowledged barrier to the systematic study of intention in psychology.

The preceding example also shows that conversation with the child about how to interpret what he has said can make a very specific semantic intention visible. It becomes clear that the potential for extremely subtle semantic intentions are present even in the one-word period of language development. An important methodological point is that we are talking not just about repetition but about repetition in a conversational context. The candidate interpretation which Matthew does not accept, made by the other participant, gives important evidence as the exact nature of his intention.

This use of repetition shows developmental continuity. Keenan (1973) has documented the same use of repetition to gain acknowledgment of specific word combinations in slightly older children. Adults use repetition with young children in exactly the same way. Indeed, in our study of adult-initiated offer sequences, there were many instances in which repetition provided evidence of an adult's communicative intention vis-à-vis the child. As with the child, what was surprising was that adult caregivers set about actualizing rather specific intents, especially considering the immaturity of their interlocutors. Consider the example shown in table 2.

Note that the child emits a number of behaviors including looking at his mother, but the mother continues to repeat the offer (for example "Wanna do it?" at 31.2.31 seconds). In the language of conversational analysis, this transcript allows us to look at candidate acknowledgments, ones which the mother does not interpret as such (Schegloff, personal communication, 1979). The child never does do anything specifically relevant to patty-cake and the mother never goes beyond offer presentation by proceeding to the next step of an offer realization. Finally the child crawls away. This example establishes the directionality of the mother's behavior by the repetition

TABLE 2

			Family Room LIZ (L) Mother			JEREMY (J) Child		
min	sec	frac	non-verbal	verbal	eye gaze	eye gaze	verbal	non-verbal
30	49	30	seated on floor		▽↓J	△ , >		holding toy to mouth seated on floor lean-ing on right hand Ia
	50	03				△		
	51	38	leans toward Jeremy	Je:remy	>↓			
		96						
	52	30	leans closer and closer to Jeremy	You wanna play patty-cake with Mo:mmy?/		<↑		
		35						
		83						toy in mouth
	53	90						
	54	68	sits up	Wan play pa: ((high pitched)) ti-cake?/				
	55	16						
		83				>		clockwise turn, leans right : ⊂ J drops toy
	56	13				> Lillian		
		28				>↓ toy		
		70						
	58	20						sits up, toy in hand: ∪ J
		48		((singing)) Patty-cake, patty cake/				
	59	11						puts toy into mouth
.31	00	60						

△ ↑ Liz
< ↓ toy ring

			Liz actions
31			
1	10	Wanna do it?↗	
2	31		
3	00		begins to drop toy
	30		
03	46	Do you wanna play with Mo:mmy?↗	toy drops into ring / picks up toy
		claps hands on Mo:mmy	
4	71	Je:remy!/	toy into mouth / turns right: ⊂ J
	18		
	43		
5	33	((singing))↓ Pa::ty: △	
	81		
6	53	claps((see arrows))↓	
7	18	↓Cake claps	crawls away→
	71		
	86	↓pa:tty claps	
8	20	sits up	
	48	↓cake/ claps	
	91	hands to lap	
	93		

of her offer. But the assessment of conditions of satisfaction is indeterminate. Repetition of the offer stopped when the child crawled away, but surely one would not want to claim that conditions of satisfaction were met. Logically, the existence of a specific intention is indeterminate: the goal or object of intention is known, having been explicitly represented in the form of a prior intention ("You wanna play patty-cake with Mommy?") and yet termination occurs in the absence of the goal. G→T does *not* apply because the goal has not been achieved. That is, it is not false as G→T does *not* imply T→G, but rather implies the possibility that conditions other than G produce T. Because G→T is a necessary condition to infer the presence of an intention, this situation ($\sim$ G $\wedge$ T) leaves the presence of an intention up-in-the-air, logically indeterminate. This corresponds to my sense of a phenomenon in person perception: if a person expresses an intention and you observe that person carrying out directed behavior relevant to the goal, but the person never attains the goal, you are left wondering whether the expressed intention was a sincere and genuine one.

Empirically, the interactive interpretation of intention can be useful in providing more information in the absence of the successful achievement of an intention. In the example under discussion, absence of an offer realization or nullification by the mother indicates that she did not interpret the child as having had the intention to acknowledge this specific offer. Still, logically definitive evidence concerning the mother's intention is lacking. It could be argued that where prior intent has been overtly represented, goal attainment is not a necessary condition to infer the presence of an intention, that in such cases the representation of the intention plus the directed behavior are sufficient. This seems possible if one does not worry about hypocrisy, that is, if the representation of an intention is taken at face value. The stiffer criterion, including G→T, in contrast, eliminates from the class of intentions cases where people verbally express an intention but do not carry it through.

The mother's repetitions of the offer in this example also illustrate a characteristic of intentional linguistic communication that is rare in the very young children with whom the caregivers were interacting: that is, what Bruner (1974) calls substitution of alternative means to correct for deviation. Thus, in table 1 each repetition of verbal offer involves a slight variation on the original theme, 'You wanna play patty-cake with Mommy?' Alternative means are even broader than these verbal repetitions: this mother, for example, uses the child's name as an attention-getting device and demonstrates the activity being offered (the intentional object in Searle's terminology) by clapping her hands. Indeed, our results showed that unless the mother's alternative means were relevant to getting the child's visual attention on the offer or to presenting it nonverbally, that is, on a sensorimotor level, linguistic repetition and variation did not succeed in actualizing the mother's intention to communicate an offer by eliciting an acknowledgment any more than did the original presentation.

When we are talking about intention-in-action, rather than prior intention, is there not a certain degree of circularity in our operationalization? The problem is this: conditions of satisfaction G are part of and identified by the intention in question. Yet without evidence of a prior intention, there seems to be no way of identifying the goal, independent of its termination of behavior. In such cases, one way of breaking this circularity is through behavioral confirmation of the goal attainment in subsequent interaction: for instance, Matthew's "yeah" in the example just presented. It need not, however, be linguistic confirmation. My informal observations suggest that, under appropriate circumstances, relaxation and smiling might, for example, serve as behavioral indices that an intention has been realized.

Children Begin to Use Linguistic Means to Accept or Reject Adult Interpretations of their Communicative Intent

The next example of communicative intentions illustrates the use of "no" and "yeah" to explicitly confirm or disconfirm the mother's interpretation of the child's communicative intent. The example (from Matthew, age nineteen months twenty-one days) also reveals once again how communicative intentions become more visible when they are not immediately realized. This example also shows how an adult repeats the child's utterance as a communication check, while the child repeats his until it is basically understood; these two phenomena were noted by Keenan (1975).

[Matthew's sister Lauren had gone out of the room.]
MATTHEW: Lara [Lauren].
MOTHER: Yeah, Lauren. What happened to Lauren?
MATTHEW: Oh [or ou, two transcribers disagreed].
MOTHER: Oh?
MATTHEW: No.
MOTHER: Hoe?
MATTHEW: Ou.
MOTHER: Out?[10]
MATTHEW: Yeah. Yaya [Lauren].

Keenan (1975) reports examples of *yeah* used to confirm an adult interpretation at two years nine days. Our data indicate that the earliest use of *no* and *yeah* in response to adult communication checks occur for Matthew during the observation session at seventeen months thirteen days, much earlier than one might think. Nonetheless, repetition and its termination appears at the very onset of language as signs of intentionality in children's speech.

10. Schegloff (personal communication, 1980) points out the importance of a list of candidate goals in the mother's mind to the process of inferring the child's intention in this type of sequence.

In addition, the foregoing example makes it clear that the child's intent encompasses more than getting the attention of his mother; he also wants to get a specific message across. Indeed, his addition of *Yaya* at the end of the discourse appears to indicate an awareness that the original topic, Lauren, may have been lost in the discussion that subsequently ensured concerning his comment.

Although both mother and child, therefore, give strong indications that communication is in the attempt to share intention, their roles in the management of the process are somewhat different. In these cases, the mother is the one who takes responsibility for the achievement. If the mother expresses an intention through an utterance or action A, and if acknowledgment of that intention fails to occur, she tries to communicate that intention to the child via alternative expressions or actions A′, A″, and so on. On the other hand, if the child expresses intention via A and similar acknowledgment fails to occur, he just repeats A and the adult varies the interpretation until she hits an expression which the child takes to be appropriate to that intention. Thus with young children the adult carries the major role in managing the sharing of intentions, a point nicely shown in the papers of Kaye and Charney, and of Brown in this volume.

Expectation or Intention?

At this point the reader may ask, is it really necessary to use such a sloppy term as "intention"? What about "expectation"?—it has future reference, as well as an honorable history in psychology. This is my reply: Speakers do not merely *expect* certain results in their hearers; they actively work to *cause* them, and this becomes overt when the effect is question is not immediately produced. Searle, in his recent analysis of intentionality (1979), sees the causal component as crucial in setting intention apart from other mental states, among which expectation would presumably be included. According to Searle, an intention is satisfied when it causes its intentional object. For example, the intention to kill someone (the intentional object) is satisfied when you poison him; the expectation that he will die may also be fulfilled at the same time. However, the intention to kill someone is not fulfilled when the person dies in his sleep from a heart attack. Thus, intention may often include expectation, but expectation does not have all the qualities of intention. Keenan, a pioneer in the application of conversational analysis to the conversations of very young children, adopts the notion of speaker expectation as central. I would like to argue that she is really talking about intention. Consider, for example, the following instance of dialogue between a pair of twins, age two years, nine months (Keenan, 1974) in which a comment is repeated until what she terms the expected acknowledgment occurs:

Twin A: e e moth moth/
Twin B: goosey goosey gander/ where shall I wander/
Twin A: e e moth moth moth moth/
Twin B: up downstairs lady's chamber/
Twin A: e e moth moth moth/
Twin B: e e le moth/

Expectation seems inadequate to explain what the speaker trying to get *moth* across does. His repetition constitutes an active attempt to have his message acknowledged. Expectation would seem more appropriate if he merely waited for an acknowledgment after the first try. (It is only fair to say that Keenan gives communicative intent a central role in general, although it does not come into her analysis of specific data. The foregoing comments are addressed less to Keenan than to those who attempt to exclude intention completely from the vocabulary of scientific inquiry into human behavior.) Psychology used to consider the person as an exclusively passive respondent to environmental stimuli; the last twenty years have witnessed a profound change in this conception. A preference for "expectation" rather than "intention" under all circumstances reflects this old view of the person as passive and needs to be rejected with it.

Repairs as Evidence for Intentional Structure

A repair as defined in conversational analysis serves to clarify mishearings and misunderstandings, or more generally, fix any trouble source in conversation (Schegloff, Jefferson, and Sacks, 1977). Reilly has studied children's repairs, both spontaneous (self-initiated) and those initiated by an interlocutor (for example by "huh?"),[11] while Käysermann has studied the latter.[12] Both investigators have noticed that the second time around, the utterance becomes more refined or expanded. Jefferson (1979) has noticed this same phenomenon in adults. Here is an example of a self-initiated repair from Reilly (1978):

NOAH [3,0; playing with a train]: De udder way
　　　　　　　　　　　　　　　　See it goes the udder way

From the point of view of intention, the first utterance apparently does not meet the terminal requirements or conditions of satisfaction set by the child. Hence, the second utterance which establishes the component of directionality: movement toward greater elaboration. Reilly concludes, "Since it is the child, in these cases, who initiated the expansion, we can infer at most that he has some intention of producing the more complex or refined struc-

---

11. Reilly, J. Children's repairs. Unpublished manuscript, 1978.
12. Käyserman, M. L. Paper was presented at the meeting of the Max-Planck-Gesellschaft Projektgruppe für Psycholinguistik, Nijmegen, The Netherlands, February, 1979.

ture, but that he needs two turns to accomplish this level of complexity. Or we can assume at least that he is unsatisfied with the first turn, and produces the second to refine his initial utterance" (p. 4). In this case, there is no evidence to infer that the intention is motivated by an intention to communicate, since the response of a hearer is not involved. A communicative intent may still be involved as the child may intend the more complex message in itself, not merely as a clarification of a first, inadequate one. This Reilly's view; she sees the division of the message into two turns as a strategy for simplifying constructions on the leading edge of the child's linguistic competence.

Other-initiated repairs have a clearer communicative intention and thus functionally resemble repetition when the first message doesn't get across. The more elaborate nature of the second turn noted both by Reilly for American children (1978) and Käyserman (1979) for Swiss children gives initiated repairs a special form of directionality going beyond the mere persistence of self-repetition. Indeed, they manifest one of the optional characteristics of intentional behavior present on Bruner's list: a substitution rule whereby alternative means can be deployed for correction of direction. Here is an example of the phenomenon from Reilly:

> JAMIE [6,3]: How an hour is long sometimes and so short another time?
> MOTHER: What, honey?
> JAMIE: How can an hour be long sometimes and so short another time?

Mother signals unsuccessful communication and Jamie constructs an alternative sentence to correct the situation.

Considering other-initiated repair as an intentional structure, one would like to know what happened *after* Jamie's second turn. Did his mother say something to show that she had understood the second version? The answer to this question is relevant to understanding Jamie's intentional object, the nature of the conditions of satisfaction for his intention. It was not, however, necessary for Reilly's purpose of examining repair as a learning strategy. This example thus illustrates how the study of intentional structures demands more information on the consequences of behavior than we, as behavioral scientists, are in the habit of collecting.

Disentangling the Intention to Communicate from a Communicative Intention

The intention to communicate is basically the intention to affect a particular audience. A communicative intention is the particular effect (illocutionary and locutionary) intended.[13] Very often these cannot be operationally separated out. But it is particularly interesting when this is possible. The following example illustrates conditions where this can be done for a child at the one-word stage. This example also shows how single words can be used to signal intentions which can be realized only through extremely complex sequential interactions. (The example is an observation of a child at the one-word stage made during a children's gym class which his mother was teaching.)

> The child goes toward his mother, whining "shoes, shoes" (he has only socks on). He comes back toward me and gets his blue sandals. I try to help him while standing up, but cannot do it. So I sit down with one shoe, put him on my lap, and put his shoe on. Then I put him down, not saying anything. He walks straight to his other shoe, picks it up, and comes back to me. I put him on my lap and put his other shoe on. He then runs toward his mother still talking, saying "shoe, shoe" in an excited voice. He lifts his foot to show her. When she attends, he points to me. She understands, saying something like "The lady put your shoes on." Both are very excited.

The intention to communicate with his mother is distinct from his message, the intentional communication, because mother and shoes are in opposite spatial directions. Note his literal directionality (in space) and note he stops repeating 'shoes' after reaching his mother. His intentional communication, in contrast, is a desire to have his shoes on. This is demonstrated by the fact that he ultimately goes toward the shoes and engages in complex interaction with me in order to get them on. He is a very active participant in this process: note where he goes to the second shoe, picks it up, and brings it back to me. This complex sequence of steps would seem another way in which directionality (D) can be operationally characterized. Once his shoes are on (G), action on my lap is terminated (G→T). Now, however, he communicates 'shoe, shoe' in an excited voice. This change from whining to excitement is an interesting candidate for an observable index of goal attainment, the fulfillment of intention. While possibly marking the attainment of one goal, it also constitutes the beginning of a second communication. Again, the intention to communicate to mother is manifest in running toward her (D) and stopping when he reaches her (G→T). The communicative intention is then revealed. He lifts his foot until his mother attends. The continuation of this position exactly until drawing his moth-

13. Cazden (1977) restricts communicative intent to illocutionary force, whereas Dore (1975) points out that "intention" has been used in he field of child language to refer to both locutionary and illocutionary aspects, in accord with my usage here. These terminological differences do not, however, affect the points under discussion.

er's attention is our only evidence of directionality; timing certainly should be useful evidence in cases where we have a video record, but we do not have one here. The termination of footlifting (only implicit in my notes) fulfills the G→T condition. This lacuna in my notes illustrates the kind of information often missing in observations because it is taken for granted. I think there is a general tendency to note onset of new behavior and take terminations for granted. The child then points to me, and his mother interprets his message. At this point, knowledge of the child's response would be needed to know if he accepts his mother's interpretation of his semantic intention. Again, my notes, taken for a different purpose, make the common error of not extending enough into the consequences of action to satisfy the complete requirements of a stringent analysis of intention. Nevertheless, this example does illustrate certain circumstances in which a group of related intentions can be disentangled through analyzing complex sequential interaction.

Conclusion

Speech act theory as developed by Searle (1969; 1975a; 1975b; 1979) makes intention intrinsic to language use. However, by leaving out the sequential course of communicative interaction, it provides little means for the operational definition required for stringent application to empirical phenomena. Conversational analysis as developed by Schegloff, Jefferson, and Sacks (for example, Schegloff and Sacks, 1973; Schegloff, Jefferson and Sacks, 1977) provides the latter, but generally prefers to talk about the functions of sentences rather than the intentions of people. I have tried to integrate these two sets of contributions in the belief that their integration will allow the issue of intentionality to be systematically and empirically investigated. Yet it is necessary to go beyond the linguistic phenomena addressed by speech act theory and conversational analysis. I hope this chapter has made it clear that our analysis is not limited to intention in linguistic interaction, but applies to nonverbal (sensorimotor) interaction, as well as interaction which uses both modes together (cf. the two transcripts of offers, tables 1 and 2). Indeed, the logic of intention and its operationalization applies to intentional action as well as interaction. Because an intention is essentially an internal cognitive state, it is only indirectly observable. One goal of this chapter was to show how, because of the mutual processes of interpretation going on in interaction, such interaction provides a context in which the intentionality of a single individual's action becomes all the more observable.

Intentionality has been with us since the beginning of psychology. Generally it has entered through the back door. My claim is that our most mechanistic, reductionistic pieces of research would not be possible for us as human beings if we did not impose an intentional structure on behavior. If you don't believe this try to make sense of the molecular transcripts in tables 1 and 2 without the labels identifying their organization in terms of the intentional structure of an offer (Ia, Ib, and so on). We need to understand much more about our own perception of intention and the basis for the perception in the actual organization of behavior. This task requires a rigorous analysis of intentionality and consideration of complex sequences of activity. The operationalization of intention requires us to study more than the stimulus antecedents of behavior; equal attention must be paid to the forward thrust of action and its interactive consequences.

Afterword

The intellectual history of this chapter—an important piece of my own intellectual history—constitutes a true acknowledgment of the contribution Jerome Bruner has made to my development.

The history of this chapter starts in 1961 when, in my junior year at Radcliffe College, I took Jerry's graduate seminar. We read three books, each of which provided themes for my later thinking and research: Inhelder and Piaget's *Growth of Logical Thinking*, Vygotsky's *Thought and Language*, and, most important for the present chapter, *Plans and the Structure of Behavior* by Miller, Galanter, and Pribram. This last mentioned book was the first clue I had that purpose and intention, so important to my personal view of human nature, could be rigorously treated in scientific psychology.

The topic of intention came up next when I returned to the Center for Cognitive Studies as a Fellow in 1968. Jerry was working on infancy and was full of observations and ideas about early intentionality. This was the ambiance which inspired a paper called "Goal as Environmental Variable in the Development of Intelligence" (1972). The paper was originally presented at the Conference on Contributions to Intelligence organized in the wake of the furor over Jensen's (1968) article on intelligence in the *Harvard Educational Review* and held at the University of Illinois in November 1969.

The most recent impetus for this chapter came when I was invited to join a language group organized by Jerry at the Netherlands Institute for Advanced Study in Wassenaar; I spent two weeks there in February, 1979. Although intentionality was not directly discussed, reactions of the group to our research on adult-initiated offers stimulated or provided a number of the ideas in this chapter. I am grateful to Jerry Bruner, Melissa Bowerman, David Olson, and Manny Schegloff for their serious and valuable discussion of our work. In addition to the NIAS group, the comments of Elena Lieven, who attended my NIAS seminar, were most useful and insightful.

With respect to this chapter, I owe a special debt to Emmanuel Schegloff whose comments on our film *Early Words* gave me my first glimpse into conversational analysis and how it could be applied to my own data. Although Manny and I are both at UCLA, it was through the experience at Wassenaar that we came to understand each other's work deeply enough to talk about it at a meaningful level. I am grateful to Jerry for masterminding the NIAS group and including me in it.

This chapter owes an intellectual debt to two other people in Los Angeles: to my student, Patricia Zukow through whom I gradually came to understand conversational analysis and, specifically, the methodological value of an interactive approach to the language acquisition process; and to my colleague Elinor Keenan whose work on child discourse furnished a brilliant background against which to develop my ideas on intentionality.

The final inspiration was the passage from Jerry's autobiography with which I opened. I hope this chapter contributes to filling the need identified therein: the need to give intentionality its rightful place in our scientific description of human nature.

References

Bates, E., Camaioni, L., and Volterra, V. The acquisition of performatives prior to speech. *Merrill-Palmer Quarterly*, 1975, 21, 205–224.

Boden, M. A. *Purposive explanation in psychology*. Cambridge, Mass.: Harvard University Press, 1972.

Bruner, J. S. The organization of early skilled action. In M. P. M. Richards (Ed.), *The integration of a child into a social world*. Cambridge, England: Cambridge University Press. 1974.

————. From communication to language—a psychological perspective. *Cognition*, 1974/1975, 3, 255–287.

————. Intellectual autobiography. In G. Lindzey (Ed.), *History of psychology in autobiography*. San Francisco: Freeman, 1980.

Garfinkel, H. *Studies in ethnomethodology*. Englewood Cliffs, N.J.: Prentice Hall, 1967.

————. Remarks on ethnomethodology. In J. J. Gumperz and D. Hymes (Eds.), *The ethnography of communication*. New York: Holt, 1972.

Greenfield, P. M. Goal as environmental variable in the development of intelligence. In R. Cancro (Ed.), *Intelligence: Genetic and environmental influences*. New York. Grune and Stratton, 1971.

Harding, C. and Golinkoff, R. Paper presented at the *Society for research in child development interdisciplinary workshop on the development of communication*. University of Delaware, 1979.

Howe, C. J. Review of *The structure of communication in early language development*. *Journal of Child Language*, 1977, 4, 479–482.

Käyserman, M. L. Paper presented at the *Max-Planck-Gesellschaft Projektgruppe für Psycholinguistik*. Nijmegen, The Netherlands, February 1979.

Keenan, E. Ochos. Conversational competence in children. *Journal of Child Language*, 1974, 1, 163–185.

————. Making it last: Uses of repetition in children's discourse. In *Proceedings of the Berkeley linguistics society*. Berkeley, 1975. Also in S. Ervin-Tripp and C. Mitchell-Kernan (Eds.), *Child discourse*. New York: Academic Press, 1977.

Miller, G. A., Galanter, G., and Pribram, K. H. *Plans and the structure of behavior.* New York: Henry Holt, 1960.

Pribram, K. H., Spinelli, D. N., and Kamback, M. C. Electrocortical correlates of stimulus response and reinforcement. *Science*, 1967, 157, 94–95.

Reilly, J. Children's repairs. Unpublished manuscript, 1978.

Reilly, J., Zukow, P. G., and Greenfield, P. M. *Facilitating the transition from sensorimotor to linguistic communication during the one-word period.* Paper presented at the meeting of the *First International Congress for the Study of Child Language*, Tokyo, August 1978.

Rodgon, M. Not the final word. Review of *The structure of communication in early language development. Contemporary Psychology*, 1977, 22, 362–364.

Ryan, J. Early language development: Towards a communicational analysis. In M. P. M. Richards (Ed.), *The integration of a child into a social world*. Cambridge, England: Cambridge University Press. 1974.

Schegloff, E. A., Jefferson, G., and Sacks, H. The preference for self-correction in the organization of repair in conversation. *Language*, 1977, 53, 361–382.

Schegloff, E. A. and Sacks, H. Opening up closings. *Semiotica*, 1973, 8, 289–327.

Searle, J. R. *Speech acts: An essay in the philosophy of language*. Cambridge, England: Cambridge University Press, 1969.

————. Indirect speech acts. In P. Cole and J. Morgan (Eds.), *Syntax and semantics III: Speech acts*. New York: Academic Press, 1975a.

————. A taxonomy of illocutionary acts. In K. Gunderson (Ed.), *Language mind, and knowledge, Minnesota Studies in the Philosophy of Science*, vol. 7. Minneapolis: University of Minnesota Press, 1975b.

————. The intentionality of intention and action. *Cognitive Science*, 1980, 4, 47–70.

Wittgenstein, L. *Philosophical investigations*. New York: MacMillan, 1953.

Zukow, P. G., Reilly, J., and Greenfield, P. M. Making the absent present: Facilitating the transition from sensorimotor to linguistic communication. In K. Nelson (Ed.), *Children's language*, vol. 3. New York: Gardner Press, in press.

12

Teaching the Young Child: Some Relationships between Social Interaction, Language, and Thought

David J. Wood

About nine years ago I was listening to one of Bruner's "Psychology 148" lectures at Harvard on the nature and development of intentionality in infancy. He was convinced that the baby showed clear signs of intentional behavior well before goal-directed activity became apparent to casual observation. One of his attempts to demonstrate this precocious intentionality had involved him in the production of a short film, made in cooperation with Allegra May. The film was about prereaching babies confronted with an extremely attractive, eye-catching, potentially graspable puppet which was kept persistently just in front of their noses. The film made the point that even though the baby was clearly unable to take the object and bring it to his mouth, there were clear signs of his intention to do so well before any potential reinforcement for an act of reaching could possibly have occurred. The baby appeared not only to be taken by the object but virtually infected by it. His mouth worked, often producing bubbles; his shoulders were raised up against gravity; his hands were opening and closing, often clutching and pulling at his clothes. Bruner claimed that all the necessary prerequisites of the reaching act were in evidence, preadapted components of the eventual movement which would fulfil the manifest intention. The process of early skill development was thus cast as the orchestration of preadapted behavioral components to fulfil intentions, whose ontogenesis lay elsewhere than in the effect of reinforcement. Eventually, Bruner went on

The author's research into the instruction of hearing children referred to in this paper was supported by research grants number HR 2520/1 and HR 2520/2 from the Social Science Research Council. The work with deaf children is currently being supported by a programme grant from the Medical Research Council held jointly by the author and Professor C.I. Howarth.

to try and identify the locus of intentionality both conceptually and physiologically in the reafference copy theory of Von Holst.

My own attention throughout the film, however, was less with the baby than with his audience. The majority of students, as the film ran on, showed clear signs of tension. The film was well made, and the director did *not* let his audience off the hook by showing his young star take the object. The film ended, as it began, with the jerky, apparently intentioned movements of the baby—no sigh of relief, no release from tension by the achievement of a reach.

Whether Bruner was right or not in this identification of intentionality is not the subject of this essay. What *is* of relevance, however, was the readiness of both Bruner and his audience, to *impute* intentions to the baby. They shared his apparent direction and tension; the infant's activity, apparently so close to success, had a catching, invitational quality to it. Subsequent research, much of which will be referred to and discussed in this volume, has gone on to demonstrate that this imputation of intentions, meanings, and wishes by the nature to the extremely immature, is a widespread and developmentally crucial phenomenon.

At the time the studies of infant intentionality were in progress we had just started a study of the acquisition of skill in three-to-five-year-olds: (Wood, Bruner, and Ross, 1976). The juxtaposition of these observations with ideas aroused by the film and other observations served to change our focus somewhat from the child's own actions on the task to his *inter*actions with an adult, in this case a female experimenter. She was following a fixed set of rules for helping the children master a complicated construction task, which we describe in some detail later. Once we elected to look at the study with an interactive framework in mind, it soon became apparent that while she was indeed systematically following the rules with all the children, they were actually drawing out different behaviors from her. Her rules of behavior were *conditional* on their ongoing task activity, and, hence, her activities formed a sort of mirror image of what the children were doing. For example, with the young children she was constantly showing them elements of the solution, trying to "lure" them into task activity. They seldom made more than one step at a time; they did what she asked, showed, or suggested but then stopped. This meant she had to react to their activity with some form of action or suggestion to keep them involved. With the eldest children, a single intervention usually engendered a whole sequence of operations as children not only did as she suggested but extrapolated from the instruction to a range of subsequent activities. They responded to the rules of the task, carrying out sequences of actions rather than simple isolated moves. The changing competence of the child was thus reflected in the uses made of the experimenter-cum-tutor.

This study, together with a reconsideration of other ongoing work, led us to the metaphor of "scaffolding." Adult and child together were achieving success on a task, but the nature of their individual contributions varied with the child's level of ability. Once the child could be lured into some form of task-relevant activity, however low level, the tutor could build around him a supporting structure which held in place whatever he could manage. That supporting activity served to connect the child's activity into the overall construction and to provide a framework within which the child's actions could lead to and mean something more general than he may have foreseen. As the child mastered components of the task, he was freed to consider the wider context of what he could do, to take over more of the complementary activity. The adult could "de-scaffold" those parts which now stood firmly on their own. Thus tutor and child shared in doing the task, the tutor helping the child succeed with those aspects he could not manage, thus supporting his gradual mastery of the task.

At the end of our report of this study, we tried to analyze the scaffolding process more explicitly and suggested a number of interacting functions which the adult might perform in helping a child toward educated mastery of a problem. A great deal more has been learned about these processes since that initial study. We shall begin with an overview of the scaffolding process and elaborate that process in the light of our more recent work. We will then move on to consider the wider theoretical implications of styles and patterns of instruction for the intellectual, linguistic, and social development of the child.

The Scaffolding Process

One concept which has come to play an important part in discussions of social interaction is that of intersubjectivity (Trevarthen, 1977; Lock, 1978). Bruner (1975) himself has identified a number of features of infant-parent interactions which help ensure that the baby is brought to attend to and participate in the "same" experiences as adults. The achievement of such early, shared, intersubjective experiences is seen as the foundation for the development of mutual understanding and eventually of language itself. The motion of scaffolding can be understood by reference to this intersubjectivity. Intersubjectivity—sharing perceptions, conceptions, feelings, and intentions—is a state or achievement; scaffolding is one of the major processes whereby it is achieved. But how can that process begin?

In the earliest stages of growth, adult and child seem more or less naturally adapted to each other. The child responds selectively and systematically to various sounds, sights, and touches, and his reactions to adult behavior are often such that they help fulfill adult expectations. His response to soothing sounds, for example, to heartbeats, to oval-shaped, eye-possessing, moving shapes, tend to fit in neatly with the adults' aspirations in providing them. The neonate may be weak and immature but he comes armed with bait and lures—he traps the attention of adults. Similarly, as the infant, for example, repeats movements which have just provoked an adult response, and thus "re-creates" that response, he reveals to adults that he can play a role in extended interactions and reinforces some of their expectations of him. However, while nature may start him on his way and naturally enmesh him in such reciprocal activities, there are many tasks to be faced and lessons to be learned which are not so immediately inviting or so readily solved. More complex tasks call for sustained adult intervention.

The hypothesis that one may leave to nature the child's total education has little to commend it. As Skinner (1968) observes, for example, Pestalozzi's attempt to apply Rousseau's noble-savage hypothesis to the education of his own son seemed to work well while the child was learning about streams, flowers, his own bodily skills, and so on but was a total failure when it came to developing an acquaintance with the artifacts of culture— with books, numbers, and other artificial skills. The child's entry into these activities, whose rewards are distant and often ill-defined, rests in the first instance on a social contract—a trust in and desire to please or to emulate another. It is just such a social contract which appears to underlie adult intervention and the growth of intersubjectivity. But it is an intersubjectivity managed mostly from the adult's side.

How can this intersubjectivity be exploited in the development of skills? The learning process is essentially one of problem solving, in which the child sets up goals and recruits, from various sources, the means to solve them. If he is to be engaged as an effective student he must be continually meeting and handling problems. But, as I pointed out, the immediate goals that the child sets for himself may not be those of greatest value, generality, or eventual significance. How does one actually facilitate the choice of appropriate goals? This, of course, was one of Dewey's central questions to educators. He saw directed thinking as a personal process of problem solving: "General appeals to a child (or to a grownup) to think irrespective of the existence in his own experience of some difficulty that troubles him and disturbs his equilibrium are as futile as advice to lift himself by his own boot-straps" (Dewey, 1933, p. 15). For Bruner, too, the process of education is viewed as one of engineering a succession of well-chosen problems with the child, whose solution represents the content of a field of study (Bruner, 1966).

How, then, does the child come to see his own goals and purposes in the task set before him by parents and teachers? One such means is shown in one of our tasks in which the child constructs objects and patterns with blocks. Many of the children displayed clear evidence of recognizing an outcome achieved by an adult before they could produce such an outcome themselves. The well-documented recognition-production gap (for example, Olson, 1966, 1971; McNeill, 1970) provides a basis for problem solving

—the child could strive to create something which he could recognize when he or the adult achieved it but for which, as yet, he had no clearly defined plan of operation. Such a mismatch between present state and desired end state is at the heart of problem solving. The discrepancy between understood goals and actual performance also provided our tutor-experimenter with scope for intervention. She was able to keep an interpretable goal before the child, continually directing and assisting him—and he could be so directed because he recognized the relevance of what he was being shown to the goal he was entertaining.

The adult may thus help the child to break down an overall problem into a series of recognizable and manageable sub-goals. But appropriate task analysis revolves around an effective diagnosis of the child's ideas and intentions—in the instructor's hypotheses about the learner's hypotheses. The central question, of course, is how an adult actually discovers the child's hypotheses and his level of task mastery—how he locates what Vygotsky (1978) called the "zone of proximal development."

In our more recent work, using the task already referred to, we have developed more explicit hypotheses about the process whereby a tutor may solve this problem. These have also revealed marked differences between parents and teachers in their strategies for trying to make and exploit such discoveries. This, in turn, led to further experiments designed to test the hypothesis that effective scaffolding exhibits certain specific properties. We turn now to a consideration of this work.

Analyzing the Instructional Process

In the first study (Wood and Middleton, 1975) we asked mothers to teach their three-to-four-year-old children how to assemble the construction toy illustrated in figure 1. We told them that after they had taught the child, we would ask him to try the task on his own. Our aim was to try and relate the instructional behavior of the mothers in the teaching phase to the child's performance in the testing phase. Our hypothesis, derived from the concept of scaffolding, was that the adult tutorial interventions should be inversely related to the child's level of task competence—so, for example, the more difficulty the child had in achieving a goal, the more directive the interventions of mother-cum-tutor should be. The eventual system of analysis was a simple one. Maternal help during the instructional phase was categorized in terms of a number of "levels of intervention." Each utterance, nonverbal indicator, and demonstration was classified into the following categories of increasingly explicit instructions.

At level 1 the mother would simply try to verbally encourage the child to enter into task activity. She might say "What are you going to do now?"

FIGURE 1 The Task

"Would you like to make something with the blocks?" and so forth. We ignored the actual syntactic form of the utterance, simply deciding that it was an attempt to prompt activity without providing any specific indications of goals to be achieved, attributes to be attended to, or operations to be performed.

At level 2, the mother attempted to verbally establish parameters which would guide the child's search for the material to be operated upon. Again, the utterance might take one of many different syntactic forms—she might say, for example, "I think you need the very big blocks, " or "Get the littlest ones," and so forth. The defining characteristic of this level was that the mother identified critical features of material but took no part in the search for material.

At level 3, the mother actually intervened in the selection process itself by indicating materials to be used. She might simply point or point and talk —"You need that little one, there" and so on. Here she is leaving the child with the task of *operating* with the material indicated, problems of proper orientation of compatible material remain.

At level 4, the mother intervenes not only in the selection of the materials but also in their actual arrangement. In fact, she leaves the child with only one degree of freedom—to perform or not to perform the act of putting together, piling, or whatever.

At level 5 the intervention is a full demonstration in which the mother takes the appropriate material, prepares and assembles it while the child looks on.

As we descend from level 1 to 5, then, mother takes over increasing control of the act of construction in question. At higher levels, the child's contribution is greatest, at the lower levels it is minimal. Where a child makes an inappropriate construction in a self-initiated act (level 0) or an error in response to a maternal instruction, the mother could loop back to any of the five levels—she might simply ask if he is satisfied with what he has done, draw attention to specific features which are at variance with a legal move, indicate what he should use to correct himself, prepare the ground for the new, appropriate move, or demonstrate what he should have done.

The task actually involved twenty distinct operations, including the final act of "topping" the pyramid with a single block. Between the initiating move for each operation and the eventual successful completion, there could be any number of maternal interventions depending upon how successful the child was. We operationalized our hypothesis about the nature of effective instruction in terms of the levels of intervention, as follows: "When the child makes an error, then immediately take over more control. So, for example, if an error occurs in response to a level 3 intervention, advance to level 4 or 5. However, if the child is successful in following an instruction (for example, level 3) relinquish some control. That is, next time an error or pause invites an instruction intervene at levels 1 or 2."

For a few of the mothers, tutorial efforts were highly contingent on their child's behavior as defined by this rule, whereas the instructional activity of others was totally noncontingent. When we examined each mother's successive level of intervention and compared this with the child's preceding move, we found the range of scores in following the hypothesized pattern ranged from 0.0 to 0.80. Some would start to *show* their child how to do the task, and this invariably motived the child to get his hands on the material. However, some mothers would ignore the early moves of the child toward such involvement, fending him off, telling him to wait until they had shown him everything. This strategy led to an almost complete failure by the child when he came to try and do the task alone. Other mothers showed an apparent reluctance to actually touch the material or to demonstrate an operation to the child. Hence, their interventions remained largely at levels 1 and 2, often involving paraphrased instructions at the same level. This strategy also did not work. In fact, the correlation between the instructor's tendency to follow our hypothetical rule and the child's subsequent ability to put the material together was extremely high (Spearman's rho (r_s) = 0.89, n1 = n2 = 12, p < 0.01, Wood and Middleton, 1975).

This study enabled us to describe more precisely, then, the actual process which successful mothers-as-instructors used in assisting young children in the solution of a well-defined problem. But, as the process is an interactional one, it remains unclear whether the mother herself had developed the strategy described by our hypothesis or if some children are more teachable, eliciting from their mentor the information they need to successfully reach their own goals. That is, it is not clear who, the instructor or the child, regulates the interaction.

From a consideration of the correlation-cause problem, two further experiments emerged. First, we asked whether a mother's performance is at all independent of her child. If she were faced with another child of the same sex and similar age, would her performance—her relative level of contingency—generalize, or would it only emerge systematically with her own child? In our first attempt to answer this question we persuaded nine of the mothers from the study just described to return to teach a "strange" child. Even with this small sample we obtained a significant correlation between their rank order performances with their own and a strange child (Wood and Middleton, 1974).

In view of the small sample employed, we reran the study with a larger sample of twenty mothers. This also enabled us to replicate the initial study. Each mother taught her own child and one whom she met for the first time shortly before the experimental session. The order was counter-balanced; ten mothers taught their own child first, ten the stranger first.

The results corroborated those of our initial studies. In the first place, maternal contingency did correlate with the children's post-test perform-ances, though not so markedly as in our initial study ($r_s = 0.62$; $n_1 = n_2 = 20$, $p < 0.01$). Another important result was that the performances of the pairs of children taught by the same adult also correlated ($r_s = 0.65$; $p < 0.01$). This provides strong evidence that the pattern of instruction gen-eralized across children. That the mothers who were effective with their own children were also successful with other people's children was also shown by the fact that the rank order performances of mothers with the pairs of children also correlated ($r_s = 0.76$; $p < 0.01$).

These experiments, then, have shown that effective instruction may be described in terms of the contingency rule relating the level of intervention to the successes and failures of the child. Furthermore, they have shown that mothers who adopt this contingent approach can apply it not only to their own child but also to unfamiliar children. It remains a possibility, however, that the contingency rule is a relatively minor part of the tutorial ability of the mother. To try and determine that we had properly identified the critical components of effective tutoring, a final experiment in this series was conducted.

If the contingency rule is a crucial part of the instructional process then it should be possible to teach it to other adults who should achieve predictable results when they apply it to new children. Four instructional strategies based on the application or violation of our contingency rule were devel-oped and applied by an experimenter-tutor to four groups of children (Wood, Wood, and Middleton, 1978). The first was the "contingent rule" defined above; the second was a purely *verbal* approach which consisted entirely of level 1 and level 2 instructions; the third was a demonstration technique which comprised only level 5 instructions. The fourth strategy which had been observed in the mother-child studies was a "swing" tech-nique in which the adult offered general verbal encouragement (level 1) but then, given the almost inevitable failure which followed, moved directly to demonstration and then back to a level 1 prompt, and so on. This latter strategy honors the turn-taking aspect of contingency, but the large jumps in level of instruction provide a poor fit to the actual performance and immediate problems of the child—the precise implications of the general prompts were not broken down into their constituent operations and decisions.

An experimenter was trained to use each of these strategies and then asked to teach four groups of eight children by using a different strategy with each group. The results were as predicted. The contingent group was by far the most successful, the verbal and swing groups gave intermediate performances, while the demonstration group managed least well. In a subsequent analysis, we went on to show that when we rank order the contingency scores for the experimenter-cum-tutor with the contingent group alone (since she was not equally successful at following the rules with all the children) here too we found a significant correlation between instructional contingency and the child's post-test performance ($r_s = 0.69$, n = 8, $p < 0.05$).

This final study thus provided additional support for the hypothesis that the contingency rule underlies effective instruction. Two additional comments may be made. The first relates to the verbal strategy. The group of children taught this way did manage to finish the task under instruction, though they were largely unable to transfer this performance to their own, unassisted efforts. This shows, then, that it is possible to get the child to cooperate in and even to complete a task without his learning much from the experience. When the verbal strategy went beyond general encouragement to contingent, specific verbal instructions, the child was sometimes successful. More often than not, however, success only came after a string of instructions at the same level. The fact that children can be "talked through" the problem in this way, without generalizing from the instruction given, further underlines the importance of contingency for learning—in this particular case, the importance of responding to the child's inability to follow a verbal instruction by immediately helping him to do the operation in question.

The second point relates to the performance of the demonstration group. Although these children were less successful than the other groups, they showed the longest involvement in the task after instruction. Providing a demonstration may not be the optimum way of explicitly teaching the child complex rules, but it may well be an effective strategy for ensuring his interest in the task at hand.

Thus, effective instruction for young children rests on a close relationship between language and action. Neither descriptions nor demonstrations are adequate by themselves. Rather, language must be interwoven with the learners' activities, sometimes the words guiding the actions, at other times the actions guiding and helping to define the words. But in all cases the language and actions are highly interdependent. Recent research in other laboratories is congruent with the hypothesis that contingent adult-child interaction is critical in intellectual growth. Margery Heber, for example (Heber, 1977, 1978, 1979) taught five- and six-year-old children a seriation task by one of four different teaching strategies and evaluated their effects by means of a post-test. Ten subjects were assigned each of the following treatments:

1. Action. The child was given a set of discs varying in diameter and asked to find ones "that go between" the largest and smallest discs. The child was then left to place items and there was no further discussion between experimenter and child.
2. Dialogue. The adult introduced the relevant verbal relations (for example, "Longer than," "Shorter than") to the child in the context of the child's ongoing activity.
3. Didactic. The adult introduced the same relevant verbal relations (for example, "Longer than," "Shorter than") to the child in the context of the adult's own activity.
4. No Intervention. The control condition.

All the teaching and the post-test sessions were videotaped and subjected to detailed analysis. The major finding of the study was that Group 2 alone showed significant progress in their ability to seriate. Although Heber's strategies do not map perfectly onto those already described, there is one important similarity. Heber stresses the importance of integrating the adult descriptions both with the child's actions and with appropriate descriptions. "Neither the child's own organizing activity nor the extrinsic influence of speech forms (action and didactic conditions) independently produce progress in seriation whereas speech and action incorporated together by discussion with the observer is effective. It seems that such guided dialogue helps the child to formulate and thus to synthesize essential serial relations. This reciprocal formulation has to be made in terms of the listener's point of view" (Heber, 1979, p. 9).

In a later study, Heber has shown that dialogues between children at a similar stage of development fail to produce an improvement in performance. Although arguments between the children were frequent, and the children were being confronted with potentially relevant arguments, these failed to produce progress. Again, these results indicated the importance both of the contingent interaction and the adults' superior knowledge in cognitive growth. We find a similar effect of appropriate instruction on cognitive development in an earlier study by Sonstroem (1966), who attemped to teach children to conserve mass across various transformations of the shape of a ball of Plasticine. The study parallels Heber's. There were four groups of children and four instructional conditions: one group simply manipulated the materials, another watched the experimenter manipulate the clay and were asked to produce descriptions. Children in the third group manipulated the Plasticine, and their transformations were described by the adult in a way which honored the conservation of mass. A fourth group served as the control. Only the third group showed a marked improvement in performance over the controls, about 80 percent achieving success as against around 30 percent in the other groups.

These results, like those arising from our own work, suggest that effective instruction with young children involves a continuous integration of language and action. It is not sufficient for learning to simply expose the child to material by allowing him to manipulate it. Nor is it sufficient that he be exposed to appropriate labels or to verbally encoded relationships between elements of a problem. Where a child is simply expected to look on while an adult shows him the elements of a task, labels them, and explains how things relate to each other, it is unlikely that he will generalize what he is experiencing to his own subsequent actions on the task. Thus, where such a technique is used, as in Sinclair-de-Zwart's (1967) study and in Heber's analagous Didactic condition, children do not make significant progress. However, where instruction is contingent on the child's own activities and related to what he is currently trying to do then considerable progress may be made.

This same emphasis on contingent interactions, the integration of the tutor's demonstrations and descriptions with the child's attempts at performance, has also figured strongly in our more recent work with young deaf children (Wood and Wood, 1979), which we now examine briefly.

Twelve severely to profoundly deaf children ranging in age from 3 and one-half to five years with little speech production and limited lip-reading skill were taught by their own teachers how to assemble the construction task described earlier. Their teaching sessions were video-taped and subsequently analyzed in terms of the levels of intervention described earlier. Although it was quite easy to score the behavior of both teacher and child using this system, it failed to reveal any significant relationships between teacher-contingency and child learning. Since these children were able to hear little or nothing of what was said to them, and unable to interpret much of what they might hear, we eventually decided to try and see the situation more from their point of view—we switched off the sound of the video-recordings! Immediately, aspects of the nonverbal behavior of teacher and child which we had overlooked became prominent and interpretable.

In our earlier analysis of the operations involved in the construction task we had isolated seventeen discrete items of information which, together, specified the structure of the task (for example, "pegs fit into holes," "pieces of the same size fit together," "small flats fit on top of larger ones"). In the new, nonverbal analysis, we found a wide variety of nonverbal devices being used by teachers to fulfil each of these functions. So, for example, the operation "find two pieces" was embodied in the following routine:

> The teacher picks up one piece and holds it, arm partially extended, toward the child. She runs her hand around its contour slowly and sketches out 'in space' the outline which a pair would make. Her facial expression is an 'open' declarative one. Then she raises her eyebrows and shoulders and, with her right hand palm upwards, sweeps over the remaining blocks.

We interpret such a routine as "you need two pieces, find the other one to go with this one."

A second format which was used in a wide variety of contexts was a "discrepancy analysis," in which the teacher makes a deliberate but informative mistake. For example, a young child has just chosen two pieces of the same size, but both had pegs and, hence, could only be partly and incorrectly assembled. The teacher operated as follows:

> Teacher gently takes the blocks from the child and holds her finger up between herself and the child with an open facial expression. She keeps the finger there until the child looks at her, she then points the finger at the two blocks which she holds in her other hand. Then she transfers one block to the other hand and orients them to tap the two pegs together. She first looks questioningly at the child, then both smile and shake their heads negatively.

We interpreted this routine as "we don't want two pieces with pegs." As the teacher had already established the critical feature which differentiated the correct from the incorrect one, it was a relatively simple matter for the child to pick out the correct one. We were thus able to reclassify these formats into our five levels of intervention. Levels 3, 4, and 5, already defined by their nonverbal content in the original system, were preserved in the revised system, but general verbal prompts and identification of critical features for search (levels 1 and 2) were redefined to subsume a range of formats illustrated above.

Armed with this revised system, we reanalyzed the teaching contingency measures on a nonverbal basis and discovered a significant correlation between the teaching performances of the teachers and the unassisted performances of the children after instructions ($r_s = 0.59$, n = 12, p < 0.05). This result again points to the centrality of the contingency rule in teaching, quite independent of the means of communication being used.

It seemed highly possible that these nonverbal forms of instruction employed with the deaf may also play a role in the teaching of hearing children. Consequently, to test for this possibility, we went back to the original video-tapes of twelve hearing children being instructed by their mothers and reanalyzed their interactions with the sound off. Although less pronounced, these interactions also involved nonverbal means of communication at levels 1 and 2, and when these were scored in terms of the nonverbal contingency rule we found an extremely high correlation between the new measure and the children's post-test performances ($r_8 = 0.94$, $p < 0.01$). These patterned forms of interaction may be compared to the formats, described by Bruner (1975), Garvey (1976), and others, which play a vital role in the linguistic development of hearing children. A communication format may be not only a means for acquiring language, but also an alternative or supplementary means of instruction. It may also be pointed out that, while there is a high correlation between the verbal and nonverbal contingency measures for mothers with hearing children ($r_8 = 0.95$, $p < 0.01$, $n = 12$), there was no significant relationship between the two measures for our sample of deaf children ($r_8 = 0.2$). This observation may be traced back to the particular requirements of deaf children. The very deaf child must watch and listen or act. The hearing child can listen while he acts. Thus, what the hearing child usually gets simultaneously, the deaf child must process in sequence. The whole process of integrating action and language is therefore quite different.

In summary, then, the teacher's sensitivity to the child's current level of activity, her ability to assign correct descriptions and explanations contingent upon the child's activity, appears to be a form of instruction which applies to both hearing and deaf children. The main means of communication may be different but the underlying principles of instructional organization remain the same. In both cases, adult intervention provides a supporting framework for the achievements of children.

If these tutorial strategies are indeed significant in the intellectual achievement of children, we may expect to find a significant relationship between a mother's tutorial style and general aspects of her child's learning and problem-solving strategies. Just such a relationship has been shown in a study by Hartmann and Haavind (1977). As we have already seen, there is good evidence that the strategy interaction described by means of the contingency rule facilitated children's achievement of a particular task. Hartmann and Haavind went beyond the immediate effects of contingency by measuring independently the teaching strategy of the mothers and the learning strategy of their children. First they examined the teaching technique the mother employed with a child other than her own. Then they examined the interactions of that mother's child in a tutorial session with an experimenter-cum-teacher. Working from a Piagetian perspective, they identified three principal strategies into which they could reliably classify the mothers-cum-teachers and three learning styles into which they could reliably sort the children. The teaching categories were as follows:

Informing Teaching involved the presentation of well-elaborated information, offered initiative to the child, and displayed little restrictive, contradictory, or logically inconsistent information.

Imperative Teaching involved a minimum of rationalization and justification, offered information which was often incomplete and contradictory, and emphasized what the child was told to do rather than what he might think about.

Competitive-Expressive Teaching focused much more on the outcome of the task and on interpersonal relations. The mother was more likely to orient toward the feelings of the child than to his information needs.

The analysis of the child's behavior with the experimenter-teacher produced categories which were mirror images of the maternal teaching strategies. The three learning styles can be briefly summarized. *Active Mastery* involved an assertive approach to learning, where the adult was seen as a resource and used as such. The child's actions often had a verbal accompaniment; he tended to think aloud, ask questions, and comment on the adult's efforts. In short, the child signaled his information needs to the adult and sought and exploited the help which he was given. *Passive Learning* was reflected in a tendency to let the adult maintain control of the task, and the child's response was largely that of imitating actions and following particular comments. The *Expressive* style was marked by the child's orientation toward the emotional, interpersonal, and competitive elements of the game. Such a child may not provide the adult with good opportunities for teaching.

As predicted, the mother's teaching strategies measured in one setting were highly correlated with the learning strategies of their children measured in an independent situation. This provides some direct evidence, then, that an instructional strategy built upon a close, contingent interaction between the learner's needs and adult intervention is important not only in the achievement of an immediate goal but also to the development of generalizable learning strategies. It is a further indication of the significance of adult intervention on the development of the child.

Summary

The importance of interaction and dialogue in the establishment and maintenance of intersubjectivity—on the assumption that we live in the same world and can trust one another—is an important theme in the recent writings of Jerome Bruner. He has argued that not only are the symbolic powers of language extremely important in intellectual development but also the child's pragmatic communications with his caretaker (under conditions of shared attention and joint action) are responsible, in part, for the child's acquisition of language in general and his mastery of semantic functions of language in particular. In this paper I have tried to indicate some of the ways in which that interaction, in the form of a tutorial dialogue between mother or teacher and child, is responsible for the solution of immediate learning tasks and for the mastery of some general intellectual skills.

It was Piaget who so forcibly drew our attention to the profound psychological implications of children's errors; to the necessity of treating them not simply as a result of poor or inadequate learning but as a basis for inferences about their view of things. Mothers, we have argued, more or less skillfully follow a similar route in teaching their child. Some pay detailed attention to the child's errors, diagnose his difficulty, and provide instruction and encouragement at the appropriate level of intervention. Others are much less sensitive to their child's difficulties and are thus less able to provide the appropriate instruction.

Beyond suggesting that instruction must be tailored to the requirements of the child being tutored, I have tried to characterize effective tutorial intervention in terms of three main principles. The first is the exploitation of the recognition-production gap. An adult may intervene in the learning process by capitalizing on the fact that children can recognize correct solutions long before they can assemble the means for achieving them. This, indeed, is the only role that modeling may usefully play in education. By seeing an adult execute a performance which he understands, the child may be induced into the action and instruction sequences I have discussed. One important characteristic of the successful teacher is that she manages to continually confront the child with just such comprehensible problems— problems which then serve as goals for the child's own activity. The development of the means to achieve these results is the acquisition of further new knowledge.

However, successful instruction involves more than the child's recognition of goals and the adult's encouragement to achieve them. It also involves what we have called the scaffolding of means. The successful teacher regulates his or her instructions, demonstrations, descriptions, and evaluations to the child's current attentions and abilities. The adult provides just that level of intervention which is necessary to get the child over his current difficulties; when the child can successfully take responsibility for a particular constituent of a task, the adult abandons that particular form of intervention and reacts at a more general level. Thus, adult intervention is contingent upon the child's activity, and that contingency is based upon the adult's interpretation of the child's errors and the fate of earlier interventions. This, backed-up with an effective analysis of the task, enables the teacher to discover and operate in what Vygotsky called the child's zone of proximal development.

Thirdly, successful tutoring involves progressive relaxation of adult control over the planning and execution of problem solving. Successful tutors thus give the child a sense of competence by offering him initiative, giving him options to choose between, and providing him with a framework for interpreting his experience. When the child understands what he is doing and what goals the tutor shares with him then he accepts problems as his own and works with energy and enthusiasm to achieve their solution. When the child fails to understand what is required of him, he is driven to short-term goals, compliance with directives, simple imitation, and general discontent and apathy.

It has been Jerome Bruner, more than any other contemporary thinker, who has provoked us into looking with some care at the processes of instruction. He promised that much of social and developmental significance would be found there. Research to date inspires a good deal of confidence that he is right.

References

Bruner, J. S. The ontogenesis of speech acts. *Journal of Child Language*, 1975, 2, 1–19.

————. *Toward a theory of instruction.* New York: Norton, 1968.

————, From communication to language—A psychological perspective. *Cognition*, 1976, 3, 255–287.

Dewey, J. *How we think.* New York: Heath & Co., 1933.

Garvey, C. Some properties of social play. In J. S. Bruner, A. Jolly, and K. Sylva (Eds.), *Play: Its role in development and evolution.* Harmondsworth: Penguin Books, 1976.

————. *Mothers as teachers and their children as learners.* Reports from the Institute of Psychology, University of Bergen, Norway. No. 1, 1977.

Heber, M. The influence of language training on seriation of 5–6 year-old children initially at different levels of descriptive competence. *British Journal of Psychology,* 1977, 68, 85–95.

————, Comparing the effects of various kinds of social interaction upon progress in seriation. Paper to the Developmental Section of the *British Psychological Society,* Nottingham, 1978.

————. Effective features of dialogue: The influence of speech on progress in seriation of children of 5–6 years. Paper to the British Psychological Society, Annual Conference, Nottingham, 1979.

Lock, A. (Ed.) *Action, gesture and symbol: The emergence of language.* London: Academic Press, 1978.

McNeil, D. Developmental psycholinguistics. In F. Smith and G. A. Miller (Eds.), *The genesis of language.* Cambridge, Mass.: MIT Press, 1966.

————. The development of language. In P. M. Musse (Ed.), *Carmichael's manual of child psychology.* New York: Wiley, 1970.

Olson, D. R. On conceptual strategies. In Bruner, J. S., Olver R. R., and Greenfield, P. M. et al., *Studies in cognitive growth.* New York: Wiley, 1966.

———. *Cognitive development: The child's acquisition of diagonality.* New York and London: Academic Press, 1970.

Sinclair-de-Zwart, H. *Acquisition du langage et développement de la pensée—Sous systèmes linguistiques et opérations concrètes.* Paris: Dunod, 1967.

Skinner, B. F. *The technology of teaching.* New York: Appleton-Century-Crofts, 1968.

Sonstroem, A. M. On the conservation of solids. In Bruner, J. S., Olver, R. R., and Greenfield, P. M., et al., *Studies in cognitive growth.* New York: Wiley, 1966.

Trevarthen, C. Descriptive analyses of infant communicative behaviour. In H. R. Schaffer (Ed.), *Studies in mother-infant interaction.* London and New York: Academic Press, 1977.

Vygotsky, L. S. *Mind and society.* Cambridge, Mass.: Harvard University Press, 1978.

Wood, D. J., Bruner, J. S., and Ross, G. The role of tutoring in problem solving. *Journal of Child Psychology and Psychiatry*, 1976, 17, 2, 89–100.

Wood, D. J. and Middleton, D. J. A study of assisted problem solving. *British Journal of Psychology*, 1975, 66, 2, 181–191.

Wood, D. J., Wood, H. A., and Middleton, D. J. An experimental evaluation of four face-to-face teaching strategies. *International Journal of Behavioral Development*, 1978, 1, 2, 131–147.

Wood, D. J. and Middleton, D. J. Instructing young children: The description and evaluation of patterns of mother-child interaction. Paper to the Social Psychology Section of the British Psychological Society, London, 1974.

Wood, D. J. and Wood, H. A. An experimental study of teaching techniques with the young deaf child. Paper to the Annual Conference of the British Psychological Society, Nottingham, 1979.

PART III

Cognitive Process
and Cultural Products

13

Preverbal Communication between Mothers and Infants

T. Berry Brazelton and Edward Tronick

Human infancy offers both infant and parents a period of interdependency more prolonged than that of most other mammals. Such a prolonged period provides the base for handing on from one generation to the next the assurance of increased individuality—among cultures, among families, and among the individuals in each family. In addition, it allows for the learning of complex tasks which are more or less unique but certainly richly refined in the human—a rich repertoire of skilled behavior and of specifically human communication, verbal and nonverbal. Prolonged infancy provides the opportunity both for the learning of these skills and for the growth of a sense of competence. This latter comes from the realization that goals, whether innate or acquired, may be successfully achieved through action coupled with sensorimotor feedback. The learning of the skills comes about in several different ways: 1. by testing and practicing alone, 2. by practice and experimentation reinforced at appropriate times by those around him, 3. by careful observation and direct imitation of the actions of behavior of others, and 4. by identification with others, in which the "quality" as well as the match of the others' actions are understood and reproduced. Thus, the human infant has both the time and the affective and cognitive information necessary to acquire the skills needed to cope with the complexity of human society.

The limitations on these acquisitions and thus on his ultimate development can arise from two sources: directly from the infant when his capacity

This work was supported by grants from the Robert Wood Johnson Foundation, the Carnegie Foundation, and the William T. Grant Foundation—NIMH (#MH14887)

The authors wish to thank Dr. Heideliese Als for her participation in this chapter and the work behind it, especially for her elegant contributions expressed in the Four Stages of Development of Mother and Infant. Drs. Barbara Koslowski and Mary Main contributed to much of the earlier work cited here.

for development is impaired, as it is in a baby with a sensory defect or with brain damage; or from the environment in which he is being nurtured. Since at least three of the four means of acquiring skilled behavior and communication are directly dependent on "others," the richness of his ultimate capacities may be highly correlated with the quality of his interaction with his caregiving environment. Thus, the two sources for potential limitation become difficult to separate, especially since his chances for optimal development are enhanced when he is rewarding to his caretakers and part of his reward value is dependent on his intactness.

From the infant's standpoint, a nurturing environment will provide not only necessary nutrients and control systems (heat, protection, and so on) but also a protective and rewarding envelope while he is learning about himself and his world. Since Bruner (1972) has demonstrated that the acquisition of knowledge is anchored in systems which are open for new information and equipped with feedback loops that produce the realization of having reached a goal, our work has been toward understanding this system within the environment's protective envelope.

In our work with Bruner at the Center for Cognitive Studies from 1966 to 1970, we first became aware of the system of nonverbal behaviors with which the infant signaled his interactions with both objects and people. At that time, Bruner (1972), Trevarthen (1977), and Bower (1971) were studying the acquisition of early reaching behavior. Their work was demonstrating how early (in the first weeks) an infant's attention to an object in "reach space" (ten to twelve inches in front of him in the midline) captured all of his behavior. Not only did he have an observable, predictable "hooked" state of attention as the object was brought into this space, but also his whole body responded in an appropriate and predictable fashion as he attended to the object.

The infant stared fixedly at the object with wide eyes, fixating on it for as long as two minutes without disruption of gaze or of attention (by six weeks). His expression was fixed, the muscles of his face tense, with eyes staring and mouth and lips protruding toward the object. This static, fixed look of attention was interspersed with little jerks of facial muscles. His tongue jerked out toward the object and then withdrew rapidly. Occasional short bursts of effortful vocalizing toward the object occurred. During these long periods of attention, the eyes blinked occasionally in single, isolated blinks. The body was set in a tense, immobilized sitting position, with the object at his midline. When the object was moved to one side or the other, the infant tended to shift his body appropriately, so it was kept at his midline. His shoulders hunched as if he were about to "pounce." Extremities were fixed, flexed at elbow and knee, and fingers and toes were aimed toward the object. Hands were semiflexed or tightly flexed, but fingers and toes repeatedly jerked out to point at the object. Jerky swipes of an arm or of a leg in the direction of the object occurred from time to time as the period of intense attention was maintained. In this interaction with an object, his attention seemed "hooked," and all his motor behavior alternated between the long, fixed periods of tense absorption and short bursts of jerky, excited movement in the direction of the object. He seemed to hold down any interfering behavior which might break into this prolonged state of attention.

Striking in all of this was the intent, prolonged state of attention, during which tension gradually built up in all segments of his body until abrupt disruption seemed the inevitable and necessary relief for him. This behavior was most striking by twelve to sixteen weeks. It could also be observed as early as four weeks of age, long before a reach could be achieved.

Additionally we have observed the cardio-respiratory involvement of infants who had congenital cardiac defects and whose circulatory balance was precarious. As they get "hooked" on and interact with an object in reach space, their breathing becomes deeper and more labored, their cardiac balance more precarious, cyanosis deepens until attention to the object is decreased momentarily, and their color returns. The return of attention to the object brings on a repetition of the same cycle of "hooked" attention, increasing autonomic imbalance, and recovery as the baby turns away briefly. From these observations it is clear that an infant's attention to an object involves behavioral, neuromotor, and autonomic systems in a predictable alternating increase and decrease in the deployment of attention and nonattention, designed to protect an immature and easily overloaded cardio-respiratory balance.

The contrast of the infant's behavior and attention when he interacted with his mother and when he attended to an object was clear even as early as four weeks of age. Indeed we felt we could see brief episodes of these two contrasting modes of behavior and attention as early as two to three weeks.

A striking way of illustrating the behaviors of the mother and the child, as well as the interaction of the two, is to present them in graphic form (from Brazelton, Koslowski, and Main, 1974). To illustrate, figures 1 to 4 are graphs drawn from interaction periods. Time is measured along the horizontal axis; the number of behaviors, along the vertical axis. Curves drawn above the horizontal line indicate that the person whose behavior the curve represents was looking *at* his partner. Curves drawn below the line indicate that he was looking *away*. Solid lines represent the mother's behavior; broken lines, the baby's. Thus, a deep, broken line below the horizontal line indicates that the baby was looking away while engaging in several behaviors.

As reflected in figure 1, the mother looks at the baby after he turns to her. As they look at each other, she adds behaviors, smiling, vocalizing,

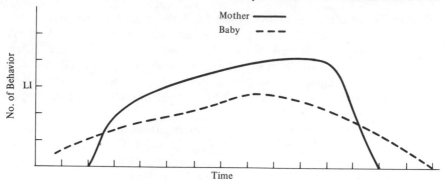

FIGURE 1   Number of behaviors added in period of sixteen-second looking interaction. Baby looking (LI: looking intent).

touching his hand, and holding his leg, to accelerate their interaction. He
responds by increasing the number of his own behaviors (smiling, vocalizing, and cycling his arms and legs) until the peak at X. At this point he
begins to decrease his behaviors and gradually cuts down on them toward
the end of their interaction. She follows his lead by decreasing her behaviors more rapidly and ends her part of the cycle by looking away just before
he does. Figure 2 shows a baby starting a cycle by looking at his mother.
She follows by looking at him and adding four more behaviors in rapid succession—touching him, smiling, talking, and nodding her head. He watches
her, vocalizes, smiles back, cycles briefly, and then begins to decrease his
responses and turns away at *a*. She stops smiling as he begins to turn away
but rapidly adds facial gestures to try to recapture his interest. She continues to talk, touch him, nod her head, and make facial gestures until *b*. At
this point she stops the gestures but begins to pat him. At *c* she stops talking briefly and stops nodding at him. At *d* she makes hand gestures in addition to her facial grimaces but stops them both thereafter. At *e* she stops
vocalizing, and he begins to return to look at her. He vocalizes briefly and
then looks away again when her activity continues.

In figure 3 the mother and infant are looking at each other; she is vocalizing, and he is smiling. As she increases her activity by patting him, he
turns away. She begins to nod at him at *a*, and he begins to look at the cur-
tain across the room. She tries to quiet him down at *b* and again at *c*. After
a period of less activity from her, he begins to turn to her at *d*. As he
returns to look at her, she begins to build up the interaction by smiling and
vocalizing; eventually at *e* she pats him. At this he begins to turn away
again.

In figure 4 the mother and baby are looking at each other, smiling,

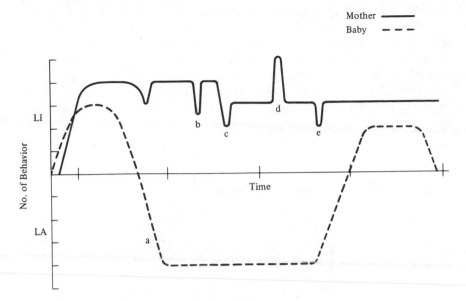

FIGURE 2 Number of behavior added in a five-second period of interaction (LI: looking interest; LA: looking away)

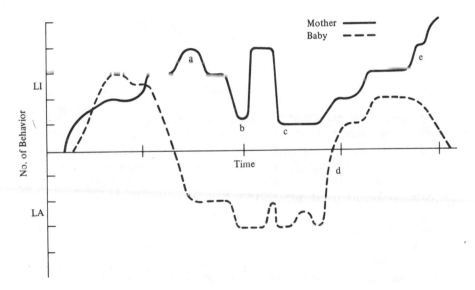

FIGURE 3 Number of behaviors added in a four-second interaction.

and vocalizing together. The baby begins to cycle and reach out to her. At *a* he begins to turn away from her. She responds by looking down at her hands and she stops her activity briefly. This brings him back to look at her at *c*. Her smiling, vocalizing, and leaning toward him bring a smiling response from him. In addition, his arms and legs cycle and he coos contentedly as he watches her. As he turns away she first adds another behavior and gestures. He, however, adds to his activities—ignoring her reminders—and turns away from her. She gradually cuts out all her activity and by *e* she looks away from him. Immediately afterward he begins to look back to her, and the cycle of looking at each other begins again at *f*.

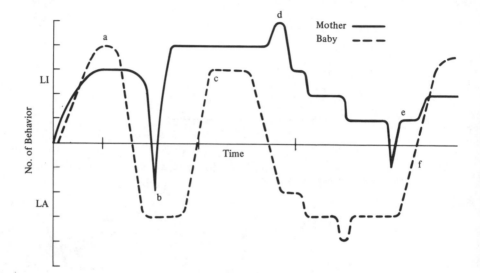

FIGURE 4   Number f behaviors added in a five-second interaction.

Of course the expectancy engendered in an interaction with a static object, as opposed to a responsive person, must be very different (Piaget, 1953, 1955). But what surprised us was how early this expectancy seemed to be reflected in the infant's behavior and use of attention. When the infant was interacting with his mother, there seemed to be a constant cycle of attention (A), followed by withdrawal of attention (W)—the cycle being used by each partner as he approached and then withdrew and waited for a response from the other participant. In each of these "states" (A and W) we found there were predicted behaviors and the use of them in clusters predicted the timing of a response of the other. Single behaviors were less predictive. But in order to predict and understand which cluster of behaviors will produce an ongoing sequence of attention, one must first understand the "state" of affective attention which has been captured and is expressed by each member of the dyad. In other words, the strength of the dyadic interaction dominates the meaning of each member's behavior. If the mother responds in one way, their interactional energy builds up (A), if another, the infant may turn away (W). The same holds true of her response to his behavior. The effect of clustering and of sequencing takes over in assessing the value of particular behaviors, and in the same way the dyadic nature of interaction supersedes the importance of an individual member's clusters and sequences.

The power of the interaction in shaping behavior can be seen at many levels. Using looking and not looking at the mother as measures of attention-nonattention, in a minute's interaction there was an average of 4.4 cycles of such attention and apparent nonattention. Not only were the spans of attention and of looking away of shorter duration than they had been with objects, but they were obviously smoother as the attention built up, reached its peak, and then diminished gradually with the mother. Both the

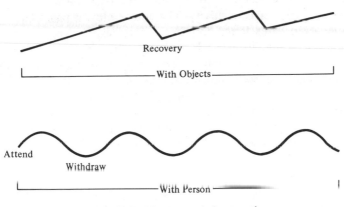

FIGURE 5 Homeostasis in attention.

build-up as well as the decrease in attention were gradual and were usually smoothly paced.

Mother's Role

In this setting, the most important role of the adult interactant seemed to be that of helping the infant to form a regulatory base for his immature physiological and motor reactions.

The most important rule for maintaining an interaction seemed to be that a mother develop a sensitivity to her infant's capacity for attention and his need for withdrawal—partial or complete—after a period of attention to her. Short cycles of attention and nonattention seemed to underlie all periods of prolonged interaction. Although we thought we were observing continuous attention to her, on the part of the infant, the stop-frame analysis uncovered the cyclical nature of the infant's looking and not-looking in our laboratory setting. Looking away behavior reflects the need of each infant to maintain some control over the amount of stimulation he can take in during such intense periods of interaction. This is a homeostatic model, similar to the type of model that underlies all the physiological reactions of the neonate, and it seems to apply to the immature organism's capacity to attend to messages in a communication system.

In the visual system it was apparent that this model was pertinent. Unless the mother responded appropriately to these variations in his behavior, it appeared to us that his span of attention did not increase, and the quality of his attention was less than optimal. For example, in the case of two similarly tense, overactive infants, the mothers responded very differently. One mother responded with increased activity and stimulation to her baby's turning away; another maintained a steady level of activity which gradually modulated her baby's overreactivity. The end result was powerfully in favor of the latter dyad. This latter baby was more responsive, and for longer periods, as our study progressed. Although this effect could have been based on characteristics of the baby that we were not able to analyze, we felt that the quality of communication changed in this pair. However, the linear tenseness of the first dyad remained throughout the twenty weeks of observation. This baby had learned "rules" about managing his own needs in the face of an insensitive mother. He had learned to turn away and stay away, to decrease his receptivity to information from her. This must be necessary for him in order to maintain a physiological and psychological homeostasis in the face of her insensitivity. These two parallel cases demonstrate that a mother's behavior must be not only reinforcing and contingent upon the infant's behavior, but also adjusted to and supportive of the infant's capacity to receive and utilize stimuli. This, then, becomes the first rule each must learn from the other.

As another example, one of our mothers was particularly striking in the way she released her demands as the infant decreased his attention to her. She sat back in her chair smiling softly, reducing other activities such as vocalizing and moving, waiting for him to return. When he did look back, she began slowly to add behavior on behavior, as if she were feeling out how much he could master. She also sensed his need to reciprocate. She vocalized, then waited for his response. When she smiled, she waited until he smiled before she began to build up her own smiling again. Her moving in close to him was paced sensitively to coincide with his body cycling, and if he became excited or jerky in his movement she subsided back into her chair.

We felt she was outstanding in her sensitivity to the importance of reciprocity in this interaction. She provided an atmosphere that led to longer periods of interaction. She seemed to teach him an expectancy of more than just stimuli from her in the guise of her sensitivity to his needs and his cues. As she allowed for these, she seemed to be teaching him how to expand his own ability to attend to stimulation, for "long-term intention" as well as "long-term interaction." Thus her role took on deeper significance as she not only established the climate for communication but also gave him the experience in pacing himself in order to attend to the environment.

Although this may look as if it were "unlearned" behavior in some mothers, its absence in other mothers may demonstrate the fact that it can be a kind of rule learning. The individuality of each member of the dyad determines the flexibility in the number of rules necessary and sets the limits on the variability within each rule that still allow the goal to be achieved.

Another rule is that the mother use her periods of interaction to "model" more and more complex routines for the baby. She times the complexity of her models to his stage of development. For example, in the early weeks imitation of his activity is limited and enlarged upon by her. This must serve as a feedback mechanism for him (Bruner, 1971, 1972)—one that enlarges upon his awareness for his behavior. He becomes aware of his action, visualizes her imitation of it, and reproduces it for himself again. As he does so, he has the opportunity to add on to it, either by serendipity or by modeling his behavior to match her enlarged version. Either way, he increases its scope. The timing of imitative reinforcement and her sensitivity to his capacity for attention and learning must depend on her having learned this "rule" about him—his capacity to accept her feedback and to use it as a method for further learning.

This interdependence of rhythms seemed to be at the root of their "attachment" as well as communication. When the balance was sympathetic to the needs of each member of the dyad, there was a sense of rhythmic interaction which an observer sensed as "positive." When the balance was not equalized, and one member was out of phase with the other, there seemed to be a "negative" quality in the entire interaction. Sander says that "each new thrust of activity in the growing infant requires a new period of interactional adjustment with the caretaking environment to reach stable coordination on the bases of new changes" (1965, p. 330). The smoothness with which these dyads made such adjustments reflected the depth of their attachment and probably contributed a further opportunity for each to learn about the other member. Certainly, the strength of the interdependence of the dyad seemed to be more powerful in shaping each member's behavior than did any other force—such as the individual member's style or wish of the moment.

A mother's behavior in a period of interaction might be summarized by five kinds of functions she serves for the infant:

1. Reduction of interfering activity.
2. Setting the stage for a period of interaction by bringing him to a more alert, receptive state.

3. Creating an atmosphere of expectancy for further interaction by her behavior.

4. Acceleration of his attention to receive and send messages.

5. Allowing for reciprocity with sensitivity to his signals, giving him time to respond with his own behavior, as well as time to digest and recover from the activation her cues establish.

The learning of these rules of interaction additionally becomes a system in which the mother learns not only about the infant, but also about herself. As she adapts to her infant, she learns a kind of self-mastery necessary for mothering as well.

The Infant's Role

The infant is equipped with reflex behavioral responses which are organized in rather primitive patterns at birth. He soon organizes them into more complex patterns of behavior which serve his goals for organization at a time when he is still prone to a costly disorganization of neuromotor and physiological systems. Thus, he is set up to learn about himself and his environment, for as he achieves each of these goals his feedback systems give him a double message: "Goal accomplished; now go on." In this way, each time he achieves a state of homeostatic control, he is fueled to go on to the next stage of disruption and reconstitution—a familiar model for energizing a developing system. We use Robert White's (1959) "sense of competence" as our idea for fueling the system from within. We also believe that the infant's quest for social stimuli is in response to his need for fueling from the world outside. As he achieves a homeostatic state, and as he responds to a disruptive stimulus, the reward for each of these states of homeostasis and disruption is thus reinforced by internal and external events. Hence, he starts out with the behaviorally identifiable mechanisms of a bimodal system—1. of attaining a state of homeostasis and a sense of achievement from within; and 2. the ability to incorporate signals from the world around him, fueling him from without. He is set up with behavioral pathways for providing both of these for himself—for adaptation to his new world, even in the neonatal period. Since very little fueling from within or without may be necessary to "set" these patterns and press him onward, they are quickly organized and reproduced over and over until they are efficient, incorporated, and can be utilized as the base for building later patterns.

With this model of a bimodal system which provides an increased availability to the outside world, one can then incorporate Sander's (1965) ideas of early entrainment of biobehavioral rhythms, Condon and Sander's

(1974) proposals that the infant's movements match the rhythms of the adult's voice, Meltzoff and Moore's (1977) work on imitation of tongue protrusion in a three-week-old, and Bower's (1971) observations on early reaching behavior to an attractive object in the first weeks of life. As each of these responsive behaviors to external stimuli contributes to a realization that he has "done it"—controlled himself in order to reach out for and respond appropriately to an external stimulus or toward an adult—his achievement encourages him to further forms of engagement. The engagement or entrainment involves the two feedback systems of internal control and external responsiveness. Thus, he can learn most about himself by responding to the world around him. This explains the observable drive on the part of the neonate to capture and interact with an adult and his "need" for social interaction.

The infant's feedback system is adaptive to stress and change and to a built-in self-regulatory goal. The immature organism with its vulnerability to being overloaded must be in constant homeostatic regulation—the physiological and the psychological. Handling input becomes a major goal for the infant, rather than a demanding or a destructive one. Such a system can handle disruption either by negative and stressful or by positive and attractive stimuli; but the organizing aspect of both is seen in the amount of growth of the system. Since positive stimuli permit growth and homeostasis with less cost, one can predict the value of a sensitive environmental feedback for the immature organism; just as one can predict with a more constantly stressful environment that there will be an attempt at precocious mastery; and finally, if the adult member or members are insensitive to the needs of the immature member of the dyad or triad, an extensive fixation or even breakdown in the system may occur. If disruption or fixation does not occur, then stress can provide a learning paradigm for handling the stress and then recovering (Als et al., 1979a). Either way there is disruption of the old balance, but in one there is the feedback which results from the successful closing of a homeostatic cycle, with the infant thereby being readied for the next task in development.

The first task for a newborn as Als (1978) has pointed out is control over the physiological system, particularly breathing, heart rate, and temperature control. For preterm and at-risk newborns, this control is more difficult to achieve then it is for healthy full-term newborns. While control over these basic physiological demands is being achieved, the newborn begins to establish organization and differentiation of the motor system, effecting the range, smoothness, and complexity of movement. The next major agendum is the attainment of a stable organization of his states of consciousness. First, the infant will have to differentiate six states, from deep sleep to intense crying, and begin to manage transitions between these states. Achieving control over transitions between states demands an integration of the control over the physiological and motoric systems and the states of consciousness. The adult caregiver can play the role of organizer (Sander, 1965) and can begin to expand certain states, e.g., the quiet, alert state, as well as the duration and quality of sleep states. In addition, the caregiver can help regulate the transitions between states for the infant.

As the state organization becomes differentiated and begins to be regulated, usually in the course of the first month, the next newly emerging expansion is that of the increasing differentiation of the alert state (Als, in press; Als, Tronick and Brazelton, in press). Hence, the infant's social capacities begin to unfold. His ability to communicate becomes increasingly sophisticated. The repertoire of facial expressions, vocalizations, cries, gestures, and postures in interaction with a social partner begin to expand. He can now use his well-modulated state organization to regulate social interactions. This, in turn, leads into the fourth state when the infant can be the leader on the signal giver. When he can seek out social cues, when he can establish games, initiate them and terminate them, when he can use toys as a bridge for communication and play with others, he is equipped to take voluntary control over his environment. This is bound to strengthen his own feelings of competence.

We first began to see the value of such a conceptual base when we were developing the Brazelton (1973) *Neonatal Behavioral Assessment Scale.* The concept underlying the assessment is that the neonate can defend himself from negative stimuli, can control interfering autonomic and motoric responses in order to attend to important external stimuli, and can reach out for and utilize stimulation from his environment necessary for his species-specific motor, emotional, social, and cognitive development. Using the baby's own control over his states of consciousness, the examiner attempts to bring the baby from sleep to wakefulness and even to crying and back to sleep again as he assesses the neonate's capacity to respond to and elicit social responses from the environment. In a twenty-minute assessment, an examiner can begin to feel a neonate's strengths in shaping those around him. The newborn responds clearly and differently to appealing and negative intrusive stimuli. Both kinds of stimulation provide some form of organization, but as one handles him and sees him achieve an alert state, using the examiner's cues, and as he then maintains a clearly alert state, one begins to realize how much a part of his organization the nurturing "other" can and must be. We work to achieve the infant's "best performance" on a series of responses to various stimuli—to voice, to face, to handling and cuddling, to the rattle, and to a red ball. As the infant becomes excited and responsive, one can see his increased and increasing sense of mastery and involvement with the adult examiner. His states of consciousness become the matrix for all his reactions; as he responds to individual stimuli and as he moves from state to state, one can see and feel him respond to the stimulus, regain his balance, then move on to respond to the next stimulus.

As one plays with a newborn, one realizes that the newborn is indeed displaying a marvelous capacity to regulate his internal physiological responses by the mechanisms of internal homeostatic control or "state" control. The newborn's "awareness" of this capacity becomes a first basis for internalizing his capacity to control himself and his environment, as well as a base for the next steps. We believe that these observations might lend perspective to Hartmann's (1958) idea of precursors of ego development.

In following the infant's interactions through the first four months of life, we were able to discern successive stages of disruption, progress, and the reachievement of homeostasis (Als et al., 1979a; Als, in press). Throughout, the infant learns about himself, and the mother's self-awareness increases as she participates in helping him achieve the goals of each of these stages. These then become a rich base for the infant's affective and cognitive development, as well as his awareness of himself—developmental accomplishments which might be equated with early ego development.

Figure 6 shows the more detailed, second-by-second analysis of the interactions of an infant boy and his mother at 25 days, 46 days, 68 days and 92 days (Als et al., 1979b; Als in press; Als et al., in press). The infant's behavior is represented on the lower part of each subgraph; the mother's behavior, on the top part of each subgraph. The partners' displays are graphed in mirror images of one another, presenting six states of interaction for each participant. The states are scaled to range from displays strongly directed away from the interaction, such as protest, avoid, and avert, through displays mildly directed toward the interaction, such as monitor and set, to displays strongly directed toward the interaction, such as play and talk. The closer the partners' respective positions to one another are on the graph, the more in heightened synchrony they are with one another; the farther away from one another on the graph their respective positions are, the more interactively distant they are from one another.

At twenty-five days, the infant observed moves mainly from cautious monitoring back to averting, then attempts to monitor again.

By forty-six days (about six weeks), the infant can repeatedly maintain a quiet, brightly alert, oriented state, labeled "set," toward the mother in this situation, and the newly emerging coo and play phase is beginning to be apparent in the initial sally. The mother's range has also widened by six weeks. She moves from intermittent averting, via monitoring, to eliciting and playing. The urgency of continuous prompting and organization exhibited in the tight cycling between eliciting and playing of the earlier interaction is no longer as intense. The infant has become more flexible, and the mother can leave some of the self-modulation up to him.

By sixty-eight days (about two months), the infant's organization has become increasingly differentiated, moving initially between protest and play, and then, from 35 seconds on, between the phases motor, set, play, and talk, until the very end, when he averts again. The repeated cycling through play and talk indicates the full emergence of the new differentiation of his alert state. He is now capable of engaging in interaction with a rich repertoire, integrating smiling and cooing, and he repeatedly achieves an amplitude of affective organization not previously attained. The mother

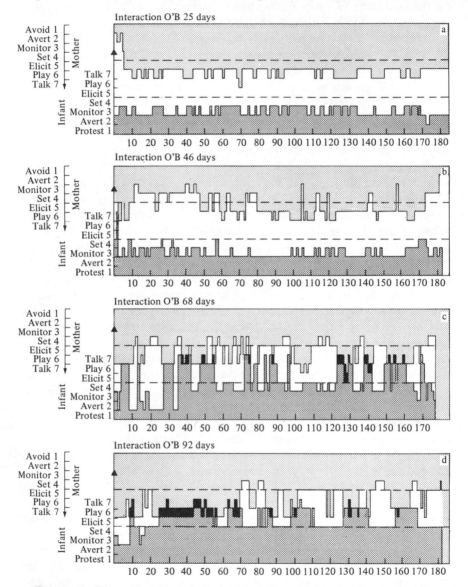

FIGURE 6   From Als (in press). Social interaction: Matrix for the development of behavioral organization. In Ina C. Uzgiris (Ed.), *Social interaction and communications in infancy: new directions for child development* vol. 4. San Francisco: Jossey Bass Publishers. Reprinted by permission of Jossey Bass.

simultaneously expands his peaks, and they achieve a high level of affective interlocking. She spends more time in set than before, indicating her expectant readiness for play and increasing ability to let him take the lead.

By three months (about ninety-two days), this new achievement of differentiation has become more solidified, as is indicated in the prolonged play episodes of the infant and the new baseline at set. The mother's new base is also at set with prolonged cycles through play and talk, indicating her confidence in the infant's self-regulation.

Figure 6 as Als (in press; Als et al., in press) describes the infant's homeostatic curve has literally moved up by two phases, from averting and monitoring at twenty-five days, with its peaks at set by forty-six days, to its base at set and its peaks at play and talk by three months. The wave lengths of the curve have also considerably increased, pointing to the smooth reintegration of the recent differentiation of both partners, now ready for new expansion of an increasingly solidifying base. This system thus gives us a way of documenting and quantifying the progress of early infant development within the matrix of social interaction.

In these interactions the mutual feedback is apparent. As Als (in press; Als et al., 1979a; Als et al., in press) has pointed out, once the infant is oriented to the parent, the parent expands the affective and attentional ambiance to maintain the infant's state. The infant begins to reciprocate with his ways of interaction. The parent maintains this interaction and gradually expands it to include the next achievement, such as, early on, the mere maintenance of alertness, then the achievement of reaching out to sound. Once the new achievement has occurred—for instance, the infant has smiled or cooed—the parent acknowledges the achievement profusely, leaving time for the infant to recognize his achievement and to integrate it into his current structure of competence. The expansion of the child's competence thus requires the sensitive gauging of the affective base necessary and the appropriate timing of the next step. It is a process of balancing support with challenge. It requires the parents' willingness to risk stressing the system when in balance and dealing with the resultant disorganization. When the limits are exceeded and disorganization results, the parent has to maintain perspective on the process and go back to that level of interaction that the child can currently manage. Once back on base, the expansion process can begin again. The levels of interaction are thus passed through over and over again.

The environment potentiates the newborn's increasing differentiation by offering him a controlling kind of organization from the outside which, because it is adapted to his level of development, provides him with appropriate feedback. This differentiation is further enchanced by a recognition of his capacity to reach out for and to shut off social stimuli. This same capacity, in turn, results in growing complexity of the interactional channels and structures and provides increasing opportunities for the individual system to become more differentiated. Given such a flexible system, the infant's individuality is continuously fitted to and shaped by that of the adult. Our model is that of a feedback system of increasing complexity, a system embedded in and catalyzed by the interaction with others.

We have come to realize a fact that must have been evident to others already, that the nurturing adult who provides the "envelope" learns as much about him or herself as does the baby. The very acts of nurturing become an inner feedback system all its own. Successful nurturance which produces rewarding responses in the infant adds further to this self-realization. And the learning about oneself as a parent can be conceptualized in developmental stages which are parallel to and dependent upon those of the infant.

In summary, this model of development is a powerful one for understanding the reciprocal bonds that are set up between parent and infant. The feedback model allows for flexibility, disruption, and reorganization. Within its envelope of reciprocal interaction, one can conceive of a rich matrix of different modalities for communication, individualized for each pair and critically dependent on the contribution of each member of the dyad or triad. There is no reason that each system cannot be shaped in different ways by the preferred modalities for interaction of each of its participants, but each *must* be sensitive and ready to adjust to the other member in the envelope. And at each stage of development, the envelope will be different—richer, we would hope.

References

Als, H. Assessing an assessment: conceptual consideration, methodological issues, and a perspective on the future of the neonatal behavioral assessment scale. In A. J. Sameroff (Ed.), *Organization and stability of newborn behavior: A commentary on the Brazelton neonatal behavior assessment scale*. Monographs of the Society for Research in Child Development, 1978, 177, 14–29.

————. Social interaction: Matrix for the development of behavioral organization. Some thoughts towards a dynamic process model. In Ina C. Uzgiris (Ed.), *Social interaction and communications in infancy: New directions for child development* vol. 4. San Francisco: Jossey Bass Publishers, in press.

Als, H., Tronick, E., and Brazelton, T. B. Stages of early behavioral organization: The study of a sighted infant and of a blind infant in interaction with their mothers. In T. B. Field, S. Goldberg, D. Stern, and A. Sostek (Eds.), *High risk infants and children: Adult and peer interactions*. New York: Grune & Stratton, in press (a).

————. Affective reciprocity and the development of autonomy: The study of a blind infant. *Journal of American Academy of Child Psychiatry*, in press (b).

————. (1979b) Analysis of face to face interaction in infant-adult dyads. In M. E. Lamb, S. J. Suomi, and G. R. Stephenson (Eds.), *Social Interaction Analysis: Methodological Issues*. The University of Wisconsin Press, 1979, 33–76.

Bower, T. G. The object in the world of the infant. *Scientific American*, 1971, 225, 30–38.

Brazelton, T. B. *Neonatal assessment scale*. Clinics in Developmental Medicine, Monograph 50. London: William Heinemann; Philadelphia: J. B. Lippincott, 1973.

Brazelton, T. B., Koslowski, B. and Main, M. The origins of reciprocity: The early mother-infant interaction. In M. Lewis and L. A. Rosenblum (Eds.), *The effect of the infant on its caregiver*. New York: Wiley, Interscience, 1974, 49–77.

Bruner, J. and Koslowski, B. Preadaptation in initial visually guided reaching. *Perception*, 1972, 1, 3–14.

Condon, W. S. and Sander, L. W. Neonate movement is synchronized with adult speech: Interactional participation and language acquisition. *Science*, 1974, 183, 99–101.

Connolly, K. J., and Bruner, J. S. *The growth of competence*. London: Academic Press, 1974.

Hartmann, H. *Ego psychology and the problem of adaptation*. New York: International University Press, 1958.

Meltzoff, A. N. and Moore, M. K. Imitation of facial and manual gestures by human neonates. *Science*, 1977, 198, 75–78.

Piaget, J. *The origins of intelligence in the child*. London: Routledge, 1953.

——. *The child's construction of reality*. London: Routledge, 1955.

Sander, L. W. Regulation and organization in the early infant caregiver system. In R. Robinson (Ed.), *Brain and early behavior*. London: Academic Press, 1965, 1–74.

Trevarthen, C. Descriptive analyses of infant communicative behavior. In H. R. Schaffer (Ed.), *Studies in mother-infant interaction*. New York: Academic Press, 1977.

White, R. W. Motivation reconsidered: The concept of competence. *Psychological Review*, 1959, 66, 297–333.

14

The Foundations of Intersubjectivity: Development of Interpersonal and Cooperative Understanding in Infants

Colwyn Trevarthen

My research with infants began at the Center for Cognitive Studies with Jerome Bruner. I am very happy to express my indebtedness to his enthusiastic plan to look for the origins of human intelligence in infancy—a plan that took in all aspects: active perception, coordination of motoric action, the antecedents of language, cognition, learning; anything a human baby might want to do.

At that time Tom Bower's early experiments (Bower, 1966), using conditioned head turning and sucking habituation to prove a priori powers of object perception, had begun his demolition of the Watsonian edifice that assumed infants had to learn, from scratch, to be aware. Operant and habituation methods in the hands of Papousek (1967, 1969), Sequeland (Sequeland and Lipsett, 1969; Sequeland and DeLucia, 1969), and others, were beginning to achieve new levels of sensitivity to the learning and perception of infants. At the same time, Roman Jakobson and David McNeil at the Center and many visitors from MIT were stirring up an intense curiosity about the inherent principles of language and possible manifestations of these in infants. Jerry was quick to follow the earliest signs that a new

Research on which this chapter is based has been carried out at Harvard and Edinburgh University. Grateful acknowledgement is given for support from the United States Public Health Service, to Professor Jerome Bruner at the Harvard Center for Cognitive Studies, from the Social Science Research Council of the United Kingdom and from the Spencer Foundation of Chicago. I am also indebted to the work of my students, Benjamin Sylvester-Bradley, Lynne Murray, Penelope Hubley and Fiona Grant.

psychology of infancy—granting the infant a true competence for cognition and for communication—was on its way. The Center for Cognitive Studies had a high sense of adventure in those days and we enjoyed ourselves hugely under his vigorous leadership in the beautifully furnished and equipped facilities he had obtained.

A film study made in 1967 at Harvard with Martin Richards and Berry Brazelton showed me the remarkable adaptations of infants for interpersonal communication. I had not realized, at least as a scientist, how expressive and how sensitive a baby could be. The actions of a month-old toward the mother were clearly not the same as efforts to make sensory and motor contact with the physical world. We had deliberately set up filming to contrast these kinds of 'object' in the infant's world. However difficult the ensuing analysis, the nature of the results was evident from the start. Moreover, the communicative behaviors in interaction seemed to become precociously rich by two months after birth. Such an infant was capable of quite different reactions to an inanimate object and to the mother, and the aptitude for communication seemed far more elaborate than any other form of action.

In subsequent research, I have made systematic studies of the development of looking at and reaching toward objects (Trevarthen, 1974a, 1975; Trevarthen and Tursky, 1969). These brought out the complexity of prenatally developed structures for intentional coordination of eye and hand, as well as massive post-natal developments of the eye-head-arm-hand system in early months. Findings in this field are reviewed in a forthcoming paper (Trevarthen, Hubley and Murray, 1979). However, most of my research has been on the responses of infants to persons, principally by analysis of film and TV records of exchanges between mother and infant and that is my primary concern here.

Before 1970 there was little curiosity about the *interactive* behaviors of young infants with their mothers. The psychoanalyst had a theoretical interest in the development of the infant ego within the protective care of the mother. This concern led to some fine observations of infant reactions, in the form of crying, cooing, and smiling, to their mothers' attention. The papers of Peter Wolff (1963, 1969) are outstanding. The problem of how language communication could begin had led to one or two attempts to observe how mothers communicate with infants before the latter speak, but I knew of only one study, then unpublished, of the pattern of face-to-face communication in early infancy—Bateson's analysis of Margaret Bullowa's films, in which she described a 'proto-conversational' behavior where infant and mother both contributed "utterances" in alternation (Bateson, 1971). Robson (1967) cast light on a central mechanism of interpersonal contact in his paper on eye-to-eye contact. But most research effort was oriented to measuring how infants responded with stereotyped smiling, looking, or changes in respiration and heartbeat to usually very artificial stimuli. That young infants, under three months, could perceive the communicative purposes of the mother as such and enter into regulation of them was not even considered. Most psychologists were concerned with perceptual discrimination of dimensions of stimuli, with variations in state of arousal and the properties of the conditioned response. We, at the Center, could approach the behavior we were observing as if discovering a rich new land.

Primary Interpersonal Understanding: The Beginning of Intersubjectivity

The most important conclusion from the film study was a radical one which has influenced the subsequent work of all participants (Bruner, 1969, 1975; Brazelton et al., 1974; Richards, 1971, 1974; Trevarthen, 1974b, 1977).

What two- to three-month-old infants do with their mothers in face-to-face interactions proves that a human is born with readiness to know another human. It suggests that the phenomenon of mother-infant communication cannot be reduced to any nonhuman description such as physical or physiological one. Nor, it would appear, is animal behavior as described by ethologists, with Fixed Action Patterns and Innate Release Mechanisms, an adequate model (Trevarthen, 1979b). The way is open to conclude that the endowment that makes possible learning how to behave from how others behave must include being to some degree human or personal to start with. We are confronted here, in the baby, with a psychological function of high order, even though it is very immature in powers of perception and of action.

An infant of this age has forms of motor expression by which considerable control is obtained over joint activity with the mother. These include apparently purposeful orientations of eyes, ears, mouth, or hands. Attentional focalizing and outline patterns of hand and arm extension move as if to grasp, leg and foot extend as if to step out in a particular direction. The movements have sufficient regularity of form and of temporospatial adjustment to environmental events for an observer, such as the mother, to have some grounds for imputing intentions to them. The babies also exhibit clear patterns of excitement, catching of interest, avoidance, and so on that are triggered by events they perceive. They seem, even as neonates, to have begun to have motives and feelings, to be aware, and to do things in adjustment to the world. But there are also purely communicative movements that can never have effect on the physical world except by influencing a human mind: remarkably rich facial expressions for changes in emotional state, gesturelike hand movements, and lip and tongue movements that are evidently precursors of verbal expression (Trevarthen, 1979a). To verify these claims that babies show well-formed, if rudimentary, purposiveness and

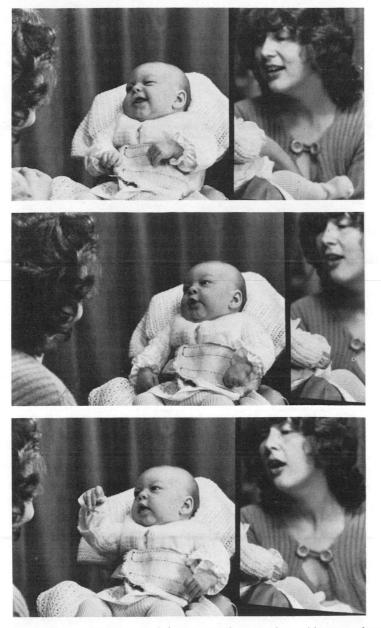

FIGURE 1 The earliest form of interpersonal expression with antecedents of speech and gesture.

A girl, six weeks old, smiles at her mother's face, then responds to gentle baby talk with cooing vocalization and a conspicuous hand movement. Such gestures above the shoulders are significantly correlated with "prespeech" movements of lip and tongue. Note that the baby ceases to smile when expressing an "utterance." In the third picture the mother is imitating the preceding vocalization of her baby.

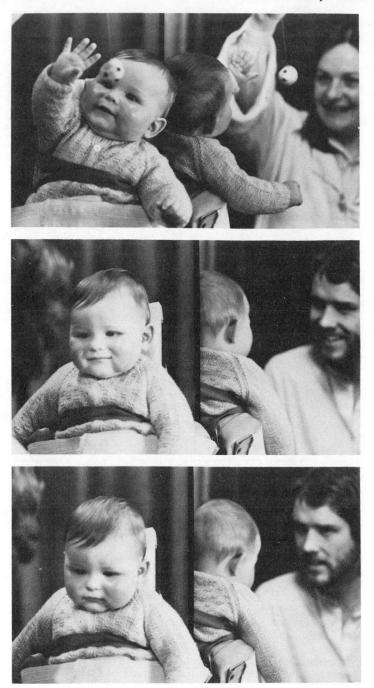

FIGURE 2   An eight-month-old boy happily plays "catch the ball" with his mother but is shy and then distressed with a friendly stranger.

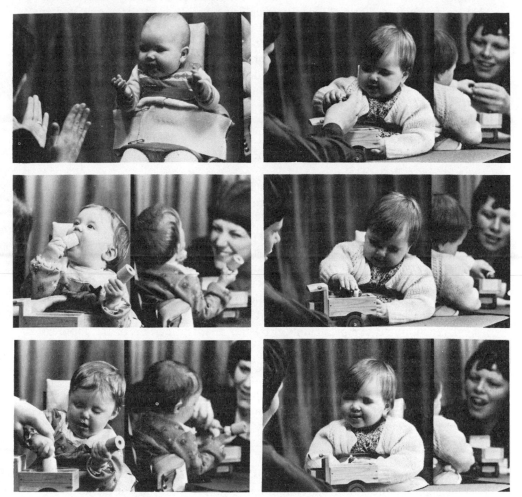

FIGURE 3 *Left* Emma, at six months, has learned clapping song—"clappa clappa handies." Esme, at nine months, plays with wooden dolls and a truck, usually ignoring her mother, and she has to be "persuaded" to follow the instruction, "Put the man in the truck." *Right* At one year Basilie is willing to cooperate in a joint task. Her mother says, "Put the man in the truck." Basilie takes the offered doll, carries out the instruction, then looks up and grins while her mother congratulates her. She is clearly enjoying their shared motives with respect to the toys.

awareness as well as preadaptations for interpersonal signaling, I have found it necessary to depend on micro-analytic descriptive techniques that are adequate to capture at least some of the complex patterns of movement that the infant brain can regulate (Trevarthen, 1977). Given there are such forms of action that make communication possible, what does one find in an ongoing interaction? How are the actions combined in sequences? How do they react to what a partner does?

In many of our samples of spontaneous communication the infant is clearly adjusting to what the mother does, not just detecting her face or her voice but modifying responses to match the particular thing she has just done. The infant watches the mother with intense focalization of gaze and an attentive expression. The mother sees this and responds with speech, touching, and changed expression. The infant may then be excited to smile, gesture, or vocalize. Examples of these interactions are shown in figures 14:1, 14:2, and 14:3.

In recent years this kind of delicate interaction has been the focus of considerable attention (Stern, 1974; Condon and Sander, 1974; Papousek and Papousek, 1974; Schaffer, 1977). That infants perceive a human face as having special relationship to themselves is supported by many experimental studies. In artificially controlled tests, infants under one month have been shown capable of specific imitation of mouth opening, tongue protrusion, simple vocalizations, and hand movements (Maratos, 1973; Meltzoff and Moore, 1977). In natural (uncontrolled) interactions with the mother, imitation like this is not important. What is important, indeed the rule, is cyclical reaction and complementation by the infant to certain of the mother's expressive acts. In the other direction, what the infant does is frequently mimicked by the mother, evidently a tactic she unconsciously adopts to gain stronger interaction (better overlap, meshing, or coaction) with the child (Stern, 1974; Stern et al., 1975; Fogel, 1977). Sylvester-Bradley suggests we use the psychoanalytical term "mirroring" to capture the sense of this sympathetic action (Sylvester-Bradley and Trevarthen, 1978).

Acts recorded in face-to-face interactions between mother and infant may closely resemble postural attitudes, facial expressions and gestures to be seen between conversing adults (Trevarthen, 1977, 1979b). It appears that some of the nonverbal component acts for being in conversation are integrated in the brain prenatally. "Proto-conversation" has been suggested as a name for this by Bateson (1971). The linguist Halliday accepts this as a necessary preparation for the phase of "proto-language" where the infant at nine or ten months begins to vocalize "acts of meaning" (Halliday, 1975, 1978). Infants of two or three months are able to act their part in a limited form of cooperative exchange of expressions with the mother.

It is important to state that turn-taking and the regular features of mother-infant interaction cannot be explained by assuming that all the significant coordinations are due to the mother alone being aware of what the infant is doing. This is proved by details in natural exchanges; for example, when the mother waits to see in what way the baby will react to a sign she has just made, she is predicting some kind of appropriate reply. It is brought out even more clearly by the results of experiments in which ongoing interactions are artificially disrupted.

We have caused the mother to act irrelevantly or to stop reacting to her infant in the middle of an exchange of expressions (Tatam, 1974; Murray, 1979; Trevarthen, 1979b). This causes a two-month-old to immediately cease to communicate pleasure and then to make elaborately patterned movements signifying distress, such as grimaces, desire to avoid or escape (gaze avoidance), and need for affectional care. Using closed-circuit TV and partially reflecting mirrors in a set-up where mother and infant perceive each other as full-face televised images, making eye-to-eye contact, Murray and I have obtained good interactions between mothers and two-month-olds. Replay of a tape of the infant's part of the interaction to the mother without warning her of the repetition, shows that, while the mother is unconscious of what actually is being done, she is unable to establish normal contact and quite put off by the televised infant's apparently irrelevant actions (Murray, 1979). Under these conditions of replay, an unresponding but normally expressive image of the infant is seen by the mother as perverse, distracted, unhappy, or withdrawn.

Condon and Sander (1974) proposed, in a highly significant paper, that a reflex entrainment of the infant's motility to coincide with patterns of adult speech gives a necessary framework for the development of language. However, two-month-olds adjust the *form* and *expressive value* of expression to the actions of their adult partner in face-to-face interaction. The infant, therefore, also possesses a qualitatively differentiated set of interpersonal motives (forms of experiencing other people and ways of responding) that act appropriately to regulate a sufficient interpersonal coordination of mood. This, too, must be taken into consideration when attempting to understand quasi-linguistic forms of mutual interest and coordination of expression between infants and adults.

Thus the evidence shows a complex interpersonal relationship formed between the infant and mother within the first few months after birth. The infant projects a rich responsive expressivity to the mother, confirming their relationship, and simultaneously learns to count on the mother's affectionate response, too. The infant smile, which has been studied experimentally, is only one of many components that reflects this interpersonal relationship. All the other acts expressed from a latent cooperative intentionality, including proto-conversation and dialoguelike play, are important.

By analysis of what mothers do and say to two-month-olds it is possible to show that the mother herself is mirroring because she is intensely identifying with the rudimentary personality of the infant. Her speech is highly informative about the interpersonal quality of the interaction (Sylvester-Bradley and Trevarthen, 1978) It is often said that the mother is "interpreting" rather ill-formed and certainly unintended acts of the baby. She is thought to be giving the infant's essentially "biological" acts mental form with her rational extrapolations, "*as if*" the baby was intending to communicate with her. Of course, in what the mother says self-conscious interpretation plays a part, especially if the exchange is being watched by another, and it is easy for the scientific observer, psychologist or linguist, to pick it up. I, personally, do not believe that such interpretation affects the infant or contributes to development of communication directly at this stage. It is the unselfconsciously intended interpersonal quality of the maternal utterances that counts, the expressed motivation to treat the infant with affectionate interest. The motivational quality of maternal speech certainly may support, or fail to support, the infant's actions.

Sylvester-Bradley (1979) subjected the motivational meaning of infant behavior to experimental test. He has found that a set of behaviors of an infant may be judged subjectively by psychologically unsophisticated females and categorized correctly in a number of adaptive modes that complement what the mother was doing, unknown to the assessor, when the infant acted in each of those ways. That is, the infant's behavior taken alone can be judged as appropriate to different forms of what the mother was doing or had just done.

The recent descriptive and experimental studies clear up two points. The infant is inherently capable, first, of differentiating himself from the world, and, second, of distinguishing things from persons. Both of these abilities are denied to newborns by reductionist physiological theories mentioned earlier, but they also are denied by the theories of Freud and Piaget. Consider these capacities in turn. First, with regard to perception of objects, Piaget, in agreement with Freud's idea of the growth of the ego, states that in the first months of life infants have no representation of events separate from their bodies in space and time. But the reaching and orienting behaviors of neonates and two-month-olds show that they possess an integrated motoric system and the ability to perceive objects at the correct exterior location, separate from the body, and to know their approximately correct form and displacement (Bower, 1974, 1978; Trevarthen, 1974a, 1974c). Infants, therefore, have some representation of objects when their prehensile actions are still ineffectual.

The totality of the baby's rudimentary powers to use external objects to satisfy perception exploration, manual prehension and the like, I call *subjectivity*—the condition of being a coordinated subject, motivated to act with purpose in relation to the world outside. While the neonate's subjectivity is rudimentary in relation to uptake of information and weak in powers of effective action, it has sufficient coordination and directedness and is sufficiently discriminating to manage simple interactions with the world.

In addition to this basic articulation with reality, the strong orientation to movements of the face, voice, and hands of the mother and the production by the infant of forms of facial expression, oral movement, hand displacement, postural change—which we take to signify human feelings of enjoyment, curiosity, puzzlement, annoyance, sadness, fear, and an effort to "say" or to "show" something—offers evidence of a specialized set of motives aimed to get the attentions of a human partner (Trevarthen,

1979a). Moreover, the sensitive adjustment of these acts to variations in the expression of the partner justifies describing the interaction as between two persons.

We may conclude that the infant is both a subject and a person. Even if the infant lacks a differentiated image of "self" and even if the communications of infants lack all referential content, the manner of expression of a two-month-old in face-to-face play with the mother has human or personal characteristics. It regulates an interpersonal field of action between them. This claim is at variance with the fundamental postulates of traditional psychoanalysis and with Piaget's conception of the sensorimotor period.

I have called the interpersonal activity of early infancy *primary intersubjectivity*. It involves psychological adaptations of both infant and mother. The term intersubjectivity has a venerable history in European phenomenology of language and it has gained importance recently in relation to the Speech Act Theory of Austin, Searle, Grice, and others (Searle, 1969). My concept of primary intersubjectivity developed from an excellent and timely presentation of the problems of language development by Ryan (1974) in which she drew on Habermas's analysis of the interpersonal basis of communication (Habermas, 1970), as well as on Speech Act Theory, to analyze behaviors of young children at the time they first use words.

Subjectivity and Intersubjectivity as Adaptive Mental Powers of Infants

I consider it to be of great importance that an intricate mechanism for interpersonal understanding develops precociously, well in advance of the cognitive machinery which will synthesize "ideas" for perceiving, identifying, and using physical things. This finding leads to extensive revision of Piaget's theory of how functions of thought develop. Most importantly, it puts a social function (I prefer to say a cooperative or an interpersonal function) in at the very beginning of human mental development and prior to the emergence of any recognizable language.

As I have indicated, in order to recover the social foundations of human cognition it is necessary to specify more precisely the human *motives;* mental structures underlying perception and action, that are active in early infancy. We may, then, contrast the motives appropriate to dealing with objects—the motives underlying subjectivity—with those appropriate to the interaction with other persons—the motives of intersubjectivity.

A word is required on the concept of "motive." What infants do may be ascribed to a set of structured states which specify both forms of action and the circumstances or affordances of stimulation which acts anticipate. To designate these, I use the word "motive" in the sense of an interior cause of action, comparable to what Piaget calls a schema. In part, motives consist of the "motor images" described by Bernstein (1967), the physiologist of movement. In part, a motive is a schema for the perception of the "affordances" of an object (Gibson, 1977). Charles Darwin believed that motives were the principal elements of mental evolution, the adaptive consequences of natural selection acting on the lives of animals (Gruber and Barrett, 1974). Of course, motives may reflect experience; they may become more specialized through learning, and they may be translated into intentions through learning how to master additional external conditions on either their activation or satisfaction (see Greenfield, this volume). But this does not imply that motives originate in experience. Many, at least, may be present in some form from birth. Let us attempt, then, to infer the set of innate motives underlying subjectivity on the one hand and intersubjectivity on the other from the patterns of behavior infants display in appropriately supportive circumstances.

MOTIVES TO KNOW THE PHYSICAL WORLD—SUBJECTIVITY

1. To seek unambiguous sensory information permitting detection of events in a single field unifying all modalities of sense.
2. To gain prehension of small objects perceived, by virtue of independent motion or by a boundary of high perceptual salience, to be discrete from their background. Then, to develop skill in knowing and using objects by exploring their perceptual "affordances" (Gibson, 1977).
3. To increase awareness by learning to attend to novel events and places, registering their occasional recurrence and their association with forms of exploratory or performatory action and with subjective benefits (rewards).
4. To maintain a coherent state of well-being while carrying out the above.

These emphasize the subject-centered view of experience. But infants by acting under the above motives also generate a particular awareness in others. Awareness in others is the environment in relation to which the interpersonal motives have evolved.

MOTIVES TO COMMUNICATE WITH PERSONS—INTERSUBJECTIVITY

1. To coordinate closely with holding, feeding, and cleaning movements of the mother and to obtain her presence in threatening circumstances by expressing alarm, hunger, pain. To learn to sense her identity (to know her from others).
2. To seek proximity and face-to-face confrontation with persons, to watch, listen to, and feel the pattern of expression and become engaged especially with movements of face and hands. To listen to the voice.

3. To respond with expressions of pleasure, then with manifestations of special human expression such as gestures and utterances, these being coordinated from the start with concurrent or intervening interests toward impersonal surroundings and objects that might be commented on or used cooperatively. Some forms of expression are clearly preadaptive to the later acquisition of cultivated forms of communication, including a true language. Most important of these are prespeech movements of lips and tongue, cooing vocalizations associated with prespeech, and gestures of the hands. These signs of expressive motivation lack mental representations of conventional topics.

4. To exhibit emotions in relation to one's cognitive and praxic performances, such as "deep serious intent" or "pleasure in mastery" (Piaget, 1966, 1962), so that others may know one's state and direction of mind.

5. To engage in reciprocal give and take of communicative initiative seeking to complement the expressed psychological state of the partner. This may involve both synchronization of motives or states of excitement and alternation in address and reply. Both partners must adjust to the actions of the other.

6. To express clear signs of confusion or distress if the actions of the partner become incomprehensible or threatening.

7. To avoid excessive, insensitive, or unwanted attempts by others to communicate, thus to retain a measure of personal control over one's state of expression to others.

Changes Beyond Primary Intersubjectivity

In early infancy, interpersonal transactions seem to be much more effective in relating the infant to the outside world than any other form of autonomous psychological endeavor. The world of the baby is mainly composed of persons. If one wants to see what an eight-week-old can do, it is sensible to confront the baby with the mother and ask her to play with the baby. Objects may be watched and even grabbed after with eagerness, but there is no skill to compare to that of communication. As an infant approaches the fourth month, however, there are signs of competition between rapidly developing motives to take hold of and become familiar with the world of impersonal but usuable objects and the already well-established will to communicate. The baby tends increasingly to break visual contact with the mother and to set out to explore or handle and mouth surroundings independently. This does not mean that the interpersonal relationship collapses or becomes weaker, but it does mean that direct face-to-face play is rejected more frequently in favor of dealing with things for oneself. The infant is as dependent as before on being in the company of the mother, especially in unfamiliar surroundings. The company of other persons may also be a source of pleasure and vitality.

Out of the conflict of motives to study or use objects and those to communicate with persons seem to be generated powerful new forms of joint intentionality that have specifically human subtlety. At least that seems, to Penelope Hubley and to me, an explanation of developments we have traced in the final months of the first year (Trevarthen and Hubley, 1978; Hubley and Trevarthen, 1979). It appears as if the cerebral control of acts of meaning that link the infant's awareness of surroundings with the awareness of the mother and that work to combine the two in new forms of purpose are the prime achievements of this period. This major watershed in mental development is reflected in all dimensions of an infant's behavior, including a sense of humor and strong emotional regulation of play, both of which are characteristic of the acts of cooperation of infants with their mothers at the middle of the first year of life.

Play with investment of humor and great energy is, therefore, seen to be a fundamental strategy in the development by which motives are elaborated for intersubjective control of both awareness and praxis. Six-month-olds are lively, playful, and curious, confidently independent when safely in familiar company, increasingly anxious when left in strange company, and likely to communicate directly with persons they know well only if they are amused by some well-adapted game, not too difficult or unfamiliar and not too aggressively pursued by the partner. These babies generally evade simple direct face-to-face exchange of expressions, such as was completely satisfying for a two-to-three-month-old, although they are very quick to recognize changes in the quality of interest others show in their behavior.

Analysis of play behavior reveals that games always involve the mother varying the conditions for the infant to satisfy his motives through action. The variation of goals and obstacles has to be controlled in such a way as to be, at least from time to time, predictable by the infant. Rules for successful games with an infant develop, frequently taking the form of reiterated "routines" as Bruner and Sherwood (1975) have pointed out. Acceptable rules are strongly influenced by the motivational patterns for cooperative action forming within the infant. The rules for games are not merely regulators of the cognitive programs of the infant as an individual actor and perceiver. For a six-month-old, games are naturally an interpersonal kind of event and the infectious expressions of an older infant in solitary play show this foundation clearly. We are definitely not in agreement with Piaget's strong bias to place solitary cognitive motives in primary position, as expressed in the following quote: "As to collective games [see Charlotte Buhler] we merely repeat that from a structural point of view, it is only the process of rules which distinguishes them from individual games" (Piaget, 1962 p. 109). The bipartisan games of mother and infant in the first year are certainly a natural part of *communication,* for which the infant has specific motivation.

Infants below six or seven months like games that allow them to explore the face, hair, eyes, tongue, hands of the mother and all her various postural, facial, and vocal reactions (Games of the Person). The babies are less involved with games in which an object that they seek to handle and explore with hands, eyes, and mouth is made to carry the partner's playful intentions (Object-Person Games). After six months, play mediated by an object (the mother making it roll, bounce, rattle, jingle, appear, and disappear) is enjoyed more. The progression has been charted in the development of a little girl over the first year by Penelope Hubley and myself (Trevarthen and Hubley, 1978), and Mrs. Hubley is in the process of extending the findings with other subjects and making quantitative estimations of changing patterns of behavior (Hubley and Trevarthen, 1979). The findings cast doubt upon the idea that games are cultural inventions applied to children to instruct them in the conventions of interacting with others. Often infants approaching nine months of age assume the initiative in creating for the mother a new direction in play. They are at all times actively involved, never simply imitating like an echo. Nevertheless, it is extremely interesting that games which succeed with infants as young as four months may be conventionalized. There are nursery rhymes that, passed down from mother to daughter, have stimulated enjoyment in generations of infants.

Recently we have observed that the games some mothers play with six-month-olds are greatly enriched by song and dance. Infants beyond this age may exhibit undisguised enjoyment of musical forms of expression. In this I see evidence that music has direct access to the motives that lead to the enjoyment of forms of movement and vocalization with others. When given sensitive help by their mothers babies really do "play" music.

Play seems always to lead toward conventional or socially integrated forms of activity. This connection may have a long evolutionary history. Are kittens when they play hard at two months of age becoming involved in the primitive conventions and cooperative routines of hunting? There does seem to be a powerful connection between play in animals and the evolution of skills of imaginative cooperation. According to Piaget (1962, p. 101), kittens "pretending" to bite are not pretending because they do not "know" what fighting is. I submit that they do pretend, if pretending is a form of acting a part to be perceived by another subject.

Communication at the middle of the first year is, though intersubjective, rather onesided. At least that is the case with the subjects we have studied most, who are predominantly middle class. Perhaps our mothers are especially encouraging or subservient to the initiatives of their infants. I think not. I believe the egocentricity of an infant at this stage is an essential factor in the emergence of knowing with others, an idea close perhaps to Vygotsky's interpretation of self-centered speech in older children. Alastair Mundy-Castle and I have begun an investigation of Yoruba subjects in

Lagos and of working class Scottish subjects to see how far cultural and social factors regulate this behavior. There do seem to be strong universal principles. The infant's motives in the middle of the first year are certainly strongly dominant in successful play. In well-practiced joint activities where the mother's knowledge and feelings are essential, like feeding, bathing, dressing, and locomoting, the infant, except when refusing in a markedly explicit way, is a skilled cooperator, accepting what the mother wants to get done. As a rule, play must be carefully adjusted to the infant's fickle state of curiosity and satisfaction. The mother must be ready to give in to a change of interest toward autonomous concentration on an object or reflection on an internal state. She is frequently an interested observer and assistant to the infant's active curiosity and her attempts to change the object of this curiosity may be pointedly rejected (Trevarthen and Hubley, 1978).

Reciprocal, Cooperative Behavior—Secondary Intersubjectivity

A change in play which we have seen after the ninth month throws the preceding period of games into relief. By some intrinsic integrative adjustment in the cerebral structures that govern motives, the infant comes to perceive the mother in a new way. She is no longer merely a source of pleasure and companionship in games in which the infant's motives remain central. She has become an interesting agent, whose own motives become something of an object or topic in themselves. This change in the way the baby sees her causes the mother to modify her actions and her speech so that entirely new kinds of cooperative action take place.

For the first time the infant appears to accept the mother as a teacher of new motives to use objects. Instead of accepting her as an amplifier, extender, and facilitator of intended actions, as well as a source of personal affection, comfort, and triumphant joy, the baby actively invites her by look, smile, and gesture, even by presentation of the object, to take initiative in a joint interaction with some common topic. In consequence, we observe a new form of spontaneous play, one that is more explicitly a joint enterprise in the managing of experiences and manipulation of objects. Given acceptance by the infant of the mother's motivating capacity, the infant can now, for the first time, learn by example. We believe that our records of mother-infant interaction at this time prove that the fundamental cause of instructive behavior by the mother is a change in the structure of motives in the infant, a change in curiosity and in intention. An observant mother is automatically capable of complementing this change so that a much more competent level of joint intentionality and cooperative awareness is quickly achieved.

When Piaget (1954) was observing his children at this age he perceptively described a number of changes of the first order of importance—key events in his theory. This is the time of transition from stage III to stage IV of the object concept—the beginning of an ability to "set in motion an intermediary capable of producing a (desired) result" (p. 203). It is also the beginning of true imitation; the infant "attributes to someone else's body an aggregate of personal powers" (p. 261). These and other descriptions of the changes toward the end of the first year have been reviewed elsewhere (Trevarthen and Hubley, 1978; Hubley and Trevarthen, 1979; Trevarthen, 1979b).

According to Piaget, acts performed in pretence without immediate perceptual support and with less real effect on the physical world begin in stage IV and stage V to stand for objects and for the performance of familiar actions. The baby starts to represent sleep by lying down, going for a walk by putting a hat on and stepping out. However, Piaget underestimates the tremendous interpersonal or cooperative significance of these playful "showing off" behaviors. They are not merely learned or imitiated rituals expressive of the cognitive act of imagining an absent object or effect. They explicitly attribute significance to other persons and what they do.

Once again, observation of the infant with the mother clarifies the infant's motives. The baby will now wait for her, watch her, and follow her instruction. We find that in cooperative play with a toy, demonstrating precisely what to do is *less* effective than an incomplete directive in the form of a brief utterance combined with a gesture (Hubley and Trevarthen, 1979). The ten-month-old is more attentive to the communicative intent expressed in an instruction and less inclined to slavishly imitate a model act. The same baby that understands instructions will reciprocate in showing and pointing, giving and taking, making these transactions with expressively inflected vocalizations (Bates, 1976; Bruner, 1975, 1977; Scaife and Bruner, 1974). This is also an age in which babies frequently act in a deliberately provocative way, for example pushing an object onto the floor after previously being told not to, then looking with a sly grin at the mother to see what she will do. In the game of "peek-a-boo" the baby increasingly plays the part of the active revealer, teasing the mother (Bruner and Sherwood, 1975). In sharing interest in a picture book, the mother and infant both point as the mother says the names of things "helping the child to master the concept of a label" (Ninio and Bruner, 1977). The routines of action and the rules behind them are accepted because of a cooperative motive, but they do not create the motive (see Trevarthen and Hubley, 1978).

At precisely the same age, in the last two months of the first year, Halliday recorded a new form of vocalization addressed by his son to others. Intentional speechlike acts transmitted the following messages in a protolanguage:

Functions of
Acts of Meaning

"I want [you to give me that]"[1]	Instrumental
"[You] Do as I say"	Regulatory
"Me and you [are interacting]"	Interactional
"Here I come [and you see me]"	Personal

1. Portions in brackets added by me.

Dore, too, has emphasized that well before they speak children adopt prosodic inflections to vocalize subtle interpersonal and intentional meaning (Dore, 1975). Greenfield (this volume) finds adequate grounds in their communicative actions for the attribution of intentions to infants.

All of these developments presage both imaginative play and the beginning of true speech with words in the second year (Trevarthen and Grant, 1979). When the baby comprehends that the other's action (vocalization, gesture, attending or use of an object) is an example for himself, he is automatically recognizing a simple sign or convention between the two of them. This sign has the power to transmit knowledge and skill. However the content of the act lacks specificity and definition and correspondingly it lacks awareness of the world. In the second year, with the advent of language, the object, the situation, and the motives and example of other persons are more explicitly recognized by the child. They become encapsulated in a symbolic movement or in a word, and they begin to seek conventional syntactical forms.

Accurate description of behaviors at this prelinguistic stage, taking care to note the integration of the infant's acts with interests of others and within the "context" of the surrounding, goes far to clarify the psychological origins of linguistic communication, and in recent years much attention has been paid to them (Ryan, 1974; Bruner, 1975; Dore, 1975; Halliday, 1975; Bates, 1976; Greenfield and Smith, 1976; Snow, 1977; Lock, 1978). It even more comprehensively gives a natural explanation for the general form of psychological cooperation that is essential to all kinds of cultural achievement, language being a special case. Transmission of rules of conduct, of techniques of praxis, of meanings established in language, and of manners in interpersonal expression all require reciprocal awareness of intentions between persons that accept one another's agency in a common field of experience and action. I believe these human behaviors to be supported by innate forms of mental process which might be called instincts for cooperative understanding (Trevarthen, 1979b).

To recapitulate the argument so far, acceptance of persons as like oneself may be implicit in the primary intersubjectivity of early infancy but it has no differentiated application to a common field of awareness. It cannot, therefore, carry any socially significant message about experience, except by coincidence. It is doubtful if the infant under eight months of age retains any impression of a symbolic, conventionalized representation of even the most familiar object in his world—a cup for example. He does like doing things with others and he might become used to the "normal" orientation or the familiar appearance of a shared toy, but the common idea of an object with a useful conventional purpose cannot be grasped. For a ten-to-twelve-month-old, however, objects have a quite new kind of identity. Because they may be recognized not only for their perceptual and manipulative affordances but also as possible entities in the awareness of others, they can begin to be used as acquired currency or tokens in a joint experiencing. By willingly giving an object to another to allow them to do something with it, a baby of this age turns the object into a potential symbol or artifact. In games, mothers and infants share jokes. A joke is a kind of symbol—for the baby it may be the early form of something stated to be significant between the two who "see the joke." However, a considerable development has occurred beyond this beginning when a serious and specific purpose inherent in a culturally defined object is shared. It is important, however, that not only the acts by infants with objects of play but also the forms of vocal utterance that they make to others may reveal the change in motivation toward a form of cooperative interest that naturally creates "acts of meaning." This is what Halliday (1975) describes as the appearance of a formal proto-language in which acts of interpersonal initiative are regulated vocally and previously shared experiences are referred to.

Evidently the achievement of a new motivational structure adapted to social cooperation in awareness and purpose liberates the infant into a new and highly productive phase of mental growth. There is, in the second year, a rapid development of comprehension of speech and of other forms of behavior that signify items of interest mentally taken out of the context of experiences and represented as significant in the companionship of mother and infant (Trevarthen and Grant, 1979). The infant's utterances also gain in power to represent familiar, jointly recognized items, even when these are taken from a memory image of their special usefulness in expression and in communication on other occasions. In Halliday's terms, the child adds a lexicogrammatical level to the levels of content and expression that were united in acts of meaning prior to the use of words.

Progress to the Act of Speaking, and to Understanding of Speech

Development of speech obviously involves maturation of the mechanisms for auditory perception and of those for oral production of utterances. Evidently, the first year of life is taken up by elaboration of neural mechanisms capable of integrating distal articulatory movement of lips and tongue, seen in rudimentary forms of activity in prespeech of neonates, with the elaborate coordination of proximal machinery inside the chest and throat. This latter pulmo-laryngeal system is essential to production of a controlled voicing. Although even six-week-olds may make bisyllabic utterances, clearly differentiated vocalizations coordinated with articulatory movements of lips and tongue begin in the second trimester after birth, and then the infant starts to babble. But this more peripheral or bodily aspect of speech production is a small part of the problem of how language develops. The psychology of language involves cerebral control of interpersonal initiatives or mutual interests, and mental representation of ideas that may be expressed to others. Meaningful speech (and the syntactical forms of language) always requires formulated motives of interpersonal initiative—including ways of explaining what one knows, wishes, intends, believes to another and ways of controlling the intentions, actions, awareness, and feelings of another. These formulations emerge as important roles of language and are of fundamental interest to linguists.

Humans speak to add information about joint enterprises that they can undertake to a limited degree without speech. Fluent, practiced speaking by which members of a society share a rich world of conscious experience and many elaborated skills becomes secondarily, though naturally, a medium for autonomous mental thought, argument, persuasion, and poetry. To be interested in developing these functions of language, humans have to be possessed by a compulsion to share their conscious understanding and wants as intimately as possible. It is this motivation, not language itself but an essential requirement for language, which, in parallel with certain actions and perceptual processes adapted to creating speech, is manifested by infants in the early part of the second year of life, just before they begin to acquire and use words deliberately to tell other people what they think and what they intend to do. Leading up to this stage and in parallel, they go through certain developments of prespeech, cooing, babbling, and protolinguistic utterances, that prepare the way for actually saying words.

The above concepts harmonize well with the theory of intersubjectivity of Habermas (1970). He proposes that intersubjectivity makes mutuality of understanding possible and that "dialogue constituent universals" of language behavior simultaneously generate and describe the intersubjectivity in the minds of language users. The first group of universals by which Habermas analyze speech are the personal pronouns enabling an "interlacing of perspectives" between people so they may keep separate their own and other people's viewpoints and understand the meaning for both of them of events in surroundings. Interlacing of subjective perspectives exists also in interactions of young infants with other persons. Infants of two months expect particular responses from a mother and make subtle changes of their behavior in response to what she does. This is what we term "primary intersubjectivity" (Trevarthen, 1979a).

The second set of Habermas's dialogue constitutive universals are deictic expressions that specify time and space, the articles and demonstrative pronouns. He says that these "link the levels of intersubjectivity on which the subjects converse and interact reciprocally with the levels of objects about which the subjects converse" (Habermas, 1970, pp. 141-42). This function appears at the end of the first year and is what we have termed secondary intersubjectivity, that is, combining communication about action on objects with direct dyadic interaction (Trevarthen and Hubley, 1978).

How do Language, Thought, and Culture Begin?

Thinking and language are essentially for and of social life and their content is certainly a product of cultural history. But, as we have seen, we are not at liberty to conclude that for this to be possible all that man requires is a brain with weak instincts and great plasticity for learning new things. The behavior of infants speaks otherwise and, in fact, such a concept of psychological growth is without foundation in brain science. The way infants enter upon the task of being members of a cultural consciousness shows that they do so because somehow their brains grow fantastically specific structures that require that kind of activity to function properly and to develop. We do not know what these structures look like neuro-anatomically nor how they function physiologically, but we can be confident that they exist in the human brain and that they have considerable definition at birth. They are intentional structures, or, more accurately, motivating structures, for intending and for being aware of how to carry out intentions. Anatomical studies of the brains of fetuses and infants would certainly lead one to expect highly complex functions anticipating those of the adult brain (Trevarthen, 1979d, 1979e).

This new view of an actively and innately motivated infant intelligence also exposes the inadequacy of some traditional language-centered, rationalist explanations of the development of the human mind. We must take a fresh approach to human natural history based on an adequate analysis of what infants try to do with the aid of other people. In consequence the basic process may appear less arbitrary, more self-organized.

Analysis of primary human motives may lead to revision of educational theory. Education is, itself, an invention of culture. By instinct and trial-and-error, practices that have success in transmitting knowledge and skills of a given society to its children have been developed and formal institutions designed to carry them out. Because it is a cultural invention, education, like language, has been thought to be shaped by the requirements of its application, whether to naturally occurring things in the physical and geographical world or to products of human artifice and convention. A concurring opinion of the child about what knowledge might be and a compliant response to its inculcation is taken for granted. But practical experience of teachers shows that rigid instruction of pupils assumed to be passively attentive does not work. Nor does it work to compel children to achieve a set performance at a given age. The only reasonable psychological theory of education is that children possess an intrinsic and growing motivation to gain knowledge from others. This is certainly the case for the knowledge acquired in out-of-school settings. Wood (this volume) and Olson (this volume) both illustrate the importance of this interpersonal contingency in various instructional settings.

Infants, most of all, are impervious to arguments about the needs of a particular society or controversy about techniques of instruction in how that society functions. Mothers of infants, likewise, tend to shake free from advice they are given, usually by men and women beyond child-bearing age or without children, about how the infant mind develops, even though mothering is quite open to serious interference in highly regulated societies with powerful technologies or authoritarian ideologies. What infants actually do to gain experience from the unconscious responses of their instructors proves that the origin of educative practice is in a rich endowment of the human brain for eliciting cooperative understanding from companions. Given this, the mastery of conventions in a human society becomes a possibility.

Implications for Theory in Sociology and Anthropology

Infants do not speak a language, nor think, nor do they make any original contribution to society or culture. For months they cannot even handle objects or move about on their own. For most anthropologists they constitute a biological factor not unlike food resources—essential to human life but passively amenable to cultivation by techniques which may change greatly from generation to generation. This is the classical view of the sociologists, too. However, if a developmental psychologist regards an infant in this way, as biological matter to be shaped into a human condition, he is no less a traitor to his subject. It is increasingly clear that we have to regard human beings as having a consistent general pattern of strategy of development in which the biological and social cannot be so easily separated.

The principle facts are these. Infants are not merely adapted to elicit care of their vital functions. They also possess rudimentary personal powers that affect their caretakers intimately so that within a short time of birth a subtle infant-caretaker relationship is established. This relationship is not social—it has too few members to warrant that name. Rather, the essential interpersonal link between infant and mother or other caretaker lies inside family and society, like a seed inside a fruit that, in turn, is in a special place of growth in a whole plant. Infants actively strengthen and enlarge their pre-adapted personal relationships by means of forms of behavior that are not merely social but, indeed, cultural in nature. In infancy these behaviors are only of presumptive functional significance. They have a temporary value as signs in a prelinguistic communication of interpersonal attitudes. Caretakers interpret these signs within their own much more developed consciousness as imitative of adult acts that are essential to collective life. They seem to be imitations, but they are really spontaneously motivated attempts to communicate.

By having such precursor behaviors, infants show that they possess structures from which effective skills of social intercourse will later be built. Furthermore, rapid developments in the course of infancy show how these structures control first steps in their own developmental transformation. They are rudimentary and essential forms of the "cultural generators" which Clifford Geertz (1966) has supposed to exist, emergent in a pre-social phase of human life.

The infant has, therefore, not ony a place inside society as a biologically coupled appendage of the mother. He or she has a prospective social potency—even a potency for making a contribution to and innovations in the collective knowledge and skills of a culture. All the conventional forms in human consciousness, including the physical artifacts and institutions, the forms of thought that organize discovery and maintenance of understanding of the world, and the various languages by means of which this understanding is communicated, discussed, clarified and stored, require a basic set of motives. These motives cause the subject to cooperate with others in action and to share mental events: ideas, images, memories, feelings, and emotions.

Modern attempts at a scientific and rational systematization of human knowledge and human social systems have claimed that cooperation is acquired through the neurophysiological association of sensory effects with elementary actions, that is, by conditioning. But the evidence from how infants behave is not in agreement with this empiricist and reductionist conclusion. The brains of infants take an active self-directing part in the development of the psychological functions of culture. They are intrinsically motivated to seek instruction and to share discovery of the conditions and techniques that make collective life effective. Thus the cultural existence of human beings, though it is clearly a product of history, is anticipated, even made inevitable or natural, by the constitution of an infant who is far too young to possess any real knowledge of effective processes in any particular social and cultural system. To understand in what way infants contribute to social life and the growth of culture, the structure and pattern of changes in their motives must be accurately described.

As with other more easily seen biological systems, the development of the human mind is prepared for by well-oriented instabilities of mental structure that anticipate dependable environmental effects, including cultural effects, in a general way.

Cultural predispositions of infants are unspecific and totally dependent on suitable exercise in a social world. But, the lesson of our research is that the fundamental motives for developing cultural forms are already active in infancy. At the earliest, the only thoughts, utterances, purposes, roles and beliefs that exist for the infant are those imputed by companions of the infant to justify or give reality to their unconscious response to the infant's complex eagerness for companionship. But before they acquire the conventional word and sentence forms of language, before they accept a decontextualized representation of a common reality, humans direct their will and experience precisely toward learning common enterprises with others and sharing common artifacts. They communicate their wants in relation to what another may do for them. They push the responses of their caretakers toward a shared understanding, and they develop in direct response to the quality and freedom of this understanding. While scarcely conscious, they are active in one or a few interpersonal relationships in a family. When in possession of a delicately personal attachment based on a shared history of tricks, pleasures, and discoveries they reach out as children to become active members of a community that goes beyond their family. What they learn has been presaged in the motives and skills they bring to the learning situation from infancy. Thus, in sharing with others, the infant is setting the stage for playing the differentiated individual roles called for in a larger society.

First Motives in the Embryogeny of Culture

Of course, human motives or cooperative life in society gain in strength throughout childhood. What has been claimed here is that they regulate the individual enjoyment of action and experience from the start of psychological existence. The best evidence for this conclusion comes from the behaviors that we have seen developing after the first few months. These behaviors are difficult to categorize because they are so far reaching in their implications and because they are so precisely adapted to and so delicately supported by the conscious understanding of the adults who share the infant's life. But let us make an attempt. Let us summarize our conclusions in a tentative list of the motives which gain command of the actions of infants in the latter half of the first year and which lead on to the beginnings of language in the second year when infancy gives way to childhood. These extend the list of motives presented on pages 326 and 327.

Motives in Play and Cooperation of Infants After Four Months

MOTIVES TO BE AWARE AND TO KNOW AND USE THE PHYSICAL WORLD

1. To develop understanding and control of the world and of objects and their uses. To explore the use of objects as instruments or as intermediaries in production of a desired result.
2. To occasionally withdraw from action and simply perceive or recollect experiences in tranquillity (contemplation).

MOTIVES FORMING COMPANIONSHIP, TRUST, AND COOPERATION
WITH PERSONS

1. To form a bond of friendship and mutual trust with those who regularly share their motives.
2. To react with humor or annoyance to the efforts of others to involve themselves with one's purposes by means of various forms of teasing.
3. To join in overlapping or complementary forms of motor expression, leading to dancelike or songlike performances involving confluent patterns of rhythmic movements.
4. To show, at times, a limited independence by avoiding or ignoring the attempts of others to obtain face-to-face play.
5. To regulate interpersonal actions with others by expressions such as laughing, teasing, or mocking.

MOTIVES FOR ACTING LIKE OTHERS AND FOR TAKING INITIATIVE IN
COOPERATION

1. To enlarge one's own motives for dealing with people and events by seeking to observe and to match or even imitate exactly the expressive or praxic acts of others—i.e., to accept the other as a potential source of motives for oneself.
2. To gain familiarity with habitual acts of caretaker/companions, especially the mother.
3. To learn by example from the acts of others.
4. To govern the degree of mixing of actions with the aid of rule-bound games learned together.
5. To assume, at times, deliberate control over the actions of another and thus to reverse the reciprocal relationship of cooperation.
6. To contribute imaginative innovation to cooperative activity with others.

MOTIVES FOR DEVELOPMENT OF COMMUNICATION WITH SYMBOLS

1. To extend play with another to incorporate an object which may be exchanged, shared, or modified by joint action within the convergent attentions of both subjects.

2. To express by vocalization or by gesture acts of meaning that transmit distinct states of excitement, of purpose, and of interpersonal relationship.

3. To use expressive acts or objects increasingly as symbols for transmission of information about one's own mental states (of recollection, of feeling, or of purpose) to others. To represent in this way familiar jointly recognized items.

4. To develop a vocal and gestural "vocabulary" by imitation of symbols used by companions in cooperative activity.

5. To practice and enlarge the skills of speaking and gesturing.

6. To become increasingly part of a culture in which expressions of consciousness and purposeful action of objects is constrained by habit and tradition.

References

Austin, J. L. *How to do things with words.* Oxford: Oxford University Press, 1962.

Bates, E. *Language and context: The acquisition of pragmatics.* New York and London: Academic Press, 1976.

Bateson, M. C. *Quarterly progress report, Research laboratory of electronics, Massachusetts Institute of Technology.* Cambridge, Mass.: MIT Press, 1971.

Bernstein, N. A. *The co-ordination and regulation of movement.* London: Pergamon, 1967.

Bower, T. G. R. The visual world of infants. *Scientific American,* 1966, 215, 80–92.

———. *Development in infancy.* San Francisco: Freeman and Co., 1974.

———. Perceptual development: Object and space. In E. C. Carterette and M. P. Friedman (Eds.), *Handbook of perception,* vol. 8. New York: Academic Press, 1978, 83–103.

Brazelton, T., Koslowski, B., and Main, M. The origins of reciprocity: The early mother-infant interaction. In M. Lewis and L. Rosenblum (Eds.), *The effect of the infant on its caregiver.* London: Wiley, 1974, 49–77.

Bruner, J. S. *Processes of cognitive growth: Infancy.* Worcester: Clark University with Barri Publishers, 1968.

———. Biological functions of infant-mother attachment behaviour: general discussion. In A. Ambrose (Ed.), *Stimulation in early infancy.* London and New York: Academic Press, 1969.

———. The ontogenesis of speech acts. *Journal of Child Language,* 1975, 2, 1–20.

———. Early social interaction and language acquisition. In H. R. Schaffer (Ed.), *Studies in mother-infant interaction.* London: Academic Press, 1977, 271–289.

Bruner, J. S. and Sherwood, V. Early rule structure: The case of peekaboo. In J. S. Bruner, A. Jolly, and K. Sylva (Eds.), *Play: Its role in evolution and development.* Harmondsworth: Penguin Books, 1975.

Condon, W. S. and Sander, L. S. Neonate movement is synchronised with adult speech. *Science,* 1974, 183, 99–101.

Dore, J. *The development of speech acts.* The Hague: Mouton, 1975.

Fogel, A. Temporal organization in mother-infant face-to-face interaction. In H. R. Schaffer (Ed.), *Studies in mother-infant interaction.* London: Academic Press, 1977, 119–151.

Geertz, C. The impact of the concept of culture on the concept of man. *Bulletin of the Atomic Scientists,* 1966, 12, 1–8.

Gibson, J. J. The theory of affordances. In R. Shaw and J. Bransford (Eds.), *Perceiving, acting and knowing.* Hillsdale, N.J.: Erlbaum, 1977.

Greenfield, P. M. and Smith, J. *Communication and the beginning of language: The development of semantic structure in one word speech.* New York and London: Academic Press, 1976.

Habermas, J. Introductory remarks to a theory of communicative competence. In H. P. Dreitzel (Ed.), *Recent Socioloy No. 2.* London: Macmillan, 1970.

Halliday, M. A. K. *Learning how to mean: Explorations in the development of language.* London: Arnold, 1975.

————. Meaning and the construction of reality in early childhood. In H. L. Pick Jr., and E. Saltzman (Eds.), *Modes of perceiving and processing information.* Hillsdale, N.J.: Erlbaum, 1978, 67–98.

Hofsten, C. von. Development of visually directed reaching: The approach phase. *Journal of Human Movement Studies,* in press.

Hubley, P. and Trevarthan, C. Sharing a task in infancy. In I. Uzgiris (Ed.), *Social interaction and communication during infancy.* New Directions for Child Development, vol. 4. San Francisco: Jossey-Bass, 1979, 57–80.

Lock, A. (Ed.) *Action, gesture and symbol: The emergence of language.* London: Academic Press, 1978.

Murray, L. *Infants capacities for regulating interactions with their mothers, and the function of emotions.* University of Edinburgh: Ph.D. Thesis (in preparation), 1979.

Ninio, A. and Bruner, J. S. Achievement and antecedents of labelling. *Journal of Child Language,* 1978, 5, 11–15.

Papousek, H. Experimental studies of appetitional behaviour in human newborns and infants. In H. W. Stevenson (Ed.), *Early behaviour. Comparative and developmental approaches.* New York: Wiley, 1967.

————. Individual variability in learned responses in human infants. In R. J. Robinson (Ed.), *Brain and early behaviour: Development in fetus and infant.* New York: Academic Press, 1969, 251–263.

Papousek, H. and Papousek, M. Cognitive aspects of preverbal social interaction between human infants and adults. In Symposium on the parent-infant relationship. M. O'Connor (Ed.), *Parent-infant interaction.* Amsterdam: Elsevier, 1974.

Piaget, J. *The child's construction of reality.* New York: Basic Books, 1954.

————. *Play, dreams and imitation in childhood.* New York: Norton, 1962.

————. *The origins of intelligence in children.* New York: International University Press, 1966.

Richards, M. P. P. M. Social interaction in the first weeks of human life, *Psychiatria, Neurologia, Neurochirurgia,* 1971, 74, 35–42.

————. Development of psychological communication. In K. J. Connolly and J. S. Bruner (Eds.), *The growth of competence.* London and New York: Academic Press, 1974.

Robson, K. S. The role of eye to eye contact in maternal-infant attachment. *Journal of Child Psychology and Psychiatry,* 1967, 8, 13–25.

Ryan, J. Early language development: Towards a communicational analysis. In M. P. M. Richards (Ed.), *The integration of a child into a social world.* Cambridge: Cambridge University Press, 1974.

Scaife, M. and Bruner, J. S. The capacity for joint visual attention in the infant. *Nature,* 1975, 254, 265–266.

Schaffer, H. R. *Studies in mother infant interaction.* London and New York: Academic Press, 1977.

Searle, J. *Speech acts: An essay in the philosophy of language.* Cambridge: Cambridge University Press, 1969.

Sequeland, E. R. and DeLucia, C. A. Visual reinforcement of non-nutritive sucking in human infants. *Science,* 1969, 165, 1144–1146.

Sequeland, E. R. and Lipsitt, L. P. Conditioned head-turning in human newborns. *Journal of Experimental Child Psychology,* 1966, 3, 356–376.

Snow, C. Mother's speech research: From input to social interaction. In C. Snow and C. A. Ferguson (Eds.), *Talking to children: Language input and acquisition.* Cambridge: Cambridge University Press, 1977.

Stern, D. N. Mother and infant at play: The dyadic interaction involving facial, vocal and gaze behaviours. In M. Lewis and L. Rosenblum (Eds.), *The effect of the infant on its caregiver.* London: Wiley, 1974.

Stern, D. N., Jaffe, J., Beebe, B., and Bennett, S. L. Vocalizing in unison and alternation: Two modes of communication within the mother-infant dyad. *Annals of the New York Academy of Sciences*, 1975, 263, 89–100.

Sylvester-Bradley, B. *The study of mother-infant relationship in the first six months of life.* University of Edinburgh: Ph.D. Thesis, in preparation, 1979.

Sylvester-Bradley, B. and Trevarthen, C. "Baby-talk" as an adaptation to the infant's communication. In N. Waterson and C. E. Snow (Eds.), *Development of Communication: Social and Pragmatic Factors in Language Acquisition.* London: Wiley, 1978.

Trevarthen, C. L'action dans l'espace et la perception de l'espace: Mécanismes cérébraux de base. In F. Bresson et al. (Eds.), *De l'Espace Corporel a l'Espace Ecologique.* Paris: Presses Universitaires de France, 1974a, 65–80.

———. Conversations with a two-month old. *New Scientist*, 1974b, 2 May, 230–235.

———. The psychobiology of speech development. In E. H. Lenneberg (Ed.), *Language and brain: Developmental aspects, neurosciences research program bulletin,* Boston: Neurosciences Research Program, 1974c, 12, 570–585.

———. Descriptive analyses of infant communication behaviour. In H. R. Schaffer (Ed.), *Studies in mother-infant interaction.* London: Academic Press, 1977, 227–270. J. M. Tanner (Eds.), *Human growth: A comprehensive treatise,* vol. 3. New York: Plenum, 1979a, 3–96.

———. Brain development and the growth of psychological function. In J. Sants (Ed.), *Developmental psychology and society.* London: Macmillan, 1979b.

———. Communication and cooperation in early infancy. A description of primary intersubjectivity. In M. Bullowa (Ed.), *Before speech: The beginnings of human communication.* London: Cambridge University Press. In press (a).

———.Instincts for human understanding and for cultural cooperation: their development in infancy. In M. von Cranach, K. Foppa, W. Lepenies, and D. Ploog (Eds.), *Human Ethology.* Cambridge: Cambridge University Press. In press (b).

———. Basic patterns of psychogenetic change in infancy. In T. Bever (Ed.), *Proceedings of the O.E.C.D. conference on "dips in the learning,"* St. Paul de Vence, March 1975. Hillsdale, N.J.: Erlbaum. In press (c).

———. Neuroembryology and the development of perception. In F. Falkner and

Trevarthen, C. and Grant, F. Infant play and the creation of culture. *New Scientist,* 22 February 1979, 566–569.

Trevarthen, C. and Hubley, P. Secondary intersubjectivity: Confidence, confiding and acts of meaning in the first year. In A. Lock (Ed.), *Action, gesture and symbol: The emergence of language.* London: Academic Press, 1978, 183–229.

Trevarthan, C., Hubley, P., and Murray, L. Psychology of infants. In J. A. Davis and J. Dobbing (Eds.), *Scientific foundations of paediatrics,* 2d ed. London: Heinemann Medical Books, in preparation.

Trevarthen, C., Hubley, P., and Sheeran, L. Les activités innées du nourrisson. *La Recherche,* 1975, 6, 447–458.

Trevarthen, C. and Tursky, B. Recording horizontal rotations of head and eyes in spontaneous shifts of gaze. *Behavioral Research Methods and Instrumentation,* 1969, 1, 292–293.

Wolff, P. Observations on the early development of smiling. In B. M. Foss (Ed.), *Determinants of infant behaviours,* vol. 2. London: Methuen, 1963.

———. The natural history of crying and other vocalizations in early infancy. In B. M. Foss (Ed.), *Determinants of infant behaviour,* vol. 4. London: Methuen, 1969.

15

Cultural Amplifiers Reconsidered
Michael Cole and Peg Griffin

It arrived in a large package and lay on my desk for some weeks before I found the time to look at it. A Ph.D. dissertation in two, thick, mimeographed volumes: *Cultural Amplifiers and Psychological Differentiation Among Khawabodosh in Pakistan*. The author was Joseph Berland, an anthropologist interested in how culture influences thought. Berland had employed several contemporary psychological concepts and data gathering techniques in his study so he was naturally anxious to see how his ideas fared among psychologists. I qualified as a reader because I am the coauthor of an article concerning inferences about cultural differences in psychological processes. My coauthor was Jerry Bruner.

In that article, which had served as one point of departure for Berland Bruner and I were attempting to come to terms with the problem of how people raised in different cultures (especially subcultures within the United States) are socialized to behave differently in response to a variety of specific intellectual tasks and to schooling in general. In our discussion, we used the notion of a cultural amplifier, which Berland had adopted as an organizing concept in his work. The matter was put as follows: "By an amplifying tool is meant a technological feature, be it soft or hard, that permits control by the individual of resources, prestige, and deference within the culture. An example of a middle-class cultural amplifier that operates to increase the thought processes of those who employ it is the discipline loosely referred to as 'mathematics.' To employ mathematical techniques requires the cultivation of certain skills of reasoning, even certain styles of deploying one's thought processes. If one were able to cultivate the strate-

The preparation of this manuscript was supported by a grant from the Carnegie Corporation to Michael Cole. The reader will note that the first person personal pronoun employed in the beginning of the paper is inconsistent with the fact that this is a co-authored effort. An early draft of this paper served as the focus of extended discussions among the authors that so heavily influenced the outcome of the paper that a joint effort resulted. This collaboration is appropriately marked as the paper progresses, reflecting the structuring of the activities that produced it.

gies and styles relevant to the employment of mathematics, then that rage of technology is open to one's use. If one does not cultivate mathematical skills, the result is 'functional incompetence,' an inability to use this kind of technology" (Cole and Bruner, 1971, p. 872).

I was very impressed with Berland's study. It was an ethnography that provided copious detail on the way traveling Pakistani entertainers and artisans organize the activities of their children. In addition, Berland tested children's and adult's responses to several phychological tasks originally designed to access cognitive and perceptual abilities. He found support for his hypothesis that nomadic groups would develop greater "field independence" (as the term is used by Witkin and his associates) than the sedentary peoples among whom they traveled. He also discovered rather striking precociousness in the speed with which some nomadic children mastered certain Piagetian tasks. Nomadic adults' techniques for organizing their children's activities are seen as the cultural amplifiers (available to nomadic but not to sedentary populations) that provide for their advantages on cognitive and perceptual tasks.

Along with my great interest in Berland's substantive findings, I experienced a sharp sense of discomfort when I thought about the term "cultural amplifiers." My discomfort had two sources. First, the notion had arisen in Professor Bruner's work, not mine. Berland had contacted the wrong predecessor! Second, I had just worked my way through two monographs, both by Soviet psychologists, that had strongly influenced my thinking about culture and cognition. I felt the need to retrace the idea of cultural amplifier which seemed not to quite mesh with the intrumental, cultural-historical approach to the study of mind offered by Lev Vygotsky (1978) and Alexander Luria (1979).

Cultural Amplifiers

The fundamental statement of the concept of cultural amplifier as it is applied in cross-cultural, psychological research is to be found in Jerry Bruner's overview to *Studies in Cognitive Growth*. The intertwining of this notion with development is here obvious. "Man is seen to grow by the process of internalizing the ways of acting, imagining, and symbolizing that 'exist' in his culture, ways that amplify his powers. He then develops these powers in a fashion that reflects the uses to which he puts [them]" (Bruner, 1966, p. 320-21).

Bruner is telling us that the supply of amplifiers in a culture and the demands of life in a culture are two cardinal, cultural determinants of the "powers of mind" that will develop. The two are staged: first there is growth by internalization of amplifiers, then development by the individual's use of those amplifiers. Unfortunately, in 1966 he also had to tell us that "Relatively little is known about . . . the culture's intellectual amplification supplies and the demands that are placed on the individual" (p. 321).

Bruner drew heavily on Weston La Barre's contention that changes in human nature in the past five hundred thousand or so years have resulted largely from a human being's capacity to incorporate external aspects of his environment into his stock of adaptations to the world, a process that La Barre referred to as "evolution-by-prosthesis."

In the evolutionary scheme of things, Bruner supposed that human evolution ("selection and survival") would be shaped by existing implement systems, such that now "We move, perceive, and think in a fashion that depends on techniques rather than on wired in arrangements in our nervous system" (p. 56).

I accepted the spirit of this line of thinking when I read it more than a decade ago, as I do now. But the more I looked at the way in which "amplifier" was used in discussions such as I have quoted from, the more I came to believe that important ambiguities, and hence important misunderstandings, lurked in its byways. In some sense, cultures do provide members with techniques for solving the problems posed by their environments, social as well as physical. But in what sense? Human achievements are thereby increased. But does the increase result from a process of "amplification?"

A Soviet Perspective

Soviet thinking about culture and thought is especially important to include in a discussion of cultural amplifiers for several reasons. As I have already indicated, my own doubts about current usage derive from my experience with the concepts evolved by Vygotsky, Luria, and their colleagues. No less important is the fact that Bruner was similarly influenced. As he recounts in the preface to *Studies in Cognitive Growth*, an exchange of visits with Luria and Alexander Zaporozhets in the late 1950s and early 1960s was important in his thinking. Jerry also wrote an outstandingly prescient preface to Vygotsky's *Thought and Language* when it appeared in 1962 (to which I will return later in this discussion). Had I understood his preface and that book in 1962, many false starts and blind alleys in my own work might have been avoided. But at that time I was just entering my first apprenticeship under Luria's guidance, and I could do little more than assimilate Vygotsky's ideas to my prior experience as a mathematical learning theorist.

However, in the mid-1970s I was engaged, along with several colleagues, in editing heretofore unpublished Vygotsky manuscripts. In the middle of this enterprise a new task came to hand—to edit, and complete, an autobiography undertaken by Alexander Luria shortly before his death. In coping with these obligations, I was forced to a deeper consideration of two sets of concepts which, in combination, form the center of the Vygotsky-Luria approach to the study of the mind.

In the mid-1920s, influenced by Marx as well as his prior experience as a philologist and educator, Vygotsky concluded that the origins of higher forms of psychological activity are to be found in the individual's social relations with the external world. Man was seen not only as the product of his environment, but also as an active agent in creating his environment. A *psychology* which sought to be a dialectical materialist enterprise needed to discover the ways in which natural processes such as physical maturation and sensory mechanisms become intertwined with culturally determined processes to produce the psychological characteristics of adults. Vygotsky liked to emphasize that we need, in a sense, to step outside the organism in order to discover the sources of specifically human forms of psychological activity.

Vygotsky called his approach variously "cultural," "historical," and "instrumental" psychology. Each term reflected different sources of the general mechanism by which societies mold the forms of activity that separate man from other creatures.

The earliest statement of this overall enterprise was a monograph called "Studies in the History of Behavior" that appeared in 1930 bearing Bacon's epigraph: "The naked hand and intellect by themselves amount to nothing: everything is accomplished with the aid of tools." This idea was at the core of Vygotsky's notion of an "instrumental" psychology that underscored the fundamentally *mediated* nature of all complex psychological functions. Unlike basic reflexes, which can be characterized by a stimulus-response process, higher functions incorporate auxiliary stimuli, which are typically produced by the person himself. The adult responds not only to the stimuli presented by an experimenter or by his natural environment, he also actively modifies those stimuli and uses his modifications as an instrument of his behavior. We know some of these modifications through folk customs such as tying a string around one's finger in order to remember more effectively. Many less prosaic examples of this principle were uncovered in Soviet studies of changes in the structure of children's thinking as they grow from the age of three to ten years (see Cole, 1978; Luria, 1979; Vygotsky, 1978).

The "cultural" aspect of the theory referred to the socially structured ways in which society organizes the kinds of tasks that the growing child faces and the kinds of tools (both mental and physical) that the young child is provided to master those tasks. One of the key tools invented by mankind is language, and Vygotsky placed special emphasis on the role of language in the organization and development of thought processes.

The "historical" aspect merged into the cultural one. The tools which man uses to master his environment and his own behavior did not spring fully developed from the hand of God. They were invented and perfected in the long course of man's social history. Language, one of the inventions, carries within it the generalized concepts that are the storehouse of human knowledge. Opportunity and methods for using and supplementing this storehouse are expanded by specialized cultural instruments like writing (and arithmetic).

Given this instrumental, cultural, and historical nature of psychological functions, a line of reasoning for investigating them is apparent: one could study the various thought operations as they are structured among people whose cultural history had not supplied them with a tool such as writing. Such people should manifest a different organization of higher cognitive processes, but a similar structuring of elementary processes, than people whose cultural history had supplied them with writing.

The close correspondence between these ideas and the idea of cultural amplifiers should be clear. The point is underlined when we look back at Bruner's introduction to Vygotsky's *Thought and Language*, where he points out that "*Thought and Language* elaborates to what sense he believed that in mastering nature we master ourselves. For it is the internalization of overt action that makes thought, and particularly the internalization of external dialogue that brings the powerful tool of language to bear on the stream of thought. Man, if you will, is shaped by the tools and instruments that he comes to use, and neither the mind nor the hand alone can amount to much" (Bruner, 1962, p, vi–vii).

But ideas of tool use and the internalization of tool-linked activity are not sufficient to capture the essence of the cultural-historical school. In addition, we need to examine Vygotsky and Luria's ideas about the nature of psychological functioning, particularly the notion of "function" itself, which, in their hands, took on a special meaning. Luria, in particular, was concerned to promote a richer understanding of the term "function" than is usually encountered in psychology. He pointed out that the term function usually refers to the function of a particular tissue. Perception of light is the function of photosensitive cells in the retina, secretion of insulin is the function of the pancreas. By analogy, hearing was said to be the function of the auditory cortex, planning the function of the frontal cortex, and so on. Such analogies, Luria repeatedly asserted, are misleading. Borrowing from his friend and colleague Peter Anokhin, Luria liked to point out that when we speak of the "function of respiration" we cannot be referring to the function of particular tissue (for example, the alveoli that transport oxygen into the blood.) The whole process of respiration is carried out by an entire *functional system* consisting of many components including the motor, sensory, and autonomic nervous systems. Functional systems are distinguished not only by the complexity of their structure, but also by the flexibility of the roles played by constituents. In the example of respiration, the activity (maintenance or restoration of homeostasis) and the result (transport of oxygen into the blood) must remain invariant if the organism is to avoid perishing. This complex function, however, can be carried out in a variety of ways should the normal system be disrupted though injury to one of its components. So, for example, if the diaphragm muscles that ordinarily operate to expand the lungs cease to work, intercostal muscles will start to work. It is the presence of an invariant goal performed by variable mechanisms that bring the process to a constant, invariant termination that is the basic feature of a functional system.

Vygotsky applied this view to child development: "I have attempted to demonstrate that the course of child development is characterized by a radical alteration in the very structure of behavior; at each new stage the child changes not only her response but carries out that response in new ways, drawing on new instruments of behavior and replacing one psychological function by another" (Vygotsky, 1978, p. 72–73). Vygotsky's emphasis on the fact that there are variable activities and variable results over the course of development, not merely a more powerful mechanism, means that he views change in the nature of functional systems as the essence of development.

It is when I considered the combined implications of applying the ideas of instrumental-mediated behavior with the notion that all higher psychological functions are in fact functional *systems* that I began to question the wisdom of using the term cultural amplifier when referring to the nature of culture's impact on cognitive development. There are several points where the Soviet perspective does not resonate with the amplifier notion. Depending upon the meaning attributed to the term "amplifier," the idea is either incomplete or misleading.

Cognitive Amplifiers and Cognitive Systems

In its everyday usage (and indeed, in the usages attributed to "amplifier" in the Oxford English Dictionary) the term "amplifier" means roughly to extend, to make more powerful, to complete. It is in this sense that we can speak of the ways in which an automobile amplifies our ability to travel, microscopes amplify our ability to see the world, and mathematics systems amplify our ability to carry out complex calculations. We can say that cultures with writing systems and aerodynamic theory can make their members more powerful, but we are left without a theory to tell us about the mechanisms that produce the added power.

It would be nice if the scientific notion of amplifier, growing out of physicists' investigations of wave-particle phenomena, could suggest a mechanism for the increased power human beings derive from culture. An amplifier in a scientific sense refers rather specifically to the intensification of a signal (acoustic, electronic), *which does not undergo change in its basic structure.* A weak oscillating signal at 60 hz remains the same shaped 60 hz signal when it is amplified; only the magnitude of the oscillations vary as a function of the amount of amplification. Any ancillary changes signal a defect in the amplification device.

In his discussion of cultural amplifiers in evolutionary perspective, Bruner adopts a position which sounds very much like "amplifier" is borrowed from the physical analogy. "Any implement system to be effective must produce an appropriate internal counterpart, an appropriate skill necessary for organizing sensorimotor acts, for organizing percepts, and for organizing our thoughts in a way that matches them to the requirements of implement systems. These internal skills, represented genetically as capacities, are slowly selected in evolution. In the deepest sense, then, man can be described as a species that has become specialized by the use of technological implements" (1966, p. 56).

This position, which posits an isomorphism between implement systems and "internal counterparts" can reasonably be adopted only by theories of culture and cognition that view cultural differences in cognitive performance as reflecting differential development of one or more basic cognitive capacities (or styles). Thus, for example, within the differentiation framework promoted by Witkin and his associates, individuals are characterized by the "level" of function that they have achieved in terms of their "field independence," the "articulation" of different parts of their cognitive structures, and other dimensions often summarized under the umbrella notion of "cognitive differentiation." (Berry, 1976; Witkin, 1978). The level of global differentiation (or one of its components) is indexed by a test that has more or less correct responses that are summed to give a criterion score (Koh's blocks test, the embedded figures test, the rod and frame test). Because such theories characterize the organism by assigning it values along one or more dimensions which are often developmentally sensitive, it seems natural to characterize the effects of a culturally organized activity such as writing, or mathematics as a quantitative change in "cognitive development." Within the context of such theories, the idea of cultural amplifier seems natural in either its everyday or its technical usage, because structural variation is not represented except in "more" or "less" terms.

But what about theories that posit qualitative changes when children move from one stage of cognitive development to another? If these theories are applied cross-culturally within an "instrumental-cultural" framework such as that proposed by Vygotsky and Luria and accepted in principle by Bruner (under the rubric of "instrumental conceptualization"), what can we make of the notion of amplifier in any other than its common sense meaning? If we accept the position that cognitive growth is characterized by qualitative changes and that these changes are best described in terms of changes in the relations among the components of complex, functional systems, we arrive at a point where the common sense notion of amplifier could seduce us into unidimensional, quantitative theorizing when we believe that systems thinking is required. From the perspective of a functional systems approach, "amplification" can refer to only one of two aspects of the performance of the system under study. On the one hand, it can refer to the overall performance measured in terms of some outcome criterion. By this product criterion, a sixth grader with a pencil in her hand has a far more powerful memory when confronted with the task of remembering a long list of words than a college sophomore asked to engage in "the same task" without a pencil and paper. On the other hand, "amplification" can refer to the hypothetical process that produces the product criterion. We can claim that the pencil "amplifies" memory power that is "in the head." But this example itself suggests that to use the term "amplification" is to mislead, for one would quickly object that "remembering" in the two cases refers to *qualitatively different activities*. The pencil did not "amplify" a fixed mental capacity. It restructured the activity so that some index of productivity was larger.

It is always a simple enough task for an academic to split words but word splitting ought to help clarify the issue at hand. I have come slowly to the conclusion that the ambiguities of the amplifier metaphor mask a widespread ambivalence (or uncertainty) among scholars about the most fruitful way to conceive of culture's impact on cognition.

When speaking of societies in a comparative way, few psychologists mind the notion that societies differ with respect to the complexity and power of their technologies. Bruner, for example, speaks of the "more evolved technical societies" that are distinguished by division of labor and the arrangement of special contexts for transmitting needed information outside of the contexts of the activity under discussion. A very similar description is to be found in our earlier speculations about the power of education (Scribner and Cole, 1973) and in the work of Greenfield (1972) and Olson (1976; 1977)—which should be no surprise, since we were all influenced by Bruner in our work.

In a common sense way, these kinds of statements are easily interpreted within an "amplifier" framework: technology increases demands on individuals so means are found to provide individuals the amplified abilities they will need. But compare this line of thinking with the interesting conclusion reached near the end of *Studies in Cognitive Growth* that ". . . the unschool Wolof child comes to terms with the idea of equivalence in a fashion that is his own, not something that is "more" or less of some unidimensional, universal pattern" (Bruner et al., 1966, p. 323). Here we have a very relativistic statement about culture and cognitive development consistent with a systems analysis. Yet on the very next page, we return to statements that lead us to believe that we can rank cognitive behaviors on some sort of scale; technological societies are said to provide a greater push toward building hierarchical connections because in less technological societies there is less reason to connect events beyond the immediate context of use. Elsewhere, we are told that some cultures push cognitive growth better and earlier than others (Greenfield and Bruner, 1966).

The ambivalence reflected in these contrasting statements about cultural comparisons in terms of the technological level of the society (as measured, for example, in Carniero's 1955 work on Guttman scaling of social complexity) is by no means restricted to one example of Bruner's work. For example, in a recent discussion of the impact of literacy on thinking, Bruner and Olson (1977–78) tell us on the one hand that literacy changes the purposes and information demands of manipulating objects in the world. On the other hand, they suggest that interaction with text may be a prerequisite in the "development of intellectual competence"; a quotation from Inhelder and Piaget about the nature of formal operations is provided as an illustration of both literate thought and developed cognition.

It is also important to note that this ambivalence is not unique to Bruner's instrumental conceptualism. It is present, too, in the work of Luria and Vygotsky, exactly the people who pushed hardest for a systems approach to understanding the growth of mind.

In the conclusion to his monograph describing the results of his cross-cultural research in Central Asia in the early 1930s, Luria clearly exhibits the duality of approach that I have attributed to Bruner. For example, he begins his summary by emphasizing the change in the structure of thought wrought by cultural change: "We have considered certain data that show the changes in the structure of mental processes associated with cognitive activity at different stages of historical development, and the major shifts that have occurred in these processes under the impact of social and cultural revolutions" (Luria, 1976, p. 161). But what is the nature of these structural changes? A list of them certainly makes one think that statements are being made about *relative intellectual power*. According to Luria, the new conditions brought about by the advent of Soviet power introduced changes in the motives (and thus the structure of activity) organizing behavior that he characterized as "complex":

These complex motives, which go beyond concrete practical activity assume the form of conscious planning of one's own labor; we begin to see interests that go beyond immediate impressions and the reproduction of concrete forms of practical activity. These motives include future planning, the interests of the collective, and, finally, a number of important cultural topics that are closely associated with achievement of literacy and assimilation of theoretical knowledge. . . . Perception begins to go beyond graphic object-oriented experience and incorporates much more complex processes which combine what is perceived into a system of abstract, linguistic categories. . . . New, theoretical thought operations arise. . . . Thinking processes begin to involve more and more abstraction and generalization. . . . Gradually we see the "transition from the sensory to the rational" (Luria, 1976, pp. 162–63).

So, while working within a framework which conceives of culturally linked cognitive change as a matter of *structural reorganization*, Luria still seems to conceive of the outcome of this process in something like mental amplification terms. Not coincidentally, it was this latter aspect of this work which caused a great deal of trouble in the USSR at the time it was done. One commentator on a theoretical monograph coauthored by Luria and Vygotsky charged that "These authors consider a primitive still not a human being. . . . Cannibals, Indians, etc., are not primitives from our point of view, but people whose culture is not a reflection of their biological capacities (as Luria and Vygotsky assert) but the result of specific means of production" (Frankel, 1930). Matters were little better following the initial reports of experimental work from the expedition, when Luria and Vygotsky were excoriated with the new charge that "[the cultural-historical theory] is a pseudoscientific, reactionary, anti-marxist and anti-working class theory that in practice leads to the anti-Soviet conclusion that the political policy of the Soviet Union is carried out by people and classes who think primitively, unable as they are to engage in abstract thought . . ." (Razmyslov, 1934, p. 83–84).

One need not agree with these intemperate criticisms to recognize their source. Despite attempts to argue that they were showing the positive effects of exposure to a socialist social and economic milieu and in spite of a theory which emphasized qualitative differences in thought associated with different cultures, Luria and Vygotsky were caught by the fact that the qualitative changes in the structure of mind that they sought to demonstrate led them into comparisons among the people involved that were distressingly quantitative in their implications. These implications were given added plausibility by the fact that the terms in which they attempted to describe the cognitive changes wrought by the advent of technological society were almost precisely the same terms that they used to describe the changes in mental function that differentiate older and younger children (c.f. Luria, 1978; Vygotsky, 1978). Moreover, they were working in a psychological tradition that had for at least fifty years, been willing to contemplate structural if not procedural, similarities between the thinking processes of young children and adults in nonliterate societies (Piaget, 1926; Werner, 1948).

I believe that the same difficulties vitiate a great deal of recent cross-cultural research. Insofar as psychologists have a theory to characterize social and economic differences among cultures, it leads them to rank cultures with respect to their degree of development (or technological sophistication, modernization, and so on). Given a "developmental" characterization of the environment, some "developmental" formulation of cultural differences in thinking seems inevitable. Thus, even when we strive to formulate a theory of culture and cognition in "systems" terms, the outcome may be virtually indistinguishable from an "amplifier" characterization that comes very close in its implications to the kind of cognitive development theories applied to children in our own society.

Examples of Two Attempts at a "Systems" Interpretation of Culture and Cognition

To sharpen the issues further, it will be helpful to examine the work of two men who have worried about the possibility that cognitive differences among members of different societies may result from reorganization of the process of thinking owing exactly to those technological features of cultures that distinguish them at the societal level.

The first is David Olson, whose recent writings often display an uncanny resemblance to those of Vygotsky and Luria. In a discussion of "culture, technology and intellect" Olson proposes a cultural model of intelligence in which ". . . it is assumed that the culture has already "worked-up" procedures for dealing with the natural environment, these procedures being embodied in the artifacts, institutions, conventions, and technologies of that culture" (1976, p. 190).

The issue of the relation between cultural technology and thought is explored by analogy with judgments of strength. What a man can lift is not determined so much by the size of his muscles as by the technology of his culture (mules, fork lifts, pulleys) *in interaction* with his muscles. The result is that "the underlying processes that go into an act of strength differ depending upon the machine that the man is hooked to" (p. 192). Olson argues, and I agree, that the analogy applies to intellectual performances such as remembering and problem solving, although the changes in mental processes are more difficult to analyze and the analogy produces some difficulties.

Drawing on the classicist Erick Havelock, Olson argues that the introduction of a written language, especially in the form of extended arguments that he characterizes as the essayist technique, biases the way in which literate people think; it facilitates the use of definitions, logical principles, and causal reasoning. Furthermore, use of literate technology places special, new demands on one's cognitive processes specifiable to the level of central nervous system functioning. For example, instead of relying on an acoustic memory in order to perform an epic such as the *Iliad*, one began to rely on "logically connected prose statements, which because they were preserved as a visible artifact, could be reflected on analytically" (p. 195).

Olson cites Ong (1971) and Havelock (1973, 1978) who suggest that intellectual life involves new systems of activity as a result of the evolving impact of literate technology: print is said to take over the role previously served by human memory as a means of preserving and transmitting cultural information; logical analysis is made possible by the reduction on memory load; logic replaces rhetoric as a means of argumentation; meaning, even theological meaning, came to reside in the text rather than the dogma of the Church. Such changes, if they indeed occur as these authors suggest, would provide a neat parallel to Vygotsky's assertion that development represents: "a change not so much in the structure of a single function (which, for example, we may call memory) as in the character of those functions with the aid of which remembering takes place; what changes is the *interfunctional* relations that connect memory with other functions" (Vygotsky, 1978, p. 49).

A great deal of practice in the literate mode of activity changes the very nature of our knowledge of the world according to Olson. He takes as his example our knowledge of cows:

One feature of cows, that they give milk, may be called concrete; another feature, that they are mammals, may be called abstract. The question is this: What is the occasion for the "detection" of these different features? *As long as one's purpose* is simply *to competently perform practical actions*, the 'give milk' feature is critical, the 'mammal' feature is a luxury. However, *as soon as one's purpose is to formulate statements from which true implications can be drawn*, one is forced to detect or create features which bear a class inclusion relation to the event in question. The application of this technique of formulating more abstract categories from which true implications can be drawn, when applied to objects, would yield the superordinate taxonomic schemes that Aristotle took to be an 'unbiased' picture of reality. I would prefer to say that taxonomic structures are the picture of reality that results from the repeated application of a particular technology—it is not a natural or unbiased or objective view of reality (Olson, 1976, p. 198).

I will return to discuss other implications that Olson draws from this work, but first I want to examine briefly the contribution of Jack Goody, an anthropologist whose work has been influential in forcing our attention to the significance of literacy as a causal agent in producing both social change and those contrasting characteristics of human intellectual performance that get labeled by such terms as "primitive and civilized modes of thought." Goody enters this discussion in a personal way because in 1974 he worked with me in Liberia and later we both spent time working with Olson, so that the lines of the discussion are by no means independent entities.

Goody's basic contention is that contrasts in mode of thought can be related to changes in the means of communication, particularly the advent of literacy. Writing provides people with new potential for thinking: ". . . [I] would go further and see the acquisition of these means of communication as effectively transforming the nature of cognitive processes. . . " (p. 18).

These transformations take several forms. Like Olson, Goody points to ways in which writing objectifies speech, shifts its information channel to vision and its "executive" channel to the hand. By giving relatively permanent form to a segment of speech, writing facilitates critical analysis, reflective thinking, and exploration of new conceptual relations.

Goody's discussion carefully traces the way in which the development of new powers in the writing system cause new kinds of intellectual activity that in turn produce further changes in literate activities in a dialectical spiral that inexorably, if not evenly, produces increasingly powerful technologies of the intellect. Each step in the process represents a *qualitative* change, but the historical effect can also be described quantitatively by criteria external to the way individuals process information.

In his examinations of very early writing practices, Goody shows how elementary tables and lists were used both as a means of transmitting stored information and as tools for changing the organization of the lists (and therefore the cultural items to which they refer). At one point he summarizes the process as follows: "We can see here the dialectical effect of writing upon classification. On the one hand it sharpens the outlines of the categories; one has to make a decision as to whether rain or dew is of the heavens or of the earth; furthermore it encourages hierarchization of the classificatory system. At the same time, it leads to questions about the nature of the classes through the very fact of placing them together. . . . The fact that no single principle of contrast is adequate to classify all cultural knowledge forces to attention the existence of contradictions, the resolution of which leads to more complex systems" (Goody, 1977, p. 102).

Goody thus suggests the basis for a link between cultural complexity and cognitive complexity, while providing a rationale for comparing cultures (and thus systems of thinking) in terms of their relative power. By linking changes in mode of thought to the nature of communication technologies, Goody proposes that

we can avoid not only the Grand Dichotomy but also the diffuse relativism that refuses to recognize long-term differences and regards each 'culture' as a thing on its own, a law unto itself. So, on one level, it is But that is not all there is to say about any set of relations, however clearly defined the boundaries may be. The set exists in the context of a specific constellation of productive relations and of a particular level of technological achievement. The technology, which creates possibilities for, and places limits upon, a wide range of social interaction, changes in the same general direction throughout human history. By 'general,' I mean to allow for some backward movement (the decay of the 'useful' arts that WHR Rivers observed in certain areas of Melanesia), as well as for the development of a plurality of differing traditions. Nevertheless, there is direction, especially in the areas of what has been called 'control over nature' and the 'growth of knowledge,' and this movement is related to developments in the technology of the intellect, to changes in the means of communication and, specifically, to the introduction of writing (p. 151).

Here, if we will accept it, is a "psychosocial" theory of how cultural and mental development are related and a way to resolve the ambiguities of previous discussions. Combining Vygotsky, Olson, and Goody, we can say that thinking is always and everywhere the internalization of the means, modes, and contents of the communications activities that exist in the culture into which one is born. These activities and the instruments invented to facilitate them have evolved to cope with the demands placed upon cultures for their survival and propagation; moreover, they also carry within them the seeds of their own undoing, seeds that will bear fruit when the proper social conditions exist, making possible further change as a consequence of interactions between new generations of technologies and peoples. In terms of our beginning metaphor, technologies transform the nature of culture and thought, increasing (amplifying) the *products* of human labor.

It is a very neat solution and, in general outline, it is probably correct. But it is incomplete as regards the mechanism by which individuals come to acquire different kinds of communication-dependent functional cognitive systems. It may also overestimate greatly the generality of the cognitive consequences of interacting with cultural technologies.

I do not propose to discuss the problem of the mechanisms by which individuals come to master complex, instrumentally mediated thought systems in the course of individual development. It may plausibly be argued that the structure of written language, the school-based uses of language, the nature of oral interaction between parents and children, the properties of an alphabetic orthography, exercise in the essayist technique, or manipulation of symbol systems that allow a reduced memory load all contribute. Careful empirical studies of this process in our own society (for example, Luria, 1978; Olson and Nickerson, 1978) as well as societies where literacy and schooling do not co-vary (Scribner and Cole, 1980) will be needed to determine *how* these tangled factors are involved in special kinds of mediated learning.

However, I do want to propose the possibility that the cognitive changes plausibly argued for in all of this work play a more restricted role in the cognitive activity of individuals than the historical record, anthropological evidence, and scanty experimental data lead us to believe.

Literacy As a Tool for Thinking: General or Specific?

I have found it useful, like Olson, to contrast our notions about intellectual power wrought by a variety of tools with the physical work that tools facilitate. To elaborate on a line of argument proposed by Olson, suppose that we were discussing cultural amplifiers for killing. Suppose further that the tools we wanted to analyze were bows and arrows on the one hand and rifles on the other. It seems pretty clear that bows and arrows are less effective cultural "kill" amplifiers than rifles and that a criterion measure like "number of deer shot in the month of November" for two groups thought equivalent in deer-finding skills would show that guns were superior to bows and arrows. Certainly Columbus's hosts in the New World and their descendants came to believe in the greater power of rifles. When, however, we consider this contrast from the perspective of the different systems of activities that are involved in their use, we must be loath to say that the use of bows and arrows or rifles led to any general difference in the "killing ability" of the individuals using these tools *when the tools were not in their hands*. The changes in "killing ability" reside jointly in the tool and the user. We might, to be sure, want to claim that there were changes in skills deemed relevant to killing ability that might be differentially promoted by the two kinds of tool use, that is, the bow and arrow hunter might have learned to get closer to her prey without being detected. This possibility is relevant to the overall argument and will be considered below.

When we look at discussions of cultural amplifiers, or more generally, at discussions of culture and cognitive growth that attempt to clarify the role of "tools of the intellect" we find that a strong predilection to assume that individuals' interactions with such tools changes them in a way that is analogous to claiming that they have different killing ability *even when they have no weapons in their hands*. At least, this is how I interpret the kinds of generalizations made by Luria based on his Central Asian data and Bruner and his colleagues when they talk about the possibility that some cultures promote cognitive growth more effectively than others. Similar claims seem to be made by Olson (1977), Goody (1977), and Scribner and Cole (1973).

How can we assess the generality of the intellectual consequences of interacting with a particular kind of cultural technology of the intellect? If we were to make a test of "killing power," we would probably put the tools at issue in the hands of people recognized to be skilled practitioners and then observe the outcome of some tests.

We don't typically do that with "tools of the intellect." Instead, as in the case of schooling (Bruner et al., 1966; Cole, Gay, Glick, and Sharp, 1971; Sharp, Cole, and Lave, 1979) we present people some "representative cognitive task" under conditions where the theoretically crucial tool is *not* available for use. In effect, we assess the residual, "general power" that is available as a consequence of interaction with the tool. It is probably not too fanciful an analogy to say that we test for the "killing" power" of bow and arrow shooters versus rifle shooters when both classes of people are barehanded.

There are a number of rationales to support the notion that interaction with intellectual tools leaves residual mental power that can be used in their absence. Although specific theories take somewhat different forms, they are all variants on the notion that an activity initially engaged in as part of an interaction with the external environment (physical or social) can be internalized. That is, the individual can mentally reconstruct essential features of the original environment using remembered representations of what went on there to guide present action. Bruner and his colleagues have emphasized language and particularly the special role that language acquires in school settings as a key mediator in the process of rendering the consequences of interaction with cultural tools general. Language is common both to the settings where "literate" and "oral" thought are engaged in, so it is a natural candidate to the mechanism of transfer. For example, Bruner and Olson (1977–78) identify writing as a tool that facilitates going back over one's experience to "re-present" it to oneself. It is a generally useful activity that is emphasized in one particular setting, highly elaborated in technological societies, the school, but applicable everywhere: "This form of metaprocessing, of re-presenting knowledge in various symbolic forms, comes into play in many circumstances—in failed communication, in our inability to interpret what we encounter, when we run into interpersonal conflict, when we run into difficulties in attempting to carry out an action or solve a problem"(p. 6).

It is in this spirit that Olson identifies writing as an example of ". . . highly generalizable and highly usable, life valuable (cognitive) operations that are responsible for intelligent behavior" (1976, p. 189).

All of these arguments are plausible, but there is more than a little evidence to suggest that while cognitive changes arising from literacy or schooling are not completely specific to literate or school tasks, they certainly do not represent general changes in the way people process information.

Consider, for example, the evidence summarized by Shweder to support his contention that the modes of thought that characterize traditional, non-literate peoples are no different from those that are employed by American college students. Shweder focuses on a class of problem-solving settings where individuals have to make judgments about the similarity and co-occurrence of events. He begins with a question: ". . . how is the student of the Azande to comprehend their attempts to cure epilepsy by eating the burnt skull of a red bush monkey or their therapeutic application of fowl's excrement in cases of ringworm?" (Shweder, 1977, p. 637). Shweder's basic contention is that such inferences are made because people have difficulty keeping track of the relevant information. One example he uses to demonstrate the problem that he thinks underlies all mundane reasoning comes from the work of Ward and Jenkins (1965).

Ward and Jenkins concocted a problem in which subjects had to determine if cloud seeding causes rainful. Subjects were presented the information in two ways. Some subjects were presented information on a trial by trial basis (for example, it rained, the clouds were seeded; it did not rain, the clouds were seeded; it did not rain, the clouds were not seeded; and so on). Over a long series of trials, the information about occurrences and nonoccurrences of the two events, seeding and rain, could lead to a correct inference about the causal significance of cloud seeding. But when the information was presented in this way, less than one in five subjects made the correct inference. However, if the information was presented in a 2 X 2 table so that the data were simultaneously available, correct inferences almost always occurred. From this kind of demonstration, Shweder concludes that "Most normal adults have the capacity to think correlationally, but they do not apply the concept in their everyday life judgments" (p. 639). Shweder goes on to show how the confusion of likelihood and correlation contribute to magical thinking in all societies. But what is of central concern to us is the question of why correlational thinking is not characteristic of the everyday life thinking of the educated adults he studied.

The answer to this question hinges upon the kind of information that is available to the individual at the point where he has to make a judgment. A good deal of evidence suggests that in the situations that Shweder refers to as "everyday," information has been lost about the relevant event co-occurrences because there is a great deal of information presented sequentially over quite a time span. Moreover, the loss is not random. Nonoccurrences of events are differentially forgotten (see Estes, 1976). The circumstance that overcomes these difficulties is one that relies on a literate technology for its efficacy; the convention of a contingency table summarizes the relevant information and reduces the memory load on the individual to almost zero, with the result that a proper inference is possible. In short, writing produces a change in the "interfunctional relations among cognitive processes," a change that produces veridical problem solving. Central to the present argument, these results suggest that it is unnecessary to posit a general change in internal cognitive activity as a consequence of literacy—*the effect requires that the tool be in the user's hand.*

Other data suggest that even paper and pencil are not sufficient to insure veridical judgments of similarity unless they are used in the right way at the right time. The seminal work here was carried out by D'Andrade (1974) in his analysis of behavioral descriptions of people interacting in small groups. D'Andrade found that when standard rating schemes were used to describe participants' interactions (friendly, helpful, aggressive, and so on) raters were strongly influenced by the meanings of the words used *independent of the participants' behaviors.* Veridical descriptions occurred only when the paper and pencil rating scheme was applied while the rater was observing the coding behavior. A brief delay between observation and judging (a delay long enough to allow memory-sans-pencil to operate) produced descriptions that were better predicted by knowing the associative network into which the rating words fit than by "remembering" what people actually do.

Still another source of data that might make us question the need to posit general consequences of literacy comes from recent work on "constructive" remembering (see Bransford, 1979). The basic phenomenon here is illustrated by the following example from the work of Paris and Carter (1973). They presented seven- and ten-year-old children with sets of three sentence "stories" like the following:

> The canary is in the cage.
> The cage is on the table.
> The canary is yellow.

The children were later asked to recognize these sentences along with sentences that they had not seen before such as "The cage is under the table" or "The canary is on the table." The children automatically integrated the information in the initial set causing them to mis-recognize sentences like "The canary is on the table" which were true inferences from the information initially given to them. This same result is true for college students as well.

In some of our recent work in Liberia we found that literacy has no noticeable impact on this process. Nonliterate adults were as likely as literates to make errors on sentences that were correct inferences from the information initially given and no less likely to reject other statements that were not in the presentation set. On the face of it, these studies suggest that literate practice and schooling (which involves a variety of literate practices) do not produce the kinds of changes in information processing which more traditional cross-cultural research has repeatedly claimed.

Literate adults' proclivity to such constructive remembering is a vexing problem in our law courts, where subtle changes in the way that a lawyer's probe of witnesses' recall of events have been shown to determine what "they remember" (Loftus, 1979). Juries have also been shown to change their decisions of guilt or innocence not on the nature of the evidence presented, but the order in which that evidence is presented (see Anderson, 1978).

We often do little better in the way that we go about solving complex problems that are presented to us daily in the course of getting around our social environments. Indeed, Bartlett (1958) was led to conclude that Cambridge students engage in two completely different kinds of thinking ("experimental" and "everyday") that proceed in very different ways.

Such differences within the experience and practice of literate adults are known to us all, but they are peculiarly missing from discussions of culture and cognitive development. The key point of resolution, I believe, is to be found in the passage quoted from Olson in which he discussed different ways to "know about cows." In the italicized passages, Olson poses two classes of purposes to which knowledge about cows might be put; to perform a practical action and to formulate statements that generate true implications. The same resolution is contained in Luria's phrase "Once we go beyond concrete practical activity" and Bruner and Olson's emphasis on the role of literacy in promoting theoretical activity. All of these statements imply that literacy will be an effective tool for a circumscribed set of human activities. They are extremely important activities, but they are not all of the purposes that engage most of us most of the time, and they are not all of a piece. Our experience as highly literate scholars urges on us the recognition that the tools of intellect acquired in the classroom and library carrel are *not* general purpose devices. This conclusion is brought home to us in a particularly powerful way by the work of Ebbesen and Konecni (1979) who compared a legal expert's decisions about the sentence to be meted out to defendants in one of two ways. First, a critical list of attributes pertaining to the crime, the defendant, and the circumstances of the cases were placed in written form before the judge who numerically weighted the contribution of each piece of evidence to his decision about sentencing. When data were collected in these same individual's courtrooms, their actual decisions were found to be arrived at quite differently. With the same information in hand and the same hypothetical purpose to their thinking, these highly literate individuals' acted as if their behavior were guided by very different purposes. And so it was. In the experiment the subject had to use (as a covert criterion) his imagined notion of what the experimenter would consider a rationale. But in the courtroom, the criterion of rationality was substituted for the social and political rationality of the society that brought the defendant to court in the first place.

I think that this line of work, when combined with the accumulating evidence that previous anthropological reports of native thinking have undervalued the cognitive power of natives' behavior (as in Hutchins', 1979a, 1979b work on legal reasoning and spatial navigation) and wide recognition of the special problems of inference that arise in the application of laboratory-style experiments in cross-cultural settings, urges on us the most extreme caution in attributing cultural differences in the ability to think "theoretically." "rationally," or in a "context free manner." There is reason to believe that such statements have a basis in fact, but the nature of the facts is not so clear as our metaphors may have seduced us into believing.

There are other difficulties with current attempts to relate cultural technologies to cognition, especially when the discussion assumes that there is a strong sense in which we can speak of both cultural and cognitive development.

For one thing, the existence of a particular technology does not mean that the technology will be exploited in the manner that we discover, *post hoc*, as in studies of the applications of writing. The wheel, certainly a cultural technology recognized to have very wide applicability in amplifying humankind's transportation capabilities, did not inevitably come to play the role that we associate with it. Archeological evidence from Mexico (Farb,

1968) indicatès that the wheel existed as a *potential* cultural technology for transportation in meso-America, but it remained instead an implement used by children in their games, or perhaps in adult ritual. It did not become part of a system of activities culminating in sophisticated transportation devices because other elements of culture necessary (or at least helpful) in creating the conditions for inventing the wheel-as-we-understand-it (beasts of burden, for example) did not exist. Similarly, proto-writing systems are known to be exceedingly old, perhaps as much as ten thousand years old (Shmandt-Besserat, 1978). The evolution of modern writing systems, however, required an intricate interplay between many different cultural technologies for its realization. A simple relationship between the existence of a form for a technology and a "level" of technological development cannot be assumed.

That a technological element has complicated relations with other elements in the cultural system is an additional problem. Above, we described how the structure of judges' reasoning varies with variations in motivations derived from the elements operating in different settings. We should also expect that the structure of various cultural tools found in different cultural systems would vary, again with motivations derived from differential relations with different elements. The rifle and bow-and-arrow analogy is an example of the problem. A culture with a rifle for deer killing may have different systems for preserving food and tanning leather and/or different population feeding needs than a culture with a bow and arrow. These differences in the systems in which the tools participate may be related to the putative measurement device we suggested; that is, killing as many deer as the tool user can during a specified period of time may be differentially affected not only by the tool but also by the structure of the tool as motivated by the differences in the systems in which it participates.

There is also the serious problem of establishing the general validity of schemes which rank cultures with respect to some developmental or evolutionary scheme. While, as Goody points out, there are seemingly undeniable contrasts to be found with respect to some cultural elements, especially those related to modern technology and its concomitants, in many spheres of experience (for example, the politics of family life) it seems virtually impossible to apply such schemes. Insofar as the rules that regulate activity in these spheres influence cognitive activity, evolutionary schemes will be inappropriate. Unfortunately, cognitive psychologists have little that is specific to offer on this problem.

The notion that writing systems and their sequelia in the modern world represent cultural tools that amplify mind has been found inadequate to represent the transformations in activity that literacy engenders. But these difficulties in no way require us to ignore the fact that the acquisition of literate powers is a landmark step forward in man's evolving capacity to operate effectively on his environment. This essay, littered as it is with the shards of previous scholarly written discussions, is testimony in form to the complex system of activities that went into its production. We think that writing down our ideas, mulling them over, coming on new sources we had not clearly understood or remembered, writing some more, getting distracted, talking intermittently to one another, and then finally sitting down to put all the pieces together is a very different process than we could possibly have engaged in without the many literate tools involved. Writing and reading did not, however, amplify our paper-writing power. They reorganized the process whereby we retrieved, compared, listed, and ordered our ideas and, eventually, transmitted them to you. Perhaps they amplified the product; that is for you to decide.

References

Anderson, Norman H. Progress in cognitive algebra. In L. Berkowitz (Ed.), *Cognitive theories in social psychology.* New York: Academic Press, 1978.

Bartlett, F. C. *Thinking: An experimental and social study.* New York: Basic Books, 1958.

Berry, J. W. *Human ecology and cognitive styles.* New York: Sage, 1976.

Bransford, J. *Human cognition: Learning, understanding and remembering.* Belmont, Calif.: Wadsworth, 1979.

Bruner, J. S. On cognitive growth. In J. S. Bruner, R. R. Olver, and P. M. Greenfield (Eds.), *Studies in cognitive growth.* New York: Wiley, 1966.

————. Introduction to L. S. Vygotsky, *Language and thought.* Cambridge, Mass.: MIT Press, 1962.

Bruner, J. S., Olver, R. R., and Greenfield, P. M. *Studies in cognitive growth.* New York: Wiley, 1966

Bruner, J. S. and Olson, D. R. Symbols and texts as the tools of intellect. *Interchange,* 1977–78, 8, 4, 1–15.

Carneiro, R. L. Ascertaining, testing and interpreting sequence of cultural development. *Southwestern Journal of Anthropology,* 1968, 24, 4.

Cole, M. (Ed.). *Soviet developmental psychology.* White Plains: Merle Sharpe, 1978.

Cole, M. and Bruner, J. S. Cultural differences and inferences about psychological processes. *American Psychologist,* 1971, 26, 867–876.

Cole, M., Gay, J., Glick, J. A., and Sharp, D. W. *The cultural context of learning and thinking.* New York: Basic Books, 1971.

D'Andrade, R. G. Memory and the assessment of behavior. In H. M. Blalock, Jr. (Ed.), *Measurement in the social sciences.* Chicago: Aldine-Atherton, 1974.

Ebbesen, E. B. and Konecni, V. J. On the external validity of decision-making research: What do we know about decisions in the real world? Proceedings of the 1978 conference on cognitive processes in choice and decision behavior. Hillsdale, N.J.: Erlbaum, 1979.

Farb, P. *Man's rise to civilization as shown by the Indians of North America from primeval times to the coming of the industrial stage.* New York: Dutton, 1968.

Estes, W. K. The cognitive side of probability learning. *Psychological Review,* 1976, 83, 37–64.

Frankel, A. Against eclectism in psychology and pedology. *Povesteniya Natsionalnostei,* 1930, no. 7–8.

Goody, J. *The domestication of the savage mind.* New York: Cambridge University, Press, 1977.

Greenfield, P. Oral and written language: The consequences for cognitive development in Africa, the United States, and England. *Language and speech*, 1972, 15, 169–178.
Havelock, E. *The Greek concept of justice*. Cambridge, Mass.: Harvard University Press, 1978
———. *Prologue to Greek literacy*. Cincinnati: University of Oklahoma Press for the University of Cincinnati Press, 1973.
Hutchins, E. Reasoning in Trobriand discourse. *The Quarterly Newsletter of the Laboratory of Comparative Human Cognition*, 1979, 1, 2, 13–17.
———. Conceptual structures in pre-literate Pacific navigation. Unpublished Manuscript. Program in Cognitive Science. Center for Human Inforation Processing. University of California, San Diego, 1979.
Loftus, E. F. *Eyewitness testimony*. Cambridge: Harvard University Press, 1979.
Luria, A. R. *Cognitive development: Its cultural and social foundations*. Cambridge, Mass.: Harvard University Press, 1976.
———. The development of writing in the child. In M. Cole (Ed.), *The selected Writings of A. R. Luria*. White Plains: M. E.Sharp,1978.
———. *Making of mind*. Cambridge, Mass.: Harvard University Press, 1979.
Olson, D. R. Culture technology and intellect. In L. B. Resnick (Ed.), *The nature of intelligence*. Hillsdale, N.J.: Erlbaum, 1976.
Olson, D. R. and Nickerson, N. The contexts of comprehension: On children's understanding of the relations between active and passive sentences. *Journal of Experimental Child Psychology*, 1977, 23, 402–414.
Ong, W. J. *Rhetoric, romance and technology: Studies in the interaction of expression and culture*. Ithaca: Cornell University Press, 1971.
Paris, S. G. and Carter, A. Y. Semantic and constructive aspects of sentence memory in children. *Developmental Psychology*, 1973, 9. 109–113.
Piaget, J. *The language and thought of the child*. New York: Harcourt Brace, 1926.
Razmyslov, P. On Vygotsky and Luria's cultural-historical theory of psychology. *Kniga i proletarskaya revolutsia*, 1934, 4, 78–86.
Schmandt-Besserat, D. The earliest precursor of writing. *Scientific American*, 1978, 238, 6, 50–59.
Scribner, S. and Cole, M. Cognitive consequences of formal and informal education. *Science*, 1973, 182, 553–559.
———. *Consequences of literacy*. Cambridge: Harvard University Press, 1980.
Sharp, D., Cole, M., and Lave, C. *Education and cognitive development: The evidence from experimental research*. Monographs of the Society for Research in Child Development. Serial No. 178, 1979, 44, (1–2). Published by the University of Chicago Press for the Society for Research in Child Development.
Shweder, R. A. Likeness and likelihood in everyday thought: Magical thinking in judgements about personality. *Current anthropology*, 1977, 18, 4, 637–658.
Vygotsky, L. S. *Mind in society*. Edited by M. Cole, V. John-Steiner, S. Scribner, and E. Souberman. Cambridge, Mass.: Harvard University Press, 1978.
Ward, W. C. and Jenkins, H. M. The display of information and the judgment of contingency. *Canadian Journal of Psychology*, 1965, 19, 231–241.
Werner, H. *Comparative psychology of mental development*. New York: Science Editions, 1961, originally published 1948.
Witkin, H. A. *Cognitive styles in personal and cultural adaptation*. Heinz Werner Lecture Series. Worcester: Clark University Press, 1978.

16

Bruner: A Case of
"Cultural Transmission"

Jacqueline J. Goodnow

How are we to describe the way societies and individuals affect one another, especially when the area of effect is as elusive as the way we "think", the way we set goals, make choices, and accept, tackle, solve, or abandon problems? A large part of Jerry Bruner's concern has been with the vehicles by which such interaction takes place. Language has been the prime candidate for analysis. The language of the culture provides the categories used or adapted by an individual: "The categories in terms of which man sorts out and responds to the world around him reflect deeply the world into which he is born . his personal history comes to reflect the traditions and thought-ways of his culture, for the events that make it up are filtered through the categorical systems he has learned" (Bruner, Goodnow, and Austin, 1956, p. 10).

In addition to language, however, is a much broader set of "symbolic tools" or "symbolic forms" proposed by Bruner as ways by which a culture is transmitted or changed:

> Theories, models, myths, cause and effect accounts, ways of looking and seeing as well as thinking are probably *the* prime prosthetic devices for assisting nervous systems beyond their naked limits . . . theories quickly become the valued property of a culture, constantly undergoing revision and often refinement toward greater abstraction as they find more compact restatement in the arts and in myth as well as in the formalism of science (Bruner, 1971b, p. 126).

Of particular help in preparing this essay has been the thesis of Keith Weeks Lyou (Kay Lyou): "In search of the sources of rationality: A study of the work of Jerome Bruner." The thesis, written for the Master of Arts degree at Lindenwood College (Missouri) and generously lent to me by Ernest Hilgard, covers the complete range of Bruner's work with a nice attention both to detail and to major themes. It also contains excerpts from interviews with Bruner, Hilgard, and Skinner, so that one has a sense both of Bruner's work and of its general context.

It is patent that the view one takes of man affects profoundly one's standard of what is humanly possible. And it is by the measure of such a standard that we establish our laws, set our aspirations for learning and judge the fitness of man's acts. It is no surprise then that those who govern must perforce be jealous guardians of man's ideas about man, for the structure of government rests upon an uneasy consensus about human nature and human wants (Bruner, 1956, p. 463).

Each culture has conceptions of the nature of a child, some conceptions of what constitutes good adults. It also has, at some implicit level, some conception of what it regards as the appropriate means of getting from the nature of a child to the nature of an adult. If a pedagogical theorist is to move that culture, he must forge a theory that relates to that range of acceptable means. The failure of a theory may be that it fails to accord with or overcome or relate to the "range of acceptable means" of a culture (Bruner, 1971a, p. 99).

The theories implicit in various social and cultural activities such as child rearing and education form a pervasive and important theme in much of Bruner's work. Two recent lines of inquiry focus directly on the conceptions and images that underlie child-rearing practices. Both explore the nature and impact of everyday theories about intellectual development on that development. (I shall later provide some examples of the impact of Bruner's own expectations on my intellectual development.)

The first stems from cross-cultural comparisons. A common line of argument is that the most interesting cross-cultural differences are not the test results per se, but the social contexts in which performance takes place: the prevailing "standard of what is humanly possible," the definitions of what is a reasonable task to work on, an "intelligent" thing to do, an "acceptable" way to ask a question, a "good" answer, a feasible way of working together, a "proper" attitude toward an investigation. Such arguments, recurring in the work of people such as Cole, Glick, Goodnow, Irvine, Nagashima, and Serpell, have recently been summarized in Goodnow (in press).

A parallel line of inquiry concerns the way in which "Images of man" held by parents affect child development. This time the parents are drawn from our "standard" Western populations. Egelund, Sroufe, and Phipps-Yonas at Minnesota, Hess at Stanford, Goodnow and Russell at Macquarie, Parke at Illinois, Sameroff at Chicago are all presently interviewing parents to elicit "accounts" of why children and parents behave as they do. The interest is based in part on the argument that parental theories are of interest in their own right (for example, Goodnow, in press) and in part on the argument that accounting for parental behaviors requires not only concern with immediately preceding events but also a knowledge of the way parents perceive and interpret those events (for example, Parke, 1978).

How are we to explore the nature and impact of such implicit theories? The work mentioned so far has relied primarily on interviews and observations. We might turn also to "psychohistory" and learn from analysis of past documents. Such sources have certainly convinced us that images of children have changed: from being useful early labor to needing protection from the job market, from being "imps of darkness" to angels "trailing clouds of glory," from having a "duty to learn" to having the "right to be educated" (see Ariès, 1962; or Pinchbeck and Hewitt, 1969, 1973). We might also turn to contemporary documents, from "masterpieces" and "heroic legends" to the fables presented for both easy reading and socialization: Dick and Jane, Charlie Brown, Horatio Alger, the boy who once stood on the burning deck, and so on.

Rather than follow any such lines of investigation, I shall present a minor case study, noting a particular moment of cultural transmission and change and the implicit theory that guided it: namely, my own response to Bruner and to Harvard. The account is not quite that of an "Ellis Island" immigrant, but there were sufficient differences in the manner of thinking and problem solving to make the interaction very real. Describing it acknowledges a debt. And it helps give a focus to that elusive area called "cultural transmission," especially elusive when it deals with what I think of as "intellectual socialization", the acquisition of ideas about ways of thinking, working, learning, teaching.

I arrived from Australia in January of 1949 and spent four and a half years at Harvard: an initial two and a half, followed by eighteen months working in Germany, and then another two years back in Cambridge. I arrived prepared for a change in speech. I was also prepared for a change in role: behind me were four years as an undergraduate plus four as a junior faculty member at the University of Sydney, and I was looking forward to being a student again. I was even prepared—by way of a massive sheepskin coat—for a major change in climate. The real test, however, was not the degree of fit between the United States and my physical baggage. It was, rather, my intellectual baggage that was altered.

Part of that baggage included some ideas about end states: *desirable goals* in the task of learning to "think," to become "educated." One particular aspect was a notion of what "breadth" meant. I regarded myself as a "general" psychologist, quite wide-ranging in my interests and knowledge. And, partly because I had started as an English major, I even regarded myself as moderately well-read. I could afford, I felt, to use my postgraduate scholarship (from the University of Sydney and applicable wherever I chose) at a place like Bryn Mawr, learning from Eugenia Hanfmann (who turned out to be at Harvard). Fortunately, others defined breadth in different ways. The advice from a senior colleague at Sydney (Cecil Gibb, then on sabbatical at Illinois) was to choose a bigger department, where I would learn from both faculty and students. He recommended Harvard, Berkeley, and Illinois, with a special stress on Harvard's relatively new Department of Social Relations, combining psychology, sociology, and social anthropology. The mixture sounded interesting, although perhaps a little exotic and possibly in conflict with my time demands (my scholarship was for two years and I had been told that a student visa meant restrictions on employment). I was, however, intrigued by the idea of learning something about sociology (anthropology I had enjoyed briefly as an undergraduate), and I was curious to see how this new department put its ideals into practice.

The reality was a nice example of what Bruner has described as the gap that can occur between behavior and "the guiding myths in terms of which men conduct their enterprises and in the image of which they set their ideals" (Bruner, 1958). Guiding myths, he points out, may vary in the extent to which they are explicit, appropriate to their time, shared by many, or put into practice.

Harvard put its belief in allied disciplines into practice in one form. It was possible then, for example, to wander across fields in the way I did, taking comprehensive exams in "clinical" and doing a thesis on probability learning with the "experimentalists." It was less easy to find ways of developing an "integrated body of knowledge," an ideal talked of. For some faculty, the ideal meant that several disciplines would be, in the words of one staff member, like "trees in a forest": separate species growing side by side but not intertwined. In effect, the student would integrate while the faculty remained as rooted as ever to their separates plots.

Fortunately for the students, there were some faculty members to whom the ideal of a diverse but integrated set of social sciences meant something more. Bruner was one. He involved himself, for example, in joint seminars. I recall, with particular pleasure, one run jointly by Bruner, Solomon, and Postman, both for its content and for the way it displayed the possibility of expressing both disagreement and respect. Bruner knew what people in other disciplines were doing, out of interest rather than a sense of duty. He wanted students to spread their wings a little and not confine themselves to one faculty member. And he had a sense of issues that often made it possible for students to see the woods that were made up of those several trees. I have kept from that time a general interest in sociology and anthropology, and a sharper ear for the theories people hold about the nature of learning, noting not only statements about ideal end states but also statements about who is to take the responsibility for achieving them. And I have kept a very different definition of "breadth" from the one I first held.

Along with a shift in the way I defined breadth of knowledge came an increased reflectiveness over what was meant by "good" thinking. We all aspire to a certain quality of thought (at least academics do), but we do not always agree on the marks of quality.

One of Bruner's criteria was expressed more in his style than in his written theory. Fortunately for this account, it became more explicit in his later writing, especially in his answer to the question, "What is worth knowing?" "I can only think of two good criteria and one middling good one for deciding such an issue: whether the knowledge gives me a sense of delight and whether it bestows the gift of intellectual travel beyond the information given, in the sense of containing within it the basis of a generalization. The middling criterion is whether the knowledge is useful" (Bruner, 1962b, pp. 108–9).

Delight was a goal Bruner sought in any dialogue with a student or any encounter with ideas. It is a goal of thought I am especially happy to see made explicit because it balances the stress of the earlier theory on what I think of as "protective" goals in thought ("reducing cognitive strain," for example, is a protective goal). In practice, Bruner seldom pursued protective goals.

For all that we agreed, however, on the importance of pleasure in thinking, we did not always agree about just what it was that provided most delight. This area yielded more information about individual and cultural differences.

Let me give two examples, both stemming in art from the educational system I had known. One of its features was an emphasis on being "clear" and making things "clear" to others: an emphasis that involved considerable practice in writing outlines and abstracts of complex (sometimes simply lengthy) material. I came to enjoy putting things into such order, deriving pleasure from dissecting out the skeleton of a problem. The rewarding end result was almost a moment of revelation, a sense of the structure of a problem, of component parts that hung together in particular ways, all previously hidden under the thicket of rhetoric or disguised by an overlay of appealing but false interconnections. The end result was also often a particular style of writing. My first drafts were often in the form of points 1, 2, 3, with subheadings; the last still tended to be lavish with headings. The skeleton was inevitably buried by Jerry: it was always there, but, like a true essayist, he felt the reader should have a sense of flesh before bones.

A second feature of my early training was a great deal of emphasis on being able to find the flaws within an argument, finding all the ways in which a statement might not be true. I did not enjoy attack for its own sake: in fact, one of the greatest pleasures in working with Jerry Bruner was his sense that adversary relationships mostly took time away from the prime task of getting on with a problem. That, combined with his attitude that theories were to use as tools and not to worship, took any "ad hominem" quality out of his critical analyses. But I enjoyed taking things apart more than he did. What I needed to learn—and did learn—was a greater readiness to use the approach Bruner often adopted: "Just suppose it were true. What would it mean if it were?" Practice in this particular form of "going beyond" had been rare in my experience, and still strikes me as rare within our schools. It lay, however, at the junction of two of Bruner's beliefs; a belief in the importance of "alternative views," and a belief in the value of the "intuitive leap": "education, by giving shape and expression to our experience, can also be the principal instrument for setting limits on the enterprise of mind. The guarantee against limits is the sense of alternatives.

Education must . . . be not only a process that transmits culture but also one that provides alternative views of the world and strengthens the will to explore them" (Bruner, 1962b, p. 117). "Two facts and a way of relating them is and should be an invitation to generalize, to extrapolate, to make a tentative intuitive leap, even to build a tentative theory. . . . Indeed, plausible guessing, the use of the heuristic hunch, the best employment of necessarily insufficient evidence—these are activities in which the child needs guidance and practice. They are among the great antidotes to passivity" (Bruner, 1962b, p. 124).

The "Tools" of Thought

So far I have been commenting on "cultural transmission" in terms of the goals of thought, the states one works toward and regards as "good." And I have been proposing that such transmission takes place in part through words and in part through finding—in the course of working with others— discrepancies between the way we and others define "good" thought. I have also suggested that some transmitted ideas fall upon more fertile or well-prepared ground than others.

One may apply the same means-to-ends analysis that Bruner often employed to the "tools of thought," that is to the techniques one uses in order to reach the goal of thinking "well" about thinking. Before my arrival at Harvard, I had already chosen "thinking" as an abiding area of interest (or it had chosen me). I was still searching, however, for ways of working on the nature of thought. Lewin had been my choice for a theoretical thesis as an undergraduate; Hanfmann and Kasanin's work on schizophrenic thinking had been my first choice—in Sydney—as a possible area for graduate work. I had completed some research on children's moral judgments and had begun work on the way people solved items on spatial tasks, hoping to tease out "visual" and "verbal" solutions and to relate these back to the factor structure of tasks, especially to the way factors were named and interpreted.

Three features continue to stand out for me in the tools of thought Bruner used and advocated: asking about functions, attending to sequence, and rephrasing problems by way of paradox and metaphor.

Hilgard (1962) has described Bruner as a "functionalist" in his studies of both perception and thought. And Bruner (1973) agrees with the description, dating his interest back to the influence of McDougall and defining "function" in broad terms: "McDougall . . . convinced me early and irreversibly that one could not understand the organization of behaviour without taking into account its directionality, its purpose, its intention—its teleological structure, however heuristically one might formulate it. The conviction has guided me into studies of selectivity in perception, into works on strategies in thinking, and now to a functionalist theory of development in an age of structuralism" (1973, p. 7). McDougall had a prominent part in Sydney's attention to the history of psychology. Perhaps that made some aspects of a "functionalist" approach attractive to me. I was usually wary of "teleology," of any statement of "distant" goals as an explanation of current behavior. But the questions "What is this individual trying to do?" "What is the meaning of this event for him or her?" struck me as useful additions to questions I seemed always to use as a first attack in a problem: "What are people actually doing?" "And why is it difficult?" The latter type of question, I have come to recognize in the course of this essay, is probably my most constant preoccupation: "Why is this task harder than that?" "Why do we ever make 'errors'?" "What is an 'error'?" "Why do we not always follow an ideal method, even when we know about it?"

Questions about "direction," about "what people are actually doing," or about sources of "error": all these made it easy to take on board the tool of attending to sequences in behavior. This particular tool was very much in the air in the department at that time. Part of the wave of information processing meant that several people—Bruner, Miller, Mosteller, and Bush in particular—were interested in the possibilities of using sequential analyses to describe the flow of behavior from one step to the next, noting the way past events were reflected in any present step or the way in which any established sequence was disrupted by stress.

In Bruner's terms, I had acquired a tool that would provide me with an always available first line of attack on any problem. It helped make manageable the notion of "strategy" in several post Harvard studies of decision making. It was useful in a study of the effects of electro-convulsive shock, and in another on sleep loss. And it remains useful. Sequence was, for instance, the first—but not the last—feature I turned to in looking at the way children draw and copy simple shapes, noting both the order of steps and the consequences of using some orders rather than others (Goodnow, 1973a; 1978b).

Why was the tool of attending to sequences and chains of behavior so attractive? It was widespread in the USA in the 1950s and was often seen as a way of finally tackling the problem of "serial" order in behavior, which Lashley had stressed as a major unsolved problem in psychology. In part, such attention provided a specific analytic tool. What made it especially attractive, however, was the way it combined with concepts such as "strategy" or "plan." In a sense, the student of thinking at that time had a choice between what were called "molar" and "molecular" approaches. The former (an example is Tolman's notion of "cognitive map") appeared closer to the way humans operated, especially in real life, but presented problems when one came to specify or "operationalize" the term. The latter (an example is any pair of associations) seemed remote from the interesting phenomena but came complete with a set of measuring tools and a batch of tasks that could be taken immediately into a round of experiments. Notions such as "strategies" and "plans" offered a constructive middle ground (perhaps similar to the position later occupied by the notion of "rule" in language). Combined with analyses of sequence, the notion of "strategy" or "plan" provided both a tool for thought and a tool for measurement.

Sequence is a tool, however, that fits some problems more happily than others. In contrast, metaphor and paradox—ways of rephrasing problems—were tools Jerry Bruner advocated and used with any problem. One I accepted happily.; the other—paradox—was a tool I always approached with suspicion.

I am still puzzled by Jerry's enthusiasm for paradox: a regular source of delight to him and only an occasional one for me. Behind its use and enjoyment (it seems the height of wit and wisdom in some circles) are probably assumptions about the nature of humor and of understanding that I do not share. I am still not clear what those assumptions are. Deep down, I suspect, there was on my part the feeling that to capture the essence of "nature" one needed to stalk quietly, without dazzle. Or perhaps I was simply too cautious about appearing "clever." Whatever the reason, the closest I came to agreeing to the virtue of paradox came in the feeling that to know more, you may need to know less. In effect, the greatest barriers to knowledge are often within the knowledge one already has. Along with this conviction went a pleasure in discarding old ideas, throwing out old baggage, a delight in "seeing" a phenomenon or a solution that had always been there but had simply not been "seen," and a conviction that we had to work to be "saved from that most common blight on human thinking: clutter" (Bruner, 1962a, p. 47).

If I found myself sometimes unappreciative of paradox as a way of thinking about a problem (suspecting perhaps a premature neatness in the way things were wrapped up, all edges tucked in), the same was not true of another heuristic Jerry often used as a way of breaking loose from the old look of a problem metaphor. He has written a great deal about metaphor as a "mode of knowing" and as a way of condensing knowledge (for example, Bruner, 1962a). He has also argued for the deliberate use of metaphor as a problem-solving device: "Good operational ideas very often have their origin in highly personal metaphors that express deep lying impulses in the person . . . this metaphoric flow of ideas . . . is a substitute for overt action. . . . One of the great sources of hypotheses, of ideas, of poetic images, seems to be the taming of such metaphoric flow" (Bruner, 1957, p. 50).

Let me give an example. Suppose we start with the question: How is parental action related to the wider society? One way is to think of parents as having an implicit contract with the wider group, a contract that says something about what kind of child—what type and level of cognitive and social skills—will be acceptable to the society at large. This is a metaphor

Bruner has in fact used: "A parent is bound by a deep, if implicit, contract to make the child into a certain kind of human being, to prepare him or her to take a place in a certain kind of society, to respect certain standards in order to be assured opportunity and reward. For its part, the study of human development mirrors these concerns: how to raise or even to define an intelligent human being, how to assure the growth of a proper moral judgment or an adequately evolved logical capability, how to increase independence or loyalty or tenderness, how to prevent alienation or anonymity. While these are questions that rarely affect our research directly, they none the less give it shape in subtle ways" (1973, p. 4).

From a notion such as contract, Bruner could move easily to a series of further questions. Who writes the contract? Is it agreed upon? Who is to say that a contract has not been fulfilled? Are there deadlines or indefinite second chances? What resources are provided for fulfilling the contract? Does the contract specify not only the end state (for example, a literate child) but also the methods and materials to be used (sending the child to school)? What opportunities exist for rewriting a contract? Do penalties really exist or are they only thought to be present? Who is held to have the major responsibility for seeing that a contract is fulfilled? Suppose, for example, that a child's intellectual achievements are not all one had hoped for. Is this outcome attributed to the child ("could have tried harder"), to the parent ("could have seen the potential or the problem earlier"), or to some agency outside the family ("the schools are awful")? If you were to write your own contract for your own child, what would you say? In what ways are any of the felt obligations between parents, children, and institutions not like the contracts we work from in other undertakings? Finally, what are the limits to any metaphor such as "contract"? The last question is crucial: "There is a cycle that runs from the open state of having an idea to the more disciplined one of recognizing it as good or fitting or appropriate. At one end, there is the taming of personal metaphor for the problem at hand, using it as a guide for constructing new and potentially fruitfully combinatorial hypotheses. At the other there is the rigorous business of recognizing the worth-whileness of an idea" (Bruner, 1957, p. 51).

Such use of metaphor as a ground-breaking device for a problem was something I enjoyed tremendously. It was a game, a form of play, and it later came as no surprise that Bruner should make very strong statements about the role of play both in individual thought and in the invention of new tools for a species (Bruner, Jolly, and Sylva, 1976).

Nonetheless, there was an aspect to this play on which we differed. I had brought with me a distinction between "private play" and "public caution," a distinction that often inhibited the translation of play into active work or the placing of work on public display. After working with Bruner, I was more sure than before that time spent finding the flaws in a piece of work was often time wasted, unless the analysis was clearly useful or constructive. But I was not so sure about the rest of the world. The better part of valor, on that basis, might be to put out very little or to wait until something had been proved several times over before even proposing it as a possibility. My largest debt to Jerry Bruner consists of losing some of this concern with making public errors, accepting instead that one does one's best and that any idea is bound to be superceded by a later idea, not because of an "error" in the earlier work but because each idea has a time and place and must fall by the wayside as better ones come along. I would have found this form of cultural transmission difficult to put into words if it were not for an interview reported by Kay Lyou, in which Bruner speaks of the role of "failure," first with regard to experimental schools and then with regard to anything one does: "The question shouldn't be about their success. The question should really be about how well they failed. I think that if they are good they are bound to fail, because the main thing in an experiment in education is that you must push to the edge of the possible, and you don't know the edge of the possible until you've gone beyond it, so you fail" (Lyou, 1978, p. 340).

Such statements might be regarded as simply another paradox, if it were not that the philosophy is meant by Bruner to apply to oneself and to be acted upon. In Lyou's words, "Bruner insists as well that you have to 'fail in public . . . private failure . . . the economy of embarrassment, is not good' " (Lyou, 1978, p. 340).

It was this readiness to be wrong, to put oneself in a position where one could be proved wrong, that I most needed to learn. It was a form of courage Jerry Bruner possessed in abundance, and I shall always be grateful for his having imparted some measure of that courage to those who worked with him. It was imparted in large degree, one should note, through dialogue he has often stressed in his approach to "cultural transmission": "One of the most crucial ways in which a culture aids intellectual growth is through a dialogue between the more experienced and the less experienced, providing a means for the internalization of dialogue in thought. The courtesy of conversation may be the major ingredient in the courtesy of teaching" (Bruner, 1971a, p. 107). Such 'courtesy of conversation" is something I felt Jerry Bruner both preached and practiced, providing a final overlap between his own style and his own theory of instruction, a final example of the way he himself transmitted ideas both about the nature of "good" thinking and the route by which this goal might be reached.

References

Aries, P. *Centuries of childhood*. London: Jonathon Cape, 1962.

Bruner, J. S. Freud and the image of man. *American Psychologist*, 1956, 11, 463–466.

————. What social scientists say about having an idea. *Printers' Ink*, 1957, 260, 48–52.

————. The need for new myths. *The Colorado Quarterly*, 1958, 7, 119–138. (Cited by Lyou, p. 134).

————. Art as a mode of knowing. In J. S. Bruner (Ed.), *On knowing: Essays for the left hand*. Cambridge, Mass.: University Press, 1962(a).

————.On learning mathematics. In J. S. Bruner (Ed.), *On knowing: Essays for the left hand*. Cambridge, Mass.: University Press, 1962(b).

————. After John Dewey, what? In J. S. Bruner (Ed.), *On knowing: Essays for the left hand*. Cambridge, Mass: University Press, 1962(c).

————. Culture, politics, and pedagogy. In J. S. Bruner, *The relevance of education*. New York: Norton, 1971 a.

————. The psychobiology of pedagogy. In J. S. Bruner, *The relevance of education*. New York: Norton, 1971 b.

————. *Patterns of growth. Inaugural lecture at the University of Oxford*. Oxford: Clarendon Press, 1973.

Bruner, J. S., Goodnow, J. J., and Austin, G. A. *A study of thinking*. New York: Wiley, 1956.

Bruner, J. S., Jolly, A., and Sylva, K. (Eds.), *Play: Its role in evolution and development*. London: Penguin, 1976.

Goodnow, J. J. Concepts of intelligence and development. In N. Warren (Ed.), *Advances in cross-cultural psychology* vol. 2. London: Pergamon Press, in press.

————. *Children drawing*. Cambridge, Mass.: Harvard University Press, 1978.

————. Visible thinking: Cognitive aspects of change in drawing. *Child Development*. 1978, 49, 637–641.

Hilgard, E. R. Introduction to distinguished scientific contribution awards, award to Jerome Bruner, *American Psychologist*, 1962, 17, 888–889.

Lyou, K. W. In search of the source of rationality: A study of the work of Jerome Bruner. Unpublished M.A. thesis, Lindenwood College, St. Charles, Missouri, 1978.

Parke, R. D. Parent-infant interaction: Progress, paradigms, and problems. In G. P. Sackett (Ed.), *Observing behavior. Theory and applications in mental retardation* vol. 1. Baltimore: University Park Press, 1978.

Pinchbeck, I. and Hewitt, M. *Children in English society*. London: Routledge & Kegan Paul, 1969 vol. 1, 1973 vol. II.

Afterword

Jerome S. Bruner

It is a delight to be invited to the party—to comment on a volume prepared by such distinguished authors without actually knowing just what it is they have said. Lewis Carroll comes immediately to mind. I think of Alice, falling down the hole, lamenting the possibility that she may never see her cat, Dinah, again. She laments the more, for Dinah might have liked it down in the hole. There might be bats around and cats like bats. Alice recites to herself a few times that "cats like bats" and then, to her surprise, she finds herself reversing things and reciting "bats like cats." On second thought she decides it doesn't matter *which* way she says it for she is not sure whether *either* statement is true. Poor Alice, trapped in the verificationist theory of meaning. I can surely do better than that. All that is needed is the appropriate metaphor to guide me, then I shall have no difficulty commenting on a volume I am not permitted to read until after I have finished commenting.

Divination, that's it. That is my metaphor. I must divine what is in the book. With the help of David Olson's splendid introduction (which I *have* been permitted to read) I must divine what others *might* have said and say now what I *would* say if they *had* said what I think they *might* have said. I am cheered by Boyd's (1979) brilliant paper on the conceptual open-endedness of metaphors. "They work by inviting the reader (or hearer) to consider the principle subject of the metaphor in the light of associated implications characteristic—typically—of the commonplace conception of the secondary subject." My notion of divination is rather Old Testament, perhaps a little Greek as well. Divining is a particularly swift and accurate way of seeing trouble ahead. Think of poor Oedipus or of Joseph and his brothers. But *that* surely is no way to approach the writing of an Afterword for a Festschrift in one's honor! Ah, but perhaps it is, given one proviso. Can I perhaps be "positive" about the troubles I divine?

Two things will surely be on everybody's trouble agenda: how the *brain* shapes the nature of cognition, and how *culture* operates to extend thought beyond its "natural" limits. How can such a group of authors possibly escape either of these fateful issues? With that much divining done, I can now settle to the task. What I would like to do now is to set down some reflections on both these issues—and here all claims to divination cease!

I am a functionalist and I believe that there are autonomous psychological explanations that are neither biological nor cultural, though dependent upon both biological and cultural processes. I like the way Hilary Putnam describes functionalism:

According to functionalism, the behavior of, say, a computing machine is not explained by the physics and chemistry of the computing machine. It is explained by the machine's *program*. Of course that program is realized in a particular physics and chemistry, and could, perhaps, be deduced from that physics and chemistry. But that does not make the program a physical or chemical property of the machine; it is an abstract property of the machine. Similarly, I believe that the psychological properties of human beings are not physical and chemical properties of human beings, although they may be realized by physical and chemical properties of human beings (Putnam, 1975, p. xiii).

I subscribe to his antireductionism, acknowledging physical constraints on mental functioning, yet insisting upon a discontinuity in explanatory principles.

Take a case in point, one close to the heart of mentalism. We know from a generation of work on perceptual recognition that human beings seem to be able to "guess" correctly about certain features of a visual display although they report that they did not "experience" the display in any conscious sense. Leave aside for the moment the question whether they were able to extract "cues" from the display that guided their later guessing. Now suppose it happens that we discover a particular brain lesion the victim of which displays an agnosia that might be called "blind sight"—he can *guess* what has been shown to him in his affected field but insists he cannot *see* it. And suppose that through assiduous neuroanatomy we also discover that there are two tracts carrying messages from the optic nerve to the brain: one goes right up to the occipital cortex and branches out into the visual association areas in the proper way; the other goes to the old optic tectum and branches out in nonobvious ways from there. Our patient, it turns out on *post mortem*, has a lesion in the former tract but not in the latter. Thereafter, suppose, we are easily and nondangerously able to implant fine recording electrodes in the two tracts and discover that, indeed, whenever a subject gives us a good guess without awareness there are currents flowing in the tectal tract but not in the cortical one, and so forth. As you know, this is not so farfetched. I am being moderately faithful to the literature and doing a little divining as well.

What would have been discovered? It is surely nontrivial that we would now know that the morphology of the nervous system has a canny way of realizing a double program for visual recognition. But the morphology surely does not tell us what that double program *is*, how it *works*, what are its constituent *routines*. That still remains as a psychological problem—or, perhaps better, as a programmatic problem. The properties of that program will have to be written in program language, not in neuromorphological language. And that will be the case, no matter how much we find out about tissue pathways and the electrical impulses that travel over them. And by the way, I would not be so churlish as to deny that neuropsychological work helped discern the double nature of the recognition program.

But two other things are true, and each of them makes the discovery of our two neural tracts a matter of capital importance. One is the brute fact that if there were *no* neural machinery to effect the double program, there would be no double program—which may not be as banal as it seems. The other, somewhat more subtle, is that the nature of the biological system through which the program is realized may itself constrain or bias the program. There may, for example, be constraints in the shunting properties of neural tissue or in the recovery rates that govern the refractory phase, and so on. It is much as in the relation between a skipper and the supertanker he commands. The skipper can signal the engine room for full speed astern, should he want to stop the ship, but the critical mass of the vessel will determine how quickly or slowly it will come to a halt. Indeed, it is inconceivable that evolution operates other than by selecting among the programs that fit the machinery that is in being—at least prior to the emergence of technology. Plainly it would be foolish to ignore the biological side of human functioning and it should be apparent that it matters greatly what kind of body the mind has to work with. I am a mentalist, yes, but I think of minds as using the apparatus of the body to get their jobs done. But the body, so to speak, is not a totally all-purpose tool nor can the nervous system do anything and everything with equal ease or at all. That makes me a nativist, I suppose.

It is fruitless, however, to make strong *general* claims about innateness. Claims become interesting to the degree that they are particular. They also lose ideological bite as they become particular. Consider a topic with which I happen to be currently concerned: the acquisition of procedures for *reference fixing* in language. Is there something "built in" to the machinery of functioning that predisposes us toward certain forms of reference fixing? (By reference fixing I mean, along with Kripke, procedures for indicating what it is that I am talking about in the world, without at the same time either defining or predicating anything about it save its existence and location.) If I assume that reference fixing is some evolved version of ostension, I have now to ask about the nature of ostension. What is the "primitive process" whereby ostension is assured? How are human beings able to know that a sound, a gesture, a word, a description, a sign *points* to something that is in *my* awareness that I want to get into *your* awareness? Is it "innate"? A claim for innateness would take the form of specifying a *parti-*

cular behavior (or a measurable event in the nervous system) that can be examined independently in its own right with respect to its innate status, the parameters within which it operates, and so forth. It is a claim that carries implications for further research into a process. This is notably *not* the case for general claims about the "innateness" of language or of intelligence or of temperament.

I want to pursue this matter a little, for it serves surprisingly to carry the discussion from the question of innateness or "naturalness" to issues having to do with the cultural and experiential patterning of cognitive processes as well. Let us take some additional steps in exploring whether or not there is an innate readiness in the species to recognize that a certain kind of "sign" indicates that the maker of the sign is attending to a particular thing in the "environment" and is trying to bring it to *your* attention by "pointing" of some kind. More particularly, is *ostension* innate and does it provide a "natural" base for *reference* in language?

The task is to find a preadapted basis for what later will turn into a behavior that is governed by rules and conventions (as reference is). An experiment immediately suggests itself. Let us take the most natural indicator that another's attention is directed to some external object: his visual line of regard. Do young, prelinguistic infants pick up the direction of another person's line of regard and follow it out to an object? The experiment is easily done, and Michael Scaife and I (1975) did it. The answer is positive, but the results are not totally without ambiguity. Yes, babies as early as four or five months *do* in fact turn to follow the line of regard of somebody with whom they have been interacting. The infants may, of course, simply be imitating head turning (although there is good reason to think that this is not the case, for the child's head displacements are different from the adult's—and why should the side to which the child's glance is directed always correspond topographically to the side toward which the adult is looking). Be that as it may, it *might* be imitation. Now we may ask about the conditions that govern the putatively innate response of the infant to adult gaze direction. A next experiment is done, this one by George Butterworth (1979). By one year of age children regularly and easily follow the line of regard of an adult with whom they have been interacting, but the constraints are interesting. For one, close examination reveals that the infant does not *begin* following the adult's gaze until *after* the adult has settled on the object at which he is looking. *Then*, the infant follows. Moreover, the infant not only "runs out" visually along the adult's gaze line but, if nothing is found "out there," he directs his gaze back to the adult's face, "as if" searching, and he then moves out again. Is he expecting to find something out there as a visual target? A proper prudence requires we answer only "Perhaps." Now one other condition gets tested. Will the child look at a target fixated by the adult that is *not* initially in the child's own visual field —I should mention that the child and adult are sitting facing each other in all these experiments. Well, yes he will, but . . . The limit seems to be a point of head turning for the child which is sufficiently extreme so that he can no longer see the adult's face in peripheral vision while searching foveally for a possible target on which to light. It would seem, then, that we are dealing with a tightly coupled *social* response that is based not only upon a "natural" understanding of the indicating or reference fixing value of another's gaze, but that this response also requires the child maintaining visual contact with the adult whose gaze is being followed (This may be attributed, of course, to infantile concreteness, but if infants are *that* concrete, why then do they so abstractly follow a projected line of sight?)

Suppose now that these results are replicated dozens of times, and we all are prepared to grant that there is a preadaptation or innate base for ostension. What other hypotheses does such a finding imply? If ostension is natural, and if things go as they were just described then at least two things seem entailed. For one, children (like adults) must believe that there is a world "out there" and, for another, they must believe that it is the same world as the one being experienced by other people—else they would not look out along other people's lines of regard to find things in the world. We cannot know, of course, what they believe. All that we can say is that they *act as if* they believed these things. "Ethnophilosophically," they must be little naïve realists rather than solipsists, as implied in the theories of initial egocentricism, proposed by either Freud or Piaget. At least they act like little naïve realists. They act as if they believed that other members of the species exist in the same external world in which they are operating and have recognizable *dispositions* toward that outside world—like paying attention.

What an interesting turn our inquiry has taken! I began by urging that claims for innateness, if they are to be substantively interesting, should be specific and amenable to empirical analysis independently of the situations in which the claim was first made. We began by asking whether linguistic reference has an initial, preadapted base in ostension (*not* whether reference is itself innate, for plainly many aspects of reference are highly conventional, as in the use of the determiners *a* and *the* in the sentence, *Yesterday I saw a bird; the bird was singing.*) We find that, indeed, ostension in some primitive form *is* natural or innate. This does not *prove* that reference is built upon or originates in the child's grasp of ostension, although one could then pursue that matter further to see *how* more abstract referential procedures are linked to ostension during their acquisition—a first step in that investigation, in fact, having already been taken by Ninio and Bruner (1978). What is especially interesting about *specific* claims for innateness is that they explore not only the *preadaptations* for language or whatever but that they derive from detailed consideration of the *psychological* program into which the innate component is claimed to fit. Rather than a claim for innateness bringing empirical research to a standstill—which most often happens in the general case—it enlivens it.

But there is one curious fallout from our pursuit thus far: it is the hypothesis that "innate ostension" requires the maintenance of social contact between addresser and addressee—that innocent babes not only seem to assume that others are looking at the same world as theirs, but also require that those others stay in view while the babes try to figure out what the adults are looking at. That is to say, social world and physical world seem to share the same locus.

Now let me say how this leads me to conclude that there is a biological basis for culture once we admit that the child is a little naïve realist who thinks he shares the same world as others around him and can find out what others are attending to in that world. We have here a primitive "intersubjectivity" based upon a naïve conviction that the things that matter—people and objects—are *out there* to be shared. The world, in Burkheim's sense, has exteriority and constraint. Our proper little naïve realist of a child, when he seems to be egocentric, is only operating on the hypothesis that others who are living in the same world as him must be having the same experience of it as he is having.* Not a bad hypothesis. Fortunately, it does not disappear with childhood though it is less likely to overgeneralize later.

I think it is important to take seriously this human tendency to *externalize* events, to put them into the world, and to assume that they are *shared* in that world by others. I think it is what leads the human species to such common-sense views as the following: categories exist not in your head but in nature; social institutions are defined by their locus not by the place they occupy in men's mind (recall the late Gilbert Ryle's rollocking pursuit of the question "But where is Oxford University?"); scientific laws and moral rules exist out there for most children and for a great many adults; history is viewed as a record of what actually happened rather than as Ranke conceptualized it. Indeed, Nelson Goodman's amusing and powerful sketch of the history of philosophy in his recent *Ways of World Making* can be read as an account of philosophy rescuing us from our powerful externalizing tendencies. First, philosophy is concerned with the nature of things, then (after Kant) with the nature of the categories of mind in terms of which we organize things, then with the symbol systems by which we express propositions about thoughts about the world. We begin life disposed to see the social world that we create by symbolic acts as existing out there just as plainly as blue, green, The Reformation, and Bismarck's shrewdness exist out there. If Durkheim were around today, I would try to convince him that here at least is one biological root for the externality and constraint of culture.

But while I firmly believe there are biological roots of culture, I believe just as strongly that human culture, once created, is autonomous and "super-

---

* I am grateful to Virginia Sherwood for this point.

organic" in Alfred Kroeber's sense. In a recent paper at Salzburg, Karl Popper comments that the most characteristic thing about man is the technology to which he is linked. In a 1972 paper, "The Nature and Uses of Immaturity," I argued that man depends for the realization of his potential upon various prosthetic devices—for using and extending his sensory, motor, intellectual, and transactional capacities. Man's evolution has depended upon his link with technology and with the "technical-social way of life" that is created by the use of technology. In no sense do the amplifiers of hand, eye, and mind "belong" to man as an individual. They have an autonomous "World Three" existence in Popper's terms.

How do the cultural-technical prostheses of World Three get into the human mind? How are they used? What is the "man-machine" relationship that goes on between me and the amplifiers of eye, hand, mind, and sociality? I certainly know what goes on when I use a lever. But that is obvious and a little trivial, e.g., I substitute *myself* as the force. But something changes. At the point where lever using becomes widespread, selection pressure within the species will no longer favor those with big pushing, pulling, and lifting muscles but those with cute ideas about new contexts in which to use levers. And the organization of the society will reflect that change in manifold ways. So the texture of our lives is changed in a larger number of subtle ways not by the lever itself but by what the lever does, once accepted, to our way of life. It is not so different when it comes to amplifiers of mind. Once the concepts and ideas of mathematics, say, become procedures that we can use in problem solving, our mental powers are amplified in much the same way as our muscular powers are amplified by using a lever. But again, the existence of mathematics and mathematicians (and the value attached to these) alters life in countless ways—even unto the magical powers attributed to a First Wrangler at Cambridge.

Our particular problem is how these amplifiers of hand, eye, mind, sociality, and so forth affect the growth of mind. This query would also have to include consideration of how the technical-social way of life that comes with technology affects the growth of mind—questions not unlike those that David Olson and Michael Cole and Jack Goody ask. One part of the answer has to do with the *specific* effects on mind of using such prosthetic devices as mathematics, casual explanation, hypothetical reasoning and the elaborate apparatus of formal operations that Inhelder and Piaget have so carefully described. Does it, as Vygotsky particularly noted, create "new" forms of intelligence by cultivating what he called the "proximal zone of development"? I believe that it does, but at the same time I also believe that it is a universal human characteristic to be capable of *using* the concepts embodied in a culture. I will even risk logical circularity by noting that concepts do not come to exist or to survive culturally unless at least *two* people can use them as adjuncts of thought—she who has the original insight and he to whom she was able to pass it on!

There is a great deal of quarrelsomeness in the history of our subject as to what *exactly* we mean in saying that the concepts and procedures that "exist" in a culture are adopted and used by people who "share" the culture in question. The extreme form of the claim has always been that it is the language that one acquires, the language *per se*, that makes the difference. That is a virtually untestable claim. Language is only come by in cultural contexts and the very act of acquiring a language gives one access to many other cultural forms and procedures. What language permits is a rapid and easy mode of access into a huge array of data, concepts, and conceptual procedures, right from the start of one's career as a member of the linguistic community. It *may* be that creatures without language could, under favorable (man-made?) circumstances, come to grasp comparably complex and powerful concepts. Their mode of access, however, would be so slow and so demanding of concentration and time that they would have to be intellectual saints to make it, renouncing most of the more primitive biological needs and satisfactions enroute!

It seems, however, that human cultures do more than equip their members with skills and concepts and views about the world and life. They also have an effect—a differential one—on the ways in which their members *use mind*. This is a topic that is only beginning to come under study, and I am sure that many of the contributors to this volume have things to say about it (if I may return to divining)—for it is a topic that was indeed first given life by Michael Cole, Patricia Greenfield, Alastair Mundy-Castle.

There is one deep trend that I see in this work on the cultural patterning of cognition. It represents a shift from emphasis upon cognitive *dispositions* to emphasis upon *contexts of appropriate use*. It is, I think, one of the important paradigm shifts in psychology in the last quarter century and is in part attributable to the emergence of the cognitive sciences. In an exquisite miniaturized way, it is illustrated by the research of one of the contributors to this volume, Peter Wason. He started his studies of negation in language by noting a disposition among human problem solvers to be slow (and often inaccurate) in comprehending negation—a characteristic that had been noted earlier by Bruner, Goodnow, and Austin and by Hovland and Weiss in their observation of the common mishandling of negative instances in concept attainment. With further probing, however, it transpired that it was not a dispositional matter at all but rather a matter of sensitivity to appropriate conditions in which negation may be conveniently used—what Wason referred to as "contexts of plausible denial." Negation is processed just as swiftly as affirmation in contexts where the status of an event is most readily definable by noting what the event is *not*.

If one extends this idea to a broader scope, it is quickly apparent that in "real life" there are occasions when, for example, it is appropriate to solve problems on one's own (rather than depending on authority), or when one should process information in one way rather than another, or when failure to reach a goal signals the need for redoubled effort rather than for giving up, and so forth. I am thinking of Patricia Greenfield's Wolof subjects treating a task as "thinkable" or of Cole and Scribner's Kpelles estimating that one rather than another model of reckoning should be used, or Luria's Uzbekis accepting the problem set them in Luria's universal terms rather than in the light of local conditions. Much of what anybody does in using mind is determined by what he reads the context to be. What turns out to be the case for using optional transformations in language—the passive, the query, the negative that George Miller studied in the early 1960s with such verve—turns out to be generally true about information processing. Transformations are used to fit appropriate contexts: to fulfill essential preparatory and sincerity conditions on types of utterance in discourse. Abstraction is used (at least in our society) when the particularity of an instance is not at issue—in talking about distances or about the economy but not in instructing this barber about how to cut my hair. The very idea of speech acts, governed by certain intentions to get particular things done with words, underlines the context sensitivity of language, for getting things done requires appreciation of appropriate contexts for communicating or for creating such contexts. It is in this sense that I meant earlier that acquiring a language entails acquiring the ways of culture—if only the "maxims" of Paul Grice's cooperative principle. I would simply want to argue that it is not only language that is used with a high degree of sensitivity to context, but also the cognitive processes in general.

You will sense that I have been talking about cultural and linguistic universals in almost the same breath as cultural and linguistic differentiation. Surely, for example, Grice's cooperative principle or something very like it operates in every society or wherever people speak with each other in ordinary language. But not all cultures prescribe in the same way the occasions on which one uses one's analytic skills or how one groups events or forms canonical prototypes of events. For a long time I have been trying to understand at what level it is interesting to talk about the latter. I was never very impressed with the anecdotal approach—that Zulus thought London bobbies very friendly because they took their raised-arm stop signals as signs of friendly greeting. If differences in the use of mind in different cultures are to be interesting, they must reflect something structural about the ways in which the culture works. How does one get from structural descriptions of a culture to differences in the use of mind? I found an interesting hint in some recent philosophical writing—and here I return to my current preoccupation with theories of reference and meaning. The take-off point is the work of Kripke and Putnam on the nature of referring, for whether they intended to or not, they have got themselves into the business of structural description. How does reference begin? They posit an initial "dubbing ceremony," to use Kripke's term, something in the world singled out by ostension of some sort. *That* is an elm tree, we are told, or *that* is electricity. The referent of such terms is given by an historical chain of events that stretches back to the original dubbing ceremony and forward to the different occasions of use in which we have used or heard the terms. We use knowledge we receive in a fashion that is far looser than a vertificationist would have us believe. If you should challenge my use of the term "electricity," I will rarely explain by reciting verifiable propositions about electricity. Rather I will refer you down the chain from which I have received my usage. "I don't know very much about it. Why not ask Gerby from whom *I* learned what little I know. He'll tell you what it refers to." Most of what we refer to and most of what we mean is not the fruit of our own cognitive acts but are hand-me-downs from past social exchanges. In that sense, in Putnam's quip, we usually mean much less than we say. What we believe is that the necessary knowledge is "out there," that somebody knows. There is, cognitively speaking, an extraordinary division of labor in a culture or in a linguistic community. And as the technology of mind moves toward written language and the possibility of storing in written form, the division of labor becomes the more complicated: scholars, scribes, libraries, journals, and other instruments of reason get added.

That is the preface to the structural description: that nobody knows everything, that knowledge is exchanged on faith, that we take as given that most of what others say they do not fully understand but that somebody else might understand better. The cognitive division of labor is inevitable and universal. The *forms* that it takes in different cultures and subcultures is what is particular. These form the presuppositions of the society. In any culture, we live on faith, or perhaps it is better to say we live on credit. We enter a linguistic or cultural community by paying the price of working with its presuppositions: the accepted reasons and explanations, the accepted occasions on which to think or deny or to accept or affirm or to promise. It is no surprise, as the ethnomethodologists tell us, that it is universally regarded as hostile to press too hard the question of what somebody really *means* by what they say. Indeed, Popper and Kuhn could tell the ethnomethodologists that such questioning is not even the rule in the paradigm-bound sciences. A great many of our programs of thought are acquired in interaction with others who are socialized just as we are. I had bitter words once with Clyde Kluckhohn when he remarked disdainfully that psychologists were a funny lot, thinking that most of what was interesting about the mind was inside the head. I would not answer him so sharply today. For in fact, we are weakest in cognitive studies just where Kluckhohn accused. I have been working hard at how very young children learn *language* through interaction. It is astonishing how little we know about how human beings acquire *any* form of knowledge through discourse. How odd of us. We carefully describe our stimulus material in this experiment or that. But we blithely take it for granted that our subjects understood the complex instructions we gave them in words. But that too is passing.

We shall need an anthropological/sociological adjunct to our sciences of cognition, indeed, we are already getting it. But it will not stop at the level of describing *systems* of thought external to the individual, much though I admire Robin Horton or Nick Colby or Dell Hymes. What is needed is an account of how such systems fare in the division of labor, how they are transmitted, now they become part of a socially regulated credit system. We need, I think, the kind of "mini-longitudinal" study that Elsa Bartlett and Sue Carey-Block (Miller, 1977) did on how kids get hold of a system of color naming by interacting with others—how they decided what *chromium* referred to, given that they almost never had enough encounters with noiseless instances to be sure. And we shall need such studies in less defined domains than color.

There. You see what I divine to be on the minds of the members of this party. I *hope* it is on their minds. For where better to look for future clarity than to such an extraordinary collection of party-makers!

References

Bartlett, E. and Carey-Block, S. Study reported in G. A. Miller, *Spontaneous apprentices: Children and language*. New York: Seabury Press, 1977.

Boyd, R. Metaphor and theory change: What is 'metaphor' a metaphor for? In A. Ortony (Ed.), *Metaphor and thought*. Cambridge: Cambridge University Press, 1979.

Bruner, J. S. The nature and uses of immaturity. *American Psychologist*, 1972, 27(8), 1–22.

Bruner, J. S., Goodnow, J. J., and Austin, G. A. *A study of thinking*. New York: Wiley, 1956.

Butterworth, G. What minds have in common is space: A perceptual mechanism for joint reference in infancy. Paper delivered to the Developmental Section, British Psychological Society, Southampton, September 1979.

Goodman, N. *Ways of world making*. New York: Hackett Publ., 1978.

Grice, H. P. Meaning. *Philosophical Review*, 1957, 66, 377–388.

Hovland, C. L. and Weiss, W. Transmission of information concerning concepts through positive and negative instances. *Journal of Experimental Psychology*, 1953, 45, 175–182.

Kripke, S. Naming and necessity. In D. Davidson and G. Harman (Eds.), *The semantics of natural language*. Dordrecht: D. Reidel, 1972.

Ninio, A. and Bruner, J. S. The achievement and antecedents of labelling. *Journal of Child Language*, 1978, 5, 1–15.

Popper, K. Creative self-criticism. *Encounter*, 1979, 53(5), 10–14.

Putnam, H. *Mind, language and reality*. Cambridge: Cambridge University Press, 1975.

Scaife, M. and Bruner, J. S. The capacity for joint visual attention in the infant. *Nature*, 1975, 253(5489), 265–266.